ENGLISH PLACE-NAME SOCIETY. VOLUME XXI
FOR 1943–44

GENERAL EDITOR
BRUCE DICKINS

THE PLACE-NAMES OF CUMBERLAND

PART II

ENGLISH PLACE-NAME SOCIETY. VOLUME XXI

THE PLACE-NAMES OF CUMBERLAND

By

A. M. ARMSTRONG, A. MAWER, F. M. STENTON & BRUCE DICKINS

PART II
ALLERDALE BELOW DERWENT AND ALLERDALE ABOVE DERWENT WARDS

CAMBRIDGE
AT THE UNIVERSITY PRESS
1971

Published by the Syndics of the Cambridge University Press
Bentley House, 200 Euston Road, London NW1 2DB
American Branch: 32 East 57th Street, New York, N.Y. 10022

ISBN: 0 521 04914 8

First published 1950
Reprinted 1971

First printed in Great Britain at the University Printing House, Cambridge
Reprinted in Great Britain by Lewis Reprints Limited, Port Talbot, Glamorgan

CONTENTS

CUMBERLAND

IV. ALLERDALE BELOW DERWENT WARD

Allerdall ward beneath the watter of Darwen 1580 Border, *Allerdale Ward beneath Darwen* 1640 HMC x (iv), *Allerdale ward below Derwent* 1671 Fleming

v. Allerdale Barony *supra* 1. Edmund Sandford, c. 1675, called Allerdale Below and Allerdale Above the West and South Wards (*A Cursory Relation*, p. 23)

1. Allhallows

ALLHALLOWS is referred to as *capellæ omnium Sanctorum de Ukmanby* 1426 NB, (*church of*) *Allhallowes* 1578 *Cocker*.

BAGGROW [bagrə] is *Baggerawe* 1332 SR (p), *Bagarey* 1560 FF, *Bagra* 1578 *Cocker*, *Baggaraye* 1581 FF, *Bagarah* 1697 PR (Bridekirk), *Baggara* 1699 ib., *Baggraw* 1794 Brayton, *Baggerhay* 1816 Lysons.

This name occurs again in BAGGARA in Nether Denton (*supra* 82), the forms for which are *le baggary* 1589 ExchKR, *Bagray* 1618 Naworth, 1699 *Boothby*, *the Bigray* 1621 Naworth, *Baggary* 1626 *Boothby*, *Bag Row* 1794 MapH; and in BAGGRA YEAT in Uldale (*infra* 328) for which the forms are *Bagrawe* 1399 IpmR, *Bagray* 1535 VE.

The triple occurrence of this name in Cumberland, not to speak of *The Bagraw* 1451 (PN Dumf 105), suggests that the first element is not the Scandinavian personal name *Baggi*, but a significant word. Zachrisson (StudNP vi, 147) urged that *bagge* is a topographical term, meaning 'low-lying place, marshland.' It may, however, be one more term like *Rattenraw*, meaning a row of tumbledown cottages such as beggars might or did inhabit. In the early 13th century *Ancren Riwle* is the saying *Hit is beggeres rihte vorte beren bagge.* Heywood (1546) has *as well as the begger knowth his bag*, Ray (1678) *It would make a beggar beat his bag*. There is rather a similar proverbial saying in Njálssaga: *Þat mun vera maklegast at fari alt saman karl ok kýll*, "It is only fair that a beggar should go with his bag." It is worth noting also that there is a remarkable contumelious use of the word *bagge* in the account by John of Hexham of the Battle of the Standard (1138). "The Scots," he said, "all slipped away from the field, flinging their sacks away from them. To the shame of this affair, that place was called Baggamor" (SD ii, 294).

UPMANBY (6″)

Vochemanby c. 1170 StB
Uckemanebi 1188 P, *Uckemannebi* 1189, 1202–6 ib.
Huchemannebi 1189 P (p), *Hukemannebi* 1190, 1192 P, *Huckemannebi* 1193 ib.
Ukemannesbi 1191 P (p), *Hukemannesbi* 1194, 1195 P
Hukemanby 1230 FF, 1305 Ipm
Uckemanby 1231 Pipe, *Ukemanby* 1278 *Ass*
Ucman(n)eby, Ukman(n)eby 1276 *Ass*, 1316 CW vi, 1347 ib. iii
Ukmanby, Ucmanby 1285 *For et freq* to c. 1479 Rose
Hucmanby 1308 Ipm
Upmanby 1501 Ipm
Hokemondby t. Hy 8 *AOMB*

In the parish was *del Wra de Ukemanneby* 1292 *Ass*, and *the olde Ringarthe of Ukmanby* 1578 *Cocker*.

Lindkvist (lvii) is probably right in deriving this name from a Scandinavian nickname *Húkmaðr (anglicised to *Hukman*), formed from the recorded *húkr*, 'bending forward, weak in the hams.' If so, the name means '*Húkmaðr's* bӯ.' The name *Hukman* is well recorded in medieval England. In 1195 (P) we have mention of *Hukeman* de Moricebi (Moresby *infra* 421). *Hucman* is found (t. Hy 3) in Lincolnshire (*Kirkstead Cartulary*) and c. 1200 in Yorkshire (YCh i, 400). In two charters in the Welbeck Cartulary (Harl. MS 3640 ff., 40*b*, 41*b*) the same man appears as *Ucckeman* and *Hucman*. In the late medieval period the guttural [k] was assimilated to the following labial nasal.

WHITE HALL is *Whithalle, Wyttehal* 1322 Ipm, *Whytehall* 1336 *Ass*, *Whitehall* 1342 FF, *Withall* 1469 Pat, *Whitehall parke* 1578 *Cocker*. Apparently 'white hall,' *v.* h(e)all.

GALLOWHOW is *mons vocatur Galahowe* 1450 *Netherhall*. Probably 'gallows hill,' *v.* g(e)alga, haugr. HARBYBROW is *Harvy Browe* 1479 IpmR, *Herwybrowe alias Harbyebrowe* 1594 FF, *Harby Brow* 1576 S. KINGGATE (6″) is *King Gate* 1581 FF, *King Yate* 1660 CantW viii. KNAPETHORN (6″) is *Napthorne, Knapthorne* 1578 *Cocker*. It stands on a cnæpp or hillock. LEESRIGG FM is *Leesrigg* 1777 NB. Cf. *Leas, the Lees* 1578 *Cocker* and *v.* hrycg. PRIESTCROFT is *Presecrofte* 1381 IpmR, *Prest(e)croft(e)* 1465 Pat, 1578 *Cocker, Priest Croft* 1777 NB. 'Priests' croft.'

FIELD-NAMES

(b) In 1578 (*Cocker*) *Crooke becke, Crosse rigges* (*Crosserig*' 1291 *Lowther.* *v.* hrycg), *Makhowe Wood*; in 1550 (NB) *Garths* (*v.* garðr). In 1635 (*Hudleston*) *Tom Close, the Withe Dike* (*v.* wiðig, dīc).

2. Allonby

ALLONBY

Alayneby 1262 *HolmC*, 1292 *Ass, Alaynby, Alainby* 1335, 1340 Pat, 1358 Fine

Aleyn(e)by 1285 *For* (p), 1307 Ch

Alanby 1306 Ch, 1308 Ipm (p), 1335 *Ass* (p), 1360 Pat, *Alandby near Skymburnesse* 1323 Cl, *Alaneby* 1485 Ipm

Allonby 1576 S, *Allonbie al. Allanbie* 1596 FF

'*Alein*'s bȳ.' A late bȳ-name, *v.* Introduction. *Alein* is a French personal name of Breton origin. Allonby is identical with Ellonby *supra* 240, to distinguish it from which *near Skymburnesse* was added in the 1323 form. Cf. also Allanton (PN Dumf 26, 1355 *Alayntoun*).

CROOKHURST is *Crookhirst* 1679 CW xxi. Cf. *Kruk*', *le Crok*' 1262 *HolmC*. *v.* krókr, hyrst. It lies between the fork of two streams.

FIELD-NAMES

(b) *freschas* 1262 *HolmC* (apparently 'pools of fresh water,' recorded in NED *s.v.* fresh, sb.[1] 3, from the 16th century), *Ruthscalys* 1262 *HolmC* (*v.* skáli), *Wrengill* 1580 Border (*v.* gil).

3. Aspatria

ASPATRIA [spi·atri, speitri]

Aspatric c. 1160 *Hesley, Aspatric, -k(e)* c. 1160 StB *et freq* to 1736 CW (OS) iii

Espatric 1171–5 (1333) CW iii, c. 1220 Weth (p), 1291 Ch (p)

Ascpatric c. 1220 BM, *As(ke)paterk* 1279 *Ass, Askpatri(c)k* 1291 Ch, 1292 QW, 1305 Cl, *Assepatri(c)k*' 1285 *For*, 1302, 1303 Ipm, *Ask Patrick* 1348 Orig

Estpateric 1224 Pat, *Astpatrik* 1292 Pat

Eskpatrike 1347 CW iii
Aspatry 1423–9 WethA, *Asspatry* 1488 *Cocker*, *Aspatre* 1491 Ipm,
1576 S, (*or Aspatrik*) 1509 LP, *Aspatria* 1734 CW (OS) iii

ASPATRIA EAST MILL (6″). Cf. *Aspatr' myln'* 1527 *Netherhall*,
Aspatria miln 1777 NB.

An inversion compound meaning '*Patric*'s ash tree,' *v.* askr and
Introduction. The second element was assimilated in modern times to
Latin *patria*.

BRAYTON

    Brayton' 1212 StBA (p), 1285 For (p), 1535 VE *et passim*, *Braytona*
    1258 *Netherhall* (p), *Braytton* c. 1265 StB
    Breyton 1255 Pipe (p), 1279 *Ass* (p)
    Breghton 1402 Pat
    Braton 1580 Border

    BRAYTON HALL is *Braiton hall* 1675 Sandford.
    Probably 'broad tūn,' *v.* breiðr. Cf. Brayton (WRY), *Breiðe-tun*
c. 1030 YCh, *Braiþatun* c. 1050 ib.

SANDWITH is (*a field called*) *Sandwath* c. 1215 HolmC. 'Sand ford,'
v. vað. Cf. Sandwith *infra* 433.

BROATS PLANTATION (6″) is *Braton brotts* 1578 *Cocker*, *North* and
South Broats 1794 *Map*. *v.* brot. COCK GATE (6″) is *the Coke yeate*
1578 *Cocker*, *High Cock-gate Field* 1794 *Map*. COCKLEE WOOD is
Cockley ib. LONG RIGG (6″) is *Langrig* 1543 *MinAcct*. 'Long hrycg.'
RANNY GILL (6″). Cf. *Raynie gill gott* 1578 *Cocker*. STOCKHILL
COTTAGE (6″). Cf. *Stock-Hill* 1794 *Map*.

FIELD-NAMES

(*b*) In 1794 (*Map*) *Dove Coat Close*, *Sour Close* (*v. infra* Des), *Town Field*,
Unflatt; in 1777 (NB) *Elnebridge close* (*v.* Ellen R. *supra*), *north Riving*;
in 1578 (*Cocker*) *Brookeholes yate*, *Clockhoe*, *Crodbitt*, *Crooks Well*, *Dolphin
Close*, *garth called Dowth wath* (*v.* vað), *Egill heade*, *Elfe Hill* (cf. *supra* 50),
Greenehowe Mose al. *gale mosse* ('bog-myrtle moss,' from OE *gagel*), *Howerigge ditche* (*v.* hryggr, under hrycg), *Hoyt* (possibly Lancashire dial. *hoyt*,
'long rod or stick'), *the Infelde*, *Langedales*, *Line Garth* (*v.* lin, garðr),
Longhey fitt (*v.* fit), *Loughe* (OE luh, 'lough'), *Lye yeate*, *olde meare ditche*,
mearegill, *mere stones* ('boundary ditch, gil and stones,' *v.* (ge)mǣre), *Mild-
ridge Close*, *the Myre stiele* (*v.* mýrr, stigel), *Nent Wath* al. *new Wath* (*v.* vað),
Orngill Towne, *the outfielde*, *Paddock myre* ('toad mýrr'), *Plaskett Close*
(*v.* plasket), *Raye Crooke*, *Ring gate*, *Saraye wathe* (*v.* vað), *Scales syke*

(v. skáli, sík, under sic), *Scurr Garth* (v. garðr), *Stone Strete*, *Swathriggs* (probably 'black hryggr,' v. svartr), *Thornsicke* (v. sic), *Trossike myre* (ON tros, 'dirt,' sík, mýrr), *Ughall Lane, White fitts* (v. fit), *Wycard, Yodall Close.* Under each of the following dates there is one field-name: *Alnfytts* (probably 'meadows by the R. Ellen' (*supra* 13), v. fit), *Crookes* 1675 *Brayton* (v. krókr), *Gresseland* 1570 *ExchKR* ('grass land'), *Northcroft* c. 1215 HolmC, *Slatestones* 1539 *MinAcct, Todhowe* 1505 *Cocker* (presumably 'fox mound,' v. haugr).

4. Bassenthwaite

BASSENTHWAITE [basnθət]

Bistunthweit c. 1160 Fountains (p)
Bastunthuait c. 1175 *Hesley* (p), *Bastunthweit, Bastuntwayt, Bastunthwait* t. John Fountains (p), c. 1240 StB, 1298 StBA (p)
Bastenethwait 1208 FF
Bastenthwyt 1212 StBA, *Bastenthwait* 1241 Cl (p) *et freq* to 1403 Pat, with variant spellings *-thwayt, -twait, -tweyt, Bastenqweyth'* 1308 *Netherhall* (p)
Bastanswayt 1256 FF
Bastanthweyt 1278, 1279 *Ass*
Bastinthwayt, Bastinthwait 1292 *Ass*, 1372 StB, *Bastynthuate* 1535 VE
Bastingthwayt 1292 *Ass, Bastingthewyt* ib. (p), *Bastingthweyt* 1308 Cl (p), *Bastingthwaite* 1547 FF
Bastonethwayt c. 1230 Fountains (p)
Bastonthwait 1303 Pat
Basyngthwaite 1492 DunBev, *Bassyngthwayte* 1540 *AOMB, Basonthwaite* 1599 FF
Bastyntwhat 1562 PR (Crosth)

BASSENTHWAITE HALLS is *Bassentwhait Halle* 1585 PR (Crosth), *Bassenthwaite Hawes* 1789 Clarke. Cf. *William of ye Halle* (1339 GDR). In the parish was *Bastingthweytbek'* 1292 *Ass.*

Ekwall (DEPN) takes the first element to be the OFr *bastun*, 'stick,' used as a personal name, noting Ernaldus *Bastun* (1191 P (Nf)), Richard *Bastun* (1303 *Ass* (Nth)). Hence '*Bastun*'s þveit. See also Introduction.

ARMATHWAITE HALL

Ermicetwayth 1278 Ch, *Ermitethwayt* 1292 *Ass, Ermethwayt* 1303 Pat, *Ermythwayt* 1333 *Ass, Ermathat* 1659 CantW viii

Armethwaite 1495 Ipm, *Armathwayte in Allerdayll* 1540 *AOMB*,
  Armathwaite Hall 1762 PR (Crosth)
Armanthwaite 1576 S

'Hermit's clearing,' *v.* þveit. Cf. the same name in Ainstable and
Hesket *supra* 168, 200.

BAKESTALL (6"). Cf. *Baikstall Pike* 1839 *Brayton*. BARKBETH is
Barkebethe 1614 PR (Crosth), *Barkboth* 1646 ib. BIRKETT EDGE (6")
is *Briket Hedge Edge* 1839 *Brayton*. BOWNESS is *Bowness* 1784 West,
Bonas 1787 ClarkeM and is so named from its shape. Cf. Bowness
supra 123. BROADNESS is *Bradness* 1784 West, *Broadness* 1787
ClarkeM. BURTHWAITE (6") is *Burthwait* 1703 NicVisit, *Birthat*
1704 ib. BURTHWAITE WOOD (6") is *Birthat Wood* 1675 Ogilby.
CASTLE HILL (6") is *Castle How* 1794 H. DYKE NOOK is so named in
1789 (Clarke). HIGH SIDE is *the High side* 1777 NB. The parish is
divided into two constablewicks, *High Side* and *Low Side* (ib. ii, 93).
MIRE HO is *Myrehouse* 1736 CW xxiv. *v.* mýrr. MOSS SIDE (6") is
Mossyd 1578 PR (Crosth). *v.* mos. PARK COTTAGE (6") and WOOD.
Cf. *the park of Bassenthwaite* 1777 NB. THE RAKE (6") is *Rakes* 1784
West. *v.* reik. SCARNESS is *Scareness* 1784 West, *Scarnhouse* 1787
ClarkeM. *Scarn* is a Cumberland dialect word for dung, from OE
scearn. ULLOCK PIKE is *Ullock* 1784 West. Cf. Ullock *infra* 367.
WHITEWATER DASH (6") is *le white waterdashe* 1594 CW x. *v.* dash.

FIELD-NAMES

(*a*) In 1839 (*Brayton*) Coalbeck (*Colebeck* 1777 NB).

(*b*) In 1789 (Clarke) *Eller Lake or Eller Stile* (*v.* elri), *Heysom-Gill*
(*Hensom Gill Beck* 1787 ClarkeM); in 1777 (NB) *Lansketh, Vothial beck*.
Under each of the following dates there is one field-name: *Karhou* 1278 *Ass*
(possibly Welsh *caer*, 'fort,' and haugr), *Rothmere* t. Eliz ChancP (*v.* rauðr,
mýrr).

5. Bewaldeth and Snittlegarth

BEWALDETH [biwɔ·dəθ]
  Bualdith 1255 FF, 1260 *Rental*
  Bowaldef 1260 *Rental* (p), p. 1500 StB, *Bowaldif* 1284 Cl (p), 1332
    SR
  Boaldith 1278 Ch, 1292 *Ass*, *Boildyth* 1279 *Ass*, *Boaldeth* 1704
    NicVisit

Boualdych, Boualdik' 1292 *Ass, Boualdith* 1318 Ipm, *Boualdyth*
1342 FF
Bowaldeth 1292 *Ass* (p), 1423–9 Weth, *Boualdeth* 1332 *Ass,*
Bowaldeth 1580 Border, 1777 NB
Bowaldehaue 1424 *CCt* (p)

This is an inversion compound meaning the '*bū* or homestead of
a woman named *Aldgȳþ,*' or, less probably, '*Aldgifu.*' For a discussion
of the name see ScandCelts 19.

Snittlegarth is *Smyttlegarth* (sic) 1580 Border, *Snittlegarth* 1608
PR (Dalston). The second element is garðr. The first may be dial.
snittle, 'noose, snare,' of uncertain origin. *v.* NED, where the earliest
example is dated 1611. Cf. also Gilderdale *supra* 175.

FIELD-NAMES

(b) *Monkholme* 1533–8 ECP (*v.* holmr).

6. Blennerhasset and Kirkland[1]

Blennerhasset [blin'reisit]

Blennerheiseta 1188 P, *Blennerhasset(t)* 1353 *Carliol* (p), 1501 Ipm
Blendherseta 1188, 1189 P
Blenh' sete 1190–2, 1195 P, *Blenherseta* 1194 ib., *Blenhersetta* 1194
CR
Blenreheyset 1230 Scotland, *Blenerheyset(e)* 1235 FF *et freq* to 1400
ib., with variant spellings *Blenyr-, Blenar-* and *-hayset, -heysat,*
-haysat, -hesset, -hasset, Blemerheyset 1276 *Ass, Blenerayset* 1290
AD vi, *Blennirhaiset* c. 1290 *Lowther, Blenerhaysette* 1308 Ipm,
Blenarhasset 1432 AD i
Blenreyset, Bleineyset 1271 Pat, *Bleneyherset* 1276 *Ass*
Blencherhayset', Blenkaysette, Blencharnsete 1278 *Ass*
Blinenhaysete 1278 Ch
Blanarhasset 1426 Cl, 1459 Pat
Blynroset 1610 Speed, *Blanrasset* 1675 Sandford, *Blinrosset* 1675
Ogilby

Blennerhasset Bridge (6″). Cf. *Adam del Brygge* (1295 *Ass*),
mentioned in connection with Blennerhasset.
Probably, as suggested by Ekwall (DEPN), the ON *heysætr,* 'hay

---

[1] Torpenhow (*infra* 325) was added to Blennerhasset in 1934.

shieling,' has been added to a British place-name containing *blaen*, 'top' (cf. Blencarn *supra* 214). The medial -*er*- is best explained by Ekwall (*loc. cit.*) on the supposition that the full first element corresponded to Welsh *blaen-dre*, 'hill farm.'

ALDERSCEUGH is *Alderschoeh* 1304 Ipm, *Aldritskow* 1306 ib., *Alderschow* 1316 AD vi, *Alderscogh* 1325 Ipm, 1395 Denton, *Alderskewgh* 1562 NB, *Alderskip* 1675 Ogilby. 'Alder wood,' *v.* alor, skógr, a hybrid formation.

FITZ is *le Fyche* 1316 AD vi, *le Maston Fittes* 1395 Denton, *The Fyttes* 1606 CantW v. This represents ME *fittes*, pl. of fit, 'meadow.'

KIRKLAND (6″) is *Chirchelanda, Chircheland* 1163 P, *Kirkeland* 1246 Misc (p), 1290 Ch, *Kirkelond* 1279 *Ass, Kyrkela(u)nd* 1286 ib., *Kirkland* 1332 SR. 'Church land,' *v.* kirkja. KIRKLAND GUARDS is *Courtland Guard* 1675 Ogilby, *Kirkland-Guards* 1704 NicVisit. *v.* garðr. The form *Courtland* is due to the common NCy pronunciation of *kirk* as [kɔ·rk] and common confusion of *k* and *t* before *l*, as in [maitl] for *Michael*.

TOSTIHOW (lost) is *Tostihow* 1291 *Lowther.* This is probably '*Tosti*'s haugr,' from ON *Tósti*, ODan *Tosti*, OSw *Toste.*

WHITEHEAD BROW (6″) may be associated with the family of Johannes *Whitehead de Kirkland* (1651 CW (OS) iii).

FIELD-NAMES

(*b*) In 1704 (Terrier) *Gate-crooks, Redmire* (*redemyre* 1276 *Ass. v.* hrēod, mýrr). Under each of the following dates there is one field-name: *Swynehou* 1292 *Ass* ('pigs' haugr'), *Walles land* 1570 *ExchKR.*

7. Blindcrake, Isel and Redmain[1]

BLINDCRAKE [blin'kreiək]

  Blenecreyc t. Hy 2 *Laner, Blenecrayc* 1268 CW vi (p)
  Blencraic t. Hy 2 *Laner et passim* to 1610 CW (OS) xv, with variant
    spellings -*creic,* -*crayc,* -*creyc,* -*crich,* -*crak(e),* -*kerck, Blenckrayk*
    1246 FF, *Blentkraych* 1278 *Ass, Blendcrayke* 1555 FF
  Blanecreck 1241 FF
  Bleyncreyk 1260 *Rental, Bleincreik* 1270 *MinAcct, Bleyncrok* 1273 ib.

---

[1] Isel Old Park (*infra* 301) and Sunderland (*infra* 324) were added to Blindcrake in 1934.

Blankrayk 1278 *Ass, Blancrake* p. 1500 StBA
Blyncrake 1555 FF, *Blindcraick* 1567 CW x

In the parish was *Blencraykmore* 1300 Ipm, *Blencrakemore* 1439 Cl. A compound of *blaen*, 'point, top' (*v.* Blencarn *supra* 214) and *creic*, 'rock' (Welsh *craig*). See ScandCelts 105.

ISEL [aisəl]

> *Ysala* 1195 P, *Isall* 1269 Pat, p. 1479 Hexham, *Isal(e)* 1279 *Ass* (p)
>   *et freq* to 1363 Ipm
> *Yshale, Ishale* c. 1235 CW xxvi *et freq* to 1344 *GDR* (p)
> *Isshale* 1295 *Ass, Issehale* 1308 Fine
> *Isehale* 1300 Ipm, 1310 Fine
> *Issell(e)* 1397 Cl, 1512 LP, *Yssel(l)* 1532 ib., *Issel* 1736 CW xxiv
> *Isell* 1485 Ipm, *Iseild* 1644 CW xvi
> *Isle* 1576 S

ISELGATE (6″) (in Isel Oldpark parish) is *Isellgait* 1623 *Brayton, Isell gate* 1777 NB. ISEL HALL is *Isill Hall* 1675 Sandford. ISEL MILL is *molendinum de Hysale* 1260 *Rental, molendinum de Ishale* 1268 *MinAcct.* ISEL PARK is *Isalepark(e)* 1363 *GDR*, 1383 *Ass.* In the parish was *Isselmore* 1507 *Cocker. v.* mōr.

This is probably an Old Anglian name, meaning '*Ise*'s haugh,' *v.* h(e)alh.

MOOTA HILL is *Mewthow, Mewtey Hill* 1537 LP, *Mewto beacon* 1576 S, *Mewtoo-beacon* 1656 Spelman, *Villare, the more of Muta* 1675 Sandford, *Moothay* 1777 NB, *Moutay* 1821 G. Cf. *Mowtay High Cow Gate* 1777 *Hudleston. v.* (ge)mōt and hōh. The hill is mentioned as a place of assembly in LP (Vol. xii, Pt. 1, pp. 80, 301, 303).

REDMAIN [ri·dmian]

> *Redeman* 1188 CW (OS) iii (p), c. 1200 Weth (p), 1281 *MinAcct*
>   *et freq* to 1332 SR (p), *Redemane* 1291 Cl (p), 1314 Ipm (p), 1357
>   FF (p), *Redemayn* 1385 ib. (p)
> *Rademan* 1198, 1202, 1203 P (all p)
> *Redman(e)* 1235 Fees (p), 1300 Ipm *et freq* to 1555 FF, *Redmain*
>   1407 ib., *Redmayne* 1572 ib., *Readmaine* 1580 Border
> *Reddeman* 1308 *Netherhall* (p)

Sir Ifor Williams suggests that this is Welsh *rhyd*, 'ford,' and *maen*, 'stone,' or its Med. Welsh pl. *mein*, as in Rhyd-y-main (near Dolgelley, Merionethshire), which means 'ford of the stones.'

B

CALFSHAW WOOD (6″) is so named in 1810 (*Map*). *v.* sceaga.
CLINTS PARK and CRAGS (both 6″). Cf. *Clints* ib. *v.* klint. CROSS
HILL (6″) is *Croshill* 1570 FF. HAGS WOOD (6″). Cf. *Redmain Haggs*
1777 NB. *v.* hǫgg. HUNTER HOW (6″). Cf. *Hunter-How Close* 1810
Map. KIRK HILL (6″) is *Kirk-hill* 1704 NicVisit. LINSKELDFIELD
is *Linskill Field* 1810 *Map*. If, as seems probable, this is to be con-
nected with *Linescales* 1300 Ipm, the second element was originally
skáli. The first element is probably lin. MILLSTONEMOOR is *Mylnaston
More* 1571 FF, *Millston mor* 1606 *Brayton*. OXPASTURE WOOD (6″).
Cf. *Ox Pastures* 1810 *Map*. SALKELD CLOSE (6″) is so named in
1777 (*Hudleston*). Cf. *Ground called Mr Salkeld Lees* ib. THACKRAY
WOOD (6″). Cf. *Thackray Park* 1810 *Map*.

FIELD-NAMES

(a) In 1810 (*Map*) Crake Wood Bank, Cushat Bank (i.e. 'wood-pigeon'),
Flatts, Frostums, Glad-mire (*v.* mýrr), Greenup's Fields (*Greenops tenement*
1699 CW xxxix), Jonathan's Fields (*Jonathan's tenement* ib.), Kirk-foot,
Kiskin Spring (cf. *infra* 348), Lun Wood, Studholme (*v.* stōd, holmr), White
Rynolds.

(b) In 1794 (H) *Chapel-Guards* (*v.* garðr), *the Trinities* (id. 1777 NB);
in 1766 (*Brayton*) *Alliston moore, Fenton Butts* (*Finting Butts* 1725 ib.),
Trinkelds (id. ib.); in 1718 (*Brayton*) *ye green gate, Lece, Orpheur gray stones,*[1]
Patrick sike (*v.* sic); in 1699 (CW xxxix) *Priorfield tenement, Washay tenement*;
in p. 1479 (Hexham) *Aldeby* ('old bȳ'), *Hoggis-crofte, le More-wra* (*v.* mōr,
(v)rá). Under each of the following dates there is one field-name: *Akergarth*
1289 *Ass* (*v.* akr, under æcer, garðr), *Brackens* 1631 *Brayton*, *ley rigge* 1606
ib., *Oxeholmes al. Oxesumer* 1571 FF (*v.* holmr), *Tongue Sharpes* 1725
Brayton.

8. Boltons

BOLTONS [boutən]

Boulton' 1200, 1201 P *et passim, Boulton' in Allirdale* 1335 *MinAcct*
Bolton 1212 StBA *et passim, Bolton in Alnerdale* 1278 *Ass*
Boeltone 1212–17 RBE, 1246 FF
Bothilton' c. 1227 *HolmC, Botheltun* t. Hy 3 CW v, *Bothelton* 1278
Ass
Bowelton 1266 *MinAcct*, 1278 *Ass*
Bolton or Bothilton 1610 Denton
Boulton 1285 *For, Boulton near Ireby* 1676 PR (Brough)

---

[1] Presumably called after one of the Orfeur family who held High Close in
Plumbland for several generations (CW (OS) iii, 99–126).

BOLTONGATE is *Bolton yate, Bolton gaite, Bolton gate* 1578 *Cocker*.
BOLTONWOOD HO (6″) is *wood of Bothilton* c. 1227 *HolmC, boscus de
Boulton* 1285 *For, boscus de Bolton* 1297 *MinAcct, Boltonwood* 1580
Border.

    v. bōōltūn. *in Allerdale* to distinguish this from Bolton *infra* 394.

BINTHWAITE PLANTATION (6″) is *Byndetwayth* 1297 *MinAcct*. The
first element is probably OE (*wudu*)*binde*, 'woodbine.' The second
is þveit.

CRUMMOCK BRIDGE (6″) is *pontem de Crumbock* 1278 *Ass. v.* Crummock Beck *supra* 10.

ELLERSHAW PLANTATION (6″) is *Ellerschogh* 1334 *MinAcct*. 'Alder
wood,' *v.* elri, skógr. The second element has been anglicised.

NEWLANDS FM is *Neweland in Boulton* 1285 *For, Newland(e)s* 1578
Cocker. NEWLANDS ROW (6″) is *Newland rowe* 1578 *Cocker, Newlands
row* 1777 NB. *v.* nīwe, land, rāw.

RESPHOLM (lost) is *Respholm* 1285 *For*. 'Sedge holmr.' The first
element, found also in Reston We, is an unrecorded OE word cognate
with OHG *hrispahi*; G *Rispe*, MLG *rispe*, 'brushwood' (DEPN).

SANDALE is *Sandeldale* 1278 Abbr, *Sanderdale Hill* 1537 LP, *Sandell*
1578 *Cocker, Sandall, Sandale hill* 1777 NB. Probably sand-dæl, with
a second *dale* added when the first was reduced by lack of stress.

SKALMALLOK (lost) is *Schallermakek in Allerdale, Scallermakek* 1292
Ass, Skelmerakeck', Sckalermakek' ib. (p), *Schallermarkek', Scallermakek* 1292 *Ass, Scalermaket* 1292 QW, *Scalermakek* 1296 *MinAcct,
Skalmallok* t. Hy 8 *AOMB*. This is an inversion compound of which
the first element is ON *skálir*, plural of skáli. The second element
appears to be a personal name, though its exact form is uncertain.
It is possibly, as Professor Jackson suggests, *Macóg*, a diminutive of
Irish *mac*, 'boy'. The forms of Skalmallok have sometimes been confused with those of Scarrowmanwick *supra* 250.

THACKTHWAITE HALL is *Takketweyt* 1278 *Ass, Thakthueyt* 1285 *For*,
Thachawyt 1296 *MinAcct, (scalinge de) Thacketwayth* 1297 ib., *Thack-
thwate* 1578 *Cocker*. The first element is ON þak, dial. *thack*, 'rushes,
(reeds for thatching)'. The second is þveit.

THORNTHWAITE is *Tornthayt* 1268 *MinAcct, Thornthweyt* 1279 *Ass* (p), *Thornethweyt* 1285 *For* (p), *Thornthwayt* 1292 *Ass, Thornwhat al. Thornethaite* 1567 FF. THORNTHWAITE HEAD is *caput de Thorne-tweyt beck'* 1300 *For, caput Thornethebek* 1540 *LRMB,* the head of *Thornthwaite beke* 1578 *Cocker,* the head of *Thornthwait* 1777 NB. 'Thorn clearing,' *v. þveit.* Lindkvist (125) compares the ODan place-name *Thornthwed.*

WEARY HALL is *Weary hall* 1578 *Cocker,* 1678 HMC xxv, *Weryehall* 1586 CW xiv, *Weery hall, Wearie Hall* 1675 Sandford. There may be an earlier reference in the name of Simon de *Wyrihal* (t. Hy 3 CW v), who was a juror in the Forest of Inglewood district, but the meaning of the name remains uncertain. Ekwall (ScandCelts 26) takes the first element to be *Werri,* as in Willow Holme in Carlisle (*supra* 43).

ANGERTON BANK is *Angerton banck* 1578 *Cocker.* Cf. *infra* 292. BURNS RIGG is probably the site of *Borance* ib. *v.* burghan. Cf. Burrance (PN Dumf 75). CARLISLEGATE (6″) is *Carleill gate* ib. CATLANDS HILL. Cf. *Cattlands* ib. CLOSE is *the Close* 1777 NB. COCK BRIDGE (6″) is so named ib. DRAYRIGG (6″) is *Dririgge, Dryrigge* 1578 *Cocker.* 'Dry ridge,' *v.* hrycg. GILL BARN (6″). Cf. *the Gill* ib. LINEDRAW is *Lynwra* 1338 *Ass* (p), *Linwra* 1381 IpmR, *Lynewray field* 1578 *Cocker.* 'Corner where flax was grown,' *v.* līn, (v)rá. MEALSGATE is *Meals Gate, Meal's Gate* 1777 NB. POW (6″) is so named in 1656 (CantW vii). QUARRYHILL is *Quarrellhill* 1578 *Cocker, Quarry hill* 1777 NB. RASH is *the Rashe* 1578 *Cocker. v.* rysc. SHAKING BRIDGE (6″) is *Shaking Bridge* 1578 *Cocker, Shakingbrig* 1687 CW (OS) xv. THISTLEBOTTOM (6″) is *Thistle bottome* 1578 *Cocker.* THORNY STONE (6″) is *Thornye Stone* ib. WAVERBANK is *Wauerbank'* 1539 *MinAcct.* On the bank of the R. Waver *supra* 30. WELLRASH is *the Well Rashe* 1578 *Cocker. v.* rysc.

FIELD-NAMES

(b) In 1777 (NB) *Great Paddock, Priest croft, Rooksbridge*; in 1578 (*Cocker*) *Beacon hill, Bengate, the brode Ings* (*v.* eng), *the Coen Ings* (*v.* eng), *Cowath Wray* (*v.* vað, (v)rá), *gravegate, the hodge mains* (*v.* mains), *parsons brigge, Rockrowe, Swale crofte* (cf. *infra* 289); in 1571 (ElizKes) *Sibenseit, Starmer* ('sedge mýrr,' *v.* star); in 1401 (DentonA) *le Wra* (id. 1296 *MinAcct, v.* (v)rá). Under each of the following dates there is one field-name: (*del*) *himpegarth* 1296 *MinAcct* (*v.* impgarth), *la launde* 1338 *Ass* ('glade,' *v.* launde), *Robertaker* 1332 Hesley (*v.* æcer).

9. Bothel and Threapland

BOTHEL [bouəl, boul]

> *Bothle* c. 1125, c. 1135 StB
> *Botla, Botlia* c. 1125 StB, *Botle* c. 1135 ib.
> *Bothel* 1230 Scotland, 1278 *Ass et passim*
> *Boyele* 1278 *Ass, Bothele* 1301 Ch
> *Bothil(l), Bothyll* 1279 *Ass et freq* to 1777 NB, *Buthill* 1796 *Brayton*
> *Bodell* 1369 Ipm, 1610 Speed, *Botill* 1421 FF
> *Bold* 1580 Border, *Bole* 1675 Sandford, *Boal* 1745 CaineCl, *Boald al. Bothel* 1756 LowtherW, *Bothill, otherwise Boald* 1816 Lysons

BOTHEL HALL (6″) is *Bothill-hall* 1816 Lysons. In the parish was *Bothelacre* 1303 Cl.

'Building,' *v.* bōðl. In 1292 (*Ass*) it was stated that certain tenements were "in *Bothel* et non in *Bostel*."

CATERLAISING (lost). This name only occurs in the name of Gilbert de *Caterlaising de Treplaund*, which occurs in a plea of 1278 *Ass*. The site is unknown, but there is a strong probability that it was in the same part of the county as Threapland. In any case, the name must be an inversion compound, consisting of OWelsh *cateir*, 'chair,' as in Catterlen *supra* 182, and ON *leysingr*, 'freedman,' often used in northern England as a personal name. Cf. Lazonby *supra* 219. The latter sense is more probable in a compound of this type.

THREAPLAND

> *Trepland* c. 1220 Fountains (p), c. 1265 Hesley (p), 1278 *Ass*
> *Threppelland* c. 1220 Fountains (p), *Threpelaund(e)* 1266 MinAcct, 1277, 1278 *Ass, Threpelond* 1279 ib., *Threpeland* 1316 AD vi *et freq* to 1591 FF
> *Threplond* 1260 Rental, 1279 *Ass, Threplaund(e)* 1276, 1278 *Ass, Threpland* 1279 ib. *et freq* to 1675 Ogilby, *Threplandes in Allerdalles* 1318 MinAcct, *Threapland* 1777 NB
> *Trepelaund(e)* 1276 *Ass,* (*in Boyele*) 1278 ib.

THREAPLAND HALL is *Threepland hall* 1675 Sandford.   × H

This name, as noted by Denton (48), signifies *contentionis terra*, 'land of dispute.' It is on the borders of the parish. The first element is the NCy *threap*, 'dispute,' from OE *þrēap*-, as in *þrēapian, brēaping*, '(to) rebuke', Cf. Threepwood (PN NbDu 196), Threepwood

(Melrose), Threpland (PN Scot 309), Threapland Gate *infra* 378, and the Debateable Land *supra* 38.

WHARRELS HILL is *Wharral Hill* 1586 CW xiv. This is a well-rounded hill and the origin of the name is perhaps OE hwyrfel or ON hvirfill. Cf. Whorlton, by Whorl Hill (PN NRY 177) and Whorwellsdown (PN W 135). The first word may, however, be *quarrel*, 'quarry', as in Quarryhill *supra* 270.

10. Bridekirk[1]

BRIDEKIRK

> *Bridekirk(e)* c. 1210 StB (p) *et passim*, (*in Alredale*) c. 1210 Guisb, *Brithekirk'* 1292 *Ass*, *Brydekyrcke* 1537 LP, *Bridechurch* 1653 CantW vii
> *Brisekirke* c. 1235 Hesley, *Bricekirk(e)* 1260 *Rental*, 1291 Tax, 1300 GDR, 1323 Pat, c. 1330 *Carliol* (p), *Briskirk'* early 14th StMaryY (p)
> *Brideschirche* 1260 *Rental* (p), *Brideskirk(e)* 1267 Misc, 1279 *MinAcct* (p), 1296 Ipm
> *Briddeskirke* 1266 *MinAcct* (p), 1292 *Ass*, *Briddeschirche* ib. (p)
> *Bridkirk(e)* 1466 Pat, 1580 Border, 1675 Ogilby
> *Birdchurch* 1631 CW xxxix
> In the neighbourhood was *Brudeskirkefeld* 1260 *Rental*.

'Church of St Bride,' *v.* kirkja and cf. Kirkbride *supra* 144.

ANNS HILL is *Ann's Hill* 1776 PR.

APPLETON HALL (6″) is *Apeltun* c. 1160 Guisb, *Apelton in Alredale* c. 1220 ib., *Appleton* 1229 ib. In the neighbourhood was *Apeltonmede* 1260 *Rental*, *Appltonemed* 1279 *MinAcct*. This is OE æppeltūn, 'orchard.' For numerous parallels *v.* DEPN.

WOOD HALL is *la Wodehall* 1278 *Ass* (p), *Woodhall* 1667 PR. 'Hall in the wood,' *v.* wudu, h(e)all.

11. Bromfield[2]

BROMFIELD

> *Brounefeld* c. 1125 StB
> *Brumfeld* c. 1155 (c. 1200) Weth, 1212 Cur *et freq* to 1576 S, *Brumfeud* 1278 *Ass* (p)

---

[1] Dovenby (*infra* 284), and Tallentire (*infra* 324) were added to Bridekirk in 1934.

[2] Blencogo (*supra* 122) and Langrigg and Mealrigg (*infra* 304) were added to Bromfield in 1934.

Brunnefeld t. Ric 1 (1308) Ch, c. 1200 Weth (p)
Brunfeld' c. 1200 *HolmC*, 1258 *Netherhall* (p) *et freq* to 1438 FF
Brunefelde n.d. *Lowther* (p), *Brunefeld* t. John BM, 1210, 1213 Cur,
   1230 Scotland
Bromfeld(e) c. 1210 Weth, 1330 Pap, 1350 Ipm, 1391 FF, 1400 Cl,
   1417 FF, *Bromfeud* 1279 *Ass*, 1303 ChancW
Bramfeld c. 1275 StBA
Braumfeld 1278 *Ass*
Brounfeld(e) c. 1308 StB, 1349 Ipm, 1399 Cl, *Brownfeld* 1494 Pat
Brimpfhild 1308 Ipm
Brundfeld 1407 Pat
Bromefeild 1576 S
Broomefielde 1578 *Cocker*

It is difficult to be certain of the etymology of this name, but the probabilities are in favour of an original *Brūnefeld*, 'brown open land.' There was early confusion (owing partly to partial assimilation of *nf* to *mf*) with **brōm**, 'broom', and even with **brame**, 'briar.' The confusion is well illustrated in the various spellings of the same man's name. The name of Thomas de *Brumefeld* (c. 1182 Weth) is also spelt *Brunnefeld, Brun(e)feld, Brumfeld*.

CROOKDAKE is *Crokydayk* 1231 Pipe, 1339 *GDR*, *Crokedayk* 1260 *Rental*, 1349 Ipm, *le Crokedhayk'* 1288 *Ass* (p), *Cruddayk* 1370 Ipm, Cl, *Crokdaike* 1438 FF, *Crukedayk* 1504 *Orton*, *Highe Crookdake* 1578 *Cocker*, *Crockdayk* 1675 Sandford, *Crooked oake* 1703 PR (Millom). CROOKDAKE MILL (6") is *Crookdake miln* 1777 NB. Cf. *le mylne rase de Crukedake* 1541 *MinAcct*. 'Crooked oak,' *v*. **eik**.

GILL HO is *la Gile de Brumfeud* 1278 *Ass* (p), (*del*) *Gylle de Brumeff*... 1292 *Ass* (p), *Gyl, Gil* ib., *La Gile, Le Gyll* 1305–6 Ipm. 'Ravine,' *v*. **gil**.

HIGH and LOW SCALES are *Scales* 1353 Pat, *Broomefielde skailes* 1578 *Cocker*, *High* and *Low Scales* 1794 H. 'Shielings,' *v*. **skáli**.

STORTH BROW (6") is named from *Storth* 1292 *Ass*. 'Brushwood,' *v*. **storð**.

HIGH and LOW AKETON are respectively *Acton heale, Ackton heade* 1578 *Cocker*. *v*. **āc, tūn**. HEATHFIELD is *Hedfield* 1567 FF. LOW ROW is so named in 1794 (H). PLASKET PLANTATION. Cf. *Plasketts Land* 1760 Brisco in Dundraw. *v*. **plasket**. MIRESIDE. Cf. *Bromfield*

Mire ib. St Mungo's Well (6″) is *Saint Mungo's Well* 1661 HMC xxi. The church of Bromfield is dedicated to St Mungo. Sandraw is *Sandwraye* 1541 *MinAcct, Sandraw* 1663 CW xvi. 'Sand corner,' *v.* (v)rá.

FIELD-NAMES

(a) Affles, Blenkin Close, Gabriel, Goodie, Grymes Field, Intake (*v.* intak), Red Dykes (*v.* dīc), Little Shares, Winnie Seymour (*Greate* and *Little Seamyre, water called siveamyre* 1578 *Cocker.* 'sedgy marsh,' *v.* sef, mýrr).

(b) In 1580 (Border) *Cowdall*; in c. 1230 (*HolmC*) *Lofthayt* (*v.* lopt, þveit), *Maskelawe* (possibly *mascle*-hlāw, 'spotted hill'); in c. 1200 (*HolmC*) *Northrig* ('north hrycg'), *Petepottes* ('peat-holes').

12. Broughton

Great and Little Broughton [brɔ·tn, brautn]

> *Broctuna* 12th Guisb, *Brocton* 1208 FF, *Brogton*' 1295 *Rental*
> *Brochton* 1231 FF, 1292 *Ass,* (*Magna*) 1260 *Rental*
> *Browcton* 1266 *MinAcct, Browhton* 1286 Ipm, *Great Browghtton, Little Browghton* 1537 LP
> *Browton* 1266 *MinAcct, Brouton*(*e*) 1267 ib., (*Magna, Parua*) ib.
> *Brouhton* 1267 *MinAcct, Brouchton* 1278 *Ass, Petit Brouthtone* 1305 Parl
> *Brougton* 1278, 1279 *Ass, Broughton* 1332 SR, (*Littell*) 1580 Border
> *Broghton* 1286 Ipm, Cl, 1292 *Ass,* 1305 Ipm, 1307 Pat, (*in Allerdale*) 1318 Misc, (*parua*) 1429 *Netherhall*

Broughton Craggs is so named in 1652 (*Cocker*). Broughton Lodge (in Broughton Moor) is so named in 1811 (PR, Bridekirk). 'Brook tūn,' *v.* brōc.

Nook (6″) is *Nooke* 1674 PR (Bridekirk).

FIELD-NAMES[1]

(a) In 1852, High and Low Barrock (*v.* Barrock *supra* 201), Boon Mire (*Boone Myre* 1652, *Bourne myres* 1697), Broad Mire (id. 1679. *v.* mýrr), Cold Fleet Close (cf. *Fleet rigg* 1720. *v.* flēot), Crook of Ellen, Cross Mire (*Crosse mire* 1684. *v.* mýrr), Dalt, East Field (*Eastfeild* 1652), Ellers (*Eller* 1684. *v.* elri), Fearon Close, Flemrigg (*Flemrigge* 1652. *v.* hrycg), Flodders, Fog Field (*v.* fog), Foul Syke (*Foule sycke* 1697. *v.* fūl, sīc), Great Close (id. 1652), Intack (cf. *a little Intack* 1585. *v.* intak), King Ings (cf. *Kinge side* 1724),

---

[1] All references, except where otherwise stated, are from *Cocker*.

Kirk Mire (*Over Kirkmire* 1688, 'church' mýrr), Ling Platt, Lot (*Lott* 1691), Palmer Cones, Pot Kiln Field (*v.* cyln), School Close (cf. *Schoolhouse Close* 1777, given as an endowment for the school), Soddy Gap (cf. *Suddocke Close* 1652), Stackmoor, Steps Field, Syke (*the Syke Close* 1652. *v.* sīc), Toad Lands, Turn Out.

(b) In 1724, *Borrance Flatt* (*v.* burghan), *Heskett Feild*, *Reading banke*; in 1720, *Butts*, *Caldgill* (*v.* gil), *Crooked hood rigg*, *Dale of Meadow*, *Gardey Ingg* (*v.* eng), *Marbell Sike Foot* (*v.* sīc), *ye Mill Field* (*the Milne feild* 1652); in 1705 (PR) *Eastgate* (*eastyeate* 1658 ib.); in 1699, *Millhow close*, *Preist Bridge gate* (cf. Thomas *le Prest* 1260 *Rental*); in 1697 *Great Broughton Outgang* (*Outganne close* 1633. *v.* ūtgang); in 1693, *Uptown Bier* (cf. *the Byer* 1652); in 1692, *Haggashill House* (cf. *Haghouse Toft* 1658), *Midleing Close* (*v.* eng), *Myles Strand* (cf. *the Strand* 1652 and *v.* strand); in 1660, *Cumerlater*, *Grayston*, *Meckinhill*, *Staverbarrow* ('hill marked by a stake or pillar,' *v.* be(o)rg); in 1652, *Coptermsrigge*, *Goodyinge* (*v.* eng), *the Halcroft* (*Haulle Crofte* 1598), *Sandayre* (*v.* sand, eyrr). Under each of the following dates there is one field-name: *Above Mire* 1684 (*v.* mýrr), *Little Carfe* 1688, *Crackenthrop* 1723, *Crosse* 1668 PR, *Curlands Dale* 1719, *Hinde Toft* 1694, *Micklefeild* 1679 (*v.* micel), (*del*) *Spute* c. 1300 Guisb (*v.* spoute), *Westgate* 1655 PR.

13. Broughton Moor

BROUGHTON MOOR is *Broghton more* c. 1187 HolmC, *mora de Broctona* c. 1215 *HolmC*, *Broughton more* 1535 *MinAcct*. *v.* Broughton *supra* 274 and mōr.

HARKER and HARKER MARSH (6″) are (*pastura voc.*) *Hartecar Tarne* 1560 *Cocker*, *Harker* 1654 ib., *Harkare* 1693 ib., *Harker Marsh* 1852 ib. 'Hart marsh,' *v.* heorot, kiarr, tiǫrn.

FOX HO is *Fox Houses* 1812 PR (Bridekirk). HENNAH HALL (6″) is *Hannah* 1682 *Cocker*, *Hennah* 1683 ib., *Henney* 1687 ib., *Hennah Hall* 1805 PR (Bridekirk). LINEFOOT is perhaps to be associated with *Linefitt Bank* 1775 *LowtherW* in Dearham. 'Flax meadow,' *v.* līn, fit. LOW CLOSE is *Loweclose* 1628 PR (Bridekirk). OUTFIELDS (6″). Cf. *Out Field Closes* 1721 *Cocker*. STOCKMOOR is so named in 1763 (PR, Bridekirk). *v.* mōr. STONEPOT is *Stanpott* 1652 *Cocker*, *Stonepott* 1668 PR (Bridekirk). 'Stone hole.'

14. Caldbeck

CALDBECK [kɔ·bek]

Caldebek 11th (13th) *Gospatric et passim*, with variant spellings *Kalde-*, *Caude-*, *Cawde-*, *Kaude-* and *-beck*, *-bec(h)*, *Caldebec in Alredal'* 1212 Cole, *Caldevek* 1404 Pat

Caldbec c. 1175 Weth, *Kaldbek* 1365 Pat
Cawlbek 1506 CW (OS) vi, *Cawdbek* 1552 Visit i, *Kolbeck* 1569
ElizKes, *Callbeck* 1569 FF
Calbeyke 1537 LP

CALDBECK FELLS are so named in 1777 (NB). They may be associated
with the names of Adam *del Fel* (1292 *Ass*) and John *del Fell* (1332
SR). *v.* fiall (under fell). In the parish was *parcus de Caldebek'* 1272
For.

'Cold stream,' *v.* kaldr, bekkr. It is called *Caldebeke Underfell* in
1519 (*FF*) to distinguish it from UPTON which is *Caldebek Upton* 1519
FF, *Uptoune* 1540 *MinAcct*, 'higher settlement,' *v.* uppe, tūn. Cf.
Uppington Yeate 1660 *Cocker*. The stream itself is referred to in
aquam de Caldebek 1292 *Ass.*

BRAE FELL is *Braythefel* 1242 *FF.* 'Broad fell,' *v.* breiðr, fiall (under
fell).

BRANTHWAITE [branθət] is *Braunthwait* 1332 SR (p), *Braunthwayt*
1345 GDR (p), *Brounthwayt* 1357 ib., *Branthwaite* 1560 *Cocker*, (*High,
Low*) 1697 ib., *Branthwaite Caldbeck* 1793 CW (OS) ix. Although no
form in *Bram-* is recorded for this name, it probably, like Branthwaite
infra 366, contains ME *brame*, 'bramble.' The second element is
þveit.

BROWNRIGG is *Brunrigg juxta Caudebec* 1209 Pipe, *Brunrigge* 1223 ib.
et freq to 1237 ib., with variant spellings *-rig'*, *-rigg'*, *-ricg*, *Brunerigg*
a. 1228 HolmC, *Brounrigg'* c. 1235 *HolmC, Brounrygge* 1504–15 ECP,
Browndrigg 1606 CW (OS) ix. 'Brown ridge,' *v.* hryggr (under hrycg).

GREENRIGG is *Greneric* 1163 P, *Grenerig* 1232 Pat (p), 1279 *Ass* (p),
1309, 1310 Ipm, 1505 *Norfolk*, (*in Caldebek*) 1286 Ipm, *Grenrig(g)*
1305, 1322, 1362 ib., *Grenrick* 1591 FF, *Greenrigg* 1658 CW xxi.
'Green ridge,' *v.* hryggr (under hrycg).

HALTCLIFF HALL [hɔ·tli]

   Halteclo 1208 FF *et freq* to 1394 IpmR, *Halteclove* 1211 Cur,
       Hauteclo 1252 Pipe (p), *Hauteclow, Hauteclou* 1258 ib. (both p),
       Hautecloch, Hauteclouch 1285 *For* (both p), *Haldeclogh, Halde-
       cloygh* 1336 Ipm (both p), *Hautteclo* 1343 *Cocker*
   Alteclo 1236 Pipe (p), 1260 Ipm, *Autoclou* 1257 Pipe (p)
   Haltclo 1332 Ipm (p), *Haltclogh* 1340 GDR (p), *Haltclugh* 1610
       Denton, *Haldclo* 1399 IpmR

Hawtecliffe 1523 *FF*, *Hawtclyff* 1535 LP, *Awtclife* 1588 *Cocker*,
Halltlife 1711 PR (Matterdale)
Hall Clyff 1540 *AOMB*, *Awcliffe*, *Aucliffe* 1579 FF
Hawcley 1569 FF, *Haltley Hall* 1715 *Devonshire*, *Hautley* 1717 *H*
Cocker

HALTCLIFF BRIDGE is *Halĭclobrig'* 1363 *GDR*, *Haltclobrigge* 1367
Ipm, *the bridge at Alteclo* t. Hy 7 CW v, *Haultley Bridge*, *Hautley
Bridge* 1565, 1574 PR (Greystoke), *Hautcliff Brigge* 1589 *LRMB*,
Hautlife Bridge 1599 PR (Greystoke), *Hotley Bridge* 1700 ib., *Hoateley
Bridge* 1715 ib.

The forms ending in *-cloch*, *-clugh*, *-clogh* show that the second
element of this difficult name is OE clōh, 'clough, ravine.' The word
has been reduced to *-clo* through lack of stress, and then replaced by
-ley, and finally by *-cliff*. The first element is more doubtful. There
is no parallel from any other name in the county to the long run of
13th-century forms in *Halte-*, *Halt-*, *Haute-*. It is on the whole most
probable that the forms in *Haute-* come nearest to the original, and
that the first element of the name is the OFr *haut*, 'high.' If so, the
forms in *Halt(e)-* will represent an inverted spelling such as is frequently found in similar sound-groups, e.g. *Oldebi* 1086 DB for
Oadby (Lei), ON *Auða býr*. *Haut* may form the first element of
Haltwhistle (PN NbDu 99–100) in which the change to *Halt-* is not
recorded before the later Middle Ages. The exact site to which the
name Haltcliff was first applied cannot be determined.

HESKET NEWMARKET
Eskhevid c. 1230 HolmC, *Eskeheued* c. 1250 *HolmC*, 1305 Ipm,
1399 IpmR, *Eskheved* 1308 Ipm, *Eskheuid* 1340 *GDR*
Hesket 1523 *FF*, 1610 Denton, *Heskethe* 1560 *Cocker*, *Hesket in the
parish of Coldbeck* 1742 PR, *Hesket New Market* 1751 CW (OS)
xiii, *Hesket...a market town* 1777 NB
Eskett 1543 CW xiv, *Eskate* 1565 *Brayton*

It is clear that this name is a hybrid compound of *esk* from ON *eski*,
'place overgrown with ash trees,' and OE hēafod, 'head, hill.' This
was reduced to *Esket* and then, in the 16th century, assimilated in
spelling to Hesket in the Forest *supra* 199. It is not known when the
right to hold a market here was granted.

HOWTHWAITE (6″)
Hothweit 1209, 1229 Pipe, *Hochthweit* 1227 ib., *Hotweit* 1228 ib.
Hathwayt 1230 P (*Haytwayt* 1230 CR)

'Hill clearing,' *v.* hōh, þveit. Cf. Huthwaite (PN NRY 177), Hucknall under Huthwaite (PN Nt 119–20) and Hewthwaite and *Hothwait infra* 434, 453.

SOKBRODLAND (lost) is *Sokbrodland* 1399 IpmR. It is at least possible that the first part of this name may be connected with the tenure of part of Haltcliff *supra* by Uctred of *Sokebred'* (probably Sockbridge, We), recorded in 1208 FF.

WHELPO [ʍelpə] is *Cuelpou* 1278 *Ass* (p), *Quelphou* 1279 ib. (p), *Whelphou* 1285 *For* (p), 1293 *MinAcct et freq* to 1344 Ipm, *Quelphowe* 1305 Ipm, *Whelpehowe* 1333 Misc, *Whelpho* 1336 Ipm, 1343 *Cocker*, *Whelpowe* 1540 *MinAcct*, *Whelphay* 1777 NB, *Whelpa* 1795 CW (OS) ix. 'Hill of the whelps or cubs,' *v.* ON hvelpr and haugr. Cf. Whelprigg (We).

WODEKOCSHOTES (lost) is *Wodekocshotes* 1318 *MinAcct*. This is (wood) cockshot, the earliest reference to which word given in NED is dated 1530.

ALCOCK FOLD and BONNERS (both 6″) are to be associated with the families of John *Aucock* (1642 CW xxi) and Hugh *Bonner* (ib.).

ASKEW MIRE (6″) is *Harskethe Myre, Heskethemyre* 1560 *Cocker*, *Haskew myre* 1578 ib., *Askewmyre* 1652 ib. Cf. *Harescow* 1242 FF, *Herskugh* 1399 IpmR. The forms are too various for any interpretation. BANNEST HILL [banəst]. Cf. *Bane-, Bainehirste Mosse* 1560 *Cocker*, *the Baniste* 1581 ib., *Banhurste* 1595 ib., *Baynehurste* 1598 ib., *Barnerhurstdale in Hautley* 1652 ib., *Bannerhurst* 1657 ib., *Bannast* 1685 ib. Possibly a hybrid compound of ON beinn, 'straight,' and OE hyrst. BIGGARDS is *Biggards* 1626 PR (Greystoke), *Bigyards* 1695 *Cocker*. The first element seems to be ON bygg, 'barley.' The second is ON garðr, 'enclosure.' THE BOG (6″) is *Boggs* 1691 ib., *Bogg* 1699 ib. BRACKENRIGGS (6″) is *Brackonrigge* 1593 ib. *v.* braken, hryggr (under hrycg). BURBLETHWAITE (6″) is so named in 1658 ib. Cf. *Burblethwaite* 1693 PR in Crosthwaite (We). *v.* þveit. CALEBRACK is *Kelebrycke* 1588 ib., *Calebreck* 1679 ib. CLAY GAP is *Claye Gappe* 1594 ib. CROOK BANK (6″) is *Crock bancke, Crookbank* 1687 ib. DYKE NOOK (6″) is *Dike Nooke* 1724 ib. *v.* dīc. FAIRY BRIDGE. Cf. *The Fairy Kettle, The Fairy Kirk* 1794 H. FAULDS is *Faldes* 1560 *Cocker*, *Folds* 1754 CW (OS) ix, *the Faulds* 1777 NB. It may be associated with the name of Henry de *Falda* (1285 *For*). *v.* fal(o)d. FELL SIDE is *Felside* 1560

Cocker. FLAT (6″) is *Fflatt* 1656 ib. *v.* flat. GILLFOOT (6″) is *Gylfoote* 1586 ib. THE GREEN (6″) is so named in 1724 ib. HARE STONES (6″) is on the parish boundary. *v.* hār, stān. HARRISON HO (6″). Cf. *Harrinson Tenement* 1680 *Cocker.* HAZELHURST is *Haslehurst* 1652 ib. 'Hazel wood,' *v.* hyrst. HEIGHT is so named ib. HIGH HO (6″). Cf. *High house meadows* 1686 ib. HIGH ROW is so named in 1723 ib. HOWK (6″) is *the Hawk* 1777 NB. Cf. *Howkbanke* 1652 *Cocker.* "A great cave or grotto" (NB ii, 136). (H ii, 388) says that this word, as a verb, is the common term in the north for scooping out earth...and digging a hole. HUDSCALES [hudskəlz] is *Hudscaille* 1560 *Cocker, Hudscales* 1777 NB. It is possibly to be identified with *hotonscal* 1285 *For, Hoton Scales* 1292 *Ass* (p). If so, it probably denotes a skáli or shieling belonging to Hutton Sceugh *infra* or Hutton Roof *supra* 210. Cf. also *Hudbeck* 1794 H, in this parish. HUTTON SCEUGH [hutn skiuf] is *Huntone Skewghe al. Heskethe pasture* 1560 *Cocker.* *v.* skógr. INTACK. Cf. *the new Intacke* 1652 ib., *Intacks* 1680 ib. *v.* intak. KNOTT is *Knot* 1794 MapH. *v.* knǫtt. LINEWATH is *Linewathe* 1560 *Cocker.* 'Flax ford,' *v.* līn, vað. LONGLEA is *Longe Lee* 1652 ib. LONNING FOOT and HEAD (both 6″). Cf. *the Lonninge* ib. and *v.* lonning. MATTHEW RUDDING (6″) is (*house called*) *Mathew Ridding* 1656 ib. Cf. *Mathew Rudding close* 1717 ib. *v.* hryding. MOOR HO is *Moorehouses* 1724 ib. *v.* mōr. NETHER ROW is *Netherraw* 1658 ib. Cf. *the nedder Close* 1592 ib., *Neather hall* 1720 ib. NORMAN is *Tenemt. called Norman* 1591 ib. Cf. *Norman Close* 1560 ib. PADDIGILL[1] is *Padokkold* 1543 CW xiv, *Paddygill* 1656 *Cocker, Pategill or Paddegill* 1777 NB, from *paddock*, 'toad.' PARKEND is so named in 1687 (CW (OS) xv). There was formerly here a red deer park (NB ii, 136). PASTURE LANE (6″) is *Pasture Loneing* 1695 *Cocker.* Cf. *Pasture Closse in Awclif* 1587 ib. *v.* lonning. PIKELESS GATE (6″) is so named in 1774 (Donald). Cf. *Pickles Gate Bridge* 1753 CW (OS) xv. POTTS GILL is *Potskailles* 1592 *Cocker, Pott gills* 1680 ib., *Pots Gill* 1697 ib. Cf. *Pottas* 1225 Scotland. RATTEN ROW is *Rattonrawe* 1581 *Cocker, Rattenrowe* 1664 CW (OS) ix. 'Rat row,' *v. supra* 98. RED SCAR (6″) is *the reade skarre* 1589 LRMB. *v.* skarð. ROUGH CLOSE (6″) is so named in 1652 (*Cocker*). SCALERIGG HO (6″) is *Skailerigg howes* 1659 ib. *v.* skáli, hryggr (under hrycg). SNAB (6″) is *Snabb* 1719 ib. *v.* snabbi. STOTGILL is *the Stotte gill* 1587 ib. *v.* stott, gil. STREET HEAD (6″) is so named in 1695 ib. Cf. *the Street* 1656 ib. TOOTHILL (6″) is *Tutehill* 1585 ib. This is an isolated look-out hill, *v.* tote.

---

[1] Add: *Paddok keld* c. 1516 *CP. v.* kelda.

TOWNEND is *the towne end of Haltley* 1652 ib. *v.* tūn. TOWNHEAD is *Townehead* 1720 ib. It is the upper end of Caldbeck village. *v.* tūn. WATH (6″) is *the Wathe* 1581 *Cocker. v.* vað. WOODHALL is *Wodhall* 1507 ib., *Woodhaulle* 1595 ib. *v.* wudu, h(e)all. WOODHALL PARK (6″) is *Woodhall Parke* 1724 ib. *v. supra.*

FIELD-NAMES[1]

(b) In 1794 (H), *Brackley beck, Brotthole-Hill* (cf. *Brocholegile* 1232 *HolmC, Brokholgyll'* n.d. ib. 'Badger-set *gil,*' *v.* brocc-hol), *Cald-Fell, Coppake, Gresgard-Gill* (*Gresgardgile* 1232 *HolmC.* 'Grass enclosure ravine,' *v.* gærs, garðr, gil), *Iscale-Bridge, Noon-Fell, Rayes-Head* (*v.* hreysi); in 1738 (*Ct*) *Pesa* (cf. *Peasay foot* 1735 ib.); in 1729 (*Ct*) *Parsons Close* (cf. *parsone close gappe* 1584); in 1724, *the Barrons flatt* (*Borwen Flatt* 1597, *Baron flatt* 1656, *Borwens Flatt* 1659. *v.* burghan), *Harrows, ye Hows* (*the Howes* 1659), *Isabell share*; in 1723, *Beckgrains* (*Beckgranes* 1657. *v.* grein), *ye High* and *Low Broad Lease* (*Brayde Leays* 1588. *v.* læs), *Charleton Wath* (id. 1694. *v.* vað), *Cole hole close* (*Coalehole closes* 1659), *Ox Parke* (*the Oxe Parke* 1587), *Parrock* (*the Parocke* 1580), *Two Railes Closes* (*Rayles close* 1660), *Wake Lodge hill* (*Wawkelodgehyll* 1584, *Walke lodge hill* 1659); in 1721, *Knowes* (id. 1685. *v.* cnoll), *Munkhouse high Nooke, Whinne close*; in 1720, *Outray* and *Out Oughtray* (*owtraye close* 1580, *Roughoutrey* 1652, *High Routery* 1679, *Low Oughtree* 1680), *Readmoor Sikes* (*Readmyre syke* 1596. *v.* mýrr, sic); in 1717, *Capen bushe* (*Caypon buske* 1584, *Cawperon Bush* 1652, *Capon-bush-bank* 1657; cf. Capon Tree *supra* 67); *Cringlands* (*Crynglande* 1586. *v.* kringla), *Force banke* (id. 1657. *v.* fors), *Mean Dalt, Needless Lees* (*v.* læs), *Steps Dale*; in 1699, *Ingmire hill* (*v.* eng, mýrr), *Pagewell*; in 1697, *Allan Loneing side* (*v.* lonning), *Cuning Garth hauce* (cf. *Cuningarthe* 1589, *Conygarthhill* 1656, 'rabbit warren h(e)als and garðr'), *Fogg Close* (*v.* fog), *Hollin, Intacks* (*v.* intak), *Kilnedale* (*v.* cyln), *Ortcherddale, Pen Ing* (*Peninges* 1589. *v.* eng), *Souerholme* (*v.* saurr, holmr), *Wad-acre, West carr* (*Westcars* 1658. *v.* kiarr); in 1695, *Crakefall* (*Craikfald* 1592. *v.* kráka), *Foulriggs close* (*Fowleriggs* 1652. *v.* hrycg), *Myresdale, Ussay Gapp*; in 1694, *Crake howes, Grandsire rood* (*Grandrood* 1658), *Piper Dockre*; in 1693, *Cottlemire* (*v.* mýrr), *Reding Bancke* (*Ruddinge Bancke* 1582. *v.* hryding), *Standingstone*; in 1691, *Abbot acre* (the Abbot of Holm Cultram held land in Caldbeck), *Barwis Loning* (*v.* lonning), *Capedale*; in 1690, *Cookdale, Kingside Brow* (*Kingside* 1652), *Sibby Close, Sillywray* (*Sellie wraw close* 1596. Cf. Sillerea *supra* 225); in 1689, *Brigflatts, Crossedales, Head raine* (*v.* rein), *Outspurns, Swineside hill* (cf. *Swynsyde* 1505); in 1687, *Akast, Brough Close, Crakey, Little Day Work* (*v.* daywork), *Harran rigg, Hurrell-hurst* (*v.* hyrst), *Low Leath* (a barn) (*Low Laith* 1659. *v.* hlaða), *Lordye Close* (*Lords Close* 1598), *Lucy Park head* (cf. *Lucyparke maner* 1394 IpmR), *Magglands Gapp, Read Stall* (id. 1657), *Todsicke* (*v.* sic); in 1685, *Butts, Quickwood* (id. 1659), *Stroberry, Wathdoore* (*Wathdoore close* 1656. 'Ford by a pass,' *v.* vað, duru); in 1683, *the Gardes* (*v.* garðr), *Greenhead, the Miry*

---

[1] Where no source is given, the reference is to *Cocker*.

Loning (*v.* lonning); in 1682, *Bank Law, Burtrice Stub* (*Burtreestubb* 1660. 'Elder-tree stump'), *Garlicke Holmes* (*v.* holmr), *Tad Crofts*; in 1680, *Bent-dales, Carnehill*; in 1679, *ye Hempe garth* (*v.* garðr), *ye Ing* (*v.* eng), *Stalker-dale*; in 1660, *Brockhills* (*Brockehill* 1582), *the Nooke or Barrow croft, Sowredale Closes* (*v.* saurr); in 1659, *Burnett* (*Burnett Land* 1591), *Mirkholme* (id. 1560. *v.* holmr), *Schoanside, the Stairs foote*; in 1658, *the Crooked rood, Wandrood*; in 1657, *Cawdaymire* (*Caldrymyre* 1652. Apparently 'Caldew mýrr.' *v.* Caldew R. *supra* 7), *Toft-Stead*; in 1656, *Holecrooke, Jersey, Meggarth, the Pickthowe* ('pointed haugr'), *Sowday*; in 1652, *Biggalls, Coakindale, Fowlegapp, Harnrigge* (*Arrandrige* 1581, *Harrenrigg* 1598), *Louse Myre* (*v.* mýrr), *Myre Intacke* (*v.* mýrr, intak), *head of Sowkar*; in 1592, *the Ham Hill, the Speldes*; in 1588, *the Carres* (*v.* kiarr), *the Ellers* (*v.* elri), *the Lawe close*; in 1587, *Swame, Watteringsted, Whirlepott* (*Whorlpotte* 1581, 'pot hole in a stream,' cf. *infra* 445); in 1586, *Ayrne Roode, Bruyd Rood, Boddom dayll, Carrecroke* (*v.* kiarr, krókr), *Kardayll, Langehowe* (*v.* haugr); in 1584, *Lyne lande* (*v.* lin), *Rayseacre, Vaupe garthe* (*v.* garðr); in 1581, *Haister Bancke, furthshote of Cringlinge, oute shote of Crinlynge, Striket wathe* (*v.* vað); in 1578, *ward flatt* (*Wardflatte* 1543 *MinAcct*); in 1560, *Brant(h)wain, Craken-thorppe et Constable*; in 1506, *Daypark, Hogehowe* (*v.* haugr); in 1399 (IpmR) *Predkinland, Tayrige*; in 1343, *Clepot* ('clay pot'), *vadum de ylesic* (*v.* vað), *luncharh*; in 1331 (Orig) *Ruddestangill* (id. 1277 *Lowther*. Possibly 'red stone gil'; if so, identical with Rudston (PN ERY 98–9); in 1330 (Cl) *Aykebanke* (*Aykebanc* 1225 Scotland. *v.* eik), *Whitewra* (*Whytewra* ib. *v.* hwit, (v)rá); in 1242 (FF) *Steynstanbeck* (apparently tautologous, 'stony stone beck,' *v.* steinn, stān, bekkr), *Swirlehow* (*v.* haugr); in 1230 (Pipe) *Grenewra* (id. 1201 P. 'Green (v)rá'); in n.d. (HolmC) *Sighrethcroft* (probably 'Sigrith's croft,' from the ON feminine personal name *Sigríðr*), *Windskalis* ('windy shielings,' *v.* skáli). Under each of the following dates there is one field-name: *Bowerhead* 1681, *Brackoine daill* 1598, *Brakhalethwayt* 1345 *GDR* (probably bræc, h(e)alh, þveit), *Bulfett myre* 1596 (*v.* mýrr), *Cotta myre* 1585 (*v.* mýrr), *Frost Croft* 1698, *helebek'* 1292 *Ass*, *Heskayth*[1] 1272 *For*, *Lawgarth syde* 1580, *Ratlandgill* 1568 *LRMB* ('rattling gil'), *Sarkhead* 1745 *Ct*, *Somerland Crosses* 1591, *le Stubriddyng'* 1348 *Lowther* (*v.* stubb, hryding), *Thwait* 1633 (*v.* þveit).

15. Camerton[2]

CAMERTON

Camerton(*a*) c. 1150 StB, c. 1174 *HolmC et passim, Camertun'* 1212 Cur, *Cammerton* 1552 CW viii

Camberton(*e*) c. 1150 StB *et freq* to 1686 CW (OS) v, *Cambirton* c. 1270 StB (p), *Kambertun'* 1212 Cur (p), *Kamberton* 1279 *Ass*, 1285 *For*

Cambreton 1307 Cl, 1332 SR (p)

---

[1] Cf. Hesket *supra* 199.
[2] Ribton (*infra* 311) was added to Camerton in 1934.

H

CAMERTON HALL is *Cammerton Hall* 1657 CantW viii, *Camberton Hall* 1636 *Hudleston*.

The first element must be considered along with that of Camberwell (PN Sr 17), Camerton (PN ERY 35–6), Cammeringham (L) and *Cameringcroft* 1257 FF (in Mumby, L). The *-ing-* suffix in the last three names might suggest that it is a personal name (possibly *Cāfmǣr*), but there is no genitival inflexion to support this in Camberwell or Camerton. Sir Ifor Williams suggests tentatively Welsh *cym(m)er*, 'confluence,' but the phonology would offer difficulties, and the stream running into the Derwent is insignificant. For the second element, *v.* tūn.

16. Crosscanonby

CROSSCANONBY and CROSBY

Crosseby 1123–50 HolmC *et freq* to 1540 *AOMB*, (*maiorem, parvam*) 1171–5 (1333) CW (OS) iii, (*Canoun*) 1285 *For*, (*in Allerdale*) 1292 *Ass*, (*Canonicorum*) ib., (*Canon'*) 1442 *Netherhall, Magna Crossebi* 1163 P

Crosbycanon' 1393 GDR, *Crosbycannonby* 1535 VE, *Crosby in Allerdaill al. Crosby Canabye* 1540 AOMB, *Croscanonby* 1552 CW (OS) viii, *Crosby Canonbye* 1576 S, *Crosby or Cross-Canonby* 1777 NB

CROSBY MILL (6″) is *molendinum aquatici de Crosseby* 1278 *Ass*, *Crosbye mylne* 1586 CW xiv.

The original name *Crosby* stands for ON *krossa býr*, 'bȳ marked by crosses.' The name *Crosscanonby* results from the gift of land in Crosbȳ with the church to the canons of Carlisle. See also *Canonbyggyng supra* 258.

BIRKBY[1]

Brettebi 1163 P, *Bretteby* 1224 Scotland *et freq* to 1443 CW xiv, (*in Allerdale*) 1443 CW xiv, *Breteby* 1260 *Rental, Bretby* 1367 Ipm, 1370 Cl, 1469 CW xiv
Byrtby 1497 Ipm, *Birtby* 1576 S
Britby 1519 FF
Birkbey 1717 *Cocker, Birkby* 1777 NB

'bȳ of the Britons.' *v.* Introduction and cf. Birkby in Muncaster *infra* 424 and PN NRY 211.

---

[1] *Brictebi* 1190 P probably refers to this place.

ELLEN BANK is *Alnebank(e)* 1308 *Netherhall et freq* to 1436 FF, *Alenbank* 1316 CW vi, *Alynbank* 1323 Misc, *Alingbank* 1324 Cl. *v.* bank and Ellen R. *supra* 13.

FIELD-NAMES

(b) In 1674 (*DandC*) *beneathbeck, Beneathgate*; in 1260 (*Rental*) *Birestede* (v. bȳre, stede), *borganes* (v. burghan), *Bryggefit* ('bridge fit'), *Hallecroft* (v. h(e)all, croft), *Heregile* (v. gil), *le Langeflatt'* ('long flat'), *Leyrebergh* (v. leirr, be(o)rg), *Lyngeflatt', Papwurthehou* (v. haugr. The first part of the name may be personal in origin and indicate possession of the site by an owner who took his name from Papworth (C))[1], *Swynessete* ('pig sætr'), *Tordebergh* (probably OE *tord*, 'dung,' and be(o)rg), *Whynnebergh, Wynne-kelde* ('whin be(o)rg and kelda'). Under each of the following dates there is one field-name: *Croguit* 1690 *DandC, Scroddale* 1270 *MinAcct, White Crooke* 1685 *DandC.*

DEARHAM
17. Dearham

Derham c. 1160 Fountains (p), c. 1210 StB *et freq* to 1456 Fine
Deram n.d. Lowther (p), 1218 Pap, 1387 FF
Derheim 1212 Cur (p)
Derehame c. 1212 Weth, 1429 *Netherhall, Dereham in Alredale* t. Hy 3 Dugd v, *Dereham* 1285 WethA, 1344 Cl, *Deareham* 1580 Border
Derhame 1308 Ipm
Direham 1437 Cl, *Deirhame* 1527 *Netherhall*
Derom 1535 VE, *Derm* t. Eliz ChancP

DEARHAM HALL may be connected with Robert de *Aula* (1332 SR). An Old Anglian compound of dēor and hām. The form from 1212 Cur, in which Scandinavian *ei* has replaced Anglian *ā*, proves that the second element is hām, not hamm. The antiquity of the settlement is shown by the fragments of early Anglian sculpture still preserved there.

HAYBOROUGH is *Hayberhe* c. 1210 StB. 'Hay hill,' v. hēg, be(o)rg.

CRAIKHOW HALL. Cf. *Crakow* (*supra* 190) and *Crakey* 1765 *LowtherW*. ROW HALL is *Derhamrawe* 1528 *Lowther, Rawe* 1578 *Netherhall. v.* rāw.

FIELD-NAMES

(b) In 1765 (*LowtherW*) *the Abby, Crook Lands*; in 1570 (*ExchKR*) *bromelande* (probably brōm, 'broom'); in 1383 (*Ass*) *le Fourstanes* ('four

---

[1] Pauperhaugh (PN NthDu 155–6) was *Papwirthhalgh* in c. 1120.

C

stones,' *v.* **stān** and cf. Fourstones (Nb) (PN NbDu 88–9)), *le Mylnefitgate* (*v.* **myln, fit, gata**), *Mylnedame* (*v.* **myln** and ME *dam* which must have been used in OE, since there is a derivative verb *fordemman,* 'to dam up,' on record. The compound is recorded in NED from 1182).

18. Dovenby[1]

DOVENBY [dɔfnbi]

Dunaneby (sic) 1230 Scotland, *Duaneby* 1260 *Rental* (p), *Douvanneby* 1265 Cl, *Donaneby* (sic) 1267 Misc, *Dovannesby* 1271 Pat, *Douonby, Douanby, Douamby* 1278, 1279 *Ass, Dovanbi, Dovaneby* 1285 Ipm, *Duuvaneby* 1286 Cl, *Duuaneby* 1292 *Ass, Duuanbi* 1318 *MinAcct, Dofanby* 1399 IpmR, *Dovenby* 1541 *MinAcct, Dovenby* or *Dolphinby* 1671 Fleming.

DOVENBY HALL is so named in 1631 (CW xxxix). DOVENBY MILL is so named in 1785 (PR, Bridekirk). It is to be associated with Benedict *Molendinarius de Douanby* (1300 *GDR*).

'*Dufan*'s **bȳ.**' This personal name is of Irish origin (OIr *Dubhán*), a diminutive of *dubh,* 'black,' but it is on record from Iceland (Lind *s.n.*). *v.* Introduction. The present pronunciation points to confusion of the first element with the personal name *Dolfin* found in Dolphenby *supra* 191.

FIELDSIDE is *Feildside* 1656 PR (Bridekirk). FOLLY BRIDGE (6″). Cf. *Folly* 1821 G. ROWBECK BRIDGE (6″). Cf. *Rowbecke* 1670 PR (Bridekirk), *Ro(e)beck* 1686, 1691 ib. SCHOOL WOODS (6″). Cf. "There are in this township an *hospital* and *school* founded by Sir Thomas Lamplugh of Dovenby in 1609" (NB ii, 104).

FIELD-NAMES

(b) In 1631 (CW xxxix) *Dowercoate, Grenerig* ('green hrycg').

19. Ellenborough and Ewanrigg[2]

ELLENBOROUGH

Alneburg c. 1160 StB *et freq* to 1664 *LRMB*, with variant spellings -*bur*', -*buru*', -*burg*, -*burch*, -*bury*, -*barrow*
Auneburg' 1237 Cl

---

[1] Added to Bridekirk (*supra* 272) in 1934.

[2] Ellenborough and Ewanrigg and Netherhall (*infra* 305) were amalgamated in 1929 into one parish styled Maryport, to which Flimby was added in 1934.

Alen(e)burgh 1260 *Rental et freq* to 1344 Cl, *Allenburg(h)* 1278, 1292 *Ass, Alenbury* c. 1300 *Netherhall*
Alyngborgh 1292 *Ass, Alingburgh* 1533–8 ECP
Aldenburgh 1304 Ipm
Alinburh 1308 Ipm, *Alinborou* 1373 *Netherhall*
Aylnburgh' 1401, 1565 *Netherhall, Ailneburgh* 1558 FF
Ellinborowe 1566 FF, *Alneboroughe al. Elenboroughe* 1578 *Netherhall, Elneboro* 1610 Speed, *Ellenburrough* 1671 Fleming

'Stronghold by the Ellen' (*supra* 13). *v.* burh.

ELLEN BRIDGE (6″) is *Alnebrigge* 1295 *Ass* (p), *Alenbrigg'* c. 1345 *Carliol.*

EWANRIGG (6″)

Ouerig' (sic) c. 1174 *HolmC, Ouerinc* 1190–5 P
Wnering 1188, 1189 P, *Unerigg(e)* 1368 NB, 1436 FF, 1610 Speed, *Onerigg'* 1391 GDR, *Hunrigge* 1578 *Netherhall, Unrigge* 1580 Border
Euenrigg' in Allerdale 1295 *Ass, Ewanrigg al. Unerigge* 1576 S, *Ewanrigg* 1703 NicVisit
Ouenrig(g') 1332 SR (p), 1341 *Ass,* 1394 GDR, *Ovenrigge, Ovynrrygge* 1406 Cl

EWANRIGG HALL is *Eunrigg Hall* 1809 PR (Crosth)   H
Probably 'ewes' ridge' (*v.* hrycg), from OE *eōwena*, gen. pl. of *eōwu,* 'ewe,' as suggested in DEPN. The present form has doubtless been influenced by the unfounded belief that "the place was called at first from one *Ewan* who was a Scotch king or chieftain" (NB ii, 113).

GILL (6″) may be associated with Thomas *del Gill* (1341 *Ass*).

SENHOUSE DOCK (6″) is named from the family of Senhouse which in 1528 came into possession of the manor of Ellenborough (CW (OS) vi, 133).

FIELD-NAMES

(b) In p. 1479 (Hexham) *flatte vocati le Ganell, le Gresse-flatte* (*v.* gærs, flat), (*del*) *Hassokis* (cf. *Hassokacre* 1303 Cl. OE *hassuc,* 'clump of sedge'), *Hexham-crofte* (from the Hexham Priory estate in Ellenborough), *Mat-wra* (*v.* (v)rá), *le Olysyk* (*v.* sic), *le See-flatte* (*v.* sǣ, flat), *le stan-brig* (*v.* stān, brycg), *Wilken-busk* ('*Wilkin's* bush.' Wilkin is a diminutive of *William,* found in the surnames *Wilkins* and *Wilkinson*); in 1399 (IpmR) *Alnefites* (*Alensyttes* 1325 Ipm. *v.* fit); in 1303 (Cl) *Ald Alensik* ('old sic of the Ellen'), *le Bradeng* ('broad **eng**'), *le Burgh* (*v.* **burh**), *le Elysicrok* (also *le Helsycroft*, probably '*Æðelsige*'s **krókr** and **croft**'), *le Estfit* ('east fit'), *le Garbrad* (*v.* **garbrede**), *le Grastanflat* ('grey stān flat'), *le Hardacre*, *le Holgat* (*v.* **holr**, under **holh, gata**), *le Keldflat* (*v.* **kelda**), *Layrsik, Layrstede, Layrwath* (*v.* **leirr, sík**, under **sīc, stede, vað**), *le Meelpot*, *le Midelfurskot* (**skot** may represent ON **skot**, 'passage,' or a Scandinavianised form of ME **shot**, 'furlong'), *le Milnehull* (*v.* **myln, hyll**. This implies a windmill and must be an early example of the compound), *le Northker*, *le Northsele* ('north **kiarr** and **sele**'), *le Out(e)gang* (OE **ūtgang**, literally 'passage out,' here probably the road by which cattle went to the pasture), *Pesebergh* ('pease be(o)rg,' cf. Peasemoor (Berks) and Peasmarsh (PN Sx 531) and Peas(e) Hill (PN C 47, 258)), *Pyonengg* (*v.* **eng**), *Ricarcsit* (probably '*Richard*'s fit'), *Rogerpot* ('*Roger*'s hole'), *le Sebanc* (*v.* **sǣ, banke**), *Seuisyk* (*v.* **sef, sík**), *la Watflat* (*v.* **vað**, flat). Under each of the following dates there is one field-name: *Nevincroft* c. 1235 HolmC (holding late of *Nevin*), *Pikehou* 1304 Ipm (*v.* **pīc, haugr**), *Rysorscarre* 1664 *LRMB*.

FLIMBY

20. Flimby[1]

Flemyngeby 1171–5 (1333) CW iii, *Flemingeby* 1201 ChR, 1279 FF, *Flemingby, Flemyngby* c. 1174 *HolmC et freq* to 1428 Pat, *Flemynby* 1279, 1292 *Ass*
Flembye t. Hy 8 *AOMB*, *Flymbye* 1571 FF

FLIMBY HALL (6") is so named in 1777 (NB). GRANGE FM (6") is *grangie sue de Flemingby* c. 1215 *HolmC*. A grange of Holm Cultram Abbey.

'**bȳ** of the Flemings,' from some Flemish settlement here. *v.* Introduction.

WHITECROFT BRIDGE (6") is named from *Waytecroft* c. 1174 *HolmC*, *Whatecroft* c. 1187 HolmC, *Waitecroft* 1198 ib., 1201 ChR. 'Wheat croft.' The forms in *wayte-, waite-*, suggest that the name contains ON **hveiti** rather than OE **hwǣte**, or at least that an OE *Hwǣte-croft* has been Scandinavianised. An East Lincolnshire example of the same name appears c. 1200 as *Wetecroft, Watecroft* and *Weitecroft*.

WOODSIDE is *Flimby Woodside* 1798 PR (Bridekirk).

FIELD-NAMES

(b) In 1546 (NB) *Reygarths* (*v.* **garðr**), *Thwaite Croft* (*v.* **þveit**); in c. 1290 (HolmC) *the Helde* (also *Heldwode. v.* **h(i)elde**); in a. 1201 (HolmC) *Aykegyle* (*Akegile* c. 1174 ib. *v.* **eik, gil**); in c. 1187 (HolmC) *Fowgill* (*Folchegile, Folkegile* c. 1174 HolmC. '**gil** of *Fulk*' (ME), or more probably 'of *Fólki*'

---

[1] Flimby was added to Maryport (*v. supra* 284) in 1934 and gives its name to a municipal ward.

(ON)), *Whytrygge* (*Wyterigg* c. 1180 HolmC. *v.* hwit, hrycg); in c. 1180 (HolmC) *Brandesdic* ('*Brand*'s dic, from ON *Brandr*), *Kirnepot* (*Kernepot* c. 1174 HolmC—pothole like a churn, one in which the water goes round like cream in a churn, from OE *cyrn*), *Middelholm* (*v.* holmr), *Nathwait* (*Natuait* c. 1174 HolmC, possibly '*Nate*'s þveit,' an ON personal name, but *v.* Lindkvist 118 and Naburn (PN ERY 274)), *the Rane* (ON rein, 'strip of land'), *Scalegill* (*Scalegile* c. 1174 HolmC. *v.* skáli, gil), *Thweregile* (ON þvergil, 'cross valley'); in c. 1174 (HolmC) *Fulwic* (*v.* fūl, wīc), *Suanesate* (possibly '*Sveinn*'s sǣtr').

21. Gilcrux

GILCRUX [gilkru·s]

Killecruce c. 1175 *Hesley*

Gillecruz 1230 *Scotland*, 1278, 1279, 1292 *Ass*, (*Parvo, Minori, Majorem*) t. Hy 3 Dugd v

Gillecruce c. 1240 *HolmC*, 1258 *Netherhall* (p), (*Magna, Parva*) c. 1272 StB, c. 1280 StBA, *Gyllecruc* 1292 *Ass*

Gilcrux 1247, 1256 FF, *Gylcroux* 1494 Ipm

Gillekrouch, Gillecrouk 1278 *Ass*, *Gillecruch* 1292 ib.

Gilcruce c. 1280 StBA, *Gilcrouce* 1303 Ipm, 1332 SR, 1344 Cl, *Gylcrous* 1332 *Carliol* (p), *Gilcrowse* 1557 *Netherhall*, *Gylcrewse* 1558 FF, *Gilcruce or Gilcrux* 1777 NB

Gillecrux 1292 *Ass*

Gilcrosse 1378 *Carliol*, *Gyllcros* 1570 *ExchKR*

This is probably, as suggested by Ekwall (DEPN), OWelsh *cil crūc*, 'retreat by a hill.' The first element was replaced at an early date by *gil*, 'ravine,' and the pronunciation of the final consonant modified under French influence. The spelling -*crux* is due to association with Latin *crux*, 'cross.'

ELLENHALL (6″) is *Ellon-Hall* 1763 PR (Bridekirk), named from the river Ellen (*supra* 13). GRANGE is *grangiam Abbatis in Gillecrouz* 1292 *Ass*. A grange of the Abbey of Holme Cultram. TOMMY TACK (6″) is so named in 1794 H. This may contain *tack*, 'tenure or tenancy of land,' sometimes used, as probably here, in the concrete sense 'leasehold tenement or farm.' See NED *s.n. tack* sb.², 2*b*. It is a salt spring with medicinal properties (Kelly).

FIELD-NAMES

(*b*) In c. 1245 (HolmC) *Duuehowes* ('pigeon hills,' from ON *dúfa*, and haugr), *Watelandes*; in c. 1245 (HolmC) *Yreipheing*' (*Threipheing* c. 1245 HolmC. Probably 'disputed meadow,' *v.* eng and Threapland *supra* 271).

HAYTON

22. Hayton and Mealo

Hayton 1278 Ch *et passim,* (*in Allerdale*) 1419 Pat, *Heyton'* 1292
Ass, Haiton 1318 Ipm

HAYTON CASTLE is so named in 1671 (Fleming).
'Hay tūn,' *v.* Hayton *supra* 88. Cf. PN Nt 32.

AIGLEGILL is *Auegyle* 1260 *Rental.* Cf. *Egill heade* 1578 *Cocker.* '*Ave*'s
gil,' with a further *gil* added when the original second element had
been obscured by lack of stress. For the Danish personal name cf.
Aveland (L).

WHINBARROW HO (6″) is *Whynnebergh, Wynnebergh* 1260 *Rental.* Cf.
Whinbarough ditch 1578 *Cocker.* 'Whin-covered hill,' *v.* be(o)rg.
c. 1400 is the earliest date recorded in NED for the word *whin.*

MEALO HO is *Melow in Allerdell* 1572 FF, *Mealeae* 1580 Border,
Mealye 1596 FF, *Meldrig al. Melrig* 1602 CW xxxix, *Mealrige al.*
Meala 1693 ib., *Mealhay* 1777 NB, *Melay* 1816 Lysons, *Mela Ho*
1821 G. MEALO HILL is *Mela Hill* ib. 'Sandhill haugr,' *v.* melr.
The 1602 and 1693 forms have presumably been influenced by Meal-
rigg *infra* 304.

FIELD-NAMES

(*a*) In 1874 (*Stainer*) Crake Hill; in 1843 (*Stainer*) Fleet (*v.* flēot), Keddy
Field.

(*b*) In 1717 (CW xxxix) *Beeckonhill, Chanell Moss Dubb, Deed Dimples,*
Greenholm (*v.* holmr), *Ladd Craggs, Pingland*; in 1578 (*Cocker*) *Loughe* (*v.* luh).

HOLME ABBEY

23. Holme Abbey

(i) *Culterham* t. Hy 1, *s.a.* 854 SD (Recapitulatio)
   Holmcoltere c. 1150 *HolmC, Holmcoltran* c. 1158, c. 1185 ib.,
      1231 P, 1300 Pat, 1323 Misc, 1512 LP, (*Insulam de*) 1292 *Ass,*
      Holm(e)coltram t. Hy 2 (1360) Pat *et freq* to 1332 SR, *Holme*
      Coltren 1512 LP
   Holmcultran s.a. 1153 JohHex, 1307 Ch, *Holmcultram* c. 1180
      (1307), 1255, 1301, 1305 Ch, *Holcultram* 1202 CR, 1226 Pap,
      1227 Ch, 1235 Cl, *Home Cultram* 1588 NCW
   Holcultr' p. 1165 Nat MSS Scotland, *Holcoltram'* 1201 P *et*
      freq to 1279 *Ass,* with variant spelling *Holkoltram*
   (*insulam de*) *Holm'* 1189 *HolmC, the Holme in the North* 1531 LP

Holmecoltrayne 1428 Pap, (*Coltryne*) 1518 DunBev, (*Colterane*)
t. Hy 8 *AOMB*

(ii) *the Abey hom* 1599 Border, *Abbey Hollm* 1622 Naworth, *Abbey*
Howm 1720 PR (Bridekirk)
the Abby quarter 1605 *LRMB*

The original place-name seems to have been a British name to
which was added OE hām. Ekwall (DEPN) suggests that it is identical
with Welsh *culdir,* 'narrow piece of land, isthmus,' from *cul,* 'narrow'
and *tir,* 'land.' Cf. Coulderton *infra* 413. Identical no doubt is
Kilter in St Keverne (Co), *Kelter* 1312 AD v, *Keltyr* 1345 Arundel,
Kylter 1504–15 ECP. To the name Culterham, the ON holmr,
'island,' was prefixed in the 12th century.

ALDOTH is *Ialdlathyt, Ialdelathyt, Aldelathe* 1292 *Ass, Aldethe* 1581–
97 CW (OS) x, *Aldlathe, Arlethe* 1604 DKR xxxviii, *Aldaith* 1604 *Ct,*
Aldath 1605 ib., *Aldeth* 1605 *LRMB, Aldoth* 1616 CW i. Named
from this was *Aldelathe Dub* c. 1230 HolmC. 'The old barn,' *v.*
(e)ald, hlaða. For dub, 'pool,' *v. infra.*

BENWRAY (field) is *Benewra* 1292 *Ass, Beanewray* 1538 *AOMB,* 1649
ParlSurv, Bennwray 1538 (1603) *Rental.* 'Bean corner,' *v.* (v)rá.

CRUMMOCK BRIDGE (6″) is *pontem de Crumbocke, Crumbok'* 1279 *Ass,*
Cromock bridge 1553 NB, *Crumbeck Bridge* 1676 CW xxi. *v.* Crummock Beck *supra* 10.

KINGSIDE HILL. Cf. *Kyngesetemire, Kyngesetemyre* 1292 *Ass, Kynge*
Syde Close 1538 *AOMB.* 'The king's sætr,' *v.* mýrr. Mireside *infra*
290 is close at hand.

ST CHRISTIAN'S CHAPEL (6″) is *Saincte Cristyans Chapell* 1538 *AOMB.*
The chapel no longer exists, but the site is marked on the 6-inch sheet.[1]

SWABIES (field) is *Swalebymire* 1292 *Ass, Swaby* 1538 *AOMB,* 1605
LRMB. The second element is bȳ. For the first, the solitary medieval
form suggests derivation from the well-recorded ON *svali,* 'swallow,'
here probably used as a personal name. A lost *Swaile Roddinges*
occurs in this neighbourhood in 1649 *ParlSurv.*

TINDALE HILL (6″) may possibly be associated with the family of
William *Tindall* (1605 *LRMB*) and Robert *Tindell* (1649 *ParlSurv*).

[1] The dedication is presumably to Christian bishop of Whithern, who in 1186
was buried in Holm Cultram where he was afterwards looked on as a saint (StB x).

ABBEY COWPER [abəku·pə] is *Abbay Cowbyre* 1538 *MinAcct*, *Abbey Cowper* eariy 17th *Rental*, *Abby Cowber*, *Abbey Cowper* 1605 *LRMB*, *Abba Cowper* 1664 ib., with reference to the cow byres or stalls belonging to the Abbey. ABBEY TOWN is *the Towne of the Abbey*, *Abbey Towne* 1649 *ParlSurv*. APPLEGARTH is *lez Appulgarthez* 1538 *MinAcct*, *Aplegarth* 1605 *LRMB*. 'Apple garðr.' BOG is *The Bogg* 1794 H. BRACKEN RIGG (6″) is so named in 1649 (*ParlSurv*). BROWN-RIGG is *Brownrigge* 1553 NB. COWFOLD is so named in 1604 (CW iii). CUNNING GARTH is *Cuninggarthe* 1581–97 CW (OS) x. *v.* coninger. Cf. *warren of conyes upon the See Banke* 1538 *AOMB*. DEER PARK (6″) is *New parke or dear parke* 1605 *LRMB*.[1] EWECROSS HILLS (6″). Cf. *Hewes Crosse* 1538 *AOMB*.[2] HIGHLAWS is *Helawes* 1538 *MinAcct*, *Hyelawes* 1548 CW i, *Highe Lowes, Loese* 1605 *LRMB*, *Hielawes* 1649 *ParlSurv*. Apparently 'high mounds,' *v.* hlāw. HILL is *The Hill* 1765 CW iii. MIRESIDE is *Myersyde* 1604 DKR xxxviii. *v.* Kingside Hill *supra* 289. NEW BRIDGE (6″) is so named in 1657 (CW xxi). Cf. *Newbridge Lane* 1649 *ParlSurv*. REDFLAT is *Readflatt* 1604 *Ct*. SANDEN HO (6″) is *Sandenhouse* 1552 March, *Sanderhouse* 1581–97 CW (OS) x. Cf. *Sandenhousegraunge* 1538 *AOMB*. SOUTHERFIELD [su·tər fild] is *Sowterfeld* 1538 *MinAcct*, *Sutterfield* 1553 NB, *Sowterfeld* 1576 S, *Southerfield* 1581 CW ix. The modern pronunciation with [t], as well as the earlier forms, suggests that the first element is *souter*, 'cobbler' (OE sūtere), possibly used as a nickname. STANKEND is named from *le Stanke* 1605 *LRMB*. 'Pond,' *v.* NED *s.v. stank*. SWINSTY is *Swynestye* 1538 *MinAcct*. WINDINGBANK is *the Wyndy Banke* 1538 *AOMB*, *the Abbotts Newland al. Windybanckes* 1649 *ParlSurv*. Cf. *Wyndybancke Lane* ib. 'Windy bank.'

24. Holme East Waver

HOLME EAST WAVER

> *East wauer quarter* 1605 *LRMB*, *manner de East Wauer* 1665 ib., *Eastwauer* 1691 *Ct*, *Eastern Waver* 1700 CW iii

This is the division of Holm Cultram which lies east of the River Waver (*supra* 30).

COCKLAYC (lost) is *Cockelayc* 1189 *HolmC*, *Cockelaic* t. Ric 1 (1307) Ch, *Cokelaye* 1201 ChR, *Coklayk* 1285 *For*, *Cokelayk* 1292 *Ass*. *v. infra* cokelayk.

---

[1] Add: DUBHIRNE (local) is *Dubhirne* 1667 PR, *Dubhurne* 1688 ib. *v.* dub, hyrne.
[2] Add: THE GALE (local) is *The Gayle* c. 1550 CW i.

ELLERCARR BRIDGE (6″) is named from *mariscus qui vocatur Ellerker* 1292 *Ass*, *Ellercarre* 1578 *Cocker*, *Alercarr Moss* c. 1640 CW i. 'Alder marsh,' *v.* elri, kiarr and cf. PN ERY 222.

MONKS DIKE (6″) is *fossatum monachorum* 1201 ChR, 1285 *For*, *the moncke ditche* 1578 *Cocker*, *Munkinge dike* 1657 CW xxi. *v.* dīc.

MORICAMBE is *Moricambe* 1616 Camden, *Moricambo* 1695 M. This name and that of Morecambe Bay (La) are due to different antiquarian attempts to locate the Μορικάμβη εἴσχυσις, the Moricambe estuary of Ptolemy, which was near the mouth of the Eden. The meaning is, of course, 'sea-bend'.

NEWTON ARLOSH

> *Arlosk* 1185, 1304 HolmC, 1332 SR (p), 1339 *GDR* (p), 1366 *Carliol*, 1393 Pat, 1411 Pap, *Arloske* 1354 *Ass* (p)
>
> *Arlossche* 1332 SR (p), *Arlossh(e)* 1379 AD vi, 1418 Pat (p)
>
> *Neutonarlosk'* 1345 *GDR*, *Newton Arloche* 1538 *MinAcct*, *Newton Erloshe* 1636 *LRMB*, *Newton Arlosh* 1649 *ParlSurv*
>
> *Newton* 1552 CW (OS) viii, *Newtowne* 1604 *Ct*
>
> *Langnewton* 1576 S

Arlosh may be compared with certain Cornish place-names, Trelask, *Trelosk* 1272 DKR xlii, 1280 *Ass*, Trelaske, *Trelosch* DB, *-losca* ExonDB, *-losc* 1272 Launceston, and Treloscan, *Treloscon* 1249 Cl, *-loskan* 1287 FF, *Ass*. The second element seems to be Welsh *llosg*, Cornish, Breton *losk, losc*, 'burning, a burning,' perhaps with reference to an area cleared by fire. In the Cumberland name *ar* may be the British preposition *ar*, 'on, upon,' or the intensive prefix, as Sir Ifor Williams suggests. The meaning is similar to that of Barnet (PN Herts 70), 'place cleared by burning.' Cf. also Arsure, les Arsures, Arsurette (Dept. of Eure), from Late Latin *arsūra*, and Usclas, Usclats (Cantal), les Usclas (High Alps), from Late Latin *ūstulātum* (Gröhler ii, 128–9).

The place was called Newton apparently because it was the 'new' town established by the Abbey of Holm Cultram to take the place of the town of Skinburness which had been destroyed by the sea. It was also known as *Kirkebi Johannis* (1305 HolmC) (*v.* kirkja, bȳ), presumably from the dedication of the church. Newton Arlosh church is dedicated to St John the Evangelist (cf. CW xxxvi, 197–8). It was called *Long* Newton to distinguish it from Westnewton *infra* 328.

RABY

> *Rabi* c. 1150 HolmC *et passim*, with variant spellings *Raby, -bye, -bie*
>
> *Raaby* 1332 SR (p)
> *Reaby* 1624 *Ct*
> *Rabby* 1636 *LRMB*

RABY COTE is *Raby(e) Cote* c. 1530 CW i, *Raby Cott, Raby Coote* 1548 ib., *Raby Coitt* 1566 ib., *Rabby Coat* 1655 ib. xxi, *Raybecott* 1656 CantW vii. *v.* cot(e). RABYCOTE MARSH (6″) is *Rabby Marshe al. Rabye Coate Marshe* 1636 *LRMB*. RABY GRANGE is *Rayby Graunge* 1538 *AOMB*.

'bȳ by the boundary mark,' *v.* (v)rá. It lies near but not on the parish boundary. Cf. Raby (Ch), *Rabie* DB, Raby (PN NbDu 161) and Roby (PN La 113). *v.* also Lindkvist 188.

SALT COTES is *Salcotes, Saltcotes* 1305 Scotland, *Salte Cote* 1538 *MinAcct*, *les Salt Cootes* 1541 *MinAcct*, *the Salcotts* 1553 NB. 'Cottages where salt was dried or stored,' *v.* cot(e). Cf. Salcott (PN Ess 322).

ANGERTON is so named in 1538 (*MinAcct*). Possibly a compound of anger and tūn; *v. supra* 144. BROOMPARK is *Broome Parke* ib., *Brumparke in Rabby* 1636 *LRMB*. KNOWEHILL is *Rabye al. Knowhill* 1616 CW i. *v.* cnoll. MOSS SIDE is *Mosse Syde* 1538 *MinAcct*. SINKS BECK (6″). Cf. *Sinkes yeate* 1635 *Ct*. *Sink* is probably used here in the sense of 'drain, sewer,' *v.* NED *s.v.* sink sb.[1], 1 *b*. SLEIGHTHOLME is *Sleight Holme* 1538 *MinAcct*, *Sletholme* 1552 March, *Slightholme* 1640 *Ct*. 'Level meadow,' *v.* slétta, holmr. STENOR SCAR (6″) is *the Stanner* 1589 *LRMB*. THE HARDS (local) is *The Herd* 1591 *PR*.

25. Holme Low

HOLME LOW

> *Lowe Holme quarter* 1605 *LRMB*, *the Loweholme* 1636 ib.

AYNTREPOT (lost) is *Antrepot* 1189 HolmC, *Amtrepot* 1201 ChR, *Aintrepot* 1285 *For*, *Ayntrepot'* 1292 *Ass*. 'Hole near, or marked by, the solitary tree.' Cf. Aintree (PN La 117) and Anthorn *supra* 123.

BLITTERLEES

> *Blatterlees(e)* 1538 *AOMB*, 1538 *MinAcct*, *Blatter-Leys* 1552 March, *Blaterleese* 1605 *LRMB*, 1635 DKR xxxix

Blitter-Leise 1538 (1603) *Rental*
Bletter Lees 1575 HolmC, 1662 CW xiv, *Blette Leyes* 1605 *LRMB,*
  the Graveshipp of Bletter Lees 1657 CW xxxix
Bletherlees 1635 DKR xxxix
The Leys 1552 March, *The Lies* 1576 S, *The Lees* 1672 Blome

BLITTERLEES BANK is *Bleterleas Bancke* 1649 *ParlSurv.*
The first element may conceivably be OE *blæcþorn,* 'blackthorn,'
but the forms are too late for certainty. The second element is *læs.*
The place is always known locally as The Lees.

GRUNE HO and POINT
  capellam voc. Sainct Johnes Chappel de Groyne 1582 CW ii, *the
  Groyne* 1618 DKR xxxviii, *St Johns Chappell of the Groyne* 1649
  ParlSurv
  the Chappell of Grune 1664 *LRMB*

This is the name of the shore here, and the name must have
reference to some defensive sea wall. *v. groyne* (NED). The forms
quoted above disprove finally Sir Frederic Madden's identification
of this place (cited by J. R. R. Tolkien and E. V. Gordon in their notes
to vv. 709 ff. of *Sir Gawayn and the Green Knight*) with the Green
Chapel of that poem.

It is perhaps worth mentioning that in Elizabethan England the
Spanish port of La Coruña (Corunna) was known as *the Groine*
(Everyman ed. of Hakluyt iv, 309 ff.).

HARTLAW is *Harclau* 1325 Cl, *Hertlawe* 14th ECP, *Hartlaw* 1538
(1603) *Rental, Hartlawe* 1586 DKR xxxviii, *Hartlowe* 1605 *LRMB.*
'Hart hill,' *v.* heorot, hlāw.

LONGCUMMERCATIFF is *Longacomercatys* 1538 *AOMB, Longacoman-
Catiff* 1538 (1603) *Rental, Longecomercatiffe, Lacun counteth al. Long
coner cater* 1605 *LRMB.* Cf. *Comercatiffe* 1649 *ParlSurv.* The forms
are too late for any interpretation to be suggested.

SEAVILLE is *Seuyll'* 1377 GDR (p), *Sevyll, Sevayll* 1538 *MinAcct,
Sevell* 1581–97 CW (OS) x, 1604 *Ct, Sevyle* 1604 DKR xxxviii,
Ceuill 1635 *Ct, Sevill* 1649 *ParlSurv.* SEAVILLE COTE is so named
in 1618 (CW iii). *v.* cot(e). It is perhaps a compound of sef and
w(i)elle, hence 'rush spring' or 'stream.' It lies in marshy ground.

SILLOTH is *Selathe* 1292 *Ass* (p), 1377 GDR, *Selathes* 1361 ib., *Seelet
medoo* 1538 *AOMB, Selythe* 1552 March, *Silluthe* 1576 S, *Silleth(e)*

1589 CW (OS) x, 1604 *Ct*, *Selleth* 1605 *LRMB*, *Sillath*, *Sellath* 1649 *ParlSurv*, *Silloth Grange* 1718 CW iii. 'Sea barn(s),' *v.* sǣ, hlaða.

SKINBURNESS [skinbərni·z]

> *Skyneburgh'* 1175 *HolmC*, *Schineburgh* 1185 HolmC, *Skynburgh* 1301 Ch
>
> *Skynburneys(e)* 1298 Cl *et passim*, with variant spellings *Skin-*, and -*ness*, -*nese*, -*nesh*, -*nessye*, -*nees*
>
> *Skineburneyse* 1298 Cl
>
> *Skymburnes(se)* 1305 Scotland, 1312, 1317 Cl, *Schymburnese* 1305 Parl, *Skimbornase* 1307 Nat. MSS Scotland, *Skymbernesse* 1323 Misc
>
> *Skinebornes* 1538 *AOMB*, *Skyburneys* 1553 CW ii, *Skinbernes* c. 1590 CW (OS) x
>
> *Skimburgh-Neese* 1538 (1603) *Rental*

'Ness or point near (a lost place) *Skinburgh*,' *v.* nes. Ekwall (DEPN *s.n.*) derives this from a Scandinavianised form of OE *scinnan burg*, 'demon or spectre haunted stronghold.' *Scinn-burg*, with the same sense, would be simpler. Cf. Shincliffe (PN NbDu 178).

STONE HO (6″) is (*del*) *Stanhuse* 1292 *Ass* (p). Cf. *Stonehousegarth* 1538 *AOMB*. *v.* stān, hūs, garðr.

WOLSTY and WOLSTY CASTLE [wusti]

> *Wolmsty* (? for *Woluisty*) 1348 Pat
>
> *Wolsty Castell* t. Hy 8 *AOMB*, *Wollstye* 1548 CW i, *Wolsty* 1649 *ParlSurv*
>
> *Ulsty* 1552 March
>
> *Wristie castell* 1563–6 Liddesdale
>
> *Wulsty* 1576 S
>
> *Woolstey Castle* 1636 *LRMB*

WOLSTY BANK (6″). Cf. *Wolsty Bancke Acre* 1649 *ParlSurv*. WOLSTYCLOSE is so named in 1775 (CW iii). Cf. also *Wolsstibay* 1324 Cl.

Probably 'wolf-frequented path,' *v.* wulf, stīg, but the forms are too late for certainty. Licence to crenellate the manor was granted in 1348 (Pat) to the abbot of Holm Cultram.

WYTHESKELD (lost) is *Wytheskeld* t. Ric 1 (1307) Ch, *rivul' de Withescalde* 1201 ChR, *riuulus de Wytheskelder* 1292 *Ass*. 'Withy spring,' *v.* wīðig, kelda.

BECKFOOT is so named in 1722 (CW i). Cf. *Beckfoote Cottages* 1649
ParlSurv. BLACKDYKE is *Blackedyke* 1590 CW (OS) x, *blackdick* 1604
Ct. v. dīc. CALVO [kɔ·və] is *Calvo(o)* 1538 *AOMB, Callffhow* 1548
CW i, *Calvoe* 1624 *Ct,* 1649 *ParlSurv.* Cf. *Caluey grange* 1605
LRMB. 'Calf hill,' *v.* haugr. Cf. *infra* 312. CAUSEWAYHEAD [kɔ·zə
hi·d] is *Causey Head* 1665 CW i, *Calseyhead* 1684 ib. iii, 1691 *Ct,
Causeway Head* 1686–8 CW iii. Cf. *Causy Flat* 1538 *AOMB, Cawsey
heade Lane* 1649 *ParlSurv.* COLDMIRE (6″) is *Culdmyre* (sic) 1647
HolmC. 'Cold mýrr.' Cf. *Caldmyer Dick* 1605 *Ct. v.* dic. COWLYERS
(sic) is *Cowbyers* 1538 *AOMB, Wolstie Cowbire* 1649 *ParlSurv.* Cf.
Abbey Cowper *supra* 290. CUNNING HILL (6″) is *Cony hill* ib. *v.*
coning. DRYHOLME is *Drye Holme* 1538 *MinAcct. v.* holmr. EAST
COTE is *Estecote* 1538 *AOMB.* Cf. *Westecote* ib. and *v.* cot(e).
FIELDHEAD is so named in 1562 (HolmC). HAYRIGG HALL is *Haryg*
1538 *MinAcct, Harrig(g)e* 1553 NB, 1664 DKR xxxviii, *Hariggs* 1575
HolmC, *Hayrigge* 1636 *LRMB. v.* hrycg. LOW WATH BRIDGE (6″).
Cf. *low waithe* 1595 CW i. *v.* vað. MEADOW LODGE. Cf. *the Meddowe*
1605 *LRMB.* NEW HO is so named in 1810 (CW iii). Cf. *Newhouse-
feild* 1649 *ParlSurv.* RODDINGS BRIDGE (6″). Cf. *the Rodinge* 1538
AOMB. This is apparently dial. *roddin(g),* 'lane, sheep-track.' SEA
DIKE [sidik] is *the Seadykes* 1570 CW iii, *the Seadyke* 1640 HolmC.
v. dīc. WAITEFIELD is so named in 1791 (CW i). Cf. *the wayte butte*
1538 *AOMB.* WATH is *the Wath* 1581–97 CW (OS) x, *Wathe* 1635
Ct. v. vað. WHINCLOSE is *Whynney Close* 1538 *AOMB, Whynnyclose*
1552 March, *Whinie close, whinclose* 1635 *Ct.* 'Whin or gorse covered
close.'

26. Holme St Cuthbert

HOLME ST CUTHBERT
   Sanct Cuthbert Chappell 1538 *AOMB, St Cuthbert quarter* 1605
   LRMB.

AIKSHAW is *Aykesom* (sic print) 1292 CW v. Cf. *Aikshawehill* 1597
Border. In spite of the form from 1292, this must be a hybrid
eik-sceaga, 'oak wood.'

BRUNSHAW MOSS (field) is *Brunselmire* 1292 *Ass, Burnt Shaw* 19th
T.B. This may originally have been a compound of ON brúnn, sel,
and mýrr, 'brown booth marsh.' The second element has been lost,
and the first, which had become unintelligible, replaced by 'burnt.'

DUBMILL POINT is (del) Dubmylne 1332 SR (p), Dubmill, Dubbemyll 1538 MinAcct, Dumbmylne, the Dubmylne 1552 March, Dubbmilne 1636 LRMB. 'Mill at the pool,' v. dub, myln.

EDDERSIDE [edərsid] is Ethersyde 1538 MinAcct, 1604 DKR xxxviii, Eddersyde 1581–97 CW (OS) x, Ederside 1605 LRMB, Etherside 1721– 34 CW iii. This doubtless gets its name from the stream which runs into Black Dub, v. ædre, 'watercourse,' and sīde. The dental stop d not infrequently becomes spirant ð before r, as in dial. lether for standard English 'ladder.'

MAWBRAY (1″) (OLD and NEW MAWBRAY on 6″)

Mayburg' 1175, c. 1187 HolmC, Mayburch 1262 ib., Mayburgh 1279 Ass, 1361 GDR, Maybroughe 1581–97 CW (OS) x

Old, New Mawbray 1552 March, Old Mawboro 1576 S, Olde, New Mawbroughe 1605 LRMB, Mawburgh or Malbray 1816 Lysons

New Mowbray 1555 CW (OS) v, Mowbrow 1783 CW xvi

Ould Mabreye 1636 LRMB

Moulburrough 1668 PR (Bridekirk)

Malbray 1809 CW xvi

MAWBRAY HAYRIGG. Cf. Mabry hayrigg Loning 1664 Ct.

The early forms of the first element seem to be from OE mæge, later replaced by Maw- from the variant māge. The second element is burh, and the name means 'the maidens' stronghold,' or, in effect, 'maidens' castle.' The reference is presumably to the Roman fort at this place. The name seems to have a duplicate in Mayburgh (We), where the original form has persisted; see also supra 255. New Mawbray is locally known as Newtown.

OVERBY [auərbi]. Cf. Ouerbybek 1292 Ass, Overbyfeld 1368 IpmR. Over or 'upper,' perhaps because it stands higher than the neighbouring marshland. For the second element, v. bȳ.

TARNS is Ternis 1185 HolmC, Ternes 1538 MinAcct, the Ternes 1552 March, Tarns 1590 CW i, Tarnes 1604 DKR xxxviii et passim. 'Tarns,' v. tiǫrn.

COCKLEY MOSS (6″) is Cockley 1610 Denton. v. infra cokelayk. COWGATE is Cowgate 1636 CW i, Cowyeat 1669 PR (Bridekirk). NEW COWPER is Newe Cowbyre 1538 MinAcct, New-couper-Causey 1552 March, New Cowper 1605 LRMB. v. Abbey Cowper supra 290.[1] FOULSYKE

---

[1] Add: EELCHIST (lost) is Eill Chist 1587, 1656 PR, Eallkist 1587 Will, Eldchist 1596 PR, Eelchist 1772 Inscription. Probably from ǣl, 'eel' and OE c(i)est, 'chest,'

[fulsik] is *Fowlesyke* 1538 *MinAcct, the Foalsyke* 1552 March, *Fullsyke* 1587 CW i, *Fulesyke* 1581–97 ib. (OS) x. 'Dirty sīc.' GILLBANK is *Gilbancke* ib. *v.* gil. GOODYHILLS is *Goodyehilles* 1538 *MinAcct, the Godyhills* 1552 March, *Guddihills* 1580 CW ii, *Godehill, Goddyhilles* 1604 DKR xxxviii. HILL HO (6″) is so named in 1691 (CW xvi). JERICHO is a lonely farm on the edge of a moss. Near it rises JORDAN BECK (6″), with which we may possibly compare Jordan Burn (Edinburgh). The names must be relatively modern. For such nicknames, *v. infra* Fan. LOWSAY is *Lowsehowe* 1604 DKR xxxviii, *Lowsay* 1649 *ParlSurv*, 1664 *Ct, Lowsey* 1718–21 CW iii, *Loosey* 1748 PR (Stanwix), *Lousey* 1768 CW xvi. This is probably 'pig-stye hill,' from OE hlōse and haugr. OLDKILN is *Old Kiln* 1682 CW xvi, *Old Kill* 1722 ib. *v.* cyln. PELUTHO [peləte, pelidə] is *Pellethowe* 1538 *MinAcct, Pellathow* 1552 March, *Pelutho* 1575 HolmC, *Pellatho(e)* 1596 CW i, 1692 *Ct, Pellathaw* 1649 *ParlSurv, Pellatha* 1652 CW xxi. The second element is haugr. The first element may be *pilloats,* 'oats whose husks peel off' (Studies[2] 105–6). PLASKETLANDS is *Plesketh Landes* 1538 *MinAcct, Plasketlands* 1580 CW ii, *Plaskett lands* 1604 DKR xxxviii. *v.* plasket. RYEBOTTOM is *Ryebothome* 1538 *MinAcct, Ryeboddome* 1581–97 CW (OS) x, *Ryebottom* 1728 CW i. Cf. *Rie Garthe, Rie Flat* 1538 *AOMB.* ST ROCHE'S CHAPEL[1] [rɑuks] (6″). Cf. *St Rooke's Cross* 1580 CW ii. SALTA is *Salto* 1688 ib. xvi. SALTA MOSS is *Sawtay Mosse* 1649 *ParlSurv.* WEST HO is so named in 1790 (CW iii).

Lands Common to Holme Abbey, Holme Low and Holme St Cuthbert

GREAT GUTTER (6″) is *Great Gutters* 1717 CW iii. STARRY HILL is *Staryhill* 1552 March. 'Sedgy hill,' *v.* star. WILSON CREEK (6″) is possibly to be identified with *Wilsons windinge* 1604 *Ct.*

not recorded in NED or EDD, but identical in meaning with Lincs dial. *eel-trunk* 'box with holes in it, in which eels were kept alive for the table.'

[1] St Roche (or Roque) was a 14th-century French saint, especially invoked in time of pestilence. He came too late to have been the patron of parish churches, but the chapel of Bonvile's Almshouse at Exeter was dedicated to him, and there were also chapels at Edinburgh, Paisley, Glasgow, Stirling and Dundee; see J. M. Mackinlay, *Ancient Church Dedications in Scotland: Non-Scriptural,* pp. 359–64 (Edinburgh 1914). Nearer home there was in 1423 a chapel of St Roche in Carlisle Cathedral (CW NS xxv, 14).

FIELD-NAMES[1]

(a) Burn Crooks, Butter Brows, Coldrigg, Gowkhills, Grigg, Hethersgill, Hornbriggs,The Wham (v. hwamm), Wiselick.[2]

(b) In 1776 (CW i) *Foulwath* (*Foulewath* 1649 *ParlSurv. v.* fūl, vað); in 1729 (CW xxxix) *Two* and *Three Clows, Garth Parrat Close, Juwiss, West Coat* (*East Coat, West Coat* 1538 (1603) *Rental, West Coate* 1659 CW xxxix. v. cot(e)), *West Loup* (probably dial. *loup,* 'a narrow channel between rocks'); in 1683 (CW i) *Craikhill* (*Craickhill* 1581–97 ib.); in 1681 (CW xxi) *Vccarasse Meadow* (*Uckerhoushills* 1538 (1603) *Rental, Uckaras* 1675 CW xxi); in 1677 (CW xxi) *Acredall* (*Acredale* 1581 CW ix, *Acredales al. Outrivings* 1649 *ParlSurv.* Cf. *Akerwall Nooke* 1538 *AOMB*. The alternative name seems to be connected with *outrive,* 'to break up (moorland or rough pasture land)'); *Kitching Crooke* (*Kyching Croke* 1538 ib. v. krókr); in 1675 (CW xxi) *Gards* (*the Gards al. Brewers Garthes* 1649 *ParlSurv. v.* garðr); *Gentleman's Meadow* (cf. *Gentilman Croke* 1538 *AOMB*), *Stenke*; in 1664 (Ct) *Barnyland, Lanse Ringe, Leuens, Mildeings* (*Middle Ing* 1538 *AOMB. v.* eng); in 1664 (LRMB) *Colt parke* (*Colte Parke* 1538 *AOMB*), *the Maynes* (id. ib. v. mains); in 1663 (CW iii) *ye lonning leading...to ye Spellgate* (*Spellyate Lane* 1649 *ParlSurv*); in 1655 (CW xxi) *Readskarth-browe* (v. skarð), *Stonie Law* (*Stoney Law* 1581 CW ix); in 1649 (*ParlSurv*) *Asketh Feilde* (cf. *John Askew hole* 1570 NB, *Askew Brigg* 1581 CW ix), *Baron Close, West Parke al. Bayly Parke, Beadehouse* (*le Bedhowse* 1582 CW ii. 'Bead-house,' originally 'house of prayer,' then 'alms-house'), *Becke marre neare ye sea, Borrowdale Close al. the Midle Close, Brownerigg Shorts* (v. hrycg), *Cowbrinehill, Crakeflatt, Dolphin Sike* (*Delphin* 1538 *AOMB, Dowllfine feild* 1605 LRMB. Cf. *Delping Ing* 1538 (1603) *Rental*), *Eighteen-men-day-worke* (*xviii men Days Work* 1538 *AOMB*), *Farmour Inges* (v. eng), *the Five menday worke* (*v men Days Wark* ib.), *East* and *West Gavel* (*the Estegavill, the Weste Gavyll* ib., *West Gavel, the East Gavell* 1538 (1603) *Rental.* Possibly dial. *gavel,* 'strip of land,' recorded from Northumberland), *Grasoneclose, Highcrosse Close al. Eastclose neare Crosse Stane, Hipping Rivings* (*Flat callyd Heppinge* 1538 *AOMB, the Hipeinge* 1605 LRMB. This is northern dial. *hipping* in the plural, 'stepping-stones.' Thoresby (1703) defines *Hippins* as "steppings; large stones set in a shallow water at a step's distance from each other, to pass over by" (v. NED, *s.v.* 'hipping')), *Hog brigg, Horseshoe, Hye Leathes* (v. hlaða), *New Intacke* (v. intak), *Laire Butts* (v. leirr), *Langlaws, Lang Leyes* (v. læs), *Langring al. Hartlow meadow, Litley Garth* (*Littley garthe* 1636 LRMB. v. garðr), *Low Closes al. Fishers Sty* (*Fisher Stye* 1538 *AOMB. v.* stig), *Mearestone* (probably 'boundary stone,' v. (ge)mǣre), *Norrenflatt, Peatehouse, Pingle* (id. 1605 LRMB. v. pightel), *Rasydike* (v. hreysi, dic), *Rodriggs, Rossecrosse* (*Rosecross* 1580 CW ii), *St Thomas Chappell* (*Sainct Thomas Chappell* 1582 CW ii), *Seavy Close* (v. sef), *East* and *West Snawden, Stanegate closes, the Stayning Stone meadowe, Stangflatt Riving* (probably stǫng), *Strickbyers* (*Stricklyer flatte* 1605 LRMB), *Waring Butts, Whart Lands,*

---

[1] This list includes the field-names for all the parishes of Holm Cultram.
[2] For the list of modern field-names we are indebted to the Rev. F. B. Swift.

Whinney Rigg (Whinny Rigg 1580 CW ii), White Inges (the White Inge 1538
AOMB. v. eng), Wythdyke (v. dic), Yad Closes (dial. yad, 'nag'); in
1636 (LRMB) Barrhouse, Burnthaite al. Burn Ing (v. þveit, eng), carrmosse
(v. kiarr), the hyemore, New Close al. Marrow Nock, Stintes pasture; in 1622
(HolmCA) the Bayes, Bayes Wath (v. vað), Feather Close, Monkmyre (may
be mosam monachorum p. 1150 HolmC); in 1605 (Ct) le heads, Swan nest
(cf. Swanwath or Womerdeal 1575 HolmCA. v. vað); in 1605 (LRMB)
Aplegarthacre (v. garðr), Bride Mead, Closed Riginge, Cowbernocks, Crickle-
flatte, Dalier sike (v. sic), Growlinge garthe, the Inges (v. eng), Jackmuche,
Lunge Inge (v. eng), Muddle flatte, Paddonflatte, Riveinges, le Saies close, Sara
crofte (Saray Crofte 1538 AOMB, Sara Croft 1538 (1603) Rental), Staine-
garth (v. steinn, garðr), Weedwood, Wheatholme (v. holmr); in 1604 (DKR
xxxviii) Brockholes (Brokholes 1363 GDR. v. brocc-hol); in 1575 (HolmCA)
Angrygillhole, Black Bog, Fleet (v. flēot); in 1538 (AOMB) Bowsers, the
Bowsers Croke, Comon Inge (v. eng), the Depe Wier, Flemeby Parke, Grasingys-
garth (v. gærs, eng, garðr), Grissgarth (v. gríss, garðr), the Gate of the Kye,
the Lange Inge (v. eng), Noddy Flat, Onyon Inge, Osmoderley Croke, Parish
Preste medoo, Redenese, Smallings, Stirebires, Wafergarthe ('garðr by the
Waver' (supra 30)); in 1538 (MinAcct) les Smeltyngs, les Stryke. Under
each of the following dates there is one field-name: Catair c. 1640 CW i,
Frankhill 1553 NB, la Galileye 1292 Ass (this is possibly galilee, 'the porch
or chapel at the entrance to an ecclesiastical building' (v. NED s.v.). Cf.
The Gallery (PN C 215)), God's house Law 1580 CW ii, the Neatts brigg 1647
HolmCA ('cattle bridge,' v. nēat), Potpurnall 1584 (1647) ib. (possibly
'Petronella's pot'), Rydingestanges (v. hryding), Studfoldrigg 1555 CW (OS) v
(v. stōdfald, hrycg), Turpene 1652 CW i.

27, 28. Ireby, High Ireby and Low Ireby[1]

IREBY, HIGH IREBY and LOW IREBY

> Irebi c. 1160 Fountains (p), c. 1175 Hesley, Ireby c. 1150 StB (p)
> et passim, with variant spelling Yre-
> Irreby 1256 FF (p), 1279 Ass (p), 1292 ib.
> Hyrby c. 1275 Scotland, Hirby 1276 Pat (p), Hyrreby 1279 Ass (p)
> Irby 1292 Ass, 1319 Ipm
> Ereby 1449 Pat

HIGH IREBY is Heghireby 1279 Ass, Magna Ireby 1291 ib., Ireby
Alta 1399 IpmR. LOW IREBY (6") is Nether Irby 1292 Ass, Market
Ireby 1305 Ipm, Lawe Irby 1333 Cl, Bassa Irby 1344 ib., Irby Base
1367 Ipm, Baserby al. Ireby 1505–15 ECP. In 1236 (Ch) William of
Ireby was granted a weekly market at his manor of Ireby and a yearly
fair.

---

[1] High and Low Ireby, together with Uldale (infra 327), were amalgamated in
1934 into one parish called Ireby.

D

HIGH and LOW IREBY BRIDGE (both 6″) are *Irebye bridge* 1578 *Cocker*, 1777 NB.

'bȳ of the Irishmen' or 'of the Irishman,' from ON *Írabýr*. *v.* Introduction. There are parallels to this name in Ireby (PN La 183), Irby on Humber and Irby in the Marsh (L), Irby (PN NRY 218), and probably Irby (Ch).

LANGTHWAITE (lost) is *Langethweit* 1171–5 (1333) CW iii, *Langethawyt* 1295 *Rental*. *v.* lang, þveit.

MAINS HALL (6″). *v.* mains.

27. High Ireby

RUTHWAITE

Rutheweyt[1] 1242 Pipe, *Ruthwayt* 1256 FF
Rughthweyt 1296 Ipm, *Rughtwait in Ireby* 1324 Lowther
Routtweyt 1300 GDR (p), *Routhwayte* 1540 AOMB
Roughthwayte 1543 MinAcct
Rowthwate 1576 S

RUTHWAITE MOSS (6″) (in Bassenthwaite parish) is *Ruthwayte Moss* 1504–15 ECP. *v.* mos.
'Rough þveit,' *v.* rūh.

SCAWTHWAITE CLOSE is *Scalethweit* 1171–5 (1333) CW iii, *Scallethwayt* 1256 FF. The form *Scallethwayt*, with double *l*, suggests that this name may be '*Skalli*'s þveit,' from the ON nick-name *Skalli*, rather than *skála þveit*, 'þveit by the shieling.' Cf. *infra* 390

BINSEY is *Binsay Hawse* 1742 Brayton, *Binsa* 1777 Hudleston, *Binsay fell, Binsell fell* 1777 NB. *v.* hals. WHITEFIELD Ho is *le Whitefielde in Iredale* (sic) 1594 CW x.

28. Low Ireby

PRIOR HALL is *Ysacby* c. 1275 Scotland, *Isacby* 1292 *Ass*, *le Priorhall'* 1391 ib., *Isakeby al. Prior Hall* 1540 AOMB, *Isaacby or Prior Hall* 1553 (c. 1686) Todd. '*Isaac*'s bȳ,' a late bȳ-name. *v.* Introduction. The estate belonged to the cathedral-priory of Carlisle 1535 VE. *v.* h(e)all.

COCKSHUT BRIDGE (6″). *v. infra* cockshot. NEWBIGGIN GRANGE is *Newbyggyne in Allerdaill* 1540 AOMB. 'New building,' *v.* bygging.

---

[1] This form almost certainly refers to this place.

29. Isel Oldpark

ISEL OLDPARK is *Old Parke* 1555 FF, *Owld parke* 1631 Brayton, *Isell-old-park* 1718 ib. *v.* Isel *supra* 267.

OUTGANG WOOD (6") is *(atte) huttegange* 1278 *Ass* (p), *Out-gang* 1810 Map. *v.* ūtgang.

MESSENGERMIRE WOOD may be associated with the family of Robert *Messenger* (1699 CW xxxix). It is *Messenger's Mire Wood* 1810 *Map*.

BRIDGE END FM (6") is *Bridge End* 1810 *Map*. BUCKHOLME is *Buckham Island* ib. HOWGILL WOOD is so named ib. JONAH'S GILL (6") is so named ib. LINGEYBANK is *Lingebanckh* 1569 ElizKes, *Lingebancke* 1629 *Brayton*, *Lingey Bank* 1810 *Map*. LINGEYBANK WOOD (6"), LONGCLOSE, NUT HILL, NUTHILL WOOD (both 6"), and ROOK HILL (6") are so named ib. PEPPERHOLME BANK (6"). Cf. *Pepper Holme* ib. PRIOR WOOD (6"). Cf. 1 *bank boscosus, vocatus le Prior-bank* p. 1479 Hexham. So called because owned by the Prior of Hexham.

FIELD-NAMES

(b) In 1718 (*Brayton*) *Mill-beck, Paper-stone*.

30. Keswick[1]

KESWICK [kezik]

Kesewic c. 1240 Fountains, *Kesewyk* 1266 Pat, 1279, 1292 *Ass et freq* to 1403 Pat, with variant spelling *-wik*, *Kesewik in Derewent-felles* 1276 Ch

Chesewyk' 1285 *For* (p)

Keswyk 1383 *Ass*, 1383 *GDR*, *Keswycke* 1550 FF, *Keswick* 1589 FF, *Kesswicke* 1648 PR (Greystoke)

Kesilwyk al. Kesewik 1489 Pat

Kestwyk 1502 CW xvi

Casewyke 1530 *FF*

Kyswyke 1563 PR (Crosth)

Keesweck 1580 Border

This is OAnglian cēse-wīc, 'cheese wīc,' with an initial K- perhaps

---

[1] An exchange of territory between Keswick and St John's (*infra* 311) was made in 1935. Brigham, Crosthwaite (*v. infra*), and St John's have given their names to the municipal wards of Keswick.

due to Scandinavian influence, as in Keswick (Nf), East Keswick (WRY) and Casewick (L). Outside Scandinavian territory, in Cheswick (Nb), which contains the same OAnglian *cēse*, and in Chiswick (PN Mx 88–9, PN Ess 522), which contain West Saxon *cīese, cȳse, the initial has remained unaltered.

BRIGHAM is *Brigholm* c. 1240, 1246 Fountains, *the Bridge holme* 1541 NB, *Briggholme* 1568 PR (Crosth). Cf. *Brigham yate* 1602 *Derwent*. 'holmr by the bridge.'

GREAT CROSTHWAITE [krɔsθət]

    Crostweit c. 1150 StB (p), *Crostwayt* c. 1160 Fountains *et passim*, with variant spellings *-twait, -thweyt, -tweit, Crosthuueit* c. 1200 Coll. Top. et Gen. (p), *Crostwaith* c. 1210 Fountains, *Great Crosthayth* c. 1220 ib., *Croswait* c. 1255 ib., *Crossethwayth* 1283 ib., *Crosthat* 1570 PR (Greystoke), 1621 ib. (Skelton), *Crostat* 1648 ib. (Matterdale)

    Croswath 1250 Fountains, *Crosswayth* c. 1255 ib., *Crosswater, Groweswetter* 1553–5 ECP

    Corsthwaite 1750 Pococke

LITTLE CROSTHWAITE (in Underskiddaw parish) is *Crosttwait* c. 1220 Fountains, *parva Crostweyt in Bastenthwayt* 1292 *Ass, parua Crosthwate* 1450 *Netherhall, Lytyll Crostwat* 1563 PR (Crosth). 'þveit marked by a cross.'

DERWENT ISLE is *insula de Hestholm* t. Ric 1 Dugd v, *Hesteholm* t. John Fountains, *Eastholm* c. 1240 ib., *Hestholm* 1327 ib., *Viker Ile* 1596 PR (Crosth). It was known in the 18th century as *Pocklington's Island or Paradise Island* (1782 ClarkeM), *Pocklington's* from the name of its owner. In the name *Hestholm*,[1] holmr must have its well-recorded sense of 'island.' *Hest* represents the ON *hestr*, 'stallion,' which occurs also in Hesket *supra* 199. The original meaning of the name must have approached closely to that of Hinksey (Berks), which is a compound of OE *hengest*, 'stallion,' and īeg, 'island.'

ISTHMUS BAY and WOOD (both 6″) may preserve the *Estpenese* of t. Ric 1 Dugdale v, *Espenese* c. 1220 Fountains. Presumably 'aspen headland,' *v.* æspe, næss.

LAIRTHWAITE (6″). Cf. *Lairewatmire* c. 1220 Fountains. Probably a

---

[1] Found also in Eastholme Ho (*supra* 120) and Hestham (*infra* 415).

compound of ON leirr, 'mud,' and vaδ, 'ford,' to which mýrr, 'marsh,' has been added.

BRISTOWE HALL (6″). Cf. *Bristow Tenement* 1619 FlemingMem. BROWTOP (6″) is so named in 1686 (PR, Crosth). CHESTNUT HILL is *Chesnut-hill* 1797 ib. COCKSHOT WOOD (6″) is *Cockshut-hill* 1770 Young, *wooded hill of Cockshot* 1789 Clarke. *v. infra* cockshot. CROW PARK (6″) is so named in 1769 (Gray). FRIAR'S CRAG is *Friar-crag* 1784 West. GRETA HALL (6″) is so named in 1805 (PR, Crosth). *v.* Greta R. *supra.* DRUID'S CIRCLE is *the druid-temple* 1784 West, *Druids' Circle* 1794 H. THE HEADLANDS (6″) is *Head Lands Lands* 1734 *Derwent*, *Heads Lords Lands, Heads and Lords Lands* 1735 ib. THE HEADS (6″) is *the heades* 1629 ib. HIGH HILL is *Hey Hill* 1563 PR (Crosth), *Hee Hyll* 1564 ib., *Hyehill* 1568 ib. KIDDAMS (6″) is *Kidhomess* 1571 ElizKes. MONK HALL (lost) is *Munckall* 1565 PR (Crosth), *Monnkhall* 1573 ib. It belonged to Fountains Abbey (CW xliii, 200–3). TOWN CASS (6″)[1] is *the Casse* 1605 *Derwent*. Cf. *Caswasts* 1723 ib and *Cass Bay infra* 363.

FIELD-NAMES

(a) Ambleside Meadow, Cabby Field, Dundubs Meadow, Green Eskhams, Eskin Beck (*Eskomebecke* 1604 PR (Crosth), *Eskambecke* 1628 *Derwent*, *Escomebeck* 1630 PR (Crosth), *Eskinbeck* 1739 *Derwent*), Fishponds (near *Monk Hall supra*), Grassings (*v.* eng), Harryman Field, Honey Pot Field (*v. infra* Fan), Howrah, Lugs Moss, Rhurrigg Field (probably 'rough ridge'), Roger Field and Meadow, Rumney Meadows, Smithy Field (cf. *Smiddy Close* 1739 *Derwent*), Swang Field (dial. *swang*, 'a low-lying piece of ground liable to be flooded; a boggy depression, swamp.' *v.* NED *s.v.*); Tenters Field (*v.* tenter), Thackrigg (*Thakerigg* t. Hy 8 W.G.C., probably ridge where reeds for thatching grew).

(b) In 1784 (West) *Castle-hill, Castlet, Goats-field* (*the Goates* 1739 *Derwent*); in 1739 (*Derwent*) *Birketts, Bridge End* (*the briggende* 1629 ib.), *Broad Doors* (*Broade dores* 1602 ib., *the broode doores* 1629 ib. *v.* duru or dor, and cf. Lodore *infra* 350), *Grisedale House* (*v.* gríss); in 1734 (*Derwent*) *Loaninghead* (*v.* lonning), *Malt Kill* (*v.* cyln), *Nan Crook* (*v.* krókr), *Wateridge Bank, Willihow Park*; in 1602 (*Derwent*) *brigstone, Le long butts*. Under each of the following dates there is one field-name: *Applegarth* t. Hy 8 W.G.C. ('apple garδr'), *Bracaneng* 1246 Fountains (*v.* braken, eng), *Ragarhheued* c. 1220 Fountains (either (v)rá' or 'roe garδr' and hēafod), *Transhag-End* 1789 Clarke, *the vennell* 1629 *Derwent* (*v.* vennel).

----

[1] Prevost, *Supp.* I, defines *cass* as 'a swampy piece of ground subject to floods,' which suits here.

LANCRIGG **31. Langrigg and Mealrigg**[1]

Langrug 1189 P, *Langrugge* 1191 ib.
Langrig c. 1230 *HolmC et passim*, with variant spellings *-rigg*, *-ryg(g)*
Langerigg' c. 1255 *HolmC* (p) *et freq* to 1439 IpmR, with variant spellings *-ryg, -rik, -rig, Langerigg' in Brumfeld* 1306 *Ass*
Lanrig(e) 1549, 1564 FF

LANGRIGG BANK (6") is *Langrige banke* 1578 *Cocker*. LANGRIGG HALL is *Langrygge hall* 1570 *ExchKR*.
'Long rigg,' *v.* hrycg.

GREENAH is *Grenhou* 1285 *For* (p), *Grenehowe* 1332 SR (p), *Greenehowe* 1578 *Cocker, Greenhow* 1777 NB. 'Green hill,' *v.* haugr.

MEALRIGG

Midelrig' 1189 *HolmC, Middelrig'* 1201 ChR, *Middelrigg'* 1292 *Ass*
Melderige 1439 IpmR, *Milrig* 1549 FF, *Mealrigg* 1576 FF, *Meldrigg* 1599 NB, *Mealdriggs* 1610 Denton

'Middle ridge,' *v.* hrycg. The reason for the name is obscure. The development to *Mealrigg* is illustrated by the 1439 form, where metathesis of *-dl-* to *-ld-* has taken place; at a later date *-d-*, the middle consonant of three, disappeared.

FIELD-NAMES[2]

(*a*) Bleabutts, Clappers, Gabriel, Honey Pot Meadow (*infra* Fan). East and West Laird Bank, Priest Acres, Sourdales (*infra* Des).
(*b*) In 1737, *Haversham or Haverum, Knott Close* (*v.* knott).

MOSEDALE [mouzdəl] **32. Mosedale**[3]

Mosedale (*in Allerdale*) 1285 Ipm *et passim*
Mosdale 1305 Ipm *et freq* to 1610 Denton, *Mosdall* 1620 Naworth
Moss(e)dale 1362 Ipm, *Mossdale* 1816 Lysons
Moysdall al. Mosedale 1568 LRMB, *Moisdaill* 1580 Border, *Moosdell* 1581 PR (Greystoke)

---

[1] Added to Bromfield (*supra* 272) in 1934.
[2] For this list of field-names we are indebted to the Rev. F. B. Swift.
[3] Added to Mungrisdale (*supra* 226) in 1934.

Mosedale Moss (6″) is *Mosedalemosse* 1568 *LRMB*.
'Valley with a moss or bog,' *v.* **mosi, dalr.**

Carrock Fell is *Carroc* 1208 FF, *Carrok* 1261 Ipm, *verticem de Carrock* 1568 *LRMB*, *the mountain Carrak, Carrick* 1610 Denton, *Carrock-Fell* 1794 H. This is a British hill-name. Cf. OWelsh *carrecc*, 'rock,' Welsh *carreg*, Co *carrec* (in place-names such as Tregarrick), identical with Cark in Cartmel (PN La 197) and Carrick (Ayrshire) (PN Scot 127).

Stone Ends is *Stane ends* 1568 *LRMB*. Swineside is *Swynesyde* ib., *Swansted* 1794 MapH.

FIELD-NAMES

(b) In 1568 (*LRMB*) *Downowcotes, Dubbend* (*v.* dub), *Ratlandgill* (*v. supra* 25), *Redmosse, Sevysike* (*v.* sef, sic), *Wynscalepyke* (*v.* skáli, pīc).

33. Netherhall[1]
Netherhall

Le Netherhall 1462 *Netherhall, Netherall* 1504–15 ECP
Ailneburgh hall al. Netherhall 1558 FF, *Aylnbroughe hall al. Nether hall* 1567 *Netherhall, Elnbrowgh' Hall* 1601 ib.

v. h(e)all. The hall lies low, but it is not clear in comparison with what particular place it is regarded as *nether*. For the alternative name *v.* Ellenborough *supra* 284.

Bank End (6″) is so named in 1794 (H).

Maryport

Aylnfoote 1656 *Netherhall, Elmefoote* 1567 ib., *Elm foot* 1675 Sandford, *Ellom-foot* 1722 Gilpin, *Elnefoot* c. 1745 CW (OS) iii *Mary-port* 1762 PR (Bridekirk)

For the original name, *v.* Ellen R. *supra* 13. For *foot* applied to a site at a river-mouth, cf. Sarkfoot *supra* 147 and Chalkfoot *infra* 331. A harbour was made here between 1750 and 1760 by Humphrey Senhouse who then named the place after his wife Mary (CW (OS) iii, 303). In the original name, medial *-n-* has been assimilated to *-m-* through the influence of the following *-f-*.

---

[1] Amalgamated with Ellenborough and Ewanrigg (*supra* 284) into one parish called Maryport in 1929.

The name of the Roman fort, built to guard the left flank of Hadrian's Wall, and situated on a hill 200 ft. in height, north of Maryport, was probably ALAVNA from the river on which it stands. *v.* Appendix.

34. Oughterside and Allerby

OUGHTERSIDE [uˑtərsed]

> *Huctretsat* 1258 *Netherhall* (p)
> *Uchtredsete* 1260 *Rental, Uctredesate* 1278 *Ass, Uchtredesate* 1279 ib.
> *Huttersete* 1276 *Ass, Huttressete* 1279 ib.
> *Hugtresate* 1278 *Ass,* *Ugtresat* 1292 ib., *Ughtreset* 1298 Ipm,
> *Hughtredsate* 1303 ib., *Hugtredsate (al Ugthtresate)* ib. (p)
> *Uthredsate* c. 1345 *Carliol*
> *Oughtrasat* 1367 Ipm
> *Ughtersyde* 1491 Ipm, *Oughterside* 1570 FF, *Utterside or Oughter-*
> *side* 1578 *Cocker, Owterside* t. Eliz ChancP

OUGHTERSIDE HALL is so named in 1612 (CW (OS) iii). OUGHTER-SIDE MILL (6″) is *Oughterside Mylne* ib.

'*Ūhtrēd*'s sætr.' According to Denton (42), the place takes its name from *Uchtred* to whom Alan, second lord of Allerdale, had given a carucate of land in Aspatria. Geographically, this identification is possible, but it should not be considered certain, for *Uhtred* was a common name in 12th-century Cumberland.

ALLERBY

> *Crossebyaylward* 1258 *Netherhall,* 1344 Cl, c. 1379 *Carliol, Crosby*
> *Aylward* 1292 *Ass, Crosseby Ayleward* 1324 Ipm
> *Aylwardcrosseby* 1260 *Rental,* 1292 *Ass*
> *Aylewardby* c. 1275 Scotland, *Aldwardby* 1383 Fine, *Alwardeby*
> 1384 ib., *Alwarby, otherwyse called Crosby Alwarde* 1552 Visit,
> *Alwarbye* 1560 FF, *Allerby* 1675 Sandford
> *Crosby Allerby* 1541 *MinAcct*
> *Crosalerbye* 1578 *Cocker*

In the parish was *Allerby Crooks* 1777 NB. *v.* krókr.

Originally '*Ailward*'s,' that is '*Æðelward*'s, Crosby,' afterwards reduced to '*Ailward*'s bȳ.'

ORMESBY (lost) is *Ormesbye* c. 1227 *HolmC,* 1230 Scotland *et freq* to 1370 Ipm, *Ormisby* 1308 ib. '*Orm*'s bȳ.' The exact situation of this place is uncertain, but charters 200–3 in the Holm Cultram Cartulary imply that it was in the neighbourhood of Allerby or Newton. Cf. Hornsby *supra* 79.

BANKEND COTTAGES (6″). Cf. *Oughterside banke* 1578 Cocker. BLUE-DIAL is so named in 1774 (Donald). Cf. Red Dial *infra* 331. COLLIER ROW (6″). Cf. *my colliery at Outersyde* 1681 CW (OS) iii. LOWMIRE (6″) is *Lowmyre* 1560 FF. *v.* mýrr.

FIELD-NAMES

(a) In 1887 (*Stainer*) Ludge, Scobra.

(b) *Langryg'* 1292 *Ass* (*v.* hrycg).

35. Oulton[1]

OULTON [uˑtən]

Ulveton c. 1200 *Laner et freq* to 1367 Ipm
Ulfton 1279 *Ass*
Ulton 1370 Ipm *et freq* to 1581 CW x, (*parva*) 1601 FF
Owton or Owlton 1570 FF, *Owton* 1576 S

In the parish was *Fites* c. 1200 *Laner*, *Ulton Fittes* 1400 IpmR (*v.* fit) and *Ulton yngs* 1570 *ExchKR* (*v.* eng).

'*Wulfa*'s tūn,' with Scandinavianising of the first element by dropping initial *W-*. This name is not found in independent use, but cf. *Wulfandun* in BCS 120.

COLMIRE SOUGH (6″) is *Colemire* 1285 *For*, *le Colemyre* c. 1285 *Hesley*, *Coll Myre*, *Olde Colmere* 1570 *ExchKR*. 'Charcoal mýrr or swampy moorland.' *Sough* may have here either its meaning 'boggy or swampy place,' or 'a small gutter for draining off water.' *v.* NED *s.v. sough*, sb.², 1, 2.

ESKRIGG is *Eskerig* t. Hy 3 *Laner*. 'Ash-tree ridge,' *v.* eski, hryggr (under hrycg).

LAWRENCEHOLM is *insulam Sancti Laurentii* 1189 *HolmC*, *insula Sči Laurent'* 1201 ChR, *Louranzholme* 1332 SR (p), *Laurenceholm(e)* 1358 Fine *et passim*, with variant spellings *Lawrence-*, *Lowrance-*. This name probably records the existence in the 12th century of a chapel dedicated to St Lawrence. *v.* holmr.

STANGS BRIDGE (6″). Cf. *Ulton stanges* 1578 *Cocker*. *v.* stǫng.

---

[1] Added to Woodside (*infra* 333) in 1934.

Wedholme Flow [wedəm flau]

> Waytheholm' 1189 HolmC, Waitheholm 1201 ChR
> Werdeholm t. Hy 3 Laner
> Waytholm 1285 For, 1292 Ass
> Wayholm 1292 Ass
> Watheholme, Watholme 1538 AOMB
> Wedholm(e) 1570 CW iii et passim
> Wedham 1630 CW iii, Weddom c. 1640 ib. i.

'Hunting holmr,' v. veiðr. The word *flow*, which is of Scandinavian origin, probably has in this instance the meaning 'watery moss,' v. NED s.v. *flow*, sb.[2], 1.

FIELD-NAMES

(b) In t. Hy 3 (*Laner*) *Appletresic* ('apple tree sīc), *Filebrig*, *Kneterlandemir*, *Lantsic* (v. sīc), *Milnepol* ('mill pool'), *Stokkebrig* ('bridge made of a tree-trunk,' v. stocc, and cf. Stockbridge (Ha)), *Winnerig* (v. hrycg). Under each of the following dates there is one field-name: *Aynolfebergh'* c. 1285 *Hesley* ('*Ainulf*'s hill,' v. be(o)rg. *Ainulf* represents OGer *Aginulf*, *Einolf*, a continental name which was current in England before the Norman Conquest), *Bornenholme* 1570 *ExchKR* (v. holmr), *Gillhead* 1686 PR, *le Kescale* 1369 Ipm, *le Kiskane* 1368 ib. (transcribed as *le Kistane* in 1368 IpmR. Compare possibly Kiskin *supra* 268 and *infra* 348).

PAPCASTLE

36. Papcastle[1]

> Pabecastr' 1260 Rental, 1278, 1279 Ass
> Papecastr' 1266 MinAcct et freq to 1399 Cl, with variant spelling
> -castre, Papecastre in Allerdale 1323 Ch
> Papecastel 1285 For (p)
> Papcastre 1302 FF, Papcastle al. Papcaster 1675 DKR xl
> Pappecastre 1332 SR (p)
> Popecastre 1381 Cl, 1383 Pat, 1385 FF
> Papscastle 1653 CantW vii
> Pope's Castle 1737 CW xxiii

The cæster, which has become 'castle' in the modern name, denoted the Roman fort at the point where the road running south-west from Carlisle branches north-west to Maryport. The first element can hardly be other than ON *papi*, 'hermit.'

[1] Part of Papcastle was added to Cockermouth (*infra* 361) Urban District in 1935.

The Romano-British name of Papcastle was DERVENTIO, from the river on which it stands.

DERWENT BRIDGE (6″) is *pons de Cokermuth super Derwent* early 14th StMaryY, *Derwentbrigg* 1358 Pap, *pons de Derwent iuxta Cokirmouth* 1366 *Carliol, Darwent bridge* 1578 *Cocker, Darwen bridge* 1693 PR (Bridekirk). *v.* Derwent R. *supra* 11.

HAMES HALL is *Le Hames in Papecastre* 1315 Ipm. We have also several references to the family of Adam *del Hames* (1308 *Netherhall*), Thomas *del Hames* (1330 StB, 1332 SR) and John *del Hames* (1367 Ipm) which probably came from here. Cf. also *Haimeshill* 1626 PR (Bridekirk), *Hemesehill* 1660 CantW viii. This can hardly be other than the northern plural of OE hām.   [?] _H

PEATMOOR WOOD (6″). Cf. *Petmyreng'* 1318 *MinAcct*. This name seems to contain an early instance of the ME *pete*, 'peat,' to which mýrr, 'swampy moorland,' and eng, 'meadow,' have been added. For a still earlier example *v. supra* 274 (*petepottes* c. 1200).

BONNY HILL is *Bownehous(e)hill* 1633, 1678 PR (Bridekirk), *Bownashill* 1669 ib., *Bonyhill* 1750 ib. Cf. *Bownesfield Hill* 1625 ib. GOAT (6″) is *Goate* 1664 ib., *ye Goat* 1704 ib. MOORSIDE is probably *Moreside* 1507 *Cocker. v.* mōr.

FIELD-NAMES

(a) In 1816 (Lysons) closes called Boroughs.

(b) In 1318 (*MinAcct*) *Spitelyng* (*Spitelenge* 1281 ib. Cf. *Spitelmede* 1273 1279 ib.); in 1283 (*MinAcct*) *Spitelbank'* (id. 1270 *Rental*. Cf. also *MinAcct*. These are 'meadow (*v.* eng), and bank, near a hospital.' The site of the hospital seems to be unknown); in 1270 (*Rental*) *Caldekeldebank'* ('cold spring bank,' *v.* kelda), *Melnebergh* ('mill hill,' *v.* myln, be(o)rg), *Middelholm* (id. 1266 *MinAcct. v.* holmr), *Sikett'* (cf. *Sicketesbank* ib.), *Weltebank*; in 1266 (*MinAcct*) *Carlisflat*.

37. Plumbland

PLUMBLAND [plimlən]

Plumbelund c. 1150 (c. 1225) RegDun
Plumlund c. 1175 *Hesley* (p) *et freq* to 1328 Banco
Plumland 1278 *Ass et freq* to 1612 CW (OS) iii, *Plumlaund* 1278 *Ass, Plumlond* 1300 Ipm, 1335 Misc
Plomland 1310 Pat *et freq* to 1439 Cl, *Plomplande* ib.
Plumpland 1425 *Lowther, Plumbland(e)* 1443 Cl, 1485 Ipm

PLUMBLAND MILL is *molendinum de Plumlund* c. 1235 CW xxvi, *Plumland Mills* 1612 CW (OS) iii. In the parish were *Plumland Mayns* ib., *the Mains* 1777 NB (*v.* mains), and *Plumland outgang* 1719 *Brayton* (*v.* ūtgang).

'Plum-tree grove,' *v.* lundr. Reginald of Durham (275) notes that the place is so called from the very dense woods with which it is surrounded, "lund denoting in the English (sic) idiom *nemus paci donatum*, i.e. grove devoted to peace."

ARKLEBY is *Arkelby* 1246 LaAss (p), 1292 *Ass* (p) *et freq* to 1580 Border, *Arkylby* 1350 *Netherhall* (p), 1361 *Hesley*, 1399 AD vi (p), *Arkilby* 1366 *Ass* (p), 1410 AD vi, *Arcleby* 1572 FF, *Arklebye* 1587 ib. ARKLEBY HALL is so named in 1704 (NicVisit). The first element is the very common Anglo-Scandinavian name *Arnketell*, generally reduced, as here, to *Arnkell* or *Arkil* (Björkman NP 8). The second element is bȳ.

HIGH CLOSE is so named in 1612 (CW (OS) iii).

PARSONBY is *Personeby* 1292 *Ass*, 1332 SR, *Personby* 1338 *Ass*, *Parsonby* 1704 NicVisit. "*Parsonby*, or the Parson's town; which is holden of the rector for the time being" (NB ii, 118).

WARD HALL [wɔ·dəl]

    sub *Wartheholis*, *Warthehol'* c. 1210 StB, *Warthehole* 1295 *Rental*, 1304 Cl (p)

    Warthole c. 1210 HolmC *et freq* to 1777 NB, *Warthol* 1256 FF, *Wartholl* 1307 Misc, 1318 Ipm, 1529–32 ECP, *Warthol'* 1314 Ipm, *Warthole Hall* 1816 Lysons

    Warthichole c. 1265 StB

    Warho, *Warhole* 1278 *Ass*

    Worthol 1279 *Ass* (p)

    Warihole 1279 *Ass*

    Wartehol 1279 *Ass* (p)

    Warthhole 1292 *Ass* (p), 1307 Pat

    Wardehole 1292 *Ass*

    Wardhole 1292 *Ass* (p)

    Worthill 1573 FF

    Wardall 1576 S, *Wardhall* 1671 Fleming, *Wardale or Warthole* 1687 DentonL, *Wardhold, corruptly Wardale or Warthole* 1777 NB, *Warthel-Hall* 1793 H

    Wordthole 1580 Border

An unusual Scandinavian compound, consisting of ON *varði*, 'beacon,' and the rare ON hóll, 'hill,' found also in Staffield *supra* 249. Cf. *Wartholl*, a lost field-name in Brackenthwaite *infra* 354.

FIELD-NAMES

(b) In 1719 (*Brayton*) *Gay lands*, *Killcroft* (*v.* cyln), *Steads* (cf. *High* and *Low Hous*(*e*)*steeds* 1704 Terrier. *v.* hūs, stede), *Yowlock*; in 1704 (Terrier) *Guards* (*v.* garðr), *West* and *Wood Lun*, *Millet*; in 1612 (CW (OS) iii) *Ffyts* (*v.* fit), *Oxholmes* (*v.* holmr); in 1366 (*Ass*) *la Legh*' (p) (*the Leye* 1338 ib.).

38. Ribton[1]

RIBTON (6″)

> *Ribelton* 12th StB
> *Ribton* 12th StB (p), 1285 *For* (p), 1332 SR (p), *Rybton*' 1260 Rental, 1558 FF, *Ribbton* c. 1260 StB (p)
> *Ribbeton* 1208 FF *et freq*, *Ribeton* 1212 Cur (p), 1279 *Ass*, *Ribbetun*' 1212 Cur (p), *Rybeton* 1278, 1279 *Ass*
> *Ripeton*', *Rypeton*' 1279 *Ass* (both p)

RIBTON HALL is so named in 1767 (PR, Bridekirk). The first element is probably the plant-name *ribbe*, 'rib-wort, hounds-tongue.' Cf. the history of Ribbesford (PN Wo 68). The form *Ribelton* is isolated and derived from a manuscript which is too late to have independent authority. The second element is tūn.

39. St John's, Castlerigg and Wythburn[2]

ST JOHN'S IN THE VALE

> *chappell of Seynte John* 1554 CW iv, *Snt. Johnes* 1567 PR (Crosth), *St John's and Castlerigg* 1703 NicVisit
> *valley of St John's* 1769 Gray, (*vale*) 1784 West

The church is dedicated to St John the Baptist. The 'Vale' is the valley through which St John's Beck runs.

ARMBOTH [armbə]

> *Armabothe* 1530 FF, *Armabeth* 1552 FF
> *Arbourth*, *Arburth* 1563, 1564 PR (Crosth)

[1] Added to Camerton (*supra* 281) in 1934.
[2] An exchange of territory between Keswick (*supra* 301) and this parish was made in 1935.

Armebutche 1571 CantW iii, *Armeboth* 1573 FF, *Armebath* 1576 S
Arneboth 1576 FF

Cf. *Armbothewhate* 1599 PR (Crosth) in this area.

The second element in this name seems to be the Old Danish bōþ,
'booth.' The first element is uncertain. It may be the ME *armite*,
ermite, 'hermit,' but an ON personal name *Armi*, short for ON
Arnmóðr, is also possible.

CALFHOW PIKE is *Calfhou* 1278 CW xxiii, 1278, 1279 *Ass*, *pyke of
Cauvey* 1589 *LRMB*, *Calevo pyke* 17th *Lowther*. 'Calf hill,' *v.* haugr.

CASTLERIGG MANOR

   Castelrig 1577–86 Furness *et passim* to 1459 FF, with variant
   spellings *Castil-*, *Kastel-* and *-ryg*, *-rigg(e)*, *-rygg(e)*, *-ridge* 1736
   Derwent, *Castrigg or Castle-Rigg* 1789 Clarke

   CASTLERIGG BROW (6″) is so named in 1725 (PR, Crosth). CASTLE-
   RIGG FELL is *Castle rigge fell* 1610 ib. *v.* fell.

DRY STONE KNOTT (6″) is *le Dristanknot*, *Drystanknot* 1303 Cl.
'Rocky hill,' *v.* cnotta (under knǫtt), or possibly 'cairn of dry stones.'
The earliest quotation given in NED for 'dry' in the sense 'without
mortar' is dated 1816, and the forms quoted above are two centuries
earlier than any example of this usage in Craigie's *Dictionary of the
Older Scottish Tongue*.

DUNMAIL RAISE is *Dunbalrase stone* 1576 S, *Dunbalrase stones* 1610
Speed, *Dunnimail or Dunmail-raise* 1610 Denton, *Drumwelrayes* 1657
HMC xxv, *Dunmaile-Raise* 1671 Fleming, *Drumelrayes* 1684 MunRec.
The second element of this name is ON hreysi, 'cairn.' The first part
is generally taken to be the Old Welsh personal name *Dunmail*, borne
by the penultimate king of Strathclyde. The history of the name is
complicated by the existence of another example of the same compound near Long Marton (We). Machell (c. 1690), who had excep-
tional local knowledge, records a place named *Dumbelraise* at the
meeting-point of the lordships of Long Marton, Milburn and Knock.
There can be no topographical connection between the two names,
and at present it can only be suggested that in the phrase '*Dunmail*'s
cairn,' there may be preserved a fragment of the lost legendary history
of the north-west.

FORNSIDE [fɔrnsit]

   Fornesate 1303 Ipm, *Fornset* 1533–8 ECP, *Fornsett* 1537 FF
   Furnesyde 1530 FF

Furnesschede 1533–8 ECP
Forneside 1552 FF
Fernside 1660 CantW viii

There can be little doubt that this is '*Forni*'s sætr,' or 'hill pasture.'
A compound of *sætr* and the ON adjective *forn*, 'old,' is intrinsically
improbable. It is curious that *Forni* and *sætr* are combined again in
this county in the inversion compound *Setforn*' which appears as a
field-name in Muncaster *infra* 426.

LEGBURTHWAITE

Legberthwait 1303 Ipm, *Legburgthwayte* 1530 *FF*, *Legbortwhat*,
 Legbourtwhat 1563 PR (Crosth), *Legberthwayte* 1573 FF, *Leig-
 burtwhaite* 1602 PR (Crosth)
Lekburnthuayte 1487 Ipm
Leybarthwaite 1552 FF

This is probably 'þveit at *Leggr*'s be(o)rg,' a personal name found
also in Legsby (L). The absence of the genitival inflexion in northern
England is not unusual. The disappearance by 1303 of the middle of
three consonants is quite explicable.

LORD'S ISLAND is *island of Derwentwatre* 1230 Scotland, *insula de
Derwentwat*' 1344 *Cocker, ye Ile upon Darwentwater* 1485 CW iv, *Iele*
1566 PR (Crosth), *Isle of Derwentwater* 1571 HMC xxv, *Lord's Island*
1784 West. On this island the Ratcliffes, lords of the manor of Derwentwater, had their manor-house.

NADDLE (6") is *Naddal(e)* 1292 *Ass* (p), 1303 Ipm *et freq* to 1734
Derwent, Naddell 1572 FF, *Naddall* 1573 ib., *Naddaile* 1580 Border.
Probably, as Professor Ekwall suggests, ON *naddr*, 'point, wedge,'
and *dalr*. *Naddle* occurs again in Naddle in Shap (We), for which
there is a form *Naddall* 1590, and as a lost field-name in Workington
infra 456. Professor Jackson adds: "It is possible that *n-* is the
Cumbric definite article, which may well have been *en, an*, as in
Cornish and Breton, rather than Welsh *y(r)*, probably a secondary
corruption of older *in*."

SETMABANNING[1] [setəne' baniən]

Satmabannyngg', *Setmabannyngg*' 1292 *Ass* (both p), *Setmabaning*
 1564 PR (Crosthwaite), *Setmabanninge* 1577 ib.

---

[1] A form *Setmabanwick* (t. Hy 3) is said in CW (OS) xv, 296 to refer to this place,
but no reference is given there, and the form has not been traced.

Settmayblessinge 1570 ib., *Settmablessinge* 1572 ib., *Setmayblessinge* 1575, 1584 ib.

Setmaybanninge 1574 ib., *Setmaybannyng* 1585 *Derwent*

This is an inversion compound (*v.* Introduction). The first element is ON sætr, 'hill pasture.' The second seems to be a Goidelic personal name. It may be *Mabanán*, *Mobanán*, containing OIr *Banán* (which Ekwall (ScandCelts 69) suggests is the first element of Bannisdale (We)), with the endearing prefix *Ma-*, *Mo-*, 'my.' When the personal name had been modified by popular etymology to *-banning*, 'cursing,' the *-blessing* form arose by conscious contrast.

SHOULTHWAITE

Heolthwaitis c. 1280 Furness

Shewltath 1564 PR (Crosth), *Shulthet* 1565 ib., *Sheweltwhait*, *Shoultwhait* 1567 ib., *Shoulethwate* 1578 *Cocker*

Shelthot 1565 PR (Crosth)

SHOULTHWAITE MOSS (6″) is *Shelthwat mosse* 1602 *Derwent*

The second element is þveit. The form from c. 1280 justifies the identification of the first element with ON *hjól*, 'wheel.' The place is on the upper course of Naddle Beck, and the name may refer to a mill-wheel. The modern initial *Sh-* results from a sound-development similar to that which has produced Shap (We) from OE *Hēap*, Shipton (PN NRY 15–16, PN ERY 228) from OE hēope and tūn, and Shetland from ON *Hjaltland*.

SHUNDRAW

Shonderhowe 1571 ElizKes, *Shunderhowe* 1571 *et freq* PR (Crosth), 1604 *Derwent*, *Schonderhawe* 1574 ElizKes

Sonderhowe 1574 ElizKes, *Sunderhow* 1591 *Derwent*

Shundrowe 1597 *Derwent*

Shoulderhowe 1603 PR (Crosth)

Shannder Howe 1615 PR (Crosth)

The forms are too late for certainty, but they suggest that the name may be identical in origin with Shunner Howe (PN NRY 130). If so, it probably represents an ON *siónar* haugr, 'look-out hill,' as is suggested by Ekwall in DEPN.

SMAITHWAITE [smiaθwæ·t]

Smathwaitis c. 1280 Furness

Smerthwayte 1530 *FF*

Smethwayte 1552 FF
Smaytwhait 1566 PR (Crosth)

SMAITHWAITE BRIDGE (6″) is *Smaytwhait Brigg* 1567 PR (Crosth),
Smathate bridge 1599 ib., *Smathods Bridge* 1675 Ogilby.
Probably 'small clearing,' from ON smá(r), 'small,' and þveit.

SOSGILL (6″) is *Saurescalls* 1208 FF, *Sourescall'* 1279 *Ass* (p), *Soskell*
1589 PR (Crosth). 'Muddy shieling(s),' *v.* saurr and skáli.

THIRLSPOT

> *Thirspott* 1616 PR (Crosth), *Thrispott* 1622 ib., *Threspat* 1774
> Donald, *Trespett* 1787 ClarkeM
> *Thirlspott* 1628 PR (Crosth), *Thurlspot* 1675 Ogilby

The forms, late as they are, point clearly to an original *þyrspott*,
'giant's pot, pool, or depression.' Thirlspot is close to Thirlmere
(*supra* 35), and the *l* in the latter name may have caused the modern
development from *Thirs-* to *Thirls-*. We may possibly compare
Therspettes (Nb), an aquatorium, 1256 AssNb. Cf. also *Transactions
of the Yorkshire Dialect Society*, Vol. VII, Pt xliii, pp. 9–23.

ULLOCK COPPICE (6″) is *magna Ulleyke in Castilrig'* 1292 *Ass*, *Great
Ulfelayth* 1235 FF, *Ullaik, Wllaik* 1301 Ipm, *Ullokclose* 1530 *FF*.
'Wolves' playground,' *v. infra* 367. *Great* in contrast to Ullock in
Above Derwent *infra* 373.

WANTHWAITE [wanθət]

> *Wannethwayth* 1301 GDR (p), *Wanthwait* 1303 Ipm, *Wanthwayte*
> 1552 FF, *Wanthott* 1564 PR (Crosth)
> *Waynthwayte* 1530 *FF*

The first element here is perhaps, as Professor Ekwall suggests,
ON hvǫnn 'Angelica archangelica'. The second element is þveit.

WYTHBURN [waibərən]

> *Withebotine* c. 1280 Furness, *Wythebocten* 1303 Ipm, *Wytheboten*
> 1345 GDR, *Whytheboden'* 1387 Lowther (p), *Wythbottom* 1552
> FF, *Wythboddome* 1566 PR (Crosth)
> *Withbone* 1554 CW iv
> *Wyeborne* 1564 PR (Crosth), *Wayborn, Weiborn* 1569 ElizKes,
> *Wybourn* 1675 Ogilby, *Wyburn* 1775 CW xl
> *Wyetbourne* 1564 PR (Crosth)
> *Withbourne, Wythbourne* 1568 PR (Crosth), *Witheburne* 1610 ib.,
> *Withburn or Wyburn* 1703 NicVisit

E

WYTHBURN CHAPEL is *Wyborn Chapel* 1675 Ogilby.

'Withy valley,' *v.* wīðig, with variation between forms from ON botn and OE botm.

ADAM'S CROSS (6″) is so named in 1787 (ClarkeM). BANK (6″) is *Bancke in Witheburne* 1610 PR (Crosth). BARROW HO (6″) is *Barrowe* 1578 ib., *Barrowhouse* 1811 ib. *v.* be(o)rg. BECKTHORNS is *Beckthones* 1592 ib., *Beckthornes* 1647 ib. *v.* bekkr. BELL CRAGGS (6″) is *Bell Craggs* 1805 *Brayton*. BIRKETT BANK is *Byrketbank* 1552 FF, *Birkedbancke* 1568 PR (Crosth), *Birkeheadbancke* 1571 ib. BIRKETT MIRE is *Bryketmyre* 1530 *FF*, *Birkheadmyre* 1567 PR (Crosth), *Birkett Myre* 1590 ib. *v.* bi(e)rce, hēafod. THE BOG (6″) is *the bogge* 1578 *Cocker*. BRAMCRAG is *Bryrincrag in Fornesyd* 1595 PR (Crosth), *Bryamcrage* 1614 ib., *Brian Cragge* 1616 ib., *Bramecragg* 1657 ib., *Bramegrage* 1701 ib. HIGH and LOW BRIDGEND is *Brighend* 1571 ib., *Bridgend* 1629 ib. BRIDGE HO is *Bryghous* 1565 ib., *Bridghouse* 1573 *Derwent*. BROADSTONES (6″) is *broodstone* 1613 ib., *Broadstone* 1701 PR (Crosth). BROTTO is *Bratto* t. Eliz ChancP, *Brottae* 1602 PR (Crosth), *Brettae* 1620 ib., *Brotthowe* 1621 ib., *Brothow* 1624 ib., *Brotta* 1649, 1657 ib. Probably a compound of brot, 'fragment,' and haugr. BROWNBECK (6″) is *Brownebeck in Naddell* 1616 ib. BROWN RIGG is *Brounewrigge* 1760 ib. *v.* hrycg. BUCK CASTLE (6″) is so named in 1789 (Clarke). BURNS is *Bournes* 1530 *FF*, *Burnys* 1537 ib., *Burnesse* 1533–8 ECP, *Burnes* 1552 FF, *Bourns* 1564 PR (Crosth), *(The) Bowrnes* 1569, 1571 ElizKes, *Burnes* 1585 *Derwent*. The forms are too late for certainty. Most of them are compatible with derivation from the plural of burghan. But the form *Burnesse* suggests that the name may be a compound with burh as the first element and næss as the second. This would suit the nature of the site. THE BUTTS (6″) is *Butts* 1622 PR (Crosth). CALFCLOSE BAY (6″). Cf. *ye calf close* 1615 *Derwent*. CASTLE ROCK (6″) is *Castle-rocks* 1784 West. This is probably so named from its appearance, and is the fairy castle of Scott's *Bridal of Triermain*[1]. CAUSEWAY FOOT is *Cassafott* 1564 PR (Crosth), *Caussafoot* 1565 ib., *Cawsayfoote* 1567 ib., *Kazyfoote* 1647 ib., *Causeway-foot* 1769 Gray. Cf. *Kawsayheade* 1602 PR (Crosth), *Casyhead* 1665 *Derwent*. 'Causeway foot' and 'head.' CHERRYTREE

---

[1] Mr W. G. Collingwood (CW xvi) asserts that the name is not due merely to the appearance of the rock. He describes the ruin of a small building actually on the rock which may have been a 'borg' or castle before Norman times, and have been the reason why the word 'castle' eventually came to be an element in the name of the place.

(6″) is *the Cherry Tree in Wyburn* 1775 CW xl. THE CITY (6″) is *City* 1787 ClarkeM. CLARK'S LEAP (6″) is so named from a man who in the 18th century leaped from this rock to drown himself (Clarke 117–18). DALE BOTTOM is *Dale bottom* 1605 *Derwent*, *Dale boddam* 1613 ib. DALEHEAD HALL. Cf. *Dalehead Parke* 1552 FF, *Daylhead* 1567 PR (Crosth), *Dalehead, at the head of Buresdale* 1777 NB (ii, 79). DODD CRAG (6″) is *dodcrage* 1615 *Derwent*. *v.* dod. EDDY GRAVE STAKE (6″) is so named in 1805 (*Brayton*). Cf. *Eddy Field* 1734 *Derwent*, in this parish. FALCON CRAG is so named in 1784 (West). FIELDSIDE is *Fieldsid* 1571 PR (Crosth), *Feldside* 1585 *Derwent*. *v.* feld. FISHER PLACE is *Fishers Place* 1787 ClarkeM. FLOUR GILL (6″). Cf. *flowery Gill Head* 1805 *Brayton*. GOOSE WELL is *Gousewell* 1567 PR (Crosth), *Goosewell* 1590 *Derwent*. *v.* w(i)elle. GREAT HOW (6″) is so named in 1789 (Clarke). *v.* haugr. GREEN (6″) is *Grene* 1564 PR (Crosth). HILL TOP is *Hill Toppe* 1595 *Derwent*. HOLLIN BROW (6″) is *Hollinge Browe* 1568 PR (Crosth), *Holline Browe* 1603 ib. *v.* holegn. HOLLIN ROOT is *Hollinge Roote* 1573 ib., *Hollyneroote* 1600 ib. HOWGATE (6″) is *Howgayt* 1564 ib., *Howgate* 1590 *Derwent*. Probably 'hollow way,' *v.* holh, holr and gata. LADY'S RAKE is so named in 1794 (H). Traditionally associated with the escape of Lady Derwentwater from Lord's Island in 1715 (ib. ii, 191). *v.* reik. LOWTHWAITE [lɔuθət] is *Lothwait* 1571 ElizKes, *Lowthwayt* 1591 *Derwent*, *Lothat* 1657 PR (Crosth). *v.* þveit. MIRE HO is *Mirehouse* 1568 ib. *v.* mȳrr. MOOR is *Moure* 1569 ib., *Mure* 1579 ib., *More* 1585 *Derwent*, *Moore* 1606 PR (Crosth). *v.* mōr. MOSS DIKES (6″) is *Mossedick* 1575 ib., *Mossedyks* 1604 *Derwent*. *v.* dīc. NAB CRAGS. *v.* nabbi. NEST is so named in 1792 (PR, Crosth). NOOK (6″) is *Newke in Appletwhaite* 1614 ib. PIETNEST (6″) is *Pyetnest* 1590 *Derwent*. 'Magpie nest.' PINFOLD HOW (6″) is *Pimfold How* 1617 PR (Crosth), *Pindfold how* 1636 ib., *Punfelhow in Wythb...* 1746 ib. *v.* pundf(e)ald, haugr. RAISE is *Highe rase* 1589 LRMB. *v.* hreysi. RAKEFOOT is *Rakefoote* 1597 *Derwent*. *v.* reik. RAMPSHOLME ISLAND (6″) is *Rampsholme* 1784 West. *v.* holmr. The form is too late for safe interpretation of the first element. ROUND MOUNT (6″). Cf. *the roundhill Dubsyd, round castell* 1604 *Derwent*, *round castell, Round Castle* 1739 ib. ROW END is *Row End* 1604 ib., *Raw End* 1739, 1743 ib. *v.* rāw. SHAW BANK is *Shabanke* 1702 PR (Crosth), *Shaw Bank* 1739 *Derwent*. *v.* sceaga. SMITHY HO (6″). Cf. *Smithey Closse* 1629 *Derwent*. SNIPES HOW (6″) is *Snipshow* 1665 ib., *Snipeshow* 1731 PR (Crosth). *v.* haugr. STABLE HILLS is *Stable Hill* 1734 *Derwent*,

Stable-hills 1770 Young. STANAH [stanə] is *Stanay* 1606 PR (Crosth).
STANDING CRAG is *Standing Cragg* 1805 *Brayton*. STEEL END is
Steelle End 1570 PR (Crosth), *Stele end* 1586 ib., *Stillend* 1610
Derwent. *v.* stigel. It is at the end of the old path from Dunmail
Raise. STENKIN is so named in 1646 (PR, Crosth). STENOCH (6″)
is *Stannick* 1578, 1634 ib., *Stannacke* 1581 ib., *Stenicke* 1668 ib.,
Steneck 1787 ClarkeM, *Stanwick* 1794 MapH. STICKS PASS. Cf.
stikes, *(the) sticks mosse* 1589 *LRMB*, *sticks* 1749 PR (Watermillock).
STYBARROW DOD. Cf. *Stibarro gill heade* 1589 *LRMB*, *Stybrow* 1794
H. STYBECK is *Styebecke* 1600 PR (Crosth), *Stibeck* 1618 ib. *v.* bekkr.
The *sty* (*v.* stig) refers to the path which becomes Stanah Gate and
leads up to Stybarrow Dod. THE SWIRLS (6″). Cf. *Swirl's Gate* 1787
ClarkeM. WALLOW CRAG is so named in 1769 (Gray). WATSON'S
PARK (6″) is *Watsons Park* 1734 *Derwent*. WEST HEAD is *Waists-hed*
1720 PR (Crosth), *Wastehead* 1734 ib. WHITE PIKE is so named in
1783 (Donald). *v.* pīc. YEWHOW WOOD (6″). Cf. *Ewhowe* 1601 PR
(Crosth), *Yewhowe* 1606 ib., *Ewehowe in Armboth* 1616 ib. *v.* haugr.
YEW TREE is *Yewtree* 1592 ib., *Yeughtree* 1616 ib., *Huetree* 1706 ib.
YEW TREE COTTAGE (6″) is so named in 1794 (H).

FIELD-NAMES

(b) In 1787 (ClarkeM) *Brow* (*Browe* 1629 PR[1]), *Scoathow* (*Skawhowe*
1565 ib., *Skaldhowe* 1566 ib., *Skothowe* t. Eliz ChancP. It is possible that
the first element here may be ON *skáld*, 'poet,' or alternatively *scalled*,
'scurvy.' The second is haugr), *Whyfold*; in 1739 (*Derwent*) *Birkhowe* (also
Brickhowsyks) (*Birkhous* 1613 PR. *v.* birki, haugr), *Bowtby*, *Chapple House*
(*Chapple* 1585 *Derwent*. Cf. *Chaplestealle* 1645 PR), *Cockbains*, *Crook* (*Crooke*
1597 *Derwent*), *High raw* (*the high rowe* 1665 ib. *v.* rāw), *Hogg close* (cf. *the
hoghouse close* 1602 ib.), *How Garth* id. 1629 ib. *v.* garðr), *Howplace* (*Howe-
places* 1619 PR. *v.* haugr), *Loanesty*, *Lonesty* (*Lonsty* 1665 *Derwent*), *Skin-
nerskill hill* (cf. *Skinerskill* 1613 ib. Cf. *Skinnerdubb* 1615 ib.), *Stockhouse*
(id. 1597 ib.), *Stone* (*the Stone* 1665 ib.), *Tentermire* (*Tentermyre* ib. *v.*
tenter, mýrr), *Walk Mill* (id. ib. 'Fulling-mill'); in 1723 (*Derwent*) *Ile Park*
(cf. *yeate called Ile* 1615 ib.); in 1722 (PR) *Tod-Crag* (id. 1604 ib. 'Fox-crag');
in 1713 (PR) *Waterhead* (*Watterhead* 1577 ib.); in 1672 (PR) *Layerhow*
(*Leyrhowe* 1670 ib. *v.* leirr, haugr); in 1665 (*Derwent*) *Bowtoakes* (*Bowdayke*
1602 ib. Probably 'bent oak,' from OE *būgan*, and āc), *Graystonhill* (*gray-
stonehill* 1604 ib.), *Helmhowe* (*v.* haugr), *ye Intake* (*the intacke* 1590 ib.
v. intak); in 1657 (PR) *Wreskay* (*Wryckehow* 1565 ib., *Wrackae* 1617 ib.);
in 1615 (*Derwent*) *Inge closse* (cf. *ingclose yeate* 1590 ib. *v.* eng), *Saterthwait*
(probably a compound of sætr and þveit, identical with Satterthwaite (PN
La 219)), *Skidgarthe* (apparently 'garth with a palisade,' from ON *skíð* and

---

[1] PR in these names refers to Crosthwaite Parish Registers.

garðr); in 1613 (*Derwent*) *the Flatte* (*Flatte* 1590 ib.); in 1610 (*Derwent*) *buckhowe* (*v.* haugr), *feresyd, the gale* (also spelled *gaile*) *mosse* ('bog-myrtle mos'), *heighleaze* (*v.* læs), *Steuthewate* (*v.* þveit); in 1604 (*Derwent*) *the burnt oke, Cotesyke* (*v.* sic), *Duch stank, henlamerhead, Ing castell* (*v.* eng), *Lynclose* (*v.* lin), *the Long Layne, Ruskellend* (cf. *Highrusgill yate* 1590 *Derwent*), *Skimelstele yate, Whitbarrey*; in 1601 (PR) *Waterend* (*Watterend*) 1568 ib.); in 1597 (*Derwent*) *Bentcastle close, the Fitts* (*v.* fit), *Henleymoore, Withenland* (this may contain *within, withen,* a ME form of wiðig, and mean 'willow land'); in 1595 (*Derwent*) *the hyghe streat, the Nout Scarraye*; in 1591 (*Derwent*) *Grassenhill, towenhead*; in 1590 (*Derwent*) *Cowdwell acre, Milkinge hill*; in 1303 (Ipm) *Crosseby, La Waterhouses.* Under each of the following dates there is one field-name: *Beetholme* 1664 *Derwent, Brodynghead* 1602 ib. (*v.* eng), *Carrgarth* 1605 ib. (*v.* kiarr, garðr), *Colland yates* 1585 ib., *Moathall Mill* 1734 ib.

40. Seaton

SEATON

Setona c. 1174 *HolmC, Seton* 1230 Scotland *et freq* to 1440 FF
Seiton 1278 *Ass, Seyton* ib. (p), 1279 ib.
Seaton 1580 Border

SEATON MOOR (6″) probably gave name to the family of Richard de *Mora* (c. 1270 StB). *v.* mōr.

Formally, this name represents OE *sǣtūn,* 'sea tūn.' On the other hand, Seaton is on rising ground and now is more than a mile from the sea. It is not impossible that the place may have been named from its proximity to the sea, but the exact significance of the name must remain doubtful. There is the same kind of topographical difficulty in the case of Seaton in Bootle *infra* 347.

ST HELENS is *St Ellens Close* 1749 *LowtherW.*

FIELD-NAMES

(*b*) In 1772 (*LowtherW*) *Bunting, Croft Rigg Gillin, Hemp Garth* (*v.* garðr), *Hunger Riggs, Kingey Closes, Moorhouse Guards* (*v.* garðr), *Roger Flatt*; in 1754 (*LowtherW*) *Tenter Meadow* (*v.* tenter); in 1749 (*LowtherW*) *Fullock, Hosterbank.*

41. Skiddaw[1]

SKIDDAW

Skythou 1260 *Rental, Skythowe* 1363 *GDR*
Sketho, Skethow 1539 *MinAcct*
Skedowe 1539 *MinAcct* (p), *Skedo* 1544 NB
Skyddowe 1570 *ExchKR, Skiddow* 1666 *Terrier*

[1] Added to Underskiddaw (*infra* 321) in 1934.

SKIDDAW (mountain)

Schydehow, Skydehow 1247 *FF, Skiddehawe* 1256 *Fountains, Skyde-howe* t. Ed 3 *Cocker, Skiddow hill* 1576 *S, Skiddowe* 1578 *Cocker, Skiddaw* 1671 Fleming, *Skiddey Topp* 1675 Sandford, *Skidda* c. 1690 *Machell*

Skythou c. 1260 Fountains, *Skythowe* 1343 Cl, *montem vocatur Skythow* 1450 *Netherhall*

Skethowe 1539 *MinAcct*

SKIDDAW FOREST

forest of Skithoc 1230 Scotland

foresta sue chacea de Skydhowe 1519 *FF, forest de Skydow* 1570 *ExchKR*

forest de Skethoo 1541 *MinAcct*

SKIDDAW MAN (6″) is "a blue slate stone, about a man's height, which they call *Skidaw man*" (NB ii, 87).

It is certain that Skiddaw is a Scandinavian name, of which the second element is ON **haugr**. But the meaning, and even the original form of the first element, are doubtful. Medieval forms, of which none is very early, are equally divided between *skid-* and *skit-*. On the other hand, if *skid-* is original, it is hard to suggest any line on which an interpretation could be found. Of the possible senses which might lie behind *skit-*, ON *skit*, 'filth,' is obviously inadmissible in the name of this great hill. *skyti*, 'archer,' sometimes found as a personal name, is possible, though such an element could hardly appear in this context unless it arose from some story or figure of mythology connected with the hill. It is more probable that, as suggested by Ekwall (DEPN), the name contains a word related to Norwegian *skut, skuta*, 'projecting crag.' The difficulty here is that the recorded forms of Skiddaw seem to imply a first element with a mutated vowel *y*, and no such word has hitherto been found. But a formation of this kind might naturally arise from the recorded ON *skúti*, which is the origin of the word *scout*, often applied to hills in the north, as in Kinder Scout (Db). On the present evidence, this explanation seems the most probable. The meaning of Skiddaw in this case would be 'craggy hill.'

GREAT CALVA is *Calva* 1794 MapH. Probably 'calf hill,' *v.* 312.

42. Underskiddaw[1]

UNDERSKIDDAW is *subtus Skedow* 1508 *Cocker, Undr Skedow* 1567 PR (Crosth), *under Skiddey* 1629 PR (Dacre), *Under-Skiddow* 1663 *Terrier. v.* Skiddaw *supra* 319.

APPLETHWAITE [aplθət]

> *Apelthwayt* c. 1220 Fountains *et freq* to 1371 IpmR, with variant spellings *-thuayt, -tweit, -thwaite, Appelthweit* 1222 Pipe (p) *et passim*, with variant spellings *-tweyt, -thwayt, -thwate, Appelethwayt* 1230 Scotland, *Appelwayth* 1278 *Ass*
>
> *Appilthwait* c. 1230 Fountains (p), *Appilthwayt* 1310 Carliol, (*in Bastenthwayt*) 1339 *GDR*
>
> *Applethweyt* 1281 *MinAcct, Aplewhaite* 1600 PR (Crosth)
>
> *Appulthuayt* 1526 CW (OS) x

> 'Apple clearing,' *v.* þveit.

BRUNDHOLME [brundəm]

> *Brundholm(e)* 1292 *Ass* (p), 1369 Ipm, 1663 *Terrier, Bruntholme* 1615 *Derwent, Brundham or Brundholm* 1777 NB
>
> *Broundholm* 1343 Cl, *Broundeholme* 1539 *MinAcct*
>
> *Brondholm(e)* 1367 Ipm, t. Jas 1 *AOMB*
>
> *Brintholme* 1376 TestKarl (p), *Bryndholm* 1397 FF
>
> *Brandome* 1564 PR (Crosth), *Brandholme* 1718 ib.

> Probably 'burnt holmr.'

CAST RIGG (6″) is *Castrig*' 1279 *Ass, Castaryg* 1563 PR (Crosth), *Castaryk* 1564 ib., *Castrigge fell* 1601 *Derwent, the Howe of Casterigge* 1574 ElizKes. *v.* hrycg. The first element may be Old Anglian cæster, though there is no trace of Roman or other ancient earthworks.

LATRIGG

> *Laterhayheved* 1220 Fountains, *Laterhayhefed* 1256 ib., *Laterayheued* c. 1260 ib.
>
> *Latterigg* 1666 *Terrier*
>
> *Latrig(g)* 1769 Gray, 1784 West
>
> *Lath-Rigs* 1789 Clarke

This contains the first recorded example in this county of an element *later*, which occurs again in Whinlatter and Latterhead *infra* 409, 410.

---

[1] Skiddaw (*supra* 319) was added to Underskiddaw in 1934.

It is discussed by Ekwall in ScandCelts 91–2 and PN La 194. Formally, the element can be derived either from an ON *látr*, 'lair,' or from a Goidelic word, represented in OIrish *lettir*, Gaelic *leitir*, and meaning 'hill' or 'slope.' The first explanation accounts most easily for the form *Later*, but it is inappropriate to the mountain height of Whinlatter and it does not suit the high and well-marked hill of Latrigg. Latterhead is in a valley, but the hills immediately to the west rise nearly a thousand feet above the settlement to which the name is applied. It is probable that the Goidelic *lettir, leitir* is the basis of this name, as of Latrigg and Whinlatter. The final element of Latrigg was originally OE **hēafod**, 'head,' afterwards changed to *rigg*. The meaning of *-hay-* is uncertain.

Lyzzick Hall

 Losaikes c. 1220 Fountains
 Lesakes 1343 Cl, *Lesake* 1563 PR (Crosth), *Lesayke* 1564 ib.,
  Lezake, Lysack 1567 ib., *Lissake* 1599 ib.
 Leasick 1570 PR (Crosth), *Lisick halle* 1608 ib., *Lizwick* 1622 ib.

The medieval forms in *Los-* and *Les-* suggest that the first element is ON *ljóss*, 'bright, shining.' The second element is **eik**, 'oak.' Cf. possibly Lysicks (137).

Millbeck is *Milnebek* 1260 *Rental* (p), *Milbeke* 1526 CW (OS) x, *Mylnebecke* 1563 PR (Crosth), *Millbeck Hall* 1732 ib. 'Mill **bekkr**.'

Ormathwaite [ɔ·rmθət]

 Nordmanthait c. 1160 Fountains, *Normanwait, Normantwait* 1246
  LaAss (p), *Northmanethwait* c. 1260 Fountains (p), *Normantweyt*
  c. 1265 ib., *Nortmannesthwayt* c. 1265 ib. (p), *Normanthuayt* 1526
  CW (OS) x
 Hormatwhat 1564 PR (Crosth)
 Ormatwhat 1564 PR (Crosth), *Ormaytwhait* 1566 ib., *Ormathwaite*
  1583 FF
 Manthwate 1570 CW (OS) x
 Hornematwhait 1581 PR (Crosth)

'Clearing of the Northmen' or 'of an individual named *Norðmann*,' *v.* þveit.

Calvert's Bridge (6") is probably to be associated with the family of William *Calvart* (1575 PR, Crosth).

BIRKETT WOOD (6″) is so named in 1677 (PR, Crosth). CROOKELTY BRIDGE (6″) is *Crooklety Bridge* 1772 ib., *Crookelty Bridge* 1789 Clarke. DANCING GATE (6″) is *Danson Yeate* 1571 PR (Crosth), *Dansinyeat* 1576 ib., *Dansingyeat* 1592 ib. Cf. *Danson Place, Dancsingeplace* 1574 ib. This may contain the personal name *Danson*. DERWENT FOOT (6″) is *Derwannt Foote* 1538 *AOMB*. The place where Derwent falls into Bassenthwaite Lake. KILN HOW (6″) is *Kilnehowe* 1644 PR (Crosth). *v.* cyln, haugr. LONG CLOSE is *Longclose, Langclose* 1563, 1566 ib. LONSCALE FELL is *Lonskell* 1566 ib., *Longskell* 1573 ib., *Loneskill* 1600 ib. Its lower slopes probably included '*the essart called Le Scales*' 1256 Fountains. *v.* skáli. LOW GROVE is *Lowgrave* 1567 PR (Crosth), *Lowgrayfe* 1576 ib., *Lowgraffe* 1577 ib., *Lowgrove* 1600 ib. MYRTLE GROVE (6″) is so named in 1805 ib. SPOONYGREEN LANE (6″) is named from *Supunaygrene, Spelmaygrene, Spimaygrene* 1577 PR (Crosth), *Sponaygrene* 1579 ib., *Spunay Greene* 1580 ib., *Spunagrene* 1583 ib. HIGH and LOW STOCK BRIDGE (both 6″) are so named in 1787 (ClarkeM). *v.* stocc, brycg. THORNY PLATS (6″) is *Thonyplett* (sic), *Thorneplete* 1581 PR (Crosth), *Thorneneplat* 1583 ib. 'Thorny plot,' THROSTLE SHAW (6″) is *Throssleshawe* 1601 ib. Apparently 'thrush wood,' *v.* sceaga. WINDEBROWE (6″) is *Windie Browe* 1594 ib. 'Windy brow.'

FIELD-NAMES

(b) In 1651 (PR, Crosth) *High* (*Hie* 1567 ib.); in 1268 (Fountains) *Ketescalerig* (*Ketescalrig* c. 1220 ib. 'Ridge and beck by *Ketil*'s shielings,' *v.* skáli, hryggr (under hrycg)), *Langrig* (id. c. 1235 ib.), *Littelrig* (id. ib. 'Little ridge'), *Strandes* (*Strindes* c. 1220 ib., *Strandes* 1225 CW xxi, *Strendas* a. 1247 CW xxiii. This is *strand, strind* (*v.* NED *s.v. strand* sb.²), 'stream, brook,' the first recorded example of which in NED is a. 1225); in c. 1265 (Fountains) *Heselrigbek* (cf. *Hesilriddyng* c. 1220 ib. *v.* hæsel, hrycg, hryding), *Pyrnebemsyk* (*v.* sic. *Pyrne-* is probably for *þyrne,* 'thorn,' to which *bēam,* 'tree', has been added later; it is an unrecorded OE compound, with which may be compared *beg-bēam,* 'mulberry tree'); in c. 1260 (Fountains) *Escaling*' (*Eskalinges* c. 1220 ib.), *Gillenukelstagge* (*Gillenuthghelstagh* (sic print) ib. The first element is the Gaelic personal name *Gillemichel*; the second is uncertain); in c. 1220 (Fountains) *Rauthecokkeridding* ('red cock hryding,' *v.* rauðr. The red cock is the common grouse), *Scippeleriding, Stalwrthemanridding* (apparently 'stalwart man hryding'). Under each of the following dates there is one field-name: *Armatt-rigg* 1787 ClarkeM (apparently 'hermit-rigg'), *Newke in Appletwhaite* 1614 PR (Crosth) (i.e. 'nook').

43. Sunderland[1]

SUNDERLAND is *Sonderland in Blankrayk* 1278 *Ass*, *Sunderlond* 1279 ib., *Sunderlande* 1299 Ipm. This is OE *sundorland*. In the OE Bede (v, 23) *on sundor lande ðæs ilcan mynstres* translates *in territorio eiusdem monasterii* (i.e. Wearmouth), the reference being to Sunderland (Du). The word glosses Latin *predia, prediolum*. *Sundor-* in OE compounds means 'private' or 'special', or 'separate' or 'remote.'

SETRAH HILL (6″) is connected with *Setteray-beck* 1718 *Brayton*, *Settera Beck* 1796 ib. Cf. Satterah, a field-name in Mardale (We), and Setterah Park (We), for which there are 15th-century forms *Satirhow*, *Setterhowe* and *Saterow*. Each of these names seems to be a compound of **sætr** and **haugr**, 'hill marked by a shieling.' SPINDLE-BANK WOOD (6″) is so named in 1810 (*Map*).

FIELD-NAMES

(b) In 1796 (*Brayton*) *High Cow Yead* (*high cow yeat* 1718 ib.), *Dobby Moss* (id. ib.), *White Hills* (id. ib.).

44. Tallentire[2]
TALLENTIRE

Talentir c. 1160 Fountains (p), c. 1210 StB *et passim* to 1584 FF, with variant spelling *-tire, Talentyr* 1171–5 (1333) CW iii *et freq* to 1535 VE, with variant spelling *-tyre, Talantir, Talantyr* 1246 FF, 1278 *Ass*, c. 1300 Guisb, *Talantyre* 1573 FF
Talghentir 1208 FF
Tallentyre 1558 FF, *Tallantire* 1580 Border

TALLENTIRE HALL is *Tallantire Hall* 1758 CW (OS) iv. TALLENTIRE HILL is *Tallentine* (sic) *hill* 1777 NB.

Ekwall (DEPN) suggests that this means 'end of the land,' from Welsh *tal* and *tir*, separated by the definite article (*-en-* in OBreton and OCornish). The normal form in Welsh is *-y-* as in Tal-y-bont, 'bridge-end,' but there is, as Sir Ifor Williams informs us, a possible instance of *-in-* in OWelsh.

THUAHOVEL (lost). In StB, as printed, there are two field-names in this parish, *Suahowes* c. 1260 and *Thuahovel* c. 1210. It is probable

[1] Added to Blindcrake (*supra* 266) in 1934.
[2] Added to Bridekirk (*supra* 272) in 1934.

that these two names are really the same and that the first element was originally ON *tví*, 'two,' or conceivably the OE cognate *twā* and the second the plural of **haugr**. In that case, the name must have meant 'two mounds.' Cf. Trehos Wapentake (L) 'three mounds' (EHN i, 59) and Forehoe Hundred (Nf) 'four mounds' (EHN i, 78).

FIELD-NAMES

(b) In 1679 (PR, Bridekirk) *Whineygill* (*Whinnickhill* 1627 ib., *Whinkels* 1647 ib., *Whiny Kill* 1678 ib.); in 1674 (PR, Bridekirk) *Pow* (*Powe* 1627 ib. v. poll); in c. 1265 (StB) *Bighou* (*Biggehoue* c. 1210 ib. 'Barley hill,' v. bygg, haugr), *Hagwrinrun*, *Hagwrinron* (sic print) ib. The second element is ON runnr, 'brushwood.' The first is ME *hagworm*, 'viper,' from ON *hǫgg-ormr*), *Harkylflat* (*Arkelflat* c. 1260 ib. '*Arnkell*'s flat,' cf. Arkleby *supra* 310), *Sandrig* (id. c. 1210 ib. 'Sand ridge,' v. hrycg); in c. 1260 (StB) *Blenkerpot*, *Fletehoumyre* (v. fljót, haugr, mýrr), *Quinahytefote*; in c. 1260 (p. 1500) (StB) *Foreland closs vel Hallwhynnes, lez infeld, lez owtfeld, Rondebank, Sothfeld, Stanbanckclosse*; in c. 1210 (StB) *Bankes, Blaakepot, Brawron* (v. runnr), *Hildirflath, Levedibuthes* ('lady booths,' v. búþ), *Routheland* ('red land,' v. rauðr), *Thorfinesakyr* ('*Þorfinn*'s acre,' the latter word probably representing ON akr, under æcer).

45. Torpenhow[1]

TORPENHOW [trə·penə], occasionally [θrə·penə, tɔ·penə]

Torpennev c. 1160 Fountains (p)
Torpennoc 1163 P (p), *Torpenno* 1222 ClR, 1223 Pipe, *Torpennoh'* 1279 Ass
Torpennoth c. 1165 Holyrood
Thorpenhou c. 1210 StB, 1243, 1247 FF, *Thorpennou* 1212 Fees, 1292 Ass, *Thorpenno* 1279 Wickwane, *Thorppennow* 1286 Ass, *Thorpenho* 1292 Ass
Torpenho 1222 ClR, *Torpenhow* 1290 Pap *et passim*, *Torpenhou* 1312 Pat
Torpeneu 1228 Pipe, *Torpenewe* 1606 PCC
Thorpeneu 1229 Pipe, *Thorpenneu* 1231 ib.
Thorpenny 1232 Pipe
Torpennou, Torpennowe 1278 Ch *et freq* to 1498 Ipm
Turpenho 1509 LP, *Turpennow* 1516 DunBev, *Turpennay* 1579 PR (Crosth)
Torpenny 1576 S, *Torpeny* 1675 Ogilby
Trepenna 1772 PR (Dalston)

[1] Added to Blennerhasset (*supra* 265) in 1934.

PARK HO. Cf. *Torpenhoweparke* 1435 IpmR.

Torpenhow Hall and church, which doubtless form the nucleus of the settlement, stand on a 'rising topped hill' (Denton 51) which is itself on the northward slope of a long hill and the name Torpenhow is doubtless descriptive of the site. The first element is the British *torr*, 'peak.' This would seem to have been compounded with British *pen*, *Torpen* then denoting 'peak-head.' To this was added in Anglian days the English hōh, dat. sg. *hō(h)e*, giving forms *Torpenho* and the like. A similar combination of *penn* and *hōh* is probably found in Pinhoe (PN D 443), c. 1050 *Peonho*.

The old story, first told by Denton (51), that the name bears witness to three successive races—British (*Pen*), Saxon (*Tor*), Danish (*How*) is incorrect; *torr*, though occasionally found in OE, is really a loan-word from British, and *torpen* may well be pure British. The added *how*, to judge by early forms in *-oc* and *-oh*, would seem to be from English hōh rather than ON haugr.

BELSAY FIELDS (6") is *Belesyse* 1399 AD vi, *Belises*, *Belysis* 1405–6 DentonA, *Bellasis(e)* 1575 NB, *Belusa field*, *Bellosa field Nook* 1742 *Brayton*, *Belliesa Field* 1777 *Hudleston*. Cf. *Bellasy Tarn* 1796 ib. This is clearly an example of the common OFr *belasis*, 'beautiful seat,' familiar in such names as Belsize (PN Mx 112), Bellasize (PN ERY 245).

CAERMOTE is *Carmalt* 1777 *Hudleston*, 1796 *Brayton*, *Caer-Mot* 1784 West. Cf. *Curmault Well*, *Carmault Well* 1742 *Brayton*. The name is recorded too late for certain interpretation, but Sir Ifor Williams suggests Welsh *caermollt*, 'fort of the wether'. *Carmalt*, *Kirmalt*, *infra* 455, also late recorded, may have the same origin.

WHITRIGG is *Whyterigg* 1278 *Ass*, *Whitrig* 1399 AD vi, 1580 Border, *Whytryg juxta Torpenhow* 1439 DentonA. 'White ridge,' *v.* hrycg.

BORROWSCALE. Cf. *Borranskell Hill* 1796 *Brayton* and Borrowscale *supra* 221. *v.* burghan, skáli. BROWN MOOR (6") is *the Brown Moor* 1703 NicVisit. COCKSHOT WOOD (6"). *v. infra* cockshot. LOW WOODNOOK (6") is so named in 1794 (H). WHITTAS PARK is *Whitt house* 1777 *Hudleston*.

FIELD-NAMES

(*a*) In 1814 (CW x) Townfallas.

(*b*) In 1796 (*Brayton*) *Gelliman Scar* (*v.* skarð), *Kill Stones Head*, *Meer Stone* (probably 'boundary stone,' *v.* (ge)mǽre), *Member Stone* (id. 1742 ib.);

in 1777 (NB) *Colebeck, Stone Cowen* (possibly for 'cairn,' cf. *supra* 213); in 1737 (*Hudleston*) *Bowflatts, Cockbridge, the Old Rivings, Tomfield*; in 1575 (NB) *Applewraye* (*Appelwra* 1292 *Ass*. 'Apple (v)rá); in 1405 (DentonA) *Thornebanke* (*Thornebank* 1399 AD vi). Under each of the following dates there is one field-name: *The Fyttes* 1606 PCC (*v.* fit), *Stampelthwayt* 1292 *Ass* (possibly 'stone peel þveit'), *Todehole* t. Eliz ChancP ('fox-hole').

46. Uldale[1]

ULDALE [uldəl]

Ulvesdal' 1216 ClR, 1279 *Ass*
Uluedal(e)[2] 1228 *For et freq* to 1399 Cl, *Uluadale* 1334 *MinAcct*
Woluedale 1286 *Ass*
Uvedale 1305 Pat
Oulfsdale 1328 Pat
Oulfdale 1329 Cl
Ulledale 1332 SR, *Uldale* 1391 FF, *Uldale al. Ulnedale* 1411 Pat,
    Uldaile in Bagray 1535 VE, *Uldall* 1570 ExchKR
Ulfdale 1359 *Carliol*

ULDALE HALL (6″) is represented in the name of Adam *del Halle de... Uldayle* (1358 CW (OS) x). *v.* h(e)all.

The earliest form suggests ON *Úlfs* dalr, '*Ulf*'s valley.' There are no means of deciding whether this, or the *úlfa dalr*, 'wolves' valley,' suggested by most of the later spellings, was the original form of the name.

AUGHERTREE [æfətri·]

Alcotewraye 1540 *MinAcct, Alkatre* 1580 Border
Ancautre 1576 S, *Ancautree Moor* 1750 Pococke
Awhatree 1777 NB

The final element is (v)rá. The first part of the name seems to be OE (e)ald cot(e), 'old cottage.'

LOWTHWAITE is *Louthweit* 1229 Pipe, *Losthawyt, Lostthawyt* 1295 Rental, *Lostethawyth* ib. (p), *Lostwaith* 1334 *MinAcct, Loftethayt, Loftthwayt* 1399 IpmR, *Lowthwate* 1539 *MinAcct*. To judge from the forms from 1399, this is ON lopt-þveit, 'clearing distinguished by a two-story building.'

---

[1] Added to High and Low Ireby (*supra* 299) in 1934.
[2] In many printed texts these forms have been wrongly transcribed *Ulnedal(e)*, and have given rise to the legend, started by Denton (48), that the place was named from *Ulne*, which was thought to be another form of Ellen (*Elne*) river.

ORTHWAITE is *Ouerthwait* 1305 *For*, *Orthwait* 1703 NicVisit. ORTHWAITE HALL (6″) is so named in 1816 (Lysons). 'Over þveit.' Why 'over' is not obvious. It lies near Over Water (*supra* 34) but the interpretation of that name is equally obscure.

STOCKDALE is *Stakedale in Uluedale* 1292 *Ass*, *Stokedale* 1539 *MinAcct*, *Stockdale* 1703 NicVisit. The first element may have been ON *stakkr*, in the sense 'pillar of rock.' The second is dalr.

CASTLE HOW and GILL BRIDGE (both 6″) are probably represented in the names of John de *Kaystre al. Castre* (1411 Pat) and William de *Gillbrigge* (1278 *Ass*).

BAGGRA YEAT. *v. supra* 259. BIRKMIRE (6″) is *Byrkmyr* 1452 Fine. 'Birch tree swamp,' *v.* birki, mýrr. DASH is so named in 1660 (CantW viii). 'Waterfall.' HORSEMOOR HILLS is so named in 1794 (H). LONGLANDS is *Langelandes* 1399 IpmR. MEAL FELL (6″) may possibly have the same history as Mell Fell *supra* 212. MIRKHOLME is *Myrkeholme* 1594 CW x. 'Dark holmr.'

FIELD-NAMES

(b) In 1777 (NB) *Bleaberrythwait* ('blaeberry þveit'), *Coppeak*; in 1542 (*MinAcct*) *le Flaske* (id. 1539 ib. *v.* flasshe); in 1508 (*Cocker*) *Netherend*; in 1493 (AD vi) *Akysbiggyng* (*ac'sbigging* 1295 *Rental*, *Ackysbyggyng'* 1409 AD vi. *v.* bigging); in 1295 (*Rental*) *Bollenardecroft*, *Heselscales* (*v.* hesli, under hæsel, skáli), *Squinstibanc* (probably 'pigstye bank').

WESTNEWTON
47. Westnewton

Neutona c. 1187 *HolmC*, *Neuton* a. 1195 *HolmC et freq* to 1399 IpmR, (*in Allerdal'*) 1285 *For*, *Neweton* 1332 SR, *Newenton* 1360 Pat, *Newton in Ardale* 1576 S, *West Newton* 1777 NB

'New tūn', *v.* nīwe. Westnewton is "So called, it is probable, in contra-distinction to *Newton Arlosh*, in the parish of *Holme Cultram*, which lies to the *east*" (H ii, 297).

STUBSGILL is *Stubscales* 1595 FF. *v.* skáli. YEARNGILL is so named in 1670 (BM).

FIELD-NAMES

(a) In 1887 (*Stainer*) Carhouse Field, Dub Field (*v.* dub), Keddy Field, Pain Ing (*v.* eng), Russcale Meadow, Tang Hill, Three Kit, Wardin Field, East and West Widah (Widow Field 1843 ib.); in 1843 (*Stainer*) Cape Leigh.

(b) *Crengale iuxta Neuton'* 1346 *GDR* (*v.* kringla).

48. Westward

WESTWARD

le Westwarde in Allerdale 1354 *Carliol, boscus de Allerdale called the Westwarde* 1365 (1578) *Cocker, le Westward* 1367 Ipm, *Westwarde in Allerdale* 1381 Cl

WESTWARD PARK is so named in 1777 (NB)

The parish corresponds generally to the free chace of Allerdale which was annexed in the 12th century to the king's forest of Inglewood (NB ii, 138) and afterwards formed the west ward, or division, of that forest.

EAST and WEST CURTHWAITE [kərθət]

Kyrkehuaite 1272 *For et freq* to 1619 *ExchKR*, with variant spellings *Kirke-* and *-thwyt, -thuait, -thweyt, -thwait(e), Kyrkthwate* 1272 *For et freq* to 1777 NB, with variant spellings *Kirk-* and *-thweyt, -thwayt, -thwait, Estkirk...wayt* 1367 Ipm, *East, West Kirkthwait* 1777 NB

Kyrthewayte 1290 NB, *Est, West Kirthwaite* 1578 *Cocker, Kirthate* 1616 PR (Dalston), *Curthwait* 1680 CW (OS) xiv, *East Curthat* 1699 PR (Orton)

This represents ON kirkju þveit, 'church þveit.' No evidence has been found bearing on the origin of the name.

CLEAHALL

Clechihouhevid a. 1228 HolmC, *Clethihowe* 1451, 1460 Fine
Cleuihowe 1272 *For, Cleuyhow* 1297 *MinAcct*, 1305 *Ass*
Clothowe 1381 IpmR
Clea 1675 CW (OS) xiii, *Clithoe al. Clea* 1675 DKR xl, *Cleah-Hall* 1715 CW (OS) xiii, *Clay Hall* 1725 ib. iii, *Clea-Hall* 1794 H

CLEAMIRE is *Cleuihoumire* 1272 *For, cleo myre* 1578 *Cocker. v.* mýrr.

The great variety of forms makes any certain interpretation impossible, but there are forms sufficient to justify the suggestion that the first element is OE *clife* or *cliþe*, 'burdock', as Professor Ekwall suggests. The second element is haugr.

FOGGYTHWAITE is *Fogithweyt* 1285 *For.* 'þveit covered by rough grass,' *v.* fog. The earliest reference to this word in NED is from the 14th century.

GREENRIGG is *Grenrig* 1285 *For* (p), *Greenrig* 1729 CW (OS) xiii. Cf. *Greenrigge closes* 1578 *Cocker* and *v.* hrycg.

HAZELSPRING is *Heselspring'* 1272 *For et freq* to 1397 FF, *Hezelspring in Ingelwod* 1305 Ipm, *Heselespring'* 1305 *For, Hesil spring* 1366 *Cocker, Hasill springe* 1578 ib., *Hassellspring* 1777 NB. 'Hazel wood,' *v.* hæsel, spring.

ISLEKIRK HALL

Hermitorium Sce' Hylde in foresta...de Engelwode 1215, 1227, 1235 HolmC, *hermitorium Sce' hilde* c. 1227 ib., *hermitorium sancte Hylde* 1227 Pipe, *land of St Hilda in Ingylwode* c. 1275 Scotland, *heremitorum Sce' hilde in foresta de Englewod* 1285 *For, hermitorum Sce Hilde in foresta R' de Engelwode* 1292, 1338 *Ass*

Hildekirk 1235, 1293 HolmC, 1338 *Ass* (p), 1374 Cl, 1375 Pat, 1377 *GDR, Hyldekerk* 1235 FF, *Hildkirk'* 1272 *For*, 1374 Cl, *Hildekyrke* 1285 *For, Hildekirke* 1292 *Ass*, 1317 HolmC, *Hyldekyrk'* 1292 *Ass, Hyldkirk* 1613 CW xiii

Heildkirk parke, heillkirke hall 1578 *Cocker, Heelkerk* 1605 *LRMB, Hylekirk* 1612 CW xiii

Ilekirke 1578 *Cocker, Ilekirk, Islekirk* 1777 NB

'(St) Hilda's kirkja', originally a hermitage.

OLD CARLISLE

Palmecastel 1272 *For, Palmecastr'* 1305 ib.

Palmcastr' c. 1275 Scotland, 1285 *For, Palmcaster* 1317 HolmC *Old Carliell al. Palme Castell* 1578 *Cocker, Olde Carlile* 1616 Camden

In spite of the early form -*castel*, the second element in the medieval name of this site is clearly Old Anglian cæster, with reference to the important Roman fort known since the 16th century as Old Carlisle. The only suggestion which can be offered for the first element is the ON personal name *Palmi* (Lind).

REATHWAITE

magna Redethwey, parua Redthueyt 1285 *For, magna Redethwayt* 1292 *Ass, Redethwaitis* 1317 HolmC

Rethwaites 1305 *For, Rethtwhayt* 1399 Pat, *Rethwate* 1578 *Cocker, Reathwait, Reethwaite or Reedthwaite* 1777 NB

'Reedy clearing,' from OE hrēod, and þveit.

ROSLEY [rɔsle] is *Rosseley(e)* 1272 *For, (magna, parua)* 1285 ib., 1317 HolmC, *Rosseleyland* 1544 *MinAcct, Rosley* 1578 *Cocker*. This is probably OE hors-lē(a)h, 'horse lē(a)h,' the OE *hors* being replaced by the equivalent ON *hross*.

WIZA HO is *Wysaye, Wisay* 1539 *MinAcct, Wysay* 1578 *Cocker, wysey* 1623 CW (OS) xiii. *v.* Wiza Beck *supra* 31.

EAST and WEST WOODSIDE is *Wodesid* 1292 *Ass* (p), *Wodside* 1519 *FF, Woddesyde* 1539 *MinAcct, Woodsyde* 1541 ib., *ye Woodside* c. 1550 CW xli. In the neighbourhood was *molendinum de Woodsyde* 1541 *ExchKR, Woodsyde Mylne* 1570 ib. 'Beside the wood,' an unusually early example of this formation.

BLAIN'S WOOD and GRAINGER HOUSES are to be associated with the families of Elzabeth *Blayne* (1601 PR, Dalston) and John *Granger* (1570 *ExchKR*). The latter is *Granger houses* 1578 *Cocker.*

BRACKENTHWAITE is *Brakenthwate* 1578 *Cocker.* 'Bracken þveit.' BROADMOOR is so named in 1757 (CW (OS) xiii). BROCKLEBANK is *Brockholebank* 1317 HolmC, *Brocklebank* 1702 PR (Crosby). 'Badger-set bank,' *v.* brocc-hol. CAUSA GRANGE. Cf. *Longcauseway* 1749 CW xxii. CHALKFOOT BRIDGE (6″). Cf. *Shawke foote* 1578 *Cocker.* *v.* Chalk Beck *supra* 8; for this use of *foot* see *Elnefoot* (305) and Sarkfoot (147). CHALKSIDE is *Shawkeside* 1578 *Cocker.* COALHOLE HILL. Cf. *Colehole* 1700 CW (OS) xiii and *Colepitts* 1608 ib. There are seams of coal in this parish (NB ii, 142). COWLAW (COWSLAW 6″) is *Cowe Wathe Lawe* 1578 *Cocker.* *v.* cū, vað, hlāw, the second element having been lost. CRAGS is *the Cragge* ib. CUNNINGARTH is *Cuniegarth, Connygarthe* ib., *Cunning garth* 1620 CW (OS) xiii. 'Rabbit warren,' *v.* coninger. ELLERS is *the Ellers* 1578 *Cocker, Eldors* 1700 CW xli. *v.* elri. FORESTER FOLD is *Fosterfall al. Foster-folde* 1578 *Cocker, Forster folds* 1777 NB. *v.* fal(o)d. GATERIGG is *Gatte rigge, Gaterigge* 1578 *Cocker.* 'Goat ridge,' *v.* gāt. GILL is *the Gill* ib. GILLHEAD is *the gill heade* ib. *v.* gil. GREENHILL (6″) is *Greene hill* ib., *Granhill* 1675 Ogilby. HEIGHT is *hurthwayte heed* 1570 *ExchKR, Vrethwate heade al. the hight* 1578 *Cocker, Hurthwaite Heads* 1790 PR. The forms are too late for definite interpretation, but the name may originally have been '*Úri*'s þveit.' HOWRIGG [hiurik] is *Howerigge* 1578 *Cocker,* possibly a compound of hōh and hrycg. LONGWATH is *Langwath, the Longwath* ib. *v.* vað. PARSON BRIDGE (6″) is *Person brigge* ib., *Parson's bridge* 1777 NB. RED DIAL is *Red-Dyal* 1685 CW i, *Red Deal* 1816 Lysons. Cf. Bluedial *supra* 307. SANDWATH (6″) is *Sandwathe, Sandewathe* 1578 *Cocker.* *v.* vað. SLACK is *Slake* ib. *v.* slakki. STONERAISE is *Staine Raies, the Staine rayes* ib., *Stone Raise* 1657 (1703) NicVisit. 'Stone cairn,' *v.* steinn,

F

hreysi. STREET is (the) street 1578 Cocker. It lies on the Roman road from Carlisle to Cockermouth. Cf. Streetebrigge 1540 LRMB in this neighbourhood. STUDFOLD is Studfall 1578 Cocker. v. stōdfald. SYKE is Sike ib. v. sīc. TOWNHEAD is so named in 1782 (Brisco). WATH HEAD is Twath head 1731 PR (Dalston), Waitehead 1787 ib. Cf. also the hight of the wathe 1578 Cocker. The first form shows the NCy t' for the. v. vað. WREAY (6") may be Wreay Hall 1654 CantW vii. v. (v)rá.

FIELD-NAMES

(a) In 1802 (CW xli) Wham (v. hwamm).

(b) In 1794 (H) Bladderslack (bradaslak 1578 Cocker. v. slakki), Hagle-thorp (Halesthorp 1777 NB), Lady Hills Quarry, Lowpgill (v. gil), Ravens-head (Rauen heade 1578 Cocker), St Ellen the Old; in 1777 (NB) Harthwait (Harethweyt 1272 For. Possibly a compound of OE hara, 'hare,' and þveit), Kirkhill ('church hill'), Manybanks (Manybanke 1539 MinAcct), Messengers of the Moss, Rook's of the bridge; in 1753 (CW (OS) xv) Priest Bridge (id. 1705 CW iii); in 1704 (Terrier) Mellsbecks, Libster-Closes; in 1616 (CW (OS) xiii) Newekirk (Newchurche 1571 CW (OS) x); in 1578 (Cocker) the Ake (v. āc), Bassengraue heade, Batle rigge, Bentie close (v. beonet), Brandreth stone (cf. infra 386), Cananbie rigge, the Cockshott (le Cokshotte 1539 MinAcct. v. infra cockshot), Cumfoorth howe (v. haugr), the daye plattle, Hagwray (v. (v)rá), Hasill rigge (v. hæsel, hrycg), Housthwate (cf. Husthwaite PN NRY 191), Hurlehurst (v. hyrst), Kell Mylne (le kildemyll 1539 MinAcct), Kidham, Margarett Tarne (v. tiǫrn), the Newe hall (Newehalle 1541 MinAcct), Oustrigge, also Howstrigge myre (v. mýrr), Prie meadowe,[1] Randall seat rayes (Randolphsete 1301 NB, v. hreysi and cf. supra 203), Reed-myre Close (v. mýrr), the Roade, Robredinge holme, beke...called Robstie (v. stig), the Rootes, Stale Lane, Stampord fielde, Starthwate rigge (Storthwayt-rigges 1367 Ipm. v. storð, þveit, hryggr, under hrycg), Stockbriggwath (v. stocc, brycg, vað), Stockdale Close, Tonngthwate (v. þveit), Warbell beke (v. bekkr), West Wauer Wathe (v. Waver R. supra 30 and vað), Wilthrom Mire, Wysaye wathe (v. Wiza Beck supra 31 and vað), White hirst (v. hyrst); in 1570 (ExchKR) le Frythe (le fyrthe 1542 MinAcct. v. fyrhþ(e)), Whynnow hall; in 1541 (ExchKR) Rabanke (held by Charles Raybanke), Slatestones; in 1540 (ExchKR) Huththawit, Whitkeldemyll (v. kelda); in 1539 (ExchKR) Foxholles, Seggiholme prope Ellercroke (v. secg, holmr, elri, krókr); in 1317 (HolmC) Eskelakes, Merton (id. 1272 For); in 1285 (For) Alnewath (v. vað), Bakstainbek' (v. bakstān, bekkr. The first example of bakestone recorded in NED is dated 1531). Under each of the following dates there is one field-name: Beethwaite 1782 CW (OS) ix, Milnstangate 1377 GDR (v. myln, stān), Whynnithweyt 1272 For (v. whin, þveit. The earliest example of whin in NED is c. 1400), Willthorne myre 1619 CW (OS) xiii (v. mýrr).

---

[1] Cf. Prye Ho (supra 178).

49. Woodside[1]

WOODSIDE is the name of a civil parish formed in 1894 (Kelly). The name is doubtless to be taken with those of East and West Woodside, just to the east in Westward parish *supra* 329.

AIKHEAD

> *wood of Aykehevid called Aykehevid scawe* 1270 HolmC, *Aykeheued* 1278 *Ass*, 1294 *Extent*, 1367 Ipm, *Aykehefd* 1286 ib., *Aykehede* 1519 *FF*
> *Eiked, Acked* 1578 Cocker, *Ackett* 1581 CW x, *Aiket* 1774 Donald
> 'Oak headland,' *v*. eik, hēafod.

DOCKRAY

> *Dokwra* 1277 *Ass*, *Docwra* 1279 ib. *et freq* to 1400 IpmR, *Dokwra juxta Wygeton'* 1285 *For*
> *Dogwra* 1292 *Ass*
> *Dockry* 1552 March, *Dockery* t. Eliz ChancP

DOCKRAYRIGG Ho (in Oulton parish) is *Docwrarig* c. 1285 *Hesley*. *v*. hrycg.
Other examples of this compound are found in

DOCKRAY in Matterdale *supra* 222

> *Docwra* 1278 *Ass et freq* to 1487 Ipm, with variant spelling *Dok-Dockewra* 1279 *Ass* (p)
> *Dockray* 1577 PR (Greystoke), *Dockera* 1589 *LRMB*, *Dockeray* 1615 CW (OS) vii

GREAT and LITTLE DOCKRAY in Penrith *supra* 230

> *Dokwra* c. 1298 *Lowther*, *Docwra* 1449 ib.
> *Dockarestrete* 1567 AD vi, *a streate called Dockeraie* 1586 CW xxix
> *Dockery* 1604 QElizSch, *Litle Dockrey* 1650 *ParlSurv*, *Dockray* 1770 PR

In the neighbourhood were *Dockray Yeate* 1626 CW i and *Dockwray-Hall* 1794 H.

DOCKRAY NOOK in Lamplugh *infra* 406

> *Dockaranooke* 1583 PR, *Dockerer-nook* 1586 ib., *Dockery-nuke* 1653 ib.

---

[1] Oulton (*supra* 307) was added to Woodside in 1934.

Probably (v)rá, notable for *docce*, 'dock, sorrel.' It is less likely that ON *dǫkk*, 'hollow' (DEPN), would have given *-o-*.

HIGH and LOW[1] LONGTHWAITE

> *Lounthwayt* 1277 *Helsey*, 1348 *GDR et freq* to 1578 *Cocker*, with variant spelling *-thwate*, *Lounethweyt* 1285 *For*, *Lounethweyt* 1316 Ipm, *Loundthwayt* 1360 Pat, *Lownthwate*, *Lownethwate* 1597 CW xl
>
> *Lonethwayte* 1549 FF

The first element here is probably the northern dialect word *lown*, 'quiet, sheltered' (see Lindkvist 117). The origin of the word has not been fully worked out, but derivation from ON *logn*, of similar meaning, is most likely. The second element is þveit.

ROSEWAIN (6″)

> *Rossiwin* 1254 Pipe, *Rossuyn(mire)* 1272 *For et freq* to 1367 Ipm, *Rossewyn(e)* 1277 *Ass* (p), 1285 *For* (p), 1357 *GDR* (p), *Rossuen* 1461 *MinAcct et freq* to t. Jas 1 *AOMB*, *Rossawen al. Rossington* 1557 *Pat*, *Rosshewen* 1562 NB
>
> *Rosewyne* 1277 *Ass* (p), *Rosawen* 1570 *ExchKR*, *Rosewan* 1821 CW xlii
>
> *Roswyne* 1292 *Ass* (p)
>
> *Ressueinge* 1655 CantW vii
>
> *Resuin* 1761 *Brisco*

This is a compound of ON *hrossa*, 'horses,' and *vin*, 'meadow, grazing place.' *vin*, though in frequent use in Norse place-names, has not so far been recorded in England. *v.* PN Shetland 116–19.

TIFFINTHWAITE is probably to be associated with the family of William *Tyffyn* (1570 *ExchKR*). It is *Tiffiethwate* 1578 *Cocker*, *Tiffinthwaite* 1777 NB.

BRACKENLANDS (6″) is *Breken lande* 1578 *Cocker*. BRIDGEBANK (6″) is *brigge banke* 1540 *LRMB*. BRIDGE HO is *brigge house* 1578 *Cocker*. BUSHGILLHEAD is perhaps *Burskall heade* ib. HAZELHEAD is *Hasillhead* ib. *v.* hæsel. HOLLINGROOT (6″) is *Hollinge roote* ib. *v.* holegn. KIRKLAND is *Kirkelande* 1557 *Pat*. 'Church land,' *v.* kirkja. LANE Ho (6″). Cf. *Lane* 1578 *Cocker*. LOWFIELD HO. Cf. *the Lowe fielde* ib. MOORHOUSE [marəs] is *the Morehouses* 1400 Cl, *Morehouse* 1440 IpmR, *Murrhouse* 1562 NB, *Moorhouse oth. Marrass* 1914 Sale Catalogue.

---

[1] Low Longthwaite is in Wigton parish.

v. mōr, hūs. MOORTHWAITE is *le Morthuayt* 1332 SR (p), *Murethwayt* 1461–7 *Norfolk, Moorethwate* 1578 *Cocker. v.* mōr, þveit. WELLHEAD (6") is *le Wellhead* 1570 *ExchKR.* WESTEND is *the Westende* 1578 *Cocker.*

FIELD-NAMES

(*b*) In 1578 (*Cocker*) *All greene, Care close, Conwray* (*v.* (v)rá), *girse close, Hauer rigge* (*v.* hafri, hryggr, under hrycg), *Keye rigge, Lancroke sike* (*v.* sic), *Moorestele rigge* (*v.* mōr, stigel, hrycg), *the Pinghill* (also *the Pighall. v.* pightel), *Ponder Close, the Scroggs* (*v.* scrogg), *the Wham* (*v.* hwamm); in 1553 (NB) *Dorestreme, Kirkwath* ('church ford,' *v.* vað), *Longstroble.*

V. ALLERDALE ABOVE DERWENT WARD

Allerdale ward above Derwent 1671 Fleming

v. Allerdale Barony and Copeland Barony *supra* 1, 2. It was known c. 1675 as the South Ward (Sandford).

1. Arlecdon

ARLECDON [aˑlkdən, æˑrəltən]

Arlauchdene c. 1130 StB (p), *Arlachadena* c. 1185 ib.

Arlokeden(e) c. 1150, 1248 StB, 1279, 1292 *Ass*, (*in Coupland*) 1262 Dugd v, *Arlokedun'* 1279 *Ass*

Arlokden(e) 1242 FF, 1309, 1334 Ipm

Arlogden 1292 *Ass*

Arlecden 1321 Ipm, *Arlekden* 1396 Pat

Arlochden early 14th StMaryY

Arloudane 1540 *MinAcct, Arladon* 1576 S

Arleyden 1552 FF, *Arleton* 1680 PR (Shap)

The forms which have recently been collected from manuscript sources are all compatible with Ekwall's suggestion that this name comes from an OE *earn-lāce* denu, 'eagle-stream valley.'

HOWGATE COTTAGE (6"), MOSSES[1] and SCALELANDS[2] are probably represented in the names of Adam de *Holegate* (1289 *Ass*), Alice de

---

[1] *Mosses* 1693 *LowtherW.*
[2] *Sckalandfeild* 1583 FF, *Scalelands* 1764 CaineCl.

La Mosse (1279 ib.) and Henry de *Scale* (1289 ib.). *v.* holr (under holh), gata, mos, skáli.

BROWNRIGG is *Brunrig(g)* c. 1180 StB, 1208, 1230 P, 1321 Ipm, *Brounrigg* 1334 ib., (*in villa de Moreton*) 1338 StB, *Morton Brownrigg* 1580 FF, *Brownridge* 1770 PR (Lamplugh). 'Brown ridge,' *v.* hrycg. *Mor(e)ton* is Murton in the neighbouring parish of Lamplugh (*infra* 406).

FRIZINGTON

> *Frisingaton* c. 1160 StB (p), *Frisintona* c. 1205 ib., *Frisington* c. 1206 FlemingMem *et passim*, with variant spellings *Frys-* and *-yng-*, *Frisinton* 1246 LaAss (p), *Phrisington* 1729 CW xv
> *Fresinton'* 1259 Pipe (p), *Fresyngton* 1338 StB, *Fressyngton* 1535 LP
> FRIZINGTON HALL is *Frisington Hall* 1579 FF. FRIZINGTON PARKS is *Frisington Parke* 1583 ib.

In view of the long series of forms with *i* in the first element, it seems clear that this name contains OE *Frīsa*, literally 'the Frisian.' The consistent succession of forms in *ing* or *in* shows that *Frisa* in this instance must have been used as a personal name. The name as a whole means 'tūn of *Frisa*' or 'of *Frisa*'s people,' the latter interpretation being strongly suggested by the early form *Frisingaton*.

HOLE GILL (6″) is *Holegile* c. 1205 CW (OS) i, facs. 'Deeply cut ravine,' *v.* holh or holr, gil. Cf. Howgill *infra* 453.

ROWRAH is *Rowray* 1535 VE, *Rowraw* 1605 Ct, *Rowrey* 1606 ib. Cf. *Rucwrabek* 1248 StB. Probably 'rough nook or corner,' *v.* rūh, (v)rá.

WHILLIMOOR FOOT is *Welingesmora* c. 1140 StB, *Welingmora* c. 1180 ib., *Quelingmor(e)* c. 1250 ib., *Welyngmore* c. 1360 ib., *Whillyngmor* 1447 ib., *Whillimore al. Wyllymore* 1559 FF. The earliest forms may represent OE **hwēoling*. It is topographically probable that the name may be connected with certain rings, presumably of standing stones, which occur as *le wheles* in a late medieval perambulation of Whillimoor (StB 487). The meaning of the name is presumably 'place with wheels or stone circles'.[1]

ASBY (6″) is *Asbie* 1654 PR (Lamplugh), *Ashby* 1713 *LowtherW*. *v.* askr, bȳ. BIG CROFT is so named in 1654 (PR, Lamplugh). Perhaps containing ON bygg, 'barley.' BIRKS. Cf. *Birks Outclose* 1743 Caine.

---

[1] The reference is not, we take it, to Whillimoor cheeses.

v. birki. COAL RACE is so named in 1818 ib. CROFTS is *Croft* 1744
LowtherW. CROSS GILL. Cf. *Hill Cross Gill* 1787 *Caine. v.* gil.
CROSSLACON is *Crosslatun* 1777 CaineCl. If the modern name is
correct, this may be an inversion compound of *cross* and the OIr
personal name *Lochán* which occurs in Lackenby (PN NRY 159), but
the solitary form is too late for any certainty. DUB HALL is so named
in 1743 (Caine). *v.* dub. HIGH HO (6″) is *Hye-house* 1637 (1664)
FlemingMem. HOLLOWDYKE FM (6″) is named from *ye Hollow Dyke*
1410 AllerA, *Hollow Dyke* 1755 CaineCl. *v.* holh, dīc. KIDBURNGILL
is *Kidbornegille* 1410 AllerA, *Kydburngill* 1592 PR (Lamplugh). Cf.
Kid Beck *supra* 18. KIRKLAND HOW is *Kirkland-howe* 1597 ib.
v. kirkja, haugr. MOORSIDE is *Moreside* 1585 FF. MOSSGILL (6″) is
so named in 1655 (PR, Lamplugh). MOWBRAY is *Mabray* 1743
Terrier. RATTEN ROW (6″) is *Rattanrowe* 1410 AllerA, *Rattenraw*
1755 CaineCl. 'Rat row,' *v. supra* 98. REDGATE FOOT (6″) is named
from *Readgate or Redgate* 1734 CW xxxviii. RHEDA is *Reeda* 1777
CaineCl. ROUTON SYKE is *Routonsicke* 1693 *LowtherW. v. supra* 25.
SKELSCEUGH. Cf. *Skelsco Closses* 1693 *LowtherW. v.* skógr. THREAP-
THWAITE is *Threapthwaite* 1608 CaineCl, *Threepthwaite* 1797 ib. 'þveit
in dispute,' cf. Threapland *supra* 271. YEATHOUSE is *Yaithowse* 1605
Ct. Presumably 'gatehouse,' from OE geat.

FIELD-NAMES

(a) Howth Gill (id. 1779 Caine), Phisica Well (mineral spring).

(b) In 1743 (Terrier) *Acre Walls Outclose, Bishop's Land, Sherwen Fields.
Wimiat Field*; in 1744 (*LowtherW*) *Maud ridding* (*Moldridding* 1693 ib.,
v. hryding), *Pearce Place* (*Pearesplace* ib.), *Sue Croft*; in 1741 ib. *Roger-
Whineys* (id. 1693 ib.); in 1725 ib. *Lausera, Stalehole*; in 1693 ib. *Crosby
Close* (*Crosby Cloose* 1635 PR (Lamplugh)), *Crowebut, Dubbe-Yeats* (*v.* dub,
geat), *Hawes mire* (*v.* mýrr), *Hungarhill* (*v. infra* Fan), *Millbeck* (id. 1410
AllerA), *Teathes.* Under each of the following dates there is one field-name:
Aspoth 1396 Pat (possibly 'ash-pit'), *Briggsfeild al. Brackenhill* 1590 *Cocker*,
Lokefeilde 1583 FF, *Lutehill* 1735 Caine.

2, 3. St Bridget and St John Beckermet

ST BRIDGET and ST JOHN BECKERMET [bek'ərmət]

Bechermet c. 1130 StB, 1262 Dugd v, 1279 *Ass, Bekhermett* 1332
SR (p), *Bekhermet* 1350 Ipm

Becheremet c. 1160 WethA, *Beccheremed* c. 1180 ib.
Bechiremd c. 1180 *Hesley*
Beckirmeth c. 1180 *Hesley* (p), c. 1185 StB, *Maiori Beckyrmeth*
    c. 1205 *Hesley*
Bekyrmet 1188 P, *Bekirmet* 1189 ib., 1278 *Ass*, *Bechirmet* 1262
    Dugd v, 1279 *Ass*, *Beckirmet* 1294 Cl
Bikermet 1190–5, *Litle Bikermet* 1578 *Cocker*
(*Major*) *Bekermet* 1242 FF *et passim*, with variant spelling *Beck-*
Bekyremet 1279 *Ass*
Beckermeth 1291 Tax, 1717 CaineCl
Beckermete 1334 Ipm, 1338 Cl
Beckermot 1385 Pat (p)
Beckermothe 1387 IpmR
Beckermouth 1583 (1664) FlemingMem
Beck Armet, Beckarmett 1570 *ExchKR*
Beckarmond 1576 S
Berkinmouth St Johns 1656 CantW vii
Beckermont 1698 PR (Whicham), 1762, 1816 Jackson
Beckerment 1722 Jackson

The two parishes are distinguished as St Bridget and St John from
the dedication of the churches. Cf. *eccl. sancti Johannis Baptistæ de
Bechermet, parochiæ sanctæ Bridgittæ* 1262 Dugd v, *Sant Jons* 1552
CW (OS) viii, *St Bride church* 1578 *Cocker*, *St Bridget's Beckermet* 1642
HMC iv. Great Beckermet is St Bridget, Little Beckermet, St John.

The references under 1570, which come from two separate documents, indicate that the present accentuation of the name is as old as
that date. They dissociate the name from Beckermonds (WRY), to
which it has sometimes been regarded as a parallel. If, as is probable,
this accentuation is original, it becomes difficult, if not impossible,
to derive the name from a compound of ON *bekkiar* (gen. pl. of bekkr,
'stream'), and OE mōt or ON *mœti*, 'meeting,' as had been suggested
by Lindkvist (6) and Ekwall (DEPN). The name should rather be
taken as an inversion compound meaning 'hermit's bekkr.'

2. St Bridget Beckermet[1]

FARMERY is *Furmery, del Fermerie* 1279 *Ass* (p), *Furmery* 1307 Cl (p),
Farmery 1754 *LowtherW*. Formally, this could be OFr *fermerie*,

---

[1] Part of Haile (*infra* 398) was transferred to St Bridget Beckermet in 1935.

'fortified place.' But the situation of Farmery, within two miles of Calder Abbey, strongly suggests that the name represents OFr (*en*)*fermerie*, '(monastic) infirmary.' The earliest example of this word in NED comes from the 14th-century Prompt Parv ('fermerye, *infirmaria, infirmitorium*'). It is known from other cases that a house for sick monks might be at a considerable distance from the main buildings of a monastery. Cf. *Fermery Hill* (348).

GODDERTHWAITE

> *Coderowhayt, Coderthweyt* 1279 *Ass* (p)
> *Godyrthayt* 1292 *Ass* (p), *Goderthwayt* 1314 Scotland, *Godarthwait in ye Townshipe of Hale* 1371 FlemingMem, *Godithwait* 1391 HMC xxv
> *Godthayt* 1396 (1664) FlemingMem

v. þveit. The first element may be either an OE personal name beginning with *Gōd*-, or the continental personal name *Godard*[1] found in *Satgodard infra* 344.

SCALDERSCEW (6″) is *Scalderscogh* 1243 *FF*, *Skelderischoth* 1287 BodlCh, *Skaldersko* 1303 Pat (p), *Skeldreskeogh* 14th Parker, *Skalder-skough* t. Hy 8 *AOMB*, *Scalderscough* 1553 FF. 'Skjǫldr's wood,' *v.* skógr. The first element is the ON personal name *Skjǫldr* (gen. *Skjaldar*). The whole name is identical with Skelderskew (PN NRY 149). *" shield-meadow " F.5.87*

HIGH and LOW SELLAFIELD and SELLA PARK are *Sellofeld* 1576 S, *Sellowfield or Sea-low-field* 1610 Denton, *Sellowfield* 1658 CW xiv, *Sellowparke* 1594 *Work*, *Sellaparke* t. Jas 1 ib., *Silla park* 1777 NB. The *Sella* or *Sellow* which occurs in all these names appears as *Sellagh* in 1278 *Ass* (p). Its meaning can hardly be gathered from this late material.

STANBRENAN (lost) is *Stainbrannan* c. 1205 CW (OS) i, facs, *Stan-brenan* 1291 ib. This is an inversion compound of the OIr personal name *Branán* and ON steinn.

STEPHNEY is *Stavenerge* 1231 Dugd v, *Stevenay* 1597 Jackson, *Steveny* 1754 *LowtherW*. It may be *Stepnay* 1612 PR (Millom). This is a compound of ON *stafn* and erg. The word *stafn* developed a number of specialised meanings in ON, such as 'stem of a ship' and 'gable-end,' but its original sense was 'stock' or 'pole' and it is probably used with this meaning here.   *✓ +eng F.J.70 .*

---

[1] *Godardus*, lord of Millom, signed the St Bees foundation charter (StB 28).

STONE PIKE is *Staynpik'* 1243 *FF. v.* steinn. The ME *pike,* 'pointed hill,' is unexpectedly rare in early local names in this county. In this example, it probably corresponds to the Norwegian *pik*, which has the same sense.

BECK COTE is so named in 1583 (*Work*). *v.* cot(e). BLACKBECK is so named in 1880 (CW (OS) v). *v.* bekkr. COLD FELL is *Caldfell* 1777 NB. *v.* fell. MIDDLEBANK is so named in 1794 (CW xvii). PRIOR SCALES is *Prior Scale* 1754 *LowtherW. v.* skáli. SIDE is *Syde* 1538 *AOMB*. STRUDDA BANK is *Strowd bank* 1594 DKR xxxviii, *The Strothie bank* 1595 ib., *Struddebanke* 1658 CW xiv. *v.* ströd, 'marsh.' THORNHOLME is *Thorneholme* t. Hy 8 *AOMB. v.* holmr. YOTTEN-FEWS is *Yottenfews* 1728 PR (Gosforth), *Yotton Fuse* 1783 Donald. No explanation can be offered of 'yotten,' but it is not unlikely that 'fews' may represent ON *féhús*, 'cattle-shed.' Cf. Fusehill *supra* 45 and Fusedale (We).

FIELD-NAMES

(*a*) In 1662 (*Will*) *Monghton Grange* (*Moughton* 1538 *Pat*, *Mougheton'* t. Hy. 8 *AOMB*, *Monghton* 1553, 1585 *FF*); in t. Hy. 8 (*AOMB*) *Haskoo* (cf. *supra* 227), *Knotte* (*v.* knǫtt), *Stocke Brydge* (*v.* stocc); in 1538 (*AOMB*) *Colman Low* (cf. William *Coleman* 1294 Cl), *Cowplandfelle* (*v.* fell), *Oystrigarth* (? ON *eystri* 'more easterly', garðr), *Ranke medoo*, *Thynne medoo*; in Dugd vi, *Patrikkeldsik* (Patrick Keld was the name of the Holy Well on the bank of the Calder east of Calder Abbey, now dry, though its site remains (*ex inf.* Miss M. C. Fair). *v.* kelda, sīc).

3. St John Beckermet[1]

BRISCOE

Brethesco 1203 Cur, *Bretscoh* c. 1205 CW (OS) i, facs. (bis), *Bretscough* t. Ed 3 (t. Eliz) *Cocker*

Bresceko 1203 Cur, *Brescou* 1291 CW (OS) i, facs.

Brisco 1204 Cur, 1338 Cl, *Briscowe* 1342 *Cocker*, *Briscoughe* 1578 ib., *Briskey* 1682 CW xvii, *Briscoe* 1710 ib.

This is *Bretaskógr*, 'wood of the Britons.'

CARLETON

Karleton by Egremond 1363 Ipm, *Carleton* ib. *et passim*, (*apud le Stanne Crosse*) t. Ed 3 (t. Eliz) *Cocker*

CARLETONMOOR WOODS (6″). Cf. *Carleton Moore* 1816 Lysons.

[1] Part of Lowside Quarter (*infra* 413) was transferred to St John Beckermet in 1935.

This represents *karlatún*, the Scandinavian equivalent of OE *ceorla tún*, 'tūn of the ceorls,' or 'peasants.' Cf. Carleton *supra* 231 and *infra* 377.

CRINGLETHWAITE TERRACE (6″), a street in Egremont, but in this parish, is on the site of *Cringlewayth* 1294 Cl, *Cringelthwayt* 1338 ib., *Cringlethwaite* 1578 Cocker. *v.* kringla, þveit. It lies within a horse-shoe bend of the Ehen.

OXENRIGGS is *Oxeregg* 1294 Cl, *Oxen rige* 1578 Cocker. 'Ridge of the oxen,' *v.* hrycg.

ULLCOATS is *ulecotes* c. 1205 CW (OS) i, facs., *Ulcoates Mill* 1799 CW xvii. 'Owl-haunted cottages,' from OE ūle, 'owl' and cot(e). It is identical with Oldcoates (PN Nt 99).

WINSCALES is *Windscales* 1294 Cl, *Wynskales* 1309 Ipm, *Winzscales* 1322 Cl (p), *Wynschales* 1323 *MinAcct*, *Wyndskales* 1338 Cl. 'Windy shielings,' *v.* skáli, and Winscales *infra* 454.

HARDHEADS (6″) may perhaps be associated with the family of Thomas *del Hard'* (1322 Cl) who held land in Carleton *supra*.

BLACK MOSS is so named in 1680 (CW xvii). CAERNARVON CASTLE (6″) is *Caernarvon-Castle* c. 1683 FlemingMem, *Carnarvon Castle* 1690 HMC xxv. Presumably an artificial name derived from Caernarvon Castle in Wales. Nothing seems to be known about its history. CONEYGARTH (6″) is *Conygarth* 1592 FlemingMem. CONEYGARTH COP is *Coney Garth Cop* 1671 Fleming, *Conygarth-Copp* c. 1683 FlemingMem. 'Rabbit warren,' *v.* coninger. The *cop* is an artificial hill, *v.* copp. COW FIELD is so named in 1778 (CW xvii). GRANGE BROW (6″) is so named in 1816 (Lysons). KERSEY BRIDGE (6″) is named from *Kersey* 1578 Cocker. This may be the *Kareswath* of c. 1260 StB, the meaning of which is probably 'Kárr's ford,' *v.* vað. LITTLE MILL (6″) is so named in 1778 (CW xvii). Low MILL is so named in 1658 ib. MILL LANE (6″). Cf. *the mill of Beckirmet* 1294 Cl. Moss DALTS is *Moss Dals* 1680 CW xvii. ST THOMAS'S CROSS is *St Thomas Cross* 1810 ib. STREETGATE BRIDGE (6″) is so named in 1753 (CW (OS) xv). Traces of a well-paved road were found near here (ib. iii, 338). THORNY (6″) is *Thornehey* 1578 Cocker. Cf. Thorney (PN Nt 207) and Thornhaugh (PN Nth 243). Near by are THORN and THORNHILL. WODOW BANK (6″) is *Waldhowholme (or Waldhowbank)* 1396 Fleming-Mem, *Waddersbank* 1625 ib., *Wotobank* 1794 H, *Wada Bank* 1821 G.

Apparently the basis of this name is a compound of OE w(e)ald, 'wood' or 'forest,' and hōh, 'mound,' to which *holm* and *bank* were subsequently added. YEORTON HALL is *Yerton* 1657 CW xiv, *Yeorton* 1792 PR (Egremont), *Yerton-hall* 1816 Lysons.

FIELD-NAMES

(a) Hallgate (may possibly be *Holegat'* 1226 Pipe, *Holegate* 1247 FF. Cf. *Holegatebeck* 1243 FF. *v.* holh, gata).

(b) In 1794 (H) *Easton-hall, green-moor-side* (*grenemore* 1338 Cl. *v.* mōr); in 1671 (Fleming) *Brawrig, Weddie*; in 1578 (*Cocker*) *Kelsley, the Kirkinges* (*Kirkeheng* 1294 Cl, *Kirkenge* 1364 Ipm. 'Church meadows,' *v.* eng.), *lyne landes, Mastalls, Reedcar* (*Le Redeker* 1322 Cl, *Redekare* 1323 *MinAcct*, *Redeker* 1338 Cl, apparently 'reedy marsh,' *v.* hrēod, kiarr'), *Skurkelde* (*v.* kelda), *the Slake* (*v.* slakki); in t. Ed 3 (t. Eliz) (*Cocker*) *bordelande* (*Bordelondes* 1338 Cl. 'Land held by a *bordar*,' cf. *supra* 50), *Brakensyke* (*v.* sīc), *Brakenstanfytt* (*v.* braken, stān, fit), *Kyrkefit* ('church fit'), *le Stanne Crosse* (*le Stanecross* 1294 Cl. 'Stone cross,' *v.* stān); in 1291 (CW (OS) i, facs) *Auenelstan* (*Auenelestan* c. 1205 ib. Possibly a compound of the OFr family name *Avenel*, and stān). Under each of the following dates there is one field-name: (*del*) *Borwanes* 1294 Cl (*v.* burghan), *Brashaw* 1754 *LowtherW*, *Milnebech* c. 1205 CW (OS) i, facs ('mill stream,' *v.* myln, bekkr), *ye Wharings* 1592 (1664) FlemingMemA.

4. Birker and Austhwaite[1]
BIRKER (6″)

Birkergh 1279 *Ass* (p), *Byrker* 1432 StBA, 1581 FF, *Birker* 1560 ib.

LOW BIRKER is so named in 1657 (CW xiv). BIRKER DUB is a pool in the Esk, *v.* dub. BIRKERTHWAITE is *Birkerthwait* 1741 *Sykes. v.* þveit.

'Birch tree shieling,' *v.* birki, erg.

AUSTHWAITE

Auestwait c. 1220 StBA, *Auesthwayt* 1255, 1257 Pipe (both p), *Auesthuayt* 1292 *Ass* (p), *Auesthwayth in villa de Millum* 1367 StBA

Anisthuayt 1272 AD iv (p), *Auisthwayte, Auisthuayte* c. 1280 StBA (both p), *Auicethwayt* 1338 Cl (p), *Auisthwaith* 1353, 1354 StBA, *Auisthwait(e)* 1354 ib., *the manor of Anisthwaith...between Esk and Doden* 1354 AD iv, *Auysthwaite* 1421 CW (OS) xii

Hauesthweyt 1292 *Ass*, (*in villa de Millum*) 1292 StBA

[1] Added to Eskdale (*infra* 388) in 1934.

Austhwayt c. 1330 CW xli
Aisthwaite 1438 StBA
Awsthwaite, now called Dalegarth 1777 NB
Auesthaitbrig c. 1282 StBA is now represented by FORGE BRIDGE (6").

Ekwall (DEPN) suggests that this is a compound of þveit and a personal name corresponding to OSw *Afaster*. *v.* Field Head Gutter *supra* 14.

From c. 1503 the manor-house of Austhwaite has been known as DALEGARTH (*Dale garthe* c. 1503 StBA) 'garth in the valley', *v.* dalr, garðr.

BLACK CRAG is *Blakrag* 1242 Furness.

BROTHERILKELD [*olim* butərilket]

> *Butherulkul* c. 1210 Furness, *Butherulkil* 1242, c. 1280 ib.,
> *Butherilkil* 1300 Pat, *Butt'elket* 1721 PR, *Butter Ilket* 1783 Donald,
> *Butter Eldkeld* 1821 G
> *Brutherulkil* 1242 Furness, *Brothurulkulle* 1292 ib.
> *Botherulkil(l)* c. 1260 Furness (p), (*in Coupland*) 1292 ib., *Botherylkle*
> 1337 ib.
> *Brotherylketh* 1537 Furness, *Brotherilkeld* 1793 PR

This is a typical inversion compound, meaning 'Úlfkell's booths,' *v.* búð (pl. búðir) and the OSc personal name *Úlfkell*, from *Úlfketill*. *v.* ScandCelts 21, NP 168–9, ZEN 91 and Introduction.

HARD KNOTT[1] and HARD KNOTT PASS

> *Hardecnuut* c. 1210 Furness, (*summitatem del*) *Ardechnut* 1242 ib.,
> *Hard-knot* 1610 Camden, 1741 *Sykes*, 1777 NB
> *Wynscarth, Wainscarth* 1242 Furness

Wainscarth, which was the original name of Hard Knott Pass, is clearly identical with Wainscarre in Blyth (PN Nt 69). It is a compound of ME *wain*, 'waggon' (from OE *wægen*) and ON skarð, 'gap' or 'cleft,' that is 'cleft through which a waggon could go.' Cf. Wainfleet (L) (DEPN).

The name Hard Knott itself is a compound of ON *harðr*, 'hard,' and *knútr*, 'knot,' meaning 'craggy hill.' A similar change of *th* to *d* occurs in Ward Hall *supra* 310, from ON *varði*, and in Guards.

It is remarkable that a doublet of this name is recorded in the

---

[1] The mountain is in Ulpha parish.

neighbourhood of Loweswater in the 13th century. A final concord of 1230 (*FF*) refers to *condosium* ('slope') *collis qui vocatur Hardecnut*. The latter hill is probably identical with Great Borne in Ennerdale (*infra* 385), of which no early forms have been found.

SEAT HOW (6″) has been identified by the Rev. W. S. Sykes (CW xxvi, 110) with *Satgodard* c. 1205 StBA. This is apparently an inversion compound consisting of sætr and the continental personal name *Godard*. Cf. Godderthwaite *supra* 339.

BRANT RAKE is so named in 1795 (*PR*, Boot). 'Steep path,' *v.* brant, reik, and cf. Bransty *infra* 452. FOX BIELD (6″) contains the Scottish and northern English *bield*, 'shelter, den, place of refuge.' Cf. "The fox will not worry near his beeld" (Abp. Sandys' *Sermons* 1585, quoted in NED). HIGH GROUND is so named in 1769 (*Sykes*). LOW GROUND, MILKINGSTEAD MIRE (*v.* mýrr), RED BROW (6″) and UNDERBANK (6″) are so named in 1741 (*Sykes*). SWORD HO (6″) is *Sword Hows* ib. Apparently 'sword hill,' from OE *sweord* and haugr, though the significance of the name cannot now be discovered. TEWIT MOSS (6″) is 'pewit mos.' WHINCOP ('whin-covered hill') is so named in 1627 (*PR*, Boot). WONDER HILL (6″) may have the same history as Under Hill *infra* 419.

FIELD-NAMES

(*a*) In c. 1840 (*TA*) High and Low Allan (*v.* allan), Allands, Ash Hagg, Ash How (*v.* haugr), Boot or Neck, Browleigh, Collin, Conning Meadow ('rabbit meadow'), High and Low Crook of Esk (cf. Crook of Ellen *supra* 274), Eller How (*v.* elri, haugr), Force Wood (*v.* fors), High and Low Frith (*v.* fyrhþ(e)), Gale Gill, Helm How, Great and Little How (cf. *How How* 1769 *Sykes*, *v.* haugr), Meg Hill, Redin, Robin Eller and Parrock (*v.* elri), Scale-field (*v.* skáli, feld), Scroggs (*v.* scrogg), Steel Moss (*v.* stigel), Tongue all Moss, Trough Hows Allen (*v.* allan), Twenty Dork (*v.* daywork), Long Wall.

(*b*) In 1794 (MapH) *Yester Field*; in 1292 (StBA) *Blakesyk* (*v.* sic), *Brindestub* (probably 'burnt stub'), *Crossithake*, *Wynterscalethayth* ('clearing for a winter shieling,' *v.* skáli, þveit); in 1242 (Furness) *Midelfel*, *Orscarth* (Miss M. C. Fair tells us that this was probably the gap (*v.* skarð) through which iron ore (OE *ōra*)[1] was taken from Eskdale into Langdale). Under each of the following dates there is one field-name: *le Frithslake* c. 1280 StBA (p) (*v.* fyrhþ(e), slakki), *Oxlesgate* c. 1282 (1594) ib. (*v.* oxa, læs, gata).

[1] Cf. Orgill in Egremont (*infra* 381).

5. Blindbothel[1]

BLINDBOTHEL (6″)

Blendebothel 1278 (bis), 1279 (bis) *Ass*, *Blendbothel* 1279 ib.
Blindbethil 1280 Cl (p), *Blyndebothill* 1333 Misc (p), *Blyndbothel* 1333 Cl (p)
Blyndboll 1563 FF

The obvious derivation of the first element from *blind* in the sense 'dark' or 'hidden' is made unlikely by the early forms in *Blende-*, *Blend-*, recently found in Assize Rolls. No help is forthcoming from the local topography, for Blindbothel is merely the name of a civil parish, and the site where the name arose is unknown. It should, however, be added that the general lie of the land within the parish does not suggest derivation from the *blaen*, 'top, summit,' found in Blencarn *supra* 214. The second element is bōðl.

6. Bootle

BOOTLE

Bodele 1086 DB, *Botele* 1251 FF
Botle c. 1135 (early copy), c. 1160 (early copy)[2] *Lowther et freq* to 1321 FF
Botel(l) c. 1170 StB *et freq* to 1440 FF
Botyl, Botil(l) c. 1200 StB *et freq* to 1513 LP, *Botil in Coupeland* 1281 Wickwane
Bothille 1228–43 DuLa, *Bothil(l)* 1291 Tax, 1309, 1396 Pap, *Botehill(e)* 1303 FF, 1401 Furness
Butile 1369 Ipm, *Butell'* 1462 *Netherhall*, *Butill* ib., 1526 *DuLa*, *Butehill* 1570 ExchKR, *Butle* 1571 CW xi
Bowtle 1568 FF, *Bootle* 1581 ib.

BOOTLE FELL is *Boothill* 1777 NB. MILL BRIDGE (6″). Cf. *the mill of Botil* 1236–52 DuLa, 1272 AD iv.
Like Bootle (PN La 116), this is simply OE bōðl, 'building.'

CORDAMOSS. Cf. *Cordhou* 13th CW xxvi, n.d. AD iv, *Cardaymoss* 1702 *LowtherW*. The second element of this is hōh.

ESKMEALS is *Eskmeal* 1610 Denton, *Eskmeals* 1777 NB, *Esk-Meols* 1842 AllerA. 'Sandbanks or sandhills by the South Esk (*supra* 14).' *v.* melr.

---

[1] Mosser (*infra* 422) and Whinfell (*infra* 446) were added to Blindbothel in 1934.
[2] The copy of this charter in StB (No. 107) gives the reading *Botell*.

GREAT and LITTLE GRASSOMS are *Gresholmes, Gressholmes* 1252 StBA. 'Grassy holmr.'

HINNING HO is (*del*) *Heyning in Bothill* 1357 TestKarl (p), *the he...ynghous* 1462 *Netherhall, Heninghouse* c. 1500 CW (OS) xii, *Heninhouse* 1646 *LowtherW, Heaninghouse* 1660 ib., *Hinninhouse* 1702 ib. *v.* haining.

HYCEMOOR is *Hysemore in Seton* 1391 AD iv, *Hytemor* n.d. AD iv, *Haysmore* 1551–3 ECP, 1568 FF, *Hysemore* 1537 *AOMB,* 1542 CW x, *Hisemore* 1571 FF, *Hismore* 1572 ib., 1613 CW ii. The forms are too late and vary too much for any certain interpretation, but the name may possibly contain the obscure OE word *hysse,* which apparently denoted some kind of water-plant. It seems to occur in Hurstbourne (Ha) and Husborne (Beds). Cf. PN BedsHu 118–19 and DEPN. For the second element, *v.* mōr.

HYTON and OLD HYTON

> *Hytona* c. 1210 Furness (p), 1201–30 DuLa (p), *Hitun* c. 1230 Furness (p), *Hyton* 1251 FF, c. 1275 StB, 1588 FF, *Hyton'* 1279 *Ass* (p), 1292 *Ass, Hytun* 13th AD iv, *Hiton* 1320 ib., 1461 HMC x, 1526 *DuLa, Hiton and Oldhiton* 1358 AD iv, *Hyton in Botyll in Caupeland* 1366 ib., *Hitone* 1537 *DuLa, Hyton al. Old Hyton* 1576 FF
>
> *Hytten in Bottell* n.d. AD iv (endorsement), *Hitton* 1531–3 ECP
>
> *Huyton* 1503, 1526 *Norfolk,* 1538 *DuLa*

As suggested by Ekwall (DEPN), this is probably OE *hȳð-tūn,* 'tūn by the landing stage, or hithe.' Huyton (La) is another example of this compound. The position of Hyton suits this derivation. Old Hyton, which must be the original settlement, stands on the Annaside Beck, a mile from the sea. At the present time this stream turns abruptly north-westwards below Hyton, and flows for a considerable distance parallel to and very near to the shore line. But the presumption is that this curious deflection is due to changes in the coastal levels, and that the river was originally easily navigable, at least as far as Old Hyton. The forms show two examples—Hytten and Hitton—of the vowel shortening which would be expected of a compound of *hȳð* and *tūn* (*v.* PN La 113), and are otherwise compatible with derivation from *hȳð.* The situation of the place, 50 feet above sea level, and overlooked by high fells a short distance to the east, rules out derivation from OE *hē(a)h,* 'high.'

MILLHOLME (6"). Cf. *Milneholm(e)bek* 1230 Furness. *v.* myln, holmr, bekkr.

MONK MOORS is *Munkemore in Cauplande* c. 1290 Furness. Presumably so named from the monks of Furness Abbey. *v.* mōr.

MOPUS (TA) is *le Malpas* c. 1195 Cockersand, *Malpase* 13th AD iv, *Malpas* 1537 *AOMB*, 1542 CW x. The modern name goes back through colloquial French to a Latin adj. + noun *Malus passus*, and like the well-known Cheshire Malpas, as interpreted by Giraldus Cambrensis (*Opera* vi, 146), means 'difficult passage.' In the Tithe Award of Corney, the name *Mopus* refers to a long strip of land along the east side of Eskmeals Pool, between the Corney-Bootle boundary and the road running westwards from Seaton Hall.

SEATON HALL

> *Seton in Couplont* 1184–90 Cockersand, *Seton* c. 1230 StB *et freq* to 1535 VE, (*in Coupland*) 13th AD iv, (*cellam de*) 1313 Greenfield, (*monialium*) 1536 LP, *Setun* c. 1235 StB, *Seeton* 1537 *AOMB*, *Seyton* 1542 CW x, 1571 FF

For this name cf. Seaton *supra* 319. The reference to 'cell' and 'nuns' in the above forms relates to Lekeley Priory, on this site. That name does not survive except possibly, as the Rev. W. S. Sykes suggests, in the field-names *Lightley Breast* and *Field* (c. 1840 *TA*), but it appears in early records as *Lekeleya* a. 1210 *HolmC*, c. 1245 *Hesley*, *Lekelay(e)* 1228 Gray, c. 1251 *HolmC*, *Lekley* 1459 *Hesley*, *Overlayclays*, *Nedderlayclays* 1542 CW x, *Leakley now called Seaton* 1610 Denton. The meaning of this name is uncertain, but it not improbably contains an OE word *lēce*, 'brook,' which seems to occur in Leek (St). Cf. DEPN under Leake and Leek. The second element is lē(a)h.

SELKER is *Seleker* c. 1205 *Hesley* (p), *Selker* 1390 AD iv, *Seltar in Bootle* 1730 PR (Millom). SELKER BAY is *Selkers Bay* 1794 H. The second element here is kiarr. The first is probably ON selja, 'willow.'

SKELDA (6") is (*mora de*) *Skeldhou*, *Eskeldhou* a. 1290 Furness, *Schelhou*, *Scheldhow* c. 1290 ib. Apparently this name consists of ON skjǫldr, 'shield,' followed by haugr, 'hill' or 'mound.' The exact meaning of this compound can hardly now be recovered.

SWALLOWHURST is *Sualewehurst* 1228–43 DuLa (p), *Swaleweherst* 1255, 1257 Pipe (both p), *Swalewehurst* 1259 ib. (p)[1], *Swaleyhyrst* 1570

---

[1] The Pipe Roll identifications are probable, but not certain.

G

LowtherW. The first element is presumably OE *swealwe*, 'swallow'; the second is hyrst, 'wooded hill.'

BECKSIDE (6″) is so named in 1646 (*LowtherW*). BROADWATER is so named in 1702 (*LowtherW*). CHARITY CHAIR (6″) is so named in 1821 (G). CROSS HO is so named in 1842 (AllerA). Cf. *the Cross* 1664 *LowtherW*. FELL SIDE is *Felsyde* 1579 PR (Whicham). *v.* fell, sīde. FLATTS is *the Flatts* 1542 CW x. *v.* flat. FORD HO is *the Ford House* ib. HIGH MILL is so named in 1767 (PR, Whicham). THE HILL is *hyll* 1570 *LowtherW*. KISKIN[1] is so named in 1702 ib. THE NOOK is *the Nooke* 1646 *LowtherW*. SIKEBECK is *Sykebeck* 1702 *LowtherW*. *v.* sík (under sic), bekkr. SOURA WELL (6″). Cf. *Sowery Sike* CW xxvi 194. STUB PLACE is so named in 1646 (*LowtherW*). THE TARN is *Tarne* ib. *v.* tiǫrn. WELLBANK (6″) is *Welbanke* 1570 *LowtherW*. WYLIE GAPP (6″) is *Wyldgapp* 1646 ib. *v.* gap.

FIELD-NAMES

(a) Abbot Ing was a possession of Calder Abbey, *v.* eng; in c. 1840 (*TA*) Barnet Croft, Barrows, Bibby Yeat (*Bibby yate* 1646 *LowtherW*), Bleamire, Blind Tarn, Bream Breast, Brierthwaite (*v.* þveit), Brilling Croft, Brots (*le Brotis* n.d. AD iv. *v.* brot), Burnbarrow (*v.* be(o)rg), Cal Close, Cockley field (*v.* cokelayk), Curley Garth (probably 'curlew garðr'), Dough Meadow, Emb Croft, Foricar (*v.* kiarr), Grandy Croft, Grimeland, Haverfold (cf. *Haverclose* 1542 CW x), Hopeless meadow (*v. infra* Fan), Jordan Ing (*v.* eng), Mans Briggs (*Mansbrig* 1646 *LowtherW*), Mordles, Parkin Thorn, Peel Croft, Pepper Know (*v.* cnoll), Pickle (*Pighelle* 1537 *AOMB*. *v.* pightel), Pinner Sykes (*v.* sík), Rails end, Far and Near Rakes (*v.* reik), Reins (*v.* rein), Robin Hole, Simon Laith (*v.* hlaða), High and Low Skiddaw Bank, Skinny Flint (*v. infra* Fan), Sneddle meadow, Sour Pasture (*v. infra* Des), Tamar Hill, Tewet Hill ('pewit hill'), Tilwell, Watlocks, Winking Moss Croft (*Winkinmoss* 1702 *LowtherW*), Wisters.

(b) In 1702 (*LowtherW*) Meals (*v.* melr), *Mountrivers*; in 1646 (*LowtherW*) Force (*Fors* c. 1260, c. 1280 StB. *v.* fors), Goukstone ('cuckoo stone'), *hossabanck, great* and *little Kell* (*v.* kelda); in 1542 (CW x) *Adings, Fermery Hill* (may refer to a *fermerie* (*v. supra* 339) belonging to Lekeley Priory *supra*), *Innermerryryddyng* (*v.* hryding), *Ormescroft* ('Orm's croft'), *Somrose Hill, Waynfeild*; in 1537 (*AOMB*) *Aldelandes* ('old lands'), *Rydding* (*v.* hryding); in c. 1500 (CW (OS) xii) *Acrelay* (*Akyrlawe* 1459 StBA), *the Lady Holme* (id. 1462 *Netherhall, v.* holmr); in 1422 (HMC x) *le Holehous* (id. 1394 ib.); in 13th (AD iv) *le Blackhacer* (*v.* æcer), *Buttes, Skyrefathe*; in 13th (Furness) *Alothriding* (*v.* hryding), *Fosseterne* (*v.* tiǫrn), *Swyneriding* ('pig hryding'); in c. 1235 (StB) *Bighusthwait* ('barley barn þveit,' *v.* bygg, hūs), *Blabec*

---

[1] Cf. Kiskin and *le Kiskane* (*supra* 268 and 308).

(*Blakbek* c. 1200 Furness), *Leuericpule* (from OE *Lēofrīc* and pōl); in c. 1225 (StB) *Staincroft* (*v.* steinn), *Swinebrechan*; in c. 1194 (Furness) *Morland* (*v.* mōr), *Waterland*. Under each of the following dates there is one field-name: *Hourd-house* 1737 PR (Millom), *Kirkevet* (cartulary copy gives *Kirkeheuet*) 1184–90 Cockersand (presumably 'church headland').

BORROWDALE [bɔrədəl] ## 7. Borrowdale

Borgordale c. 1170 (n.d.) StBA
Borudale 1209, 1215, 1241, 1337 Furness
Borcheredale c. 1209, 1215, 1292 Furness
Borcherdale c. 1210 Furness
Burhedale, Borhedale 1211, 1240 Furness
Bordale 1215 LaCh
Borowedale 1391 GDR, *Borowdale* ib., 1398 Furness
Boroudale 1396 Furness, *Borodale* 1423 Pat, 1505 Cocker
Boradell, Borradell 1564, 1569 PR (Crosth)

BORROWDALE FELLS is *Borowdale Fells* t. Hy 8 DuLa.
The explanation of this name may proceed on one or other of two lines. It may represent ON *borgar dalr*, 'valley of the *borg*, or fortress,' the first element preserving the genitive case of the ON word *borg*. But it is also possible that the first element is a compound *borgar á*, 'river of the fort,' with reference to the course of the upper Derwent. The latter river appears as *Borghra* in the Fountains Cartulary. The three 13th-century forms *Borcheredale* for Borrowdale may preserve a trace of the *á* in the *e* which connects *Borcher-* and *-dale*. Borrowdale (We) seems to be derived from a stream name *Borgar á*, now called Borrow Beck, and the Cumberland Borrowdale probably has the same origin. It is possible, though far from certain, that the *borg* from which in any case Borrowdale derived its name, was the fort which is believed to have existed near Castle Crag *infra* 353.

ASHNESS is *Esknese* 1211 Furness, *Eskenese* 1211 Fountains, *Eskness* 1541 NB, *Exnesse* 1586 PR (Crosth), *Eshnese* 1588 ib., *Ashnes* 1604 ib. Cf. also *Esknebec* 1209 Furness, *Eschenesbec* c. 1210–12 ib. 'Ash headland,' *v.* eski, nes (under næs), with later anglicising to 'ash-ness.'

BROWN DODD is *Broundodde* 1272 For, *Browndodd* 1285 ib. 'Brown dod.'

BURTHWAITE BRIDGE (6") is named from *Butherthwait, Burthwayt* 1211 Fountains. The first form shows that this is an ON genitival compound, representing an original *búðar þveit,* 'clearing around, or adjacent to, a booth.' *Butherhals* 1211 Fountains, in which *búðar* is followed by **hals,** 'pass,' was in this neighbourhood.

GLARAMARA is *Hovedgleuermerhe* 1209–10 Furness, *Gleuermerghe* 1211 ib., *Glaramara* 1784 West. In the first form *Hoved* is from OWSc hǫfuð, 'head,' clearly used here of the mountain itself, and the whole name, which is an inversion compound, may be interpreted 'Glaramara head.' The first element in the difficult Glaramara can be explained without violence to the early forms as *(at) gliúfrum,* 'at the ravines,' the dative plural of ON *gliúfr,* to which erg, 'shieling,' was subsequently added. For the formation cf. Carhampton (So), the first element of which is *(æt) carrum.*

GRANGE is *grangia nostra de Boroudale* 1396 Furness, *The Grange* 1576 S, *Grange-in-Borrodell* 1669 PR (Crosth). GRANGE CRAGS (6″) is *Grainge-Cragg* 1789 Clarke. A grange of the monks of Furness.

GREENUP EDGE is *Grenehope, Parva Grenehope* c. 1211 Scotland. 'Green **hop** or valley.'

LODORE (6″)
　Laghedure 1209–10, 1211 Furness, 1211 Fountains, c. 1210–12 Scotland
　Lawdoore, Lawdowre, Lawdure 1567 PR (Crosth) *et freq* to 1615 Derwent
　Lowdore 1601 PR (Crosth), 1784 West
　Lodore 1789 Clarke

LODORE CASCADE is *Lowdore waterfall* 1769 Gray.

Lodore is so called in contrast to *Heghedure* 1209–10 Furness, *Hie Dore* 1588 PR (Crosth), probably the present HIGH LODORE. Their relative positions were further emphasised in the name *Low-low-Door,* said in Clarke's *Survey of the Lakes* (74) to be used locally of Lodore itself. The name seems to be a hybrid compound, consisting of ON lágr, 'low,' and OE *duru,* 'door.' The *dure* is the 'door' or gap through which Watendlath Beck makes its way. According to Clarke *(op. cit.),* "these houses [High and Low] are not improperly called *Low-Doors* for between them is an opening into Borrowdale which is almost shut up between the rock and water at the place now called Great Inin."

LONG STRATH is *Langestrothe* t. Ric 1 CW iv, *Langestrohe* t. John Fountains, *Langestrode* 1211 Furness. See also Longstrath Beck *supra* 20. 'Long marsh,' *v.* strōd and cf. WRY Langstroth Dale (DEPN).

HIGH SCAWDEL is *Hovedscaldale* c. 1210–12 Scotland. The early form of this name is an inversion compound, the first element of which is ON hǫfuð, 'head.' The second is probably a compound of ON *skalli*, 'bald head', used as a nickname *infra* 390, and dalr, 'valley.'

SEATHWAITE [si·ʍæ·t] is *Seuethwayt* 1292 *Ass*, *Seuythwayt* 1340 *GDR*, *Sethwayt*, *Sethwait* 1542 *DuLa*, *Sethtwhat* 1564 PR (Crosth), *Seatwhait* 1566 ib., *Sethat* 1576 ib., *Seathwaite* 1600 ib. 'Sedge clearing,' *v.* sef, þveit. The 1340 form would seem to be from the adjective *sevy*, 'overgrown with sedge.' Cf. Seavy Carr (PN ERY 248) and Seavy Sike *supra* 26.

SEATOLLER is *Settaller* 1563 PR (Crosth), *Seitaller*, *Seataller* 1566 ib. SEATOLLER FELL is *Seatallor fell* 1777 NB. The forms are late, but suggest that the name is an inversion compound consisting of sætr and alor, 'alder-tree.'

STOCKLEY BRIDGE is named from *Stokeleye* 1285 *For.* *v.* stocc, lē(a)h.

STONETHWAITE is *Staynethwayt* t. Ric 1 CW iv, *Stainthwait* 1211 Fountains, *Staynthwait* 1302 ib., *Stanthwait* 1546 NB, *Stontwhat* 1563 PR (Crosth), *Stonwhat* 1564 ib., *Stantwhat* 1565 ib., *Stonetwhait* 1566 ib. 'Stone clearing,' *v.* steinn, þveit. Identical with Stainfield (L).

STY HEAD is *the Stey heade* 1540 *LRMB*, *the Stime* (or *Stye*) *head* 1578 *Cocker*, *Stye Head* 1774 Donald. 'Head of the path,' from OE stig. The original name for STY HEAD PASS (6″) was *Edderlanghals*, *Hederlanghals* 1209–10 CW xx, *Edderlanghalf* (sic) 1322 Cl, while that for STYHEAD TARN was *Edderlangtern* 1209–10 CW xx, *Edderlangtirn* 1322 Cl. Cf. also *Ederlangebeck* 1294 Cl. *hals* is OE *h(e)als*, or ON hals, 'neck, col, hause.' The name *Edderlang* was doubtless first applied to the tarn. The second element, which seems to be derived from *lang*, 'long,' may be compared with that of Swedish lake-names such as *Eklången* and *Lelången*. The *Edder* will then be the earlier name of the tributary of the Derwent which runs down Sty Head Gill. By 1294, it had come to be known as *Ederlangebeck*. There are alternative explanations of *Edder*. It may be from OE *ǣdre*, 'water-course,' or from the adjective which gives the OE adverb *ǣdre*, 'quickly, at once.' The latter would be admirably suited to a stream with so rapid a fall. See Ekwall RN 156. *Edderlanghals*, now known as Sty Head Pass, is the hause or col between Great Gable and Seathwaite Fell which is crossed by the *sty* or path leading from Derwentwater to Wastwater.

Tongue Head is *caput de Tunghe, del Tung* 1242 Furness. So called from its shape, as it lies between Angle Tarn Gill and Allen Crags Gill. The name is derived from OE **tunge**, 'tongue,' or more probably from ON **tunga** which is in frequent use in Iceland as an independent word and as a place-name element. Cf. also Tongue in N. Sutherland.

Watendlath

> *Wattendlane* t. Ric 1 CW iv, *Watendelair* 1209–10 Furness, *Wattendelan* t. John, 1213 Fountains, *Wattenland* 1546 NB
>
> *Wathenthendelan*[1] 1211 Fountains, *Wattintindelan*[1] 1210–12 Scotland, *Wathendeland* c. 1250 Fountains
>
> *Wateleth* 1563 PR (Crosth), *Wayteleth* 1564 ib., *Waidendleth* 1567 ib.
>
> *Wat(t)endleth* 1564, 1565 PR (Crosth), *Watanlath* 1784 West, 1786 Gilpin
>
> *Wantendlethe* 1600 PR (Crosth)

The first part of this name may well be a compound of ON **vatn** and **endi**, with the meaning 'end of the lake.' The *vatn* in question is presumably Watendlath Tarn. Ekwall (DEPN) compares Vassenden, from ON *vatns endi*, a common place-name in Norway. The forms of the final element vary too widely for any interpretation to be suggested.

Airy's Bridge, Mitchell Cove, Patterson's Fold (all 6″), Sergeant's Crag[2], Taylorgill Force and Wilkinson's Dub (6″) are probably to be associated with the families of Christopher *Airaie* (1603 PR, Crosth) and Jane *Araye* (1634 ib.), Thomas *Mitchel* (1793 ib.), Mary *Paterson* (1768 ib.), William *Sargyante* (1602 ib.), William *Taylor* (1718 ib.) and Francis *Wilkynson* (1566 ib.).

Base Brown is *Bess Brown* 1774 Donald. It may be noted that a

---

[1] Transcribed with final *u* in the printed edition of the Furness Coucher Book, but the later *land* forms make this very unlikely, and Watendlath is certainly not a *law* or hill.

[2] *Sergeant-crag* 1784 West.

William *Basbroun* appears under Santon in 1332 SR. BIRCH HOW (6″) is *Birkhow* 1695 PR (Crosth). 'Birch hill,' *v.* birki, haugr. BOWDER STONE is *bowders stone* 1751 GM, *Boother-stone* 1786 Gilpin, *Bowder-stone*, *Powder-Stone* or *Bounder-Stone* 1789 Clarke. Cf. *Bowtherstone house* 1807 PR (Crosth). A dial. form of 'boulder.' BULL CRAG is so named in 1784 (West). CAPELL CRAG is so named in 1570 (*ExchKR*). This is probably ME *capel*, 'nag,' ultimately from Latin *caballus*. CASTLE CRAG is so named in 1769 (Gray). CHAPEL Ho (6″) is *Capella* 1542 DuLa, *Chappell in Borrowdell* 1576 PR (Crosth), *Borrowdale Chapelhouse* 1746 ib. DOVENEST CRAG (6″). Cf. *Dove's nest* 1769 Gray. EAGLE CRAG[1] is so named in 1777 (NB). "Here...is every year an airy or nest of eagles" (ib. ii, 69). ELLERS is *Ellers or Ellersfielde* 1578 *Cocker, Ellars in Borradaill* 1703 PR (Crosth). 'Place overgrown with alders,' *v.* elri. FIELD Ho is so named in 1762 ib. GOAT CRAGS is *Gate-Cragg* 1789 Clarke. GREAT END is *the Wastall great ende* 1578 *Cocker, hill called Great End* 1805 *Brayton*. *Wastall* is Wasdale *infra* 390. HANGING KNOTTS (6″) is *Hanging Knot* ib. HIGH SEAT (6″) is *High Seatt* 1569 ElizKes. HIND SIDE (6″) is so named in 1794 (H). HOLLOWS is *Hollas* 1565, 1569 PR (Crosth), (*in Boradaille*) 1610 ib., *Howlas* 1571 ib. HOLLOW STONE (6″). Cf. *Hallow-stone crag* 1784 West. HOW (6″) is *Howe* 1542 DuLa, *the Hoowe* 1600 PR (Crosth). *v.* haugr. LEATHES COTTAGE (6″) is *Leades* ib., probably from hlaða, 'barn.' LONGTHWAITE is *Longtwhayte* t. Hy 8 DuLa. 'Long þveit.' MANESTY [manəsti] is *Manistie, Maynister* 1564 PR (Crosth), *Manistae* 1565 ib., *Manistye* 1601 ib. The second element is probably stīg, 'path.' REECASTLE CRAG (6″) is *Ree-Castle* 1794 H. RIGGSIDE is *Rigesyde* 1626 PR (Crosth), *Rigsyde in Borradaille* 1631 ib. *v.* hrycg. ROSTHWAITE is *Rasethuate* 1503 *Cocker, Rastwhat* 1563 PR (Crosth), *Raystwhat, Raistwhat* 1564 ib., *Restwhait* 1566 ib., (*in Boradell*) 1603 ib., *Rosthwait* 1786 Gilpin. 'Clearing marked by, or surrounding, a cairn,' *v.* hreysi, þveit. SHEPHERDS CRAG (6″) is *Shepherd's Crag* 1794 H. SHIVERY KNOTT is so named in 1805 (*Brayton*). STAKE (6″) is *the Stake of Borrowdall* 1784 West. This may be *stake*, 'columnar rock,' as in EDD *s.v. stake*, sb.[1], 2. HIGH TOVE is *High Toue* 1805 *Brayton*, possibly dial. *tove*, 'tuft.'

FIELD-NAMES

(*a*) In 1805 (*Brayton*) Bowfellend (named from Bow Fell (We)), Floodstangs gill, Uttersil of raise, Uregap.

[1] There is also an *Eaglescrag* in Barton We (NB i, 410).

(b) In 1787 (ClarkeM) *Eea ffoot* (probably 'river foot,' *v.* ēa), *Hardindale Knott*, *Spaw* or *Borrowdale Well*; in 1784 (West) *Falcon's-nest, Lady's-leap, Shuttenoer*; in 1670 (PR, Crosth) *Loft* (*Lofte* 1620 ib.); in 1651 (PR, Crosth) *Rigge in the Grange* (*Riggat Grange* 1592 ib.); in 1614 (PR, Crosth) *Park Yeat* (id. 1589 ib.); in 1546 (NB) *Applegarth* ('apple garðr'), *Monk acre, Pykerigg, Thakerigg* (*v.* þak, hryggr, under hrycg); in 1542 (*DuLa*) *Alla, hedgarth, Hehowse*; in 1399 (*DuLa*) *the Blakehall, Gaytshale*; in 1209–10 (Furness) *Arneraid* (possibly '*Arni*'s road,' from Scottish and NCy *raid*), *Bredinebrigge* ('plank bridge,' from OE *breden*, adj. of *bred*, 'plank'), *Marcebuthe* (possibly 'boundary búð,' *v.* mearc), *Windheg*. Under each of the following dates there is one field-name: *Clyne* 1537 Furness, *Killhowe* 1656 PR (Crosth) (*v.* cyln, hōh), *Newke* 1643 ib. (i.e. 'nook'), *Shepe Oodde* 1542–4 Furness, *Whitedale-pike* 1769 Gray.

8. Brackenthwaite[1]

BRACKENTHWAITE

Brakenthwayt 1230 Scotland *et freq* to 1541 *MinAcct*, with variant spelling *-thweyt, -tweyt, -twheyt, -thwayth, -twhait*

Brakanthweit 1286 StB *et freq* to 1731 PR (Bridekirk), with variant spelling *-thwayt, -thwait, -thwate*

Brankanthuait 1349 *Cocker*, *Braukanthwait* (sic print) 1367 Pat (p)

Brackenthate 1602 CW xii

'Bracken clearing,' *v.* þveit. The forms beginning in *Brank-* are due to anticipation of the *n* of the second syllable.

MILLBECK is represented in the name of Adam de *Milnebeck* (1279 *Ass*). *v.* myln, bekkr.

CORN HOW is so named in 1655 (CantW vii). *v.* haugr or hōh. DALE HOW (6″) is *Dalehowes* 1550 NB. The haugr above Rannerdale *infra* 356. GRASMOOR is *Grasmire* 1784 West. LANTHWAITE GREEN is named from *Langthwate* 1505 *Cocker*. 'Long þveit.' PICKET HOW is *Pichthow* 1653 CantW vii. Presumably 'piked hill,' *v.* haugr and cf. Picket How *infra* 381. SCALEHILL and WHITESIDE are so named in 1784 (West). *v.* skáli. TURNERHOW (6″) is *Tannerhow* 1821 G. *v.* haugr.

FIELD-NAMES

(b) In 1506 (*Cocker*) *Gylysfeld*, *Wartholl* (this is possibly another example of a compound of varði and hóll, *v.* Ward Hall *supra* 310). Under each of the following dates there is one field-name: *Braunthebank* 1285 *For* (probably 'steep bank,' *v.* brant), *le Fyshegarth* 1570 *ExchKR* (*v.* Fishgarth Holm *supra* 79), *riuulum de Caluegille* (also *Kaulegill*) c. 1227 StB.

---

[1] Added to Buttermere (*infra* 355) in 1934.

9. Brigham

BRIGHAM

Briggham c. 1175 StB *et passim*, with variant spelling *Brig-*
Bricgaham 1185 StB, *Briggaham* 1210–10 Furness (p)
Briggeham 1210 Pipe, 1266 *MinAcct*, 1279 *Ass* (p), 1311 Ipm,
    Bryggeham 1267 FF
Bricham c. 1230 StB, *Brikam* 1250 Fees (p)
Brugeham 1278, 1279 *Ass* (both p), *Breggeham* 1292 ib. (p)
Bridgeham 1610 Speed
Brigholme 1649 PR (Bridekirk)

'Homestead near the bridge,' *v.* brycg, hām and Introduction.

ELLERBECK is *Ellerbek* 1541 *MinAcct*. 'Alder stream,' *v.* elri, bekkr.

THE FITZ is *del Fit* 1300 Cl (p), *Fytt* 1570 *ExchKR*, *Fitts* 1811 PR
(Bridekirk). FITZ MILL (6″) is *Fitts Mill* 1798 ib. FITZ WOODS (6″)
is *Fitts-Wood* 1794 H. *v.* fit, 'meadow.'

FIELD-NAMES

(b) In 1578 (*Cocker*) *Bouchfitt* (*Bouchefit* 1399 IpmR, *Bowchesfitt* 1519 FF.
v. fit. The first element is probably the family name *Bouch*); in 1544 (NB)
Brunthwait (*Brunthwayt* 1399 IpmR. *v.* þveit), *Dunthwait* (*Dunthwayt* ib.
v. þveit); in 1315 (Orig) *Swinesset* (*Swynsete* 1310 Pat. 'Pig sætr'). Under
each of the following dates there is one field-name: *Boutherbeck* 1663 DKR xl
(probably 'stream by the booth or booths,' from ON búðar, or -ir, and bekkr),
Kirkecroft 1399 IpmR ('church croft'), *Mayfield* 1744 PR (Lamplugh).

10. Buttermere[1]

BUTTERMERE [butrmiᶾr]

Butermere 1230 Scotland, *Buttermer'* 1260 *Rental*, *Buttremere* 1283
    MinAcct, *Buttermyre* 1539 ib.
Bottermere 1256 FF, *Botermer'* 1278 *MinAcct*
Bouttermer' 1279 *MinAcct*

BUTTERMERE DUBS (6″) is *Buttermere dubbes* 1561 FF. *v.* dub. Also
in the parish was *Buttermergreynes* 1293 *MinAcct*. *v.* grein.
The village takes its name from the lake *supra* 33. Cf. *Buttermere*
in Tyndall 1346 GDR in this county.

BUTTERMERE HAUSE is *Ravenerhals* c. 1170, c. 1175 (n.d.) StBA,
Ravenhals c. 1250 ib., *Randon-knot or Buttermere-hawse* 1784 West.

[1] Brackenthwaite (*supra* 354) was added to Buttermere in 1934.

Linked with this is the adjacent RANNERDALE in Brackenthwaite parish, *Ranerdall* 1508 *Cocker*, and *Ranerthwate* 1507 ib. *Ravenerhals* is *hrafn-erg-hals*, 'raven shieling pass' (*v.* **erg**, **hals**). For the other two names, *v.* **dalr** and **þveit**.

GATESGARTH

Gatescarth(e) 1260 *Rental et freq* to 1562 *Brayton*, with variant spelling *-skart*, *Gaitescarth* 1318 *MinAcct*, *Birknesfield or Gatescath* p. 1550 NB

Gascard 1268 *MinAcct*, *Gascarth* 1273 ib., *Gaskarth* 1567 PR (Crosth), *Gaskaith* 1805 *Brayton*

Gadschard 1268 *MinAcct*, *Gatscharth* 1278 ib.

Gasgarth 1273 *MinAcct*, *Gasgath* 1616 CW xxviii

Geyte garth 1570 *ExchKR*

LITTLE GATESGARTHDALE (6″) (in Borrowdale) is *Gascadale* 1786 Gilpin. In the neighbourhood was *Gatescartheheved*, *Gatescardeheved* c. 1211 Scotland.

'skarð, or gap of the goats.' The original name seems to have contained the OE gen. pl. *gáta* which in some forms is scandinavianised to *geita*. In the second element, *garth* (*v.* garðr) was later substituted for skarð.

HONISTER CRAG is *mountain called Unnisterre* 1751 GM, *Honister Crag* 1784 West. The forms are too late for certainty, but this may conceivably be '*Húni*'s staðir,' twice recorded in Norway in the form *Hunastad(h)r*. For the preservation of inflexional *r*, cf. Burton Stather (L).

BOWDERBECK (6″) is *bowderbeck* 1570 *ExchKR*, *Boldebeck*, *Bolderbeck* 1578 *Cocker*. Probably 'boulder **bekkr**.' FLEETWITH is *Fleetwath* 1783 Donald, *Fleetwith* 1784 West. Probably from fljót and vað. HASSNESS is *Hosenesse*, *gate of hessnesse* 1578 *Cocker*. This may be a compound of ON **hals** and **nes**. HIGH CRAG is so named in 1784 (West). HIGH HO (6″) is so named in 1578 (*Cocker*). HIGH STILE (6″) is *High Steel* 1783 Donald, *High Stile* 1784 West. *v.* **stigel**. NEWLANDS HAUSE is *Newland Hose* 1783 Donald, *Newland hawse* 1784 West. *v.* **hals**. SWINSIDE GILL (6″) is named from *Swynsed*, *Swynsyde* 1570 *ExchKR*.

FIELD-NAMES

(b) In 1578 (*Cocker*) *Donninge Coue beck*, *Drigg Garwite*, *fishgarth called Ealinge* (cf. Fishgarth Holm *supra* 79. This may conceivably be a formation from *eel*, parallel to *fishing* (for fishery) from *fish*), *Grademoore heade*, *grise-garth* (*v.* gríss, garðr), *hallinghowe* (*v.* haugr), *karfielde* (*v.* kiarr), *Rowemyre* (*v.* mýrr); in 1570 (*ExchKR*) *Blackrygge*, *Cardale* (*v.* kiarr), *Waudopp beck*. Under each of the following dates there is one field-name: *Lughborowe* 1540 NCW, *Scarf* 1784 West (*v.* skarð).

11. Cleator[1]

Cleator [kliˑtər]

Cletertha c. 1185 StB

Cletern(e), *Kletern(e)* c. 1220 StB (p), 1241 Pipe *et freq* to 1322 Cl

Cleterhe c. 1225 Furness, 1201–30 DuLa, *Cletergh* c. 1260 StB (p) *et freq* to 1338 Cl, *Cleterh'* 1291 CW (OS) i, facs.

Cleter(e) c. 1250 StB (p), 1279 *Ass*, 1291 Tax, (*in Copland*) 1478 Lowther

Cleterwe 1279 *Ass*, *Cleterue* ib., 1301 GDR (p)

Cletter early 14th StMaryY, 1490 Ipm, 1542 *MinAcct*, 1594 NCW

Cleeter 1503 Norfolk, *Cleyter* 1567 FF, *Cleator* 1579 ib.

Clotter 1526 Norfolk, *Clotter al. Cleter* 1538 ib.

Cleytor 1569 FF

Cleator Moor is so named in 1732 (CaineCl). In the parish was *Cletergil* 1272–9 CW xli.

The forms imply that this name is a compound of ON **klettr**, 'rock, cliff,' and **erg**, 'shieling' (cf. DEPN). This interpretation suits the site. CaineCl x observes: "It might be said that this interpretation—'the outlying pasture among the rocks'—in no way answers to the configuration of the district. But I am not sure that this is so. Towering above the cultivated lands there was a majestic outcrop of limestone now known as 'Clints.'...This hill is now a series of 'cliffs.' But this is not all. The limestone also asserted itself in large outcrops at Jack-trees, Todholes, notably at Aldby, and other places. After this is stated, there are still the outcropping 'slates' of Dent, and other rocks, left unnoticed. The derivation of the word *Cleator* from **klettar** is consistent, therefore, with the physical aspects of the place." That the forms in *-erne* are clearly errors of transcription for *-erue* is shown by the 13th-century form in *-erwe*, which is a regular development of *-erg(e)*.

Aldby is *Aldeby* 1278, 1279 *Ass* (both p), (*H*)*aldeby* 1279 ib. (p), *Oalby* 1697 Caine, *Aldby, or Oldby* 1783 CaineCl. 'Old **bȳ**,' *v.* (e)**ald**.

[1] Styled Cleator Moor since 1934.

CROSSFIELD is *Crosfeld* 1279 *Ass* (p), *Crossefeld* 1292 ib. (p), *Crossfield* 1616 CaineCl. This may take its name from Fawn Cross *infra*, half a mile to the south-east.

DENT is *mons Dinet* c. 1200 StB, *Denthill* 1576 S, *Dint* 1690 CW xvii, 1779 CaineCl, *Dennt* 1754 ib. As noted in DEPN, this is the same name as Dent (PN WRY 58), for which the earliest form is *Denet* c. 1200 Ass. It is certainly Celtic in origin. Cf. OIr *dind*, 'hill.' Dent Hill in Stainmore (We) may be another example of this name, but no form has so far been found earlier than 1724 PR (Brough) (*Dent House*). Cf. also Dent in Millom (421).

LONG BARROW is *Langeberh* c. 1205 CW (OS) i, facs. *v.* be(o)rg. In this district 'barrow' probably descends from ON berg rather than from OE be(o)rg.

SUNTON (lost) is *Suntun* c. 1205 CW (OS) i, facs., *Sunton'* 1278 *Ass*, 1291 CW (OS) i, facs., (*in Cleterge*) 1518–29 ECP. The name survives in Sunton Sike (*supra* 28) and in the fields Far and Near Sumpton, and possibly contains the OE word *sunt*, 'swamp,' which occurs in Sunt and Sompting (PN Sx 191, 201).

TODHOLES (6″) is *Todholes* 1260 *Rental*, *Toodhooles* 1660 CantW viii. 'Fox holes.'

WATH is so named in 1717 (CaineCl). It may represent *mill of Thoraldewath*, *Thoraldwath* 1294 Cl, *Thoraldwait* 1322 Cl, *Thoroldwath* 1350 Ipm. '*Thor(v)ald*'s ford,' *v.* vað.

BLACK HOW is so named in 1717 (CaineCl). *v.* haugr or hōh. BOW-THORN is *Bowthorne* 1410 AllerA, 1655 CantW vii. 'Thorn tree in the curve,' *v.* boga. FAWN CROSS (6″). Cf. *Fallen Cross Gate* 1743 CaineCl. THE FLOSH is *Howthorne vel Flosh* 1685 CaineCl. A tributary of the Ehen once ran through these lands, but was later led under the road (CaineCl 113). *v.* flasshe. JACKTREES is so named in 1731 ib. KEEKLE GROVE is so named in 1804 ib. *v.* Keekle R. *supra* 18. ROW is *Cleator al. Cleator Rawe* 1582 FF, (*Rowe*) 1583 ib. ROW FOOT is *Roefoot* 1759 CaineCl. *v.* rāw. TROUGHTON HO may be connected with Nicholl *off Troghton* 1432 StBA. It is possible that he derived his surname from Troughton (La).

FIELD-NAMES

(a) Borrans (*Burwan* 1279 *Ass* (p). This may also be *ye Borren of Stones* 1410 AllerA 74. *v.* burghan), Burnt How Foot (*v.* haugr), Crowgarth (id. 1659

CantW viii. *v.* garðr), Crugarth (distinct from Crowgarth, cf. *supra* 229), Esp Dale (i.e. 'aspen'), Hemp Garth (id. 1744 *LowtherW*), Hingrihow (*Ingrehowe* 1410 AllerA, possibly from the ON feminine personal name *Ingiríðr* and haugr), Hollin, Holsters (*the holster* 1578 *Cocker, Holsters* 1752 CW xxxix), How Guards (*v.* garðr), Linethwaite (may be *Lynthwayt* 1338 Cl. *v.* lín, þveit), Lobby Ley, Mathew Rae, Moor Plat, Outriggside, Parrock, Priest Croft (id. 1686 CaineCl), Riddings (cf. *Reddinghead* 1752 CW xxxix and *v.* hryding), Roger Ridding (*v.* hryding), Rose Dykes, Side Bram, Sour Dale (probably from *saurr*), Stoneraise (*v.* hreysi), Stubbing Ing (*v.* eng), Tinkler Holm ('tinker holmr,' from Scottish and Northern *tinkler*), Townsteads (*Townesteads* 1686 CaineCl), Trumpet, Warlock How (this may be OE *wǣrloga*, 'wizard,' or possibly dial. *warlock*, 'mustard.' The second element is haugr), Wha Meadow; in 1819 (CaineCl) Gatroy (*Gaytwray* 1410 AllerA, probably 'goat corner,' *v.* geit, (v)rá).

(*b*) In 1752 (CW xxxix) *Kicklethwaite* (*v.* Keekle R. *supra* 18 and þveit), *Kirkstool*; in 1717 (CaineCl) *Cat Kill How* (may be *Gaitkethow* 1670 ib.); in 1410 (AllerA) *ye Black Moss, Damage Dubb, Lynebank Cragg, Tharsagamell, Uter Croft* (probably 'outer croft'), *ye Crooke of Wenar*. Under each of the following dates there is one field-name: *Gibing* 1707 CaineCl, *Hawcroft* 1686 ib., *Melthwaite* 1533–8 ECP (possibly mel(r) and þveit, as *infra* 404).

12, 13. Great and Little Clifton

GREAT and LITTLE CLIFTON

> *Cliftona* c. 1160 (early copy) *Lowther*,[1] *Clifton* 1210 Cur *et passim*, with variant spelling *Clyf-*, *Cliftun'* 1210 Cur
> *Clifton Gamel* 1212 Cur, *Kirkeclifton'* c. 1260 Hesley, *Parua Clifton* 1278 Ass, *Alta Clifton* 1284 Hesley, *Great Clifton* 1300 Ipm

In the parish was *Cliftonbankes* c. 1276 Hesley, *Cliftonbanckes* c. 1330 ib.

'Cliff tūn,' taking its name from the "*cliff* or steep precipice which hangs over Derwent at the mouth of Marron" (NB ii, 56). *Alta, Kirke* are Great Clifton. Clifton *Gamel* may be named from *Gamel*, the holder in 1212 (Cur).

12. Great Clifton

BOTLANDS BLAWITH (field) is connected with *Blawathlinays* c. 1330 *Hesley*. The first element in the 14th-century form is 'dark ford,' *v.* blá(r), vað. The second element looks like the plural of ME *linhay*, 'shed,' but this word seems to be specifically a south-western form,

---

[1] The copy in StB (No. 107) gives the reading *Clyfton*.

and here, as also in *Stallardlinays* c. 1330 *Hesley*, in this parish, a compound līn-. (ge)hæg, 'flax enclosure,' is more probable. No explanation can be given of *Botlands* in the modern name. It occurs again in the existing Botlands and Lords Botland—fields in this parish—and in *Botland* 1789 *LowtherW*, also in this parish.

BRACKENBARROW is *Brakanberscahe* c. 1270 StB, *Brackenbarrow* 1550 (1687) Whellan, 1725 *Work*. 'Bracken-covered be(o)rg.' In the earliest form, OE sceaga is added to the name.

BRAITHMOOR (field) is *Braithemire* c. 1250, c. 1258 StB, *Braizemire* c. 1258 ib., *Brade Moor* 1773 *LowtherW*. 'Broad mýrr,' v. breiðr.

COLDFITZ WOOD (6″) is named from *Kaldefite* c. 1330, c. 1335 *Hesley*. 'Cold meadow,' v. fit.

CROSSBARROW is *Crossebergh* 1279 *Ass*, *Crossbarrow* 1725 *Work*. 'be(o)rg marked by a cross.'

WIGGON HOW (6″) may perhaps be associated with the family of Michael de *Wyghayn* (1279 *Ass*), which must have come from Wigan (La).

13. Little Clifton

BRIGGETHORFIN (lost). A charter of c. 1260 (*Hesley*) relating to Clifton, refers to half an acre of meadow in *Briggethorfin*, and another charter (*Hesley*) of about the same date mentions an acre of land *super Aynthorfin*. The first of these names is an inversion compound meaning '*Thorfin*'s bridge.' The second name is also an inversion compound containing the same personal name *Thorfin*, but the first element is uncertain. It may conceivably be ON *eign*, 'holding.' It is possible that the name BRIDGEFOOT in this parish refers to the bridge recorded in *Briggethorfin*. *Thorfin* was a common name, especially in northern England, and it would be unsafe to attempt any identification of the *Thorfin* from whom these local names are derived.

Another inversion compound is recorded from Clifton—*Fitbrandan* c. 1250 *Hesley*, *Sitbrandan* (sic print) c. 1260 StB, *Fit Brundon* 1789 *LowtherW*, which means '*Brandán*'s meadow,' v. fit, *Brandán* being an OIrish personal name. In *Polgauer* 1279 Ass we have probably British *poll gafr*, 'goat brook'; cf. RN 329. These three names are all discussed in ScandCelts, 20–1, 24, 29–30.

GOOSETAIL (6″) is *Goose Taile* 1750 CW xiv.

STARGILL is *Stargl'* c. 1230 StB (p), *Stargile, Stargyle* 1292 *Ass* (p), *Starrgill Well* 1682 *Work*. 'Sedge ravine,' from ME *star* or ON *storr, star-*, and gil. Cf. Icelandic *Starmýrardalr* (Kålund ii, 261) and Starnmire *supra* 246.

FIELD-NAMES

(a) Crinelmas Meadow, Graystones Lot (*Great Greystones* 1782 *LowtherW*), Harris Lots, Hover Croft, Lograys Folds, Moor Flatts (*Morplath* c. 1250 StB, *Moor Flatt* 1773 *LowtherW*), Nichol Style, Open Lots (*the Lott* 1782 *LowtherW*), Portlands, Reelfitz (*v.* fit), Shuttle, Whithams Meadow.

(b) In 1789 (*LowtherW*) *the Hemplin* or *Hemplin Garth, Swinside* (*Swinesett* 1773 ib. Apparently 'pig sætr')[1]; in 1773 (*LowtherW*) *Murplilett, Skirth Head* (ON *skurðr*, OSw *skyrþ*, 'cutting, watercourse'), *Swineson Gill*; in c. 1330 (*Hesley*) *le Haygate, Laythild* (*v. infra* 362); in 1282 (*Hesley*) *Milneholm* (*Milneholm'* c. 1276 ib. *v.* myln, holmr); in c. 1260 (*Hesley*) *Meleberg'* (*Milneberch'* c. 1250 ib. 'Mill hill'), *Scaleberg'* (*v.* skáli, be(o)rg); in c. 1258 (StB) *Buttes, Rocheland* (*Rocheland* c. 1215 ib., *Rotheland* c. 1250 ib.), *Segland de Hothaches* (id. ib.), *Withebuthes* (*Witebuttes* c. 1215 ib. *v.* wiðig), *parva Wynsath* (id. c. 1215, c. 1250 ib.). Under each of the following dates there is one field-name: *Busy bitt* 1782 *LowtherW, the Stanges* n.d. Whellan, *Stodfaldrunes* 1284 *Hesley* (*v.* stöðf(e)ald, runnr).

14. Cloffocks[2]

CLOFFOCKS (6″) is *Fyt Cloffhow* n.d. Whellan, *Two Clofocks* 1660 (1723) CW v, *High Cloffock, Middle* and *Low Cloffocks* 1749 *LowtherW, High* and *Low Cloffock* 1793 H. Ekwall (ScandCelts 24) compares with this name that of Clougha (PN La 169), from OE clōh, 'ravine' and hōh, 'spur.'

15. Cockermouth[3]

COCKERMOUTH

Cokyrmoth c. 1150 StB, *Cokirmowth* c. 1220 ib., *Cokirmouth* 1381 AD iii

Kokermue 1194 CartAnt, *Cokermue* 1247 FF, 1277 *CP*, *Cokermu* 1310 Greenfield iv, *Cokermwe* 1317 Ipm

---

[1] Add: in 1777 (*Hudleston*) *Hemboale, Sunderboales*.
[2] In the parish and borough of Workington (*infra* 454).
[3] Part of Papcastle (*supra* 308) was transferred to Cockermouth, and part of Cockermouth to Setmurthy (*infra* 433), in 1935.

Cocremuth' 1221 ClR, *Kokermuth'* 1260 Cl, *Cokermuth* 1278 *Ass*, *Cokermouth'* 1308 *Netherhall* (p), *Cockermouth* 1547 FF COCKERMOUTH CASTLE is *Castr' de Cokermue* 1266 *MinAcct*.

'Mouth of the river Cocker' (*supra* 9).

NOTE. CASTLEGATE is *Castle Street* 1737 CW xxxiii. *v.* gata. GALLOW-BARROW is *Gallabargh(e)* 1578 *Cocker*. 'Gallows hill,' *v.* be(o)rg. KIRKBANK is *Kirkbancke, Kirkbanck* ib. KIRKGATE is *Kirkgatestreete* ib. 'Church road,' *v.* kirkja, gata. MAIN ST is *the wide street between Cocker and Derwent bridges* 1777 NB. MARKET PLACE is *ye merket place* 1578 *Cocker*. ST HELENS ST is *Sanct Elyns gaitt* 1540 *Netherhall, St helen street* 1578 *Cocker*. It leads to St Helens *infra*. HIGH SAND LANE. Cf. *the Sande* 1578 *Cocker*. SULLART ST is connected with *Sullerd Sand* 1737 CW xxiii, *Sullart Sand Went* 1761 *Cocker, Sulloth Sand* 1785 ib., *Sulwath Went* 1802 ib., *Sulwath Sand Went* 1811 ib., *Sullart Went* 1816 ib. These forms are too late to establish the derivation of this name, but it seems clear that the second element was originally vað, 'ford.' For *went v.* went. WASTE LANE. Cf. *the Waste* 1578 *Cocker*.

A lost name is *the Shambells in the merkett place* 1578 *Cocker*, from OE *sceamol*, 'butchers' stall.'

LAITHWAITE [leiθət] (field) is *Leycheld* 1300 Cl, *Leychell* 1300 Ipm, *Ouer-, Netherlatheld iuxta Cokermouth* 1519 FF, *Laythell iuxta Cokermouth* 1570 *ExchKR, Latheldes* 1578 *Cocker, High, Low Laithed* 1688 ib., *Low Lythwaite* 1737 CW xxiii. These fields are at the west end of Cockermouth. This is probably 'barn slope,' *v.* hlaða, helde, the second element being replaced by the more familiar þveit. Cf. *Laythild* c. 1330 *Hesley*, in Clifton, and *Latholds* 1578 *Cocker*, in Lorton.

THE MOOR (6") is *la More* 1278, 1279 *Ass* (both p), *le Moore* 1570 *ExchKR*. Cf. *moore closses, moorehills* 1578 *Cocker*. *v.* mōr.

RUBBY BANKS (6")

Ruggebagbanks 1300 Ipm
Rybabank 1519 FF, *Rubbe banke* 1570 *ExchKR, Rubby banck* 1578 *Cocker*

In the neighbourhood was *Ruggbaggecroft* 1300 Ipm.

This name preserves the surname of Thomas *Ruggebag*, son and heir of Robert *Ruggebag*, who held land in Cockermouth in 1300 (Cl).

ST HELENS takes its name from the *capella Sancte Elene* 1342 *Cocker*. It is *Sayntelyne Closse* 1539 *MinAcct, clausum vocatum Sancte Ellinge* 1560 *Cocker*.

SIMONSCALES (6″) is probably identical with *Simondescales* 1279 *Ass* (p), *Simonscales* 1286 ib. (p). It appears as *Symondskell* 1578 *Cocker*. *v.* skáli. The personal name *Simond*, which forms the first element, may equally well be derived from OE *Sigemund* or ON *Sigmundr*. The latter is more probable in this county.

UREBY FIELD (lost) is *Ourebyfeld* 1260 *Rental*, *Urebyfeld* 1399 IpmR, *Ureby feilde* 1578 *Cocker*, *Upperby Field* 1757 ib., *Ureby Field* 1809, 1827 ib., *Upperby Field otherwise Radcliff Field* 1812 ib. There was more than one field of this name, but all were in the east end of Cockermouth, adjoining or near Waste Lane[1]. In 1757 (*Cocker*) Richard Radcliffe became customary tenant of these fields. The forms clearly represent a lost village-name ending in bȳ. The first element is uncertain, but may be the ON personal name *Úri*. Professor Ekwall prefers OE *uferra*, 'upper', which may have replaced ON *øfri* or *efri*.

HORSECLOSE WOOD (6″) is so named in 1578 (*Cocker*). Cf. *Horse Close* 1560 ib. HOWFOOT (6″). Cf. *Howfyt* ib., *the howe fitts* 1578 ib. The meadows (*v.* fit) lie by the Derwent under a hill (*v.* haugr). PARK HO. Cf. (*clausum sub*) *Parco* 1260 *Rental*, (*iuxta*) *Parcum* 1279 *MinAcct*, *Cokermouth park* 1381 AD iii. STRAWBERRY HOW is *Strowbery how* 1578 *Cocker*, *Strawberry How* 1777 Donald. 'Strawberry hill,' *v.* haugr or hōh. TUTE HILL (6″) is *Toot-Hill* 1794 H. This is a tumulus, formerly used as a look-out point, *v.* tote.

FIELD-NAMES

(b) In 1737 (CW xxiii) *Birkett Bank, Buck, Bull Tree Garden, Butts Towne Head, Cass Bay* (*Casbay* 1578 *Cocker*. Cf. Town Cass in Keswick *supra* 303), *Grandy Croft, Kitty Went Head* (*v.* went), *Morden Close* (*Mawkyn closse al. Carlton closse* 1578 *Cocker*. *Mawkyn*[2] is a diminutive of *Matilda*, through the short form *Mald* > *Maud*), *Tenter Holm Garden* (*Tentreholme* ib. *v.* tenter, holmr); in 1578 (*Cocker*) *Badskyne* (*Badeskyn* 1570 *ExchKR*), *Baliffe garth* (*v.* garðr), *the frith* (*Ffreythe* 1560 *ExchKR*. *v.* fyrhþ(e)), *graystone close, heyninge Bekk* (*v.* haining), *Lingecloses* (*v.* lyng), *New Rents, St Leonards Closse* (cf. *capella sancti leonardi* c. 1280 Hesley), *the settinge, Sowter closes* ('cobbler closes,' from OE sūtere), *Wallbekk, Wooland*; in 1519 (*FF*) *Spitelhowse* (cf. *Spytelenge* 1260 *Rental*. 'Hospital meadow,' *v.* eng); in 1399 (IpmR) *Collenland* (*Collauland* 1367 Ipm); in 1292 (*Ass*) *atte Styghele*

---

[1] *Ex inf.* Mr T. Blacklock.

[2] Perhaps here, as often in Scots and NCy dialect, applied to a hare (NED *malkin*).

H

(p) (*attestiwghele* 1268 Scotland (p). *v.* stigel); in 1273 (*MinAcct*) *le holm sub castro* (id. 1260 *Rental.* *v.* holmr); in 1260 (*Rental*) *Braythemyre* (*v.* breiðr, mýrr), *le Cragges, Kirkemyre* (*v.* kirkja, mýrr). Under each of the following dates there is one field-name: *Bowtherdall Close* 1560 Cocker, *Hay fell* 1777 NB, *Horford* 1570 *ExchKR* ('dirty ford,' *v.* horh), *le Vsterland* 1342 Cocker.

16. Corney[1]
CORNEY

Cornai c. 1160 (early copy)[2] *Lowther et passim*, with variant spellings -*ay*(*e*), *eie*, -*ey*(*e*), -*ye*, *Cornaie* 1228–43 DuLa (p), *Kornai* c. 1230 StB (p), *Kornay* c. 1235 ib. (p), *Little Cornay* 1386 AD iv
Gornay 1291 Tax
Corna 1391 AD iv, *Kornau'* 1478 Furness, *Corno* 1576 S

HIGH CORNEY is so named in 1657 CW xiv. CORNEY FELL and CORNEY HALL are so named in 1685 (*LowtherW*). CORNEY MILL is *the mill of Cornay* 1391 AD iv. Two settlements are referred to in (*inter*) *duas Cornays* 1190–1200 Cockersand.

Probably 'heron ēg,' from **corn, *cron*, a side-form of OE cran. Derivation from *corn*, 'grain,' is made unlikely by the situation of the place.

BORROWDALE GROUND (6″). Cf. *Borughdalemylnegrym, Borughdalemyngrym* 1336 *Ass* (both p), *Borrowdale Milnegrund* 1399 DuLa. No explanation of this name can be offered. The last form in all probability refers to this place.

HIGH, MIDDLE (6″) and LOW KINMONT

Kinemund 1201–16, 1236–52 DuLa, *Kynemund'* 1235, 1236 Pipe (both p), 1319 Dugd vi
Kenemund 1236–52 DuLa, 1278, 1279 *Ass*
Kinnemuth 1278 *Ass*, *Kinnmuh* 1279 ib.
Kynmont 1526 *DuLa, Kyntmounte al. Kydmonte* 1536 *MinAcct*
Kynmonde 1537 *DuLa*

This name is identical with Kinmont in Annandale and in Methven and in Banffshire, for which Watson (400–1, 404) gives forms *Kynmund* (1529), *Kynmonth* (1578), *Kynmonthe* (1407), and Kinmonth in Glenbervie, for which he gives no early forms. Cf. also Kinmont

---

[1] Added to Waberthwaite (*infra* 439) in 1934.
[2] The copy in StB (No. 107) gives the reading *Cornay*.

(Dumfriesshire), *Kynemund* 1194–1214 HMC, *Kinnemoth* 1329 ib. The name is derived from the Gaelic *ceann monaidh*, 'head (or end) of the moor (or mountain)'; cf. Kintyre, 'end of the land'.

LANGLEY

Langliuerh' c. 1225 StB (p), *Langlivere* ib. (p), 1315 FF, *Langliferhe* 1228–43 DuLa, *Langliveregh* 1235 StB (p), *Langliuerhg* 1252 Pipe (p), *Langliver* 1254, c. 1255 StB (both p)
Langelivere c. 1225 StB (p), *Langeliuerh* c. 1240–50 Hesley (p), *Langelyve Erghe* 1240–56 Furness, *Langelive* c. 1290 ib.
Langauergh' 1235 Pipe (p)
Laglivesherge 1236, 1228–43 DuLa (both p)
Langalyver c. 1275 Chronicle of Man
Langler 1397 Furness, *Langley* 1572 FF

LANGLEY PARK is so named in 1702 (*LowtherW*).
"The erg or shieling of a woman bearing the ON personal name *Langlíf*," as first suggested by W. G. Collingwood (CW iii, 89). The name is well recorded in Danish England in the form *Langliva*.

NORMOSS is *Northmose* 1190–1200 Cockersand. 'North moss.'

SKELLERAH[1] (6″). Cf. Cecilia f. Eme de *Skelhare*, who is associated with Millom in 1292 (*Ass*).

BARRAS MEADOW (6″). Cf. *Barwise* c. 1840 *TA* and *v. supra* 70. BUCK BARROW is *Bokkeberghes* 1319 Dugd vi, *Blakbery or Bukbury* 1548 FF, *Klerkburre al. Lukberry* 1571 CW xi, *Buckberry al. Luckbary* 1613 ib. In spite of some widely differing forms, this is apparently 'bucc-be(o)rg.' FOLDGATE may be *Foulyate* 1702 *LowtherW*. *v.* fūl, geat. GILLFOOT (6″). Cf. *Mikilgile quae est inter duas Cornays* 1190–1200 Cockersand. *v.* gil. MIDDLETON PLACE is *Midletonplace* 1657 CW xiv. MIREGROUND, PARK NOOK and WELCOME NOOK are so named in 1702 (*LowtherW*). WHIT CRAGS (6″). Cf. *Little Whitt Cragg End* 1685 ib. WHITESTONES is so named in 1660 ib.

FIELD-NAMES

(a) In c. 1840 (*TA*) Aickre, Barrows (*v.* be(o)rg), Borrans (*v.* burghan), Brunkers Hill, Brunt Hill, Groudle Ground, Hallsteads, Harclay, Hard work (*v. infra* Fan), Haverdale (*v.* hafri, dalr), Honey pot meadow, Hungry Moor (*v. infra* Fan), Lapboard Field (*v.* lapboard), Look out, Melderteen, Murth-

---

[1] It can hardly be identified with *Selekere* (StB 170) as suggested in the note to that charter.

waite (*v.* mōr, þveit), Pickle (*v.* pightel), Pinning, Priest Ridding (*v.* hryding), Low Rains (*v.* rein), Roger cell Flatts, Scroggsfield (*v.* scrogg), Spout Meadow (*v.* spoute), Summerwork Field, Tewit Park (i.e. 'pewit'), Toota (*v.* tote).

(b) In 1461 (HMC x) *Graynes* ((*del*) *Greynes* 1279 *Ass* (p). *v.* grein); in 1437 (HMC x) *Whitwra* (*Wytewra* 13th ib. 'White corner,' *v.* (v)rá). Under each of the following dates there is one field-name: *Crumwelbothye* a. 1292 CW xli (*v.* bóð), *dobcroft* 1462 *Netherhall*, *Flecherland* 1387 AD iv, *Flickebec* 1236–52 DuLa, *Whynwray* 1494 HMC x ('whin corner,' *v.* (v)rá).

17. Dean[1]

DEAN is *Dene* c. 1170 StB *et passim* to 1385 FF, *Deen* 1367 Ipm, 1375 Cl, 1404 Pat, *Deane* 1559 FF, *Deyn* 1576 S. DEAN MOOR (6″) is *Deane Moore* 1589 *Cocker*. DEANSCALE is *Deneschall* 1278, 1279 *Ass*, *Denescal'* 1279 ib., *Deenskalis* 1391 GDR. *v.* skáli. This is simply 'valley,' *v.* denu.

BRANTHWAITE [branθət]

Bromthweit 1210 Cur

Bramtweit 1212 Cur, *Bramthuait* c. 1260 *Hesley* (p), *Bramthwayt* 1285 *Ass*, 1369 Ipm

Branthwayt 1230 Scotland *et freq* to 1570 *ExchKR*, with variant spellings -*thwayte*, -*tewayth*, *Brancthweyt* 1278 *Ass*

Brampeweyt 1276 FF, *Bramptweyt* 1279 *Ass*, *Brampthwayte* 1544 *MinAcct*

Brannthwayt cum Dene 1278 *Ass*, *Braunthwait* 1279 FF, 1367, 1370 Ipm

Brayntheweyt 1279 *Ass*, *Braynthwayt* 1294 ib.

Branthate 1602 CW xii

BRANTHWAITE BRIDGE (6″) is so named in 1753 (CW (OS) xv). BRANTHWAITE EDGE is *the common called the Edge* 1777 NB, *Branthwaite Edge* 1800 PR (Lamplugh). BRANTHWAITE HALL (6″) is so named in 1611 (CW (OS) iv). BRANTHWAITE Row is so named in 1809 (*EnclA*).

Apart from the 1210 form, the evidence favours ME **brame**, 'bramble,' for the first element. In *Bromthweit* the *o* may represent the rounding of *a* before a nasal, rather than the ō in OE **brōm**, 'broom.' The second element is þveit.

[1] Eaglesfield (*infra* 378) was added to Dean in 1934.

CALVA HALL [kɔ·və] is *Caluowe* 1395 *Ass*, *Calva Hall* 1809 *EnclA*. 'Calves' hill,' *v.* c(e)alf, haugr. CALVA HILL (6") is *Calva Great Hills*, *High Calva Hills* 1809 *EnclA*.

CRAKEPLACE HALL is *Crakeplace* 1288 Orig (p), 1392, 1399 *Ass* (both p), *Crakplace* c. 1382 StB (p), *Crakeplase* 1383 *Ass* (p), *Crackplace Hall* 1617 CW (OS) iv, *Crakeplace Hall* 1727 CW (OS) iv. This would seem to be a British place-name from OWelsh *creic*, 'rock.' Cf. Crake (PN La 191). *Place* is used here in the sense 'manor-house,' as in Sir Gawayne and the Green Knight v. 398, and the common Welsh *Plas Newydd*.

PARDSHAW [pa·rdzə]

> *Perdishaw, Perdishau* c. 1205 (n.d.) StBA, *Perdishou* c. 1300 StB, *Perdyshowe* 1370 Ipm, 1397 FF, *Perdishewe* 1537 CW (OS) xiv, *Perdissow* 1570 FF
> *Pardishou* c. 1260 StB (p), *Pardisou* 1266 *Ass*, *Pardyeshou* 1290 Cl, *Pardishow(e)* 1292 *Ass et freq* to 1578 *Cocker*, with variant spelling -*ys*-
> *Perdeshow* 1266 *MinAcct* (p)
> *Pardeshou* 1338 Cl (p), *Pardeshowe* 1369 Ipm
> *Paradyshowe* 1382 Ipm (p)
> *Prodessowe* 1399 IpmR
> *Bardsey Hall* 1576 S, *Pardsey* 1578 *Cocker*, *Pardshawe* 1601 FF, *Bradsey Hall* 1672 Blome, *Pardsey or Bardshaw* 1794 H
> *Pargay* 1660 CantW viii

PARDSHAW CRAG (6") is *Pardsey Cragg* 1544 NB.
The second element is haugr. The first is doubtless identical with that of *Perdiswell* (PN Wo 113). Both contain a metathesised form of *Preed*, an OE name found in the Liber Vitae of Durham (DEPN).

SNAB MURRIS (*EnclA*) is *Snabmorris* 1684 *Cocker*, *Snab Murris* 1809 *EnclA*. An inversion compound consisting apparently of snabbi, and the personal name *Maurice*, found also in the nearby Moresby *infra* 421.

ULLOCK

> *Ulnelaike* (sic print) 1248 StB (p), *Uluelaykes* c. 1265 Hesley (p), *Uluelaik* 1279 *Ass* (p)
> *Wluelaykis* 1277 For
> *Ulleyk* 1295 Ipm (p), *Ullayk(e)* 1334, 1367 Ipm, 1338 Cl
> *Ullocke* 1570 FF

ULLOCK MAINS is *Ullocke Maines* 1633 *Cocker*. *v*. mains.
'Place where wolves play,' *v*. úlfr, leikr. Cf. Ullock *supra* 315,
infra 373.

ACREWALLS (6″) is *the Acrewall* 1654 *Cocker*. BROOMY HILL (6″) is
Broomhill 1809 *EnclA*. BROWTOP is so named ib. BUTTS WOOD (6″).
Cf. *Butts* 1689 *Cocker*. COCKSHOT WOOD (6″) is named from *Cockshot*
1809 *EnclA*. *v*. cockshot. CROFTHOUSE is so named in 1652 (*Cocker*).
It may be connected with (*del*) *Croftes* 1281 *MinAcct*. CROOKELTY
SPOUT (6″). Cf. *Crooklet* 1809 *EnclA* and *Spout Close* ib. *v*. spoute.
CUP and RING (6″) may be *Cuppleriggs* ib. FIFKETTLE BROW (6″) is
named from *Fif Kettle* ib. FOULKNOTT HILL (6″) is named from *Foul
Knott* ib. FRITH WOOD (6″) is so named ib. Cf. *the Frith* 1689
Cocker. *v*. fyrhþ(e). GATEBARROW. Cf. *Gatebarrow Sike* 1777
Hudleston. GREENCASTLE BROW (6″) is named from *Greencastle* 1619
CW (OS) iv. There was traditionally a castle in the Glebe field called
Greeny Castle (ib. 108). HIGHFIELD HO is named from *High Field*
1809 *EnclA*. KIRBY BROW (6″). Cf. *Kirkby Close* 1684 *Cocker*.
LONGCROSS INTACK (6″). Cf. *Longcross head* 1809 *EnclA*. LUSTY
CLOSE is *Lucye Close*, *Lusye Close* 1590 *Cocker*, *Lucy Close* n.d.
Whellan. OUTFIELD PLANTATION (6″) is named from *the outfeild* 1652
Cocker. PARK HILL (6″) is so named in 1794 (H). Cf. *the parke* 1689
Cocker. RAISE (6″) is an isolated hill, *v*. hreysi. RYE COTTAGE (6″).
Cf. *Rye Close* 1809 *EnclA*. SHAWBANK BROW (6″). Cf. *Shaw Banks*
ib. SMITHYBANKS WOOD (6″). Cf. *Smithy* 1658 *Cocker*, *Smiddy Banks*
1809 *EnclA*. NEAR and FAR STOCKBECK (6″). Cf. *Stockbeck Close* 1689
Cocker. TOOT WELL (6″) is so named in 1809 (*EnclA*). WHITEKELD
is so named in 1633 (*Cocker*). 'White kelda.' WOODHALL BROW (6″)
is (*del*) *Wodhall* 1332 SR, *Wodhall* 1399 IpmR. *v*. wudu, h(e)all.
WOODSIDE is so named in 1809 (*EnclA*). WRIGHT GREEN (6″) is so
named in 1776 (PR, Lamplugh).

FIELD-NAMES

(*a*) In 1809 (*EnclA*) Arnowhill (*Arney-Close* 1660 *Cocker*), Askew (*Ascoe*
1684 ib.), Bainwash, Baldreading (*v*. hryding), Baxonwath hill ('bakestone
vað'), Bear lisle, Bleaze, Blind Keld ('hidden spring,' *v*. kelda), Borrans (and
Burrangarth) (*v*. burghan), Bow Thorn, Brandy Butts, Burbury Dale, Bur-
tree Butts (i.e. 'elder-tree'), Cockfitt (*v*. fit), Cold Keld (*v*. kelda), Colin
Croft (cf. possibly Thomas *Collan* 1332 SR and John *Collan* 1338 Cl, the
holder of land in Ullock), Cring Ing (*v*. eng), Cringlemer Meadow (*v*.
kringla), Day Thorn, Dohiver (*Doughiver* 1689 *Cocker*), Dubberton Meadow,

Espgarth ('aspen garðr'), High and Low Fleck, Four Nooked Close, Gale
Moss (*Gale Mosse* 1689 *Cocker*, probably from OE *gagel*, 'bog-myrtle'),
Gammer, Gazum (*Gazam Meadow* 1693 *Cocker*), Grandy Close, Greystone
or Cootlass bottom, Guards (cf. Gilbert *del Garth* 1355 *Ass. v.* garðr), Gully
Slack (*v.* slakki), Hannah Close, Harnings, Harrow, Hemplin, Honey Pot,
Hunger Hill (*v. infra* Fan), How Rudding (*v.* hryding), Intack (*v.* intak),
Kellbarrow (*Keldbarrow* 1652 *Cocker. v.* be(o)rg), Kirkthwaite meadows,
Lamberiux, Lamps Close, Landrew, Lickbank, Likewilling, Mains (*v.* mains),
Mean bit (probably from (ge)mǣne), Middlescugh Meadow, Middlesboro',
Mill Fitts (*v.* fit), Moping Butts, Morrison Yoaking (*v.* yoking), Mother
Brows, Moudy Butts, Mowdrop, Muedale, Murrans, Murway (*Murweray*
1689 *Cocker*), Neulags, Norman Close, Noutgill, Nutay (*Newtay* 1720
Cocker), Ottergill, Out Mains (*v.* mains), Plaskettfield (*v.* plasket), Poak,
Pudding How, Rainbow, Rattanlands (possibly 'rat lands,' cf. *supra* 98),
Ringrime, Roangrune, Rudding (*v.* hryding), Scallows, Scroggs (*v.* scrogg),
Selace, Shurma, Slamperon, Spittle Croft (i.e. 'hospital'), Spout Close (*v.*
spoute), Street (cf. *Streetgate* 1689 *Cocker*), Studfold Plantation (*v.* stōdfald),
Teas, Thistlewra (*v.* (v)rá), Tinsley, Toms Daywork (*v.* daywork), Trenell
Hill, Underraise (*v.* hreysi), Whatelands, White Wall, Wrea (*ye Wray* 1719
Cocker, v. (v)rá).

(*b*) In 1695 (*Cocker*) Huran, Saydale Rigg, *West raine firth* (*v.* rein,
fyrhþ(e)); in 1652 (*Cocker*) Roger Raynes (*v.* rein), *Salmon dayles*; in 1777
(*Hudleston*) Eminoth, Emmy Hole, Flaskey. Under each of the following
dates there is one field-name: *Banakrow* 1797 PR (Lamplugh), *Cozenhow Beck*
n.d. Whellan, *Dulbarofyld* 1473 *Cocker*, *Jaythorne* 1689 ib., *Waldeylond*
(*Waldethland*) 1338 Cl (probably 'Waltheof's land'), *Went puddle ends* 1690
Cocker (from dial. went, 'path, passage'), *Whynnymore* 1590 FF ('whin
covered mōr'), *Woodyat-green* 1612 PR (Lamplugh).

18. Above Derwent

ABOVE DERWENT. Cf. *Beyond Darwent* 1612, 1616 PR (Crosth).

BIRKRIGG is *Birkeryg'* 1293 *MinAcct*, *Byrkayryg* 1564 PR (Crosth),
Brikrig 1579 ib. 'Birch-tree ridge,' *v.* birki, hryggr (under hrycg).

BRAITHWAITE

Braithait c. 1160 Fountains, *Braythwayt(e)* 1230 Scotland *et
passim*, with variant spellings *Brai-* and -*thwait(e)*, -*thweit*,
-*twhayt*, *Braythethwayt* 1286 *Ass*, Great, Mikkel, Lytyll *Bray-
twha(i)t* 1563, 1566, 1569 PR (Crosth)
Bratheweit t. John Fountains, *Brathweyt* 1284 *Ass*, *Bratwheyt* 1292
ib., *Brathwaite* 1595 FF, *Bratwhaite* 1600 PR (Crosth)
Brayquat 1323 Cl
Brethwayte in Derwent felles 1570 *ExchKR*

BRAITHWAITE HOW (6″) is *Braythwatehowe* 1507 *Cocker. v.* haugr.
BRAITHWAITE MOSS (6″) is *Brathwate mosse* 1578 ib. In the neighbour-
hood was also *Braythwatebek* 1507 *Cocker, Brethwaytebeck* 1570
ExchKR.
'Broad, or wide, clearing,' *v.* breiðr, þveit.

HIGH and LOW COLEDALE are *Coldale* 1260 *Rental et freq* to 1578
Cocker, Colledale 1339 *GDR, Cowdall* 1569, 1670 *PR, Cowdale* 1689
DKR xli. The form from 1339 suggests that in spite of earlier forms
without a medial vowel, this may contain a personal name. If so, the
early and very common ON *Kolli* seems the most probable. The
second element is dalr.

COPPERHEAP BAY (6″), *v.* Introduction.

DERWENT FELLS is *Derwentfelles* 1256 FF, *Darwentfell* 1578 *Cocker,*
Dawenfells 1616 PR (Crosth). 'Fells above Derwent Water,' *v.* fell,
and *supra* 33.

FAWEPARK is (*ate*) *fal* 1260 *Rental* (p), *la Falle* 1278 *MinAcct* (p),
Falpark 1369 Ipm, *Fawe parke* 1578 *Cocker, Foe-park* 1784 West.
The position of Fawepark between Swinside and Derwent Water
suggests that the name contains *fall* in the sense 'slope' or 'declivity'
(*v.* NED *s.v. fall* sb.[1], 8). Professor Ekwall suggests, however, *fall,*
'forest clearing', an element well-evidenced in Lancashire (PN La 10).

GOLDSCOPE MINE is *Gottesgab* 1569 ElizKes, *Golld-scalp* 1741 PR
(Crosth), *Goldscope, or rather I would call it Gold-Scalp* 1789 Clarke,
Goldscalp 1816 Lysons. "The Germans (i.e. German miners) called
this rich new coppermine '*Gottesgab,*' '*Gotzgab*'—God's gift" (Eliz-
Kes 10).[1]

GUTHERSCALE is *Goderyscales* 1293 *MinAcct, Goderikeschales* 1318
ib., *Gutterskell* 1573 PR (Crosth), *Gudderscille* 1601 ib. 'Gōdrīc's
shieling(s),' *v.* skáli and cf. Gutterby *infra* 380, 448.

How is probably (*del*) *hou, la howe* 1292 *Ass* (p), *Le Howe* 1399 IpmR,
Howe 1564 PR (Crosth). HOWEND PLANTATION (6″) is named from
howend 1507 *Cocker. v.* haugr, 'hill.'

KESKADALE is *Keskeldale* 1260 *Rental,* 1268 *MinAcct,* 1339 *GDR,*
Ketelschaledal 1268 *MinAcct, Schescheldale* 1278 ib., *Keskedale* 1369
Ipm. 'Valley by *Ketil*'s shieling,' *v.* dalr, skáli.

[1] Other mines in the neighbourhood mentioned by Robinson (1709) were *Long*
Work, and *St Thomas' Work.*

LONG BRIDGE (6″) is *Langebrigge* 1287 Cl.

NEWLANDS is *Neulandes* 1318 *MinAcct*, *Neweland* 1369 Ipm, *Noulandes* 1370 ib. 'Land newly taken into cultivation.'

PORTINSCALE is *Porqeneschal* c. 1160 Fountains, *Portewinscales* c. 1265 ib., *Portewynscales* 1285 *For* (p), *Porwinescall* 1278 *Ass*, *Portanskale* 1399 IpmR, *Portenscales* 1543 *MinAcct*, *Portinskaille* 1568 PR (Crosth). This is a compound of OE *portcwene*, 'townwoman, harlot,' and skáli, 'shieling.'

REVELIN MOSS (6″) is *Reavolinge mosse* 16th CW xiv. This contains the word *riveling*, 'rivulet,' found in Rivelin (WRY) and Tackriveling (PN NRY 7). See also RN 343.

ROGERSIDE (lost) is *Rogersat(e)* 1260 *Rental et freq* to 1369 Ipm, *Rogeressete, Rogereshat* 1278 *MinAcct*, *Rogersette* 1293 ib., *Rogersett* 1505 *Cocker*, *Rogersyd* 1563 PR (Crosth), *Rogerside* 1616 ib., *Rogersett Pike* 1805 *Brayton*. '*Roger*'s sætr or hill pasture.'

ST HERBERT'S ISLAND is *island of Herbertholm* 1343 Cl, *insulam Herberti* 1374 NB, *S. Herebertes isle* c. 1540 Leland, *Sancte Harbartes, Insula voc. Sancte Harbart Isle* 1560 *Cocker*. This is the island in which *Hereberht*, the friend of St Cuthbert, lived the life of a hermit in the 7th century (Bede, *Historia Ecclesiastica* iv, 28). The addition of the Scandinavian holmr, in the precise sense of 'island', to St Herbert's name is remarkable. *v. supra* Derwent Water 33.

SKELGILL is *Scalegayl* 1260 *Rental*, 1290 *MinAcct*, *Scalgeyl* 1278 ib., *Scalgill in Derewentfell* 1334 Ipm, 1338 *Fine*, *Scalgill in the town of Braythwait* 1338 Cl, *Scagill in Derwentefell* 1363 Ipm, *Skellgell* 1564 PR (Crosth). 'Narrow ravine with a shieling,' *v.* skáli, geil.

SWITHENTHATE (lost) is *Swithenthate* 1578 *Cocker*. The second element is þveit. The first is ON *sviðinn*, 'land cleared by burning,' found several times in the North Riding of Yorkshire (PN NRY 330). It has given rise also to Sweden (We), 1275 *le Swythene*.

THORNTHWAITE [θɔ·nθɔt]

> *Thorn(e)thwayt, -thweyt, -thwait* 1230 Scotland *et passim*, (*in Derewentefelles*) 1275 FF, (*in the Fells*) 1515 ECP, *Thornthat* 1605 PR (Crosth)
> *Thornewaith in the fells* 1543 RichWills
> *Thornythwaite beyond Keswicke* 1623 PR (Greystoke)
> 'Thorn clearing,' *v.* þveit.

UZZICAR

Huseker c. 1160, c. 1270 Fountains
Husaker c. 1160 Fountains, *Husacre* 1231 FF *et freq* to 1578 *Cocker*,
with variant spellings *-aker, -akre*
Hosakre 1283 *MinAcct* (p)
Usakredale 1369 Ipm, *Usaker* 1563 PR (Crosth), *Usayker(e)* 1566,
1567 ib., *Usseker* 1600 ib.
Hussaker 1565 PR (Crosth)

Apparently a compound of OE hūs, 'house,' and æcer, which here
may have the general sense of tillage or cultivated land. The name
probably arose to denote a patch of cultivation adjacent to an isolated
farmstead.

AIKIN HO is *Haykin* 1569 PR (Crosth), *Aykinge* 1576 ib., *Akone* 1587
ib., *Akine* 1591 ib., *Akinge* 1593 ib., *Ekine in Newlands* 1606 ib., *Akin*
1620 ib. The forms are too late for interpretation. BARF is *Barrugh*
Fells 1821 G. *v.* be(o)rg. BAWD HALL is *Boodhole* 1575 PR (Crosth),
Bodehole 1578 *Cocker*, *Boadholle* 1632 PR (Crosth). Cf. Boadhole
infra 418. BECKSIDE (6″) is *Beckside* 1578 *Cocker*, (*in Thornetwhaite*)
1668 PR (Crosth). BECKSTONES is so named in 1574 ib. Probably
'place where bakestones are found,' *v.* bakstān. BLACK CRAG is *Black*
cragge 1569 ElizKes. BRANDELHOW is *Brandelaw, Brandelow* 1569
ElizKes, 1573 PR (Crosth), *Brandell Howe* 1615 ib. Cf. *Brandelholme*
1574 ElizKes, *Brandle* 1578 *Cocker*. BRANDELHOW PARK is *Branley*
Park 1787 ClarkeM. CALFCLOSE WOOD (6″). Cf. *Calfe close* 1578
Cocker. CAT BELLS is *Catbels* 1794 H. CAUSEY PIKE is *Cawsey-pike*
1784 West, *Causey Pike* 1794 H. Cf. *Causey* 1546 NB, *the Cowsey*
1578 *Cocker*. THE CROFT (6″) is *the Crofte* ib. DALE BOTTOM (6″)
is *Daylbothom* 1565 PR (Crosth), *Daleboddome* 1579 ib. *v.* botm.
DERWENT BAY is *Derwentwater Bay* 1811 ib. DERWENT HILL (6″) is
so named ib. ELLAS CRAG (6″). Cf. *Elis closse* 16th CW xiv. GILL
(6″) is so named in 1573 (PR, Crosth). *v.* gil. GILL BANK is *Gylbanke*
1564 ib. GILLBROW is *gilbrowe* 1578 *Cocker*. GRAY STONES (6″). Cf.
Grastone Hill 1597 PR (Crosth). GREENAH HILL (6″). Cf. *Grenhowe*
1574 ElizKes, *greene howe* 1578 *Cocker*. *v.* haugr. HALLGARTH (6″)
is so named in 1739 (*Derwent*). HAWSE END is *Hausend* 1567 PR
(Crosth), *Hosend* 1649 ib. *v.* hals. HIGHGATE (6″). Cf. *Higgatt end*
medowe 1578 *Cocker*. HOLLINS (6″) is *Hollinge* 1577 PR (Crosth),
Hollings 1739 *Derwent*. *v.* holegn. JENKIN HILL (6″) is *Genkin-hill*
in Thorntwhate 1646 PR (Crosth), *Jenkin Hill* 1648 ib. KING'S WOOD

(6″) is *Kyngeswood* 1570 *ExchKR*. LADSTOCK WOOD (6″) is named from *ladstocke* 1686 *Derwent*, *Lanstockside*, *Landstock Grasses* 1739 ib. LANEFOOT is *Lane-foot* 1731 PR (Crosth). LINGHOLME is *Ling Holm* 1787 ClarkeM. 'holmr covered with ling,' holmr having here the sense 'islet.' LITTLE DALE (6″) is *Liteldale* 1332 SR (p), *Litledell* 1573 PR (Crosth). 'Little dalr.' LITTLE TOWN is *Litleton* 1578 *Cocker*, *Litletowne* 1595 PR (Crosth). LOW HO (6″) is *Lawehouse* 1599 ib., *Lowhouse* 1739 *Derwent*. HIGH MOSS. Cf. *the Mosse* 1570 *ExchKR*. OTTERBIELD BAY (6″). Cf. *Otterbeth*, *Otterbetts close* 1578 *Cocker*, *Otterballstones* 1629 *Derwent*. OTTER ISLAND (6″) is so named in 1787 (ClarkeM). OVERSIDE WOOD (6″). Cf. *Overside* 1578 *Cocker*. PAN HOLES (6″) may be *Penhaus* 1573 ElizKes. POW HO (6″) is named from *Poe in Portinskell* 1669 PR (Crosth), *the Powe* 1673 ib. The poll is Pow Beck. POW HOW (6″) is so named in 1578 (*Cocker*) and is near Pow Ho. Cf. also *Powegarthe* ib. POWTER HOWE (6″) is *Puther howe* 1577 PR (Crosth), *Powther howe* 1578 ib., *Powter Howe* 1581 ib. ROODLANDS (6″) is *Roode lande* 1578 *Cocker*. ROSETREES (6″) is so named ib. ROWLING END is so named in 1784 (West). SILVER HILL (6″) is so named in 1797 (PR, Crosth). HIGH and LOW SNAB are (*le*) *Snabb* 1503, 1505 *Cocker*, *Farrsnabb* 1570 PR (Crosth), *Lawsnabb* 1573 ib., *Hyesnabb* 1589 ib. This is a nose-like hill. *v.* snabbi. STAIR is *Stayre* 1565 ib., *Stare* 1566 ib. Presumably so called from the rise in the road here. STILE END is *Steelend* 1573 ib., *Stealehend* 1577 ib. *v.* stigel. STONYCROFT is *Stanycroft* 1505 *Cocker*, *Stonicrofte* 1563 PR (Crosth). SWINSIDE is *le Swynesyde* 1507 *Cocker*, *Swynsyd* 1564 PR (Crosth). THWAITEHILL (6″) is *Thwatehill* 1578 *Cocker*. *v.* þveit. ULLOCK may be *Uloke* 1564 PR (Crosth). ULLOCK MOSS (6″) is *Illuck* (sic) *Mosse* 1570 *ExchKR*, *Ullocke Mosse* 1663 *Terrier*. Cf. *Ullaikmire* 1304 Ipm. *v.* mýrr. This is identical in meaning with Ullock *supra* 367. VICTORIA BAY is *Mutton Pye Bay* 1787 ClarkeM. WINDYHILL WOOD (6″) is named from *Wyndhyll*, *Wyndell* 1570 *ExchKR*, *the Wynehills*, *Wyndhills* 1578 *Cocker*. WOODEND (6″) is *Woodend* 1564 PR (Crosth), (*in Thornetwhaite*) 1613 ib.

FIELD-NAMES[1]

(b) In 1787 (ClarkeM) *Fold* (id. 1647 PR), *Foul Sike or Ew Tree* (*Foul Syke* 1739 *Derwent*. *v.* fūl, sīc and cf. also *the Ewe* 1605 PR), *Trippett Holm*, *Walker Gate* (id. 1739 *Derwent*), *Woad holes*[2] (probably *wad* (*v.* NED *s.v.*

---

[1] PR is Crosthwaite Parish Register.
[2] There is a Wad Mine just across the upper Derwent from Seathwaite in Borrowdale (*supra* 351).

wad sb.[3]), 'black lead, plumbago'); in 1739 (Derwent) *Borenskill* (also *Borrowskill*) (*v.* burghan), *Bowe, Broading* (*broade Inge* 1578 *Cocker. v.* eng), *Slacke Brea* (*Slackbraye* 1669 PR. *Brea* probably represents ON *brá* 'eyelid', Scots *brae*. For Slack, *v.* slakki); in 1714 (PR) *Wreckey* (*Wirckay* 1681 ib.); in 1703 (PR) *Coatsike* (id. 1642 ib. *v.* sic); in 1697 (PR) *Mousefald* (*Mousefeild* 1582 ib.); in 1695 (PR) *Millhowe* (*Mylnhowe* 1565 ib. *v.* haugr), *Scorans* (*Skoryngs* 1565 ib.); in 1687 (PR) *Highleyes* (*Hee Lees* 1574 ib.); in 1682 (Derwent) *Chapwell, Hiathfeilds* (probably 'heath fields'); in 1680 (PR) *Bowtbie* (*Bowtbybrowe* 1654 ib. Cf. *Boughtlieh* 1578 *Cocker*); in 1672 (PR) *Laythehowe* (*Leathowe* 1634 ib. *v.* hlaða, haugr); in 1670 (PR) *Parkside* (*Parkesyd* 1565 ib.); in 1664 (PR) *Frankhisshow* (*Frankeshowe* 1570 ExchKR. *v.* haugr); in 1647 (PR) *Howhill* (id. 1614 ib.); in 1643 (PR) *Hye Rawe* (*Hee Rawe* 1577 ib. *v.* rāw); in 1636 (PR) *Knipeshow* (*Knipthowe* 1600 ib. *v.* haugr); in 1630 (PR) *Readscare* (*Reedskarr* 1592 ib.); in 1615 (PR) *the Church Stile* (*Kirksteyll* 1565 ib. *v.* stigel); in 1614 (PR) *Todcrage* (id. 1577 ib., 'fox crag'); in 1602 (PR) *Howgraue* (id. 1574 ib.); in 1600 (PR) *Pyetnest* (*Pyatnese* 1564 ib., i.e. 'magpie'), *Scaldhowe* (*v. supra* 318), *Skinnerscell* (*Kynnerskell* 1565 ib., *Skennerskell* 1568 ib.); in 1595 (PR) *Haueksyd* (*Hauksyd* 1562 ib. 'Hawk slope,' *v.* side); in 1585 (PR) *Ratton Rawe* (*Rattanrow* 1564 ib. *v. supra* 98); in 1578 (Cocker) *the Allands* (*v.* allan), *Askhill, Bitts, Brake, Brathmyre* (*Braithemyre* 1369 Ipm. *v.* ON breiðr, mýrr), *the butts, Byld frith* (*v.* bield, fyrhþ(e)), *the Claredubbs, Coteacre, Crooke of the beck* (cf. Crook of Ellen *supra* 274), *Ellergill* (*v.* elri, gil), *Eveninge browe, farshyerers, Fyshe Shuttle* (*v.* NED *s.v.* shuttle sb.[3] 1. 'Flood gate'), *gale common* (probably OE *gagel*, 'bog-myrtle'), *gangh, gard rigge* (*v.* garðr), *the goote hill, grise garth* (*v.* gríss, garðr), *gruske, gubbrigge, guddholme* (cf. *Godbrigholm* c. 1280 Fountains, possibly '*Gūðbeorht*'s holmr'), *Hawtherud Inge* (*v.* eng), *hennings* (*v.* haining), *Hexam close, Hivinge stye, Hockiner Ridding* (*v.* hryding), *huthwate* (*v.* þveit), *Knowes* (*v.* cnoll), *Langthuate* (id. 1503 *Cocker*. 'Long þveit'), *the lath* (cf. Adam de *Lathes* 1260 *Rental* and *v.* hlaða), *Lendingefielde, Leyate, Low myre* (*v.* mýrr), *overthwartlands* ('upper crosswise lands'), *paycock, pompehole, Raselandes* (probably from hreysi), *reddinges* (*v.* hryding), *rokreden, Salt seller, Seavyend* ('sedgy end,' *v.* sef), *Segdale, Shailehow* (*v.* haugr), *Sinkinge Cragg, Skarlone* (presumably 'gap lane,' *v.* skarð, lonning), *Slaipestange* (probably 'slippery stọng,' from OE slǣp), *Stange crofte, Tallowe fielde, Thaw Inge* (*v.* eng), *Thwate* (*v.* þveit), *Tuppendon, Utin Close, Womphowe* (*v.* haugr); in 1574 (ElizKes) *Cackhawe, Jandar ent* ('yonder end'), *Parsonthwait* (*v.* þveit); in 1571 (ElizKes) *Breckhowrigge* (*v.* hryggr, under hrycg), *Rigges* (*Riggs* 1503 *Cocker. v.* hrycg), *Satertwaith* ('clearing by a sætr,' *v.* þveit. Identical with Satterthwaite (PN La 219)); in c. 1520 (ECP) *Fishgarthede* (*Fisgardheued* c. 1200, c. 1270 Fountains. 'Head of the fish garth,' *v. supra* 79); in 16th (CW xiv) *Geavyd close, Hawkriggsike, the mosse dubbe* (*v.* dub), *Rysphowe* ('sedgy hill,' from risp, 'sedge' and haugr); in 1503 (Cocker) *Waterok, Withmyr* (*v.* wiðig, mýrr); in c. 1270 (Fountains) *Pikerig* (id. t. John ib.). Under each of the following dates there is one field-name: *Apleyte* 1706 PR, *Arklobe* 1606 ib., *Armatrigg* 1771 ib. (possibly 'hermit hrycg'), *Barron Moss* 1569 ElizKes, *Birkhead Knot* 1589 PR (*v.* birki), *Byrkness* 1473 *Cocker* ('birch tree headland,' *v.* birki, nes),

Brodhowe 1571 PR (*v.* haugr), *Dallathorne* 1565 ib., *Kaugart* 1568 ElizKes, *Loaneing foote* 1671 *Derwent* (*v.* lonning), *Loftskales* 1369 Ipm ('shielings with an upper story,' *v.* ON lopt, skáli, and cf. *infra* 416), *Moshows* 1331 *Work* (*v.* mos, haugr), *Starebridge* 1646 PR ('sedge,' *v.* star), *Swynethwayte* 1570 *ExchKR* ('pig clearing,' *v.* þveit).

19. Distington

DISTINGTON [disiŋtən, disəntən]

> *Distingtona* a. 1230 *HolmC, Distington, Distyngton* 1256 FF *et passim, Distinton* 1256 FF, 1292 *Ass, Distincton* 1294 Cl, c. 1305 StB, *Distynton'* 1342 FF
> *Dustinton* c. 1230, 1295 StB, *Dustyngton* 1291 Tax, *Dustincton'* 1292 *Ass* (p)
> *Drisington* 1291 Tax
> *Dissington* 1671 Fleming, 1761 *Work*, 1797 PR (Skelton)

No satisfactory explanation of this name can be offered. The forms suggest very strongly that the name is an OE compound ending in -ingtūn, and the series, as a whole, is definitely against the suggestion (DEPN) that the first element may be an OE adjective *dysten, 'dusty.' All that can at present be said is that the name is a survival from the Old Anglian nomenclature of the north-west, and that its original form appears to have been *Dystingtūn*.

FEATHER KNOTT (6″) is *Frotheu* a. 1230, a. 1246 *HolmC, Frotheouflatte* a. 1246 ib., *Frothou* 1292 *Ass* (p), *Frodhou* 1321 Ipm, *Froichou otherwyse callyd Frostyknotte* 15th *HolmC, Frothowe* p. 1500 StB. So far as can be seen, the first element here is the ON personal name *Fróði*. The second is certainly haugr. The eccentric form *Froichou* comes from a late and ill-written note on the fly-leaf of the Carlisle copy of the Holm Cultram cartulary.

GILGARRAN is *Gillegarran* a. 1230 *HolmC, Gilgerra* 1292 *Ass, Gilgarran* 1321, 1334, 1348 Ipm, *Gilgaran* 1338 Cl, *Gylgaron* 15th *HolmC, Gilgarren* 1503 *Cocker, Gilgarron Bek* n.d. Whellan. As noted by Ekwall (ScandCelts 25) this is probably an inversion compound (Introduction) with gil as the first element. The second may be Gael *gearrán*, 'gelding,' used as a nickname. If so, '*Gearrán*'s ravine.' The medieval use of Garran as a surname in Cumberland is shown by the names of David and Robert *Garran*, villeins in Beckermet in 1294 (Cl).

SPRING HILL may perhaps, as suggested in StB (101, n. 3), be associated with *le Keldlandes, le Keldland, le Keldhows* (c. 1270–1392 StB). But the whole land is full of springs; cf. KELMORE HILL to the north in the same parish, with springs close at hand, doubtless a compound of kelda and mōr. The note referred to above under Feather Knott mentions a place-name relating to this district which is hard to decipher, but apparently reads *Becynkeld heid*. It may be a compound of OE *bē(a)cn*, 'beacon,' kelda and hēafod.

STUBSGILL is *Stubscales* c. 1210 StB, 1321, 1348 Ipm, 1544 *MinAcct*, 1595 FF, *Stubskailes* 1338 Cl, *Stubscale* 1542 *MinAcct*, *Stubskill* 1743 *LowtherW*. 'Stub shielings,' from stubb and the plural of skáli. The vowel in the second element has been fronted, shortened and raised, thus leading to re-formation, as though from gil. The same change has taken place in Gaitsgill *supra* 133.

STUDFOLD is *Stodefald'* a. 1230 *HolmC*. *v.* stōdf(e)ald.

WHINBANK (6″) is *Quinebank, Quenbank'* 1292 *Ass* (p), *Whinbank* 1743 *LowtherW*. 'Gorse bank,' *v.* whin.

BARFS (6″). Cf. *Little Baurgh* 1737 *LowtherW* and *supra* 372. *v.* be(o)rg. BARNGILL and BOTTOM BANK (both 6″) are so named in 1743 ib. CASTLE MILL and CASTLERIGG (both 6″). Cf. *Distington...cum castro ibidem* 1392 IpmR. The latter is *Castlerigg* 1743 *LowtherW*. *v.* hrycg. DYAN HALL (6″). Probably ODan *dyande*, 'marsh.' Cf. Dian Ho *supra* 140. HAYES CASTLE is *Hay Castle* 1610 Camden, *Hayes Castle* 1777 NB. HIGH HO is so named in 1697 (CW xv). HINNINGS is so named in 1774 (*LowtherW*). *v.* haining. STONE-FIELD GATE (6″) is *Stonefoldgate* 1743 ib. WEST CROFT. Cf. *West Crofthead* ib.

FIELD-NAMES

(b) In 1774 (*LowtherW*) *Blackett tree* (*Blackatrey* 1758 ib., cf. *Blackett Mire* 1743 ib.); in 1743 (*LowtherW*) *Above Wood, Courtfoot, Law*; in 1338 (Cl) *le Milnstangrene, le Millenstongrove* (OE *mylenstān* seems to mean 'grindstone' (cf. also *mylenscearp*)); in p. 1500 (StB) *Inveregh*.

DRIGG

20. Drigg and Carleton

Dreg 1175–99 *DuLa*, c. 1180 StB *et freq* to 1363 Ipm, *Dreg in Coupland* c. 1290 StB, *Drege otherwise Dregge* 1557 *Netherhall Dregg(e)* 1279 *Ass et freq* to 1514 BM, *le Dregg* 1279 *Ass Drigg* 1572 FF, *Drigge al. Dregge* 1579 ib.

DRIGG CROSS. Cf. *Drigg crosse feilde* 1578 *Cocker*. DRIGG HOLME (6") is *Drige holme* ib. In the parish was *la Sale de Dreg'* 1292 *Ass* (p) and *Dreglowe more* 1578 *Cocker*. *v.* hlāw, mōr.

In the first edition of DEPN, Ekwall suggested that this name represents an OScand **dregi*, the dative case, with mutated vowel, of ON *drag*, 'portage.' The latter word may occur in *dragg myre infra* 393. In view of the situation of Drigg, it is not unreasonable to assume the existence of a portage between the sea and the river Irt at this point. In the Addenda to the second edition of DEPN, Ekwall quotes a Swedish place-name, Dräg, which apparently stands for a mutated nominative *drægh*, identical in meaning with *drag*, which would give a simple explanation of the Cumberland name. Derivation from ME *dreg*, 'filth,' though possible (cf. Adel (WRY) and Mixon (St)), is less likely, for at present no other example of this word has been found in place-names.

BARN SCAR is *Barnesker* 1338 Cl. To judge from the solitary form, this name means '*Barni*'s sker.' The *sker* is a reef off the coast west of Drigg.

CARLETON (6")

> *Karlton* c. 1240 Furness, *Karelton'* 1279 *Ass* (p), *Carleton* 1334 Ipm *et passim*

CARLETON HALL is *Carlton hall* 1578 *Cocker*. HALL CARLETON is so named in 1733 (CW x). For the order of the elements, cf. *infra* 417. *v.* karlatún and cf. *supra* 148, 340. NB (ii, 25) renders this *villa rusticorum*, 'a town of husbandmen.'

STONY HOW is *Stanihous* (sic) c. 1280 StB. The first element is OE *stānig*, 'stony,' the second probably ON haugr.

WHITRIGGS and WRAY HEAD (6") may be recorded in the names of Richard de *Whitrig* (1338 Cl) and William *del Wra* (ib.). *v.* hrycg, (v)rá.

BELLHILL is *Belhill* 1658 CW xiv, *Bell Hill* 1777 ib. xv. BRIDGESTONES (6") is *Brigston* 1806 PR (Gosforth). CARL CRAG is so named in 1842 (AllerA). CUMBLANDS is *Cumerlandes* 1578 *Cocker*, *Cumlands* 1799 CW xiv. GRUNDY CROFT is *Groundy Croft* 1774 Donald, *Grundy Croft* 1821 G. HOLMROOK is *Holmronk* (sic) 1332 SR (p), *Holmcrooke* 1569 FF, *Holmrook* 1647 CW x. If the *c* is correct, the second element is krókr, 'bend.' Holmrook lies by a bend in the Irt. *v.* holmr.

MAUDSIKE (6″) is *molde sike, malde sike* 1578 *Cocker*. Probably '*Maud*'s sīc,' from a ME form of OFr *Mahaut*, such as *Mald* or *Mold*. MIRE-SIDE may be *Myre side* ib. *v.* mýrr. MITEBANK is so named in 1754 (CW xiv). *v.* Mite R. *supra* 22. PANOPE is said by Parker (38) to have been named after a ship, presumably a ship with a sea-nymph for figure-head; cf. Lycidas 99, "sleek Panope with all her sisters play'd." SALTCOATS is so named in 1657 (CW xiv). Cf. Salt Cotes *supra* 292, and *Saltcotecroft* 1578 *Cocker* and *supra* 147. STONE ACRES WOOD (6″) is named from *the Stone acre* ib. THORNFLAT is *Thornflatt* 1656 CW (OS) vi.

FIELD-NAMES

(a) Far and Near Oxey, Scubbra, Slemming Mire (*v.* mýrr), Threapland Gate ('land in dispute,' *v.* þrēap-. This lies on the parish boundary).

(b) In 1578 (*Cocker*) *the bell mosse, Hugga Well, little morehooke, Oxnamsike* (*v.* sīc), *Powle acre, little Slake banck* (*v.* slakki), *Skugh* (*v.* skógr), *Tubman-howe green closse, White howe* (*v.* haugr); in 1338 (Cl) *Brockholmbank* (*Brokyl-banks* t. Ed 3 (t. Eliz) *Cocker*), *Hirthgarth* (this was a salmon garth on the estuary of the Irt (*supra* 17)), *Segarth in Barnesker* (this was a fish-garth off Barn Scar (*supra*)). Under each of the following dates there is one field-name: *Quinhou* c. 1235 StB ('whin hill,' *v.* whin, haugr), *Sandlandis* c. 1250 ib.

EAGLESFIELD

21. Eaglesfield[1]

Eglesfeld c. 1170 StB *et freq* to 1357 FF, with variant spelling -*feud*,
    Egglesfeld 1333 Cl, *Egglesfeild* 1586 FF
Eglisfeld 1277 *Ass*, 1292 QW, *Eglisfild* 1312 *Lowther*, *Eglysfeld* 1560
    FF
Egelesfeld a. 1290 *Netherhall* (p), *Hegelisfild* 1373 ib. (p)
Eggesfeld' early 14th StMaryY
Eklesfeld 1489 Pat
Egglishfeild 1659 CantW viii

'*Ecgel*'s open land,' *v.* feld. The personal name *Ecgel*, suggested by these forms, is not found in independent use, but is a normal diminu-tive of compound names such as *Ecglaf*, or *Ecgwulf*. Cf. Egglestone (PN NRY 301).

CUMELKELDFOT (lost) is *Cumelkeldfot* c. 1200 StBA. *v.* kelda, fot. *Cumel* may represent ON *kumbl, kuml*, 'grave mound' or 'cairn,' recorded in the dative plural (*i Kumblum*) as a place-name in Norway.

---

[1] Added to Dean (*supra* 366) in 1934.

MOORLAND CLOSE is *Mourland* 1332 SR (p), *Moorland Close* 1749 CW (OS) iv. *v.* mōr, land.

SNECKYEAT PLANTATION (6") contains the northern dialectal *sneck*, 'latch' and *yeat* from OE geat, 'gate.' SNECKGATE (6") in Gosforth probably has the same meaning.

SOUTHWAITE[1] and SOUTHWAITE MILL are *molendinum de Sowewad* 1308 Greenfield iii, *molend. de Sowthudytt* 1527 *Netherhall, Southwayte* 1543 *MinAcct, Southwath Mylne* 1570 *ExchKR. v.* vað. There is still a ford by the Mill. The first element is uncertain. In view of the form of 1308 it cannot be 'south.' It is not impossibly ON *sauðr*, 'sheep,' which occurs in *sautheberch infra* in this parish.

FIELD-NAMES

(*b*) In a. 1290 (*Netherhall*) *Wodecoclandes* ('woodcock lands,' from OE *wuducocc*); in c. 1265 (StB) *Kyrkecroft* (cf. *Kyrketoft* c. 1225 ib. *v.* kirkja), *Scortgayle* (cf. (*del*) *gail* c. 1230 Hesley. 'Short geil'); in c. 1225 (StB) *Capherou, Lastrikhouhe, Milnbek* (*v.* myln, bekkr), (*sub*) *Ulfel* (presumably 'wolf fiall'); in c. 1200 (*Hesley*) *berkelund* ('birch grove,' *v.* birki, lundr), *duwelangside, sautheberch* (probably 'sheep hill,' from ON *sauðr*, 'sheep' and be(o)rg), *Westwra* ('west (v)rá'); in c. 1200 (St BA) *Hwitestan* ('white stone'), *Normanneskoende* (sic print).

22. Egremont

EGREMONT, occasionally [egə·məθ, egə·mət]

  Egremont c. 1125 StB, c. 1180 *Hesley et passim*
  Echermund c. 1130 StB, *Egermund* c. 1205 CW (OS) i, facs. *et freq*
    to 1327 Ipm, *Egermond* 1294 Cl, *Egermount* 1338 StB
  Egremunt c. 1135 (early copy) *Lowther et freq* to 1281 FF, *Egremund*
    c. 1160 StB *et freq* to 1317 Misc, *Egrèmond* 1231 FF, 1291 Tax,
    1428 FA, *Egremound(e)* 1278 *Ass*, c. 1310 BM
  Agremunt c. 1165 StB, *Agremonde* 1537 CW (OS) xiv
  burgenses de Acrimonte c. 1200 CW (OS) i, facs.
  Eggermuth 1260 Cl
  Egyrmunde 1278 StB, *Egirmond* 1363 Ipm, *Egirmound* 1386 Pat

EGREMONT BRIDGE (6"). The names of Robert de *Ponte* (1279 *Ass*), Roger de *Ponte* (1322 Cl) and Roger and John *del Brig(g)* (1338 ib.) apparently provide early references to Egremont Bridge. It is *Egre-*

---

[1] Southwaite is in Blindbothel parish.

mont Bridge 1753 CW (OS) xv. EGREMONT CASTLE is *castellum de Egremundia* c. 1125 (15th) CW xiv, *castellum...de Acrimonte* c. 1205 CW (OS) i, facs., *castrum de Egermundia* early 14th StMaryY.

This is an artificial name, representing a French compound *aigre mont*, 'sharp-pointed hill.' At least three examples of the name Aigremont are recorded in France, in Gard, Haute-Marne and Yonne (Gröhler ii, 74), but no connection has been traced between any of the places so named and the early medieval lords of Copeland. It is probable that the name was a new formation, descriptive of the castle site.

NOTE. CHURCH ST. Cf. *Church lane* 1774 CW xvii. EAST RD. Cf. *the Easte rowe* 1578 *Cocker*. GREENDYKES is so named in 1681 (CW xvii). *v.* dīc.

BIGRIGG is *Bigrig* 1235 StB *et passim*, with variant spellings *Byg-* and *-rigg, -ryg, Byggerik'* 1295 *Ass* (p), *Biggerig* 1342 *Cocker*, *Bigrigshagh* 1363 Ipm. 'Ridge where barley grows,' *v.* bygg, hryggr (under hrycg). *-shagh* in the form from 1363 represents OE sceaga.

CARODALE (lost). Cf. *Caraldhill, Keraldhill, le Keraldeng* 1338 Cl, *Caraldehilheng* t. Ed 3 (t. Eliz) *Cocker*, *Keraldhill* 1363 Ipm, *Carodale* 1578 *Cocker*. The derivation of this name is uncertain. For *eng, v.* eng. Professor Ekwall suggests that we have here ME *carald*, 'cask', recorded in Patience, v. 159, from ON **karald* (cf. ON *kerald*), Swed. dial. *karale*, though it is difficult to say why the place should have been so named—unless the Devil's Beef Tub (Dumf) be a parallel.

CATGILL HALL is *Catgyll* 1278 StB (p), *Catgill* 1338 Cl, (*near White-haven*) 1786 MunRec, *the Parke al. Catgill parke, Catkellhowe* 1578 *Cocker*. 'Wild-cat ravine,' *v.* gil.

FLASHINGE DYKES (lost) is *Flashinge Dykes* 1578 *Cocker*. Cf. *Flessyng-holm* 1338 Cl, probably from ON poetical *fles*, 'green spot among bare fells,' with eng added as the original word became obsolete.

GUTTERBY (6″) is *Godrikeby, Godrickeby* 1235 StB, *Goderikby* 1312 Pat (p), *Godrigby* 1378 StB (p), *Guderby* c. 1500 ib., *Goodrigbye* 1590 FF. '*Gōdrīc*'s bȳ,' from the OE personal name *Gōdrīc*. Cf. the same name *infra* 448.

HAGGET END is *Haygate* 1278 StB (p), 1279 *Ass* (p), *Haggett End* 1680 CW xvii. 'Hay road,' *v.* hēg, gata.

ORGILL is *Orgilcroftes* 1342 *Cocker*, *Orgill* 1656 CantW vii. The first element here[1] may well be OE *ōra*, 'ore.' There are iron workings in the immediate neighbourhood of Orgill. The second element is gil.

SCALEGILL HALL is *Scalgaill* 1321 Ipm, *Scalegilen* 1338 Cl, *Scalgill*, *Skalegille* 1363 Ipm, *Skalegyll* p. 1500 StB, *Skellgill* 1578 *Cocker*, *Skaylgill nigh St. Bees* 1656 Jackson. If the first form is correct, this may, like Skelgill *supra* 371, be a compound of skáli and geil. If the first form is not correct, the second element is gil.

SNELLINGS is *Sneelinges* 1578 *Cocker*, *Sniling* 1717 CW xv, *Snelings* 1719 ib. xvii, *Snillings* 1774 Donald. Cf. *Snelehow whynnys* p. 1500 StB. The forms are late, but suggest that the first element may be OE *snegel*, 'snail.' The second is probably ON eng, 'meadow.'

STANDING STONES (6″) is *Stanes* 1278 StB (p), *Stanes de Egremund* 1292 *Ass* (p), *Standingstones* 1628 *Work. v.* stān.

THIRNEBY (lost) is *Thirnebi* c. 1205 CW (OS) i, facs., *Tyrneby* 1278 *Ass*, *Thyrnby* 1321 Ipm, *Thirnby* 1322 Cl, *Thirneby* 1334, 1363 Ipm, 1338 Cl. The second element is bȳ. The first may be ON *þyrnir*, 'thorn bush,' or the genitive of the OScand personal name *Thyrne*, recorded in England as *Þirne* c. 1050. *v.* DEPN *s.n.* Thrimby, and cf. Thrimby (We) and Thurnby (Lei), and *Thyrnby Closes supra* 50.

WHANGS is *le Wayng* 1338 Cl, 1363 Ipm, *le Wange* 1578 *Cocker*, *the Wangs* 1769 *LowtherW*. This may be from ON vangr or the OE *wang* having the same meaning.

CROFTEND HO (6″). Cf. Alan de *Croffend* (1279 *Ass*).

BLACK LING is *Blakelinge* 1578 *Cocker*. BOOKWELL (6″) is *Bowoke well, Bowake well* ib. CLINTS is *Clynt* ib. Cf. *Clint Hill* 1675 Ogilby and *v.* klint. CROSS SIDE COTTAGE (6″). Cf. *Crofside* (sic) 1793 PR. GILL is *the Gill* 1633 ib. *v.* gil. GILL FOOT is so named in 1685 (CW xvii). GOOSEKNOTT WOOD (6″) is so named in 1690 ib. HOW BANK (6″) is *Howe banke* 1578 *Cocker*. Cf. *ye How* 1670 PR and *v.* haugr. MOOR ROW is *More Rawe* 1515–18 ECP, *morowe* 1578 *Cocker*. *v.* mōr, rāw. NEW BRIDGE (6″) is so named in 1711 (CW xvii). PALLAFLAT is *Palla flat(t)* 1578 *Cocker*, 1658 PR. PARK HO. Cf. *park of Egremound* 1322 Cl. PICKET HOW is *Pikethowe* 1338 Cl, *Picked How* 1769 *LowtherW*, probably with reference to the irregular contour

---

[1] Cf. Orgrave (PN La 207) and *Orscarth* (*supra* 344).

of the hill, with its many corners. *v.* haugr and cf. *supra* 354. RAVEL-
SAYE HO (6″) is possibly named from *Rameleshowe* 1338 Cl. *v.* haugr.
SOUTHAM is so named in 1578 (*Cocker*). TOWNHEAD (6″) is *ye Head
of ye Towne* 1662 PR. WOODEND is *le Wodehend* 1338 Cl. Clearly
'wood end.'

FIELD-NAMES

(*a*) Gibbet Holme (*gibbit holme* 1578 *Cocker*; cf. *Gybetflat, Gibbekeld* 1338
Cl, *gibbit flatt, gibbit gate* 1578 *Cocker*), Stoolings, Summerhow (*v.* haugr).

(*b*) In 1775 (CW xvii) Housesteads (*Hussestedecroft* 1294 Cl, *House steade*
1578 *Cocker*. *v.* hūs, stede); in 1771 (CW xvii) Stuarding Gate (*Stuardeng*
1338 Cl, *le Stiwardenge, Stewardhenges* 1363 Ipm, 'steward's meadow,' *v.*
eng); in 1769 (*LowtherW*) Calldikes (*v.* dic), *Causeway End* (cf. *Cawser banke*
1578 *Cocker*), Collon Ings (*Callan inges* 1578 *Cocker*; cf. *Collaneleye* 1338 Cl
and Colin Croft in Dean (*supra* 368)), Crackenflatt (*Craconflat* 1338 Cl,
Craken flatt 1578 *Cocker*, possibly containing ON krakande, 'crawling,' used
as a nickname, as suggested by Ekwall (DEPN) for Crackenthorpe (We)),
Crook of Viver (cf. *Viuerside* 1578 *Cocker*. This is ME vivēre, 'fishpond,' from
OFr vivier, Latin vīvārium. Viver in Stainton (We) appears as "the fishery
of the vivary of Henecastre" in 1237), Crowdallow (*Crowdelow* 1685 CW xvii),
Headabusk (*Huredowebushe* 1578 *Cocker*, *Head-a-busk* 1753 CW xvii), *Heal-
bank* (*Healde banke* 1578 *Cocker*. *v.* h(i)elde), Hendon Busk (*v.* buskr), *Jenkin
Dale, Moor Thorns* (*moorethorne* 1578 *Cocker*), Tarnbanks (*Ternebanck* 1294
Cl. *v.* tiǫrn), Whitecross al. *Crosthwaite Close*; in 1756 (CW xvii) *Firtellfields*
(*Firtilsit* 1338 Cl, *Firtlefeilde* 1578 *Cocker*. *-sit* in the form from 1338 must
be a mistake for sīc or fit. *Firtil* may conceivably represent OE fyrhþ(e)hyll,
'wooded hill,' as in Firber (PN La 87); in 1709 (CW xvii) Langhorn (*Lang-
horne* 1578 *Cocker*); in 1660 (Caine) *Dawlands, Whitkills* (*Whitekelde* 1578
Cocker. 'White spring,' *v.* kelda); in 1633 (CW xviii) *Chappell close, Gunnalt-
holme* (id. 1578 *Cocker*. *Gunnalt* seems to represent a personal name such
as *Gunnhildr* (fem.) or more probably *Gunnvaldr* (masc.)); in 1578 (*Cocker*)
Aplegarthe (*le Overapelgarth, Netherapelgarth* 1338 Cl. *v.* æppel, garðr),
Armitt banke (presumably ME ermite, 'hermit'), *Bell butt* (*Belbut* 1338 Cl),
Blindekelde ('hidden spring,' *v.* kelda), *Boradell close, Bradinge* (*v.* eng),
Brownehow (*v.* haugr), *Catter banke, Clackbutt, Cole garthe* (may be *Calgarth*
1338 Cl, possibly, as in Calgarth (We), 'garðr for calves'), *Coupeholme*
('holmr which had been bought,' *v.* kaupa and Copeland *supra* 2), *Crowcockett,
Crusteade, Daleloupes* (*v.* loup), *Ellys Close, Eskeron* (also *Eskorne*) ('ash
thicket,' from ON eski and runnr), *Gappow heade, Grabarrowe* (*Grabergh*
1338 Cl, 1363 Ipm. 'Gray hill,' *v.* be(o)rg), *griscall myre* (*v.* mýrr), *Gunflatt*
(*Gunflat* 1338 Cl), *Hangingdale, Hardecar inge* (*Hertker* 1294 Cl, probably
'hart marsh,' *v.* heorot, kiarr, eng, and cf. *supra* 275), *Harie Knotts* (*v.* knǫtt),
Kell flett banke (*v.* kelda), *Langers Tarne, latebutts* (*Lathebutthe* 1294 Cl.
v. hlaða), *Lovalands, Lownabanke, Pertholme, Roswelinge, Rosewellgarthe,
Longe Sandwith, Short butts, Slatbaroweclosse* (also *Sleet barrowes*) (*v.* be(o)rg),
Starkelde butts (from star- and kelda, 'sedgy spring'), *Stirland Syke* (*v.* sīc),

Thwarterdale, Under Tour Horne cragge, Walt Closse, Whirnestone (probably OE cweorn-stān, 'millstone'), *the Wyge*; in 1363 (Ipm) *Blaikstansyt* (*Blakestanefitte* 1294 Cl, *Blaystanfit* 1322 Cl, *Blakestanfoyt* 1323 *MinAcct, Blakestansit, Blaikestansit* 1338 Cl. 'Black-stone meadow,' *v.* fit), *Brakanthwayt* (*Brakanthwait* ib. *v.* braken, þveit), *Cambanacre* (id. ib.), *Cannonheynges* (*Canonenges, Canounenges* 1338 Cl. Cf. *Canoneriges* 1363 Ipm. This is OE *canon* or ME *canoun* (from OFr), 'canon,' and eng. The 'canons' cannot be identified), *Crosflat* (*Crosseflats* 1338 Cl), *Halforthbank, Kemecroft* (cf. *Kempeflatte* 1294 Cl, *v.* flat. *Kempe* may be either OE *cempa*, 'warrior,' 'professional fighter or wrestler' or a family name of the same derivation), *Listerkroft* (cf. Richard *Lister* and *Watecroftlister* 1338 Cl, the latter meaning '*Lister*'s wheat croft,' and *Listra closse* t. Ed 3 (t. Eliz) *Cocker*), *le Pele* (*le Poll* 1338 Cl), *Richardkroft* (*Richardecroft* ib.), *Tacknot* (id. ib.), *Thornebank* (*Thornbanks* ib.), *Wetecroft* (*Watecroft* ib. 'Wheat croft'), *Williamfeld* (id. ib.); in 1338 (Cl) *Anneislandes* (*Anneslands* t. Ed 3 (t. Eliz) *Cocker*, from ME *Anneis*, colloquial form of *Agnes.* Cf. possibly Anniesland (Glasgow)), *Brakenholm, Brombankes* (*Bromebank* 1294 Cl, probably brōm), *Butterstaynes, Caldfordbank, Crakeslane, Craikestan, le Croklandes* (*Crokelandes* 1294 Cl. *v.* krókr), *Dounecroft, Fisgarthbank* (*v. supra* 79), *Frauncishowes, Goldflat, Gretehou* (probably from ON griót, 'gravel or loose stones,' and haugr), *the hailath of John del Stanes* (apparently 'hay barn,' *v.* hlaða), *Helmescogh* (possibly 'helmet-shaped wood,' from ON hjálmr and skógr), *Hugeraymosse, Hug(h)landes, Hungerhowe* ('hunger hill,' *v.* haugr), *Huntereng* (*v.* eng), *Yvehowe, Kylnegarth* (*Le Kilngarth* 1322 Cl. *v.* cyln, garðr), *Mikelflat* ('big flat,' *v.* micel, mikill), *Mochelhoweeast, le Monedyck, Mulnagarth* ('mill-garth'), *Sirithlandes* (containing the ON feminine personal name *Sigríðr*[1]), *Trathousyk, le Turfbanke, le Whetlathe* (*Whitlathe* t. Ed 3 (t. Eliz) *Cocker.* Apparently 'wheat barn,' *v.* hlaða); in 1294 (Cl) *Blaketteflatte, Cultercoubeck, Gillinglandes, Hanckehow, Hardened, Hungrehayre, Langehowes, Langeflatte, Lonckebanck, Lonckehow, Le Nethergarth* (*v.* garðr), *Le Netherheugh* (*v.* hōh), *Ossehowes* (*v.* haugr), *Rebor', Le Redebanck, Silmertern, Stabelgarth, Stapelstanecroft* (*Stapelstaynes* 1278 *Ass* (p). 'Pillar-stones,' from OE stapol and stān or steinn), *Stodehou* (*v.* stōd and haugr); in 1292 (*Ass*) *Oxholm* (p) ((*H*)*oxolm* 1279 ib. (p)). Under each of the following dates there is one field-name: *Balnesferme* 1539 *MinAcct, Burras Bridge* 1683 CW xvii, *Jonney Gards* 1766 CW xvii, *the Meckins* 1689 CW xvii, *Middelward* 1497 Pat, *Mordin Parkes* 1677 (:710) CW xvii, *Low Ridding Nooke* 1681 CW xvii (*v.* hryding).

23. Embleton

EMBLETON [emǝltn]

Emelton 1195 FF, 1364 AD iv, 1369 *Hesley*, 1407 FF
Emilton' 1195 FF, *Emylton* 1438 StBA
Embelton' 1233 Pipe (p) *et freq* to 1322 Ipm, *Embulton* 1544 FF
Embleton 1243 Cl *et passim*

---

[1] Recorded in Cu (StB 50, 258).

Emmelton 1369 Ipm
Elmeton 1428 FF
Emilton al. Embleton 1601 DKR xxxviii

v. tūn. Formally, the first element may be OE *emel,* 'caterpillar,' but, as suggested by Ekwall (DEPN), OE *Ēanbald* is a more likely base.

LAMBFOOT is *Langfite* c. 1210 StBA, *Langfit* 1363 AD iv. 'Long meadow,' *v.* fit. The development is [laŋgfit] > [laŋfit] > [lanfit] > [lamfit]. The second element was confused with *foot* which was pronounced [fit] in this area.

SHATTON is *Shaton* 1322 Ipm, 1323 Cl, 1455 FF, *Schaton* 1399 Ipm. The forms are inconclusive, but they make it possible that this is identical with Shatton (Db), which is probably derived from OE scēat, 'point' or 'corner, of land,' and tūn.

STANGER is *Stangre* 1298 FF, 1332 SR (p), *Stanger* 1322 Ipm, 1323 Cl, 1323 Fine, 1455 FF, 1777 NB, *Stanker* 1340 GDR, *Stangard* 1578 *Cocker, Stonger Houses* 1657 CantW viii. Apparently from *Stangir,* plural of stǫng, 'pole', as suggested by Lindkvist.

FELL CLOSE (6″) and WESTRAY may be recorded in the names of Robert *del Fel* (1279 *Ass*) and Roger de *Westwra* (1292 ib.). *v.* fell, (v)rá.

BOUCH HO is perhaps to be associated with the family of Percival *Bowche* (1570 *ExchKR*), mentioned in a Cockermouth context.

ABBEY is *The Abbey* 1655 CantW vii. The origin of the name seems to be unknown. BECKHOUSE is so named in 1658 (ib. viii). EAST HO (6″) is *the Esthouse* 1578 *Cocker.* HIGH SIDE is *Higheside* ib. How END (6″) is *the How end* 1655 CantW vii. *v.* haugr. SCALES (6″) is *Skale* 1578 *Cocker. v.* skáli. STANLEY HALL is *Stanley hall, Standley heale* 1578 *Cocker, Stanlehale* 1658 CantW viii. The form from 1578 suggests that 'hall' in this name is OE h(e)alh. If Stanley itself is an ancient name, it represents OE stān-lē(a)h.

FIELD-NAMES

(a) Miss M. C. Fair tells us that Hand How (by Wythop Mill) is locally said to be the provenance of the La Tène sword and other weapons now in the British Museum. *v.* haugr.

(b) In 1578 (*Cocker*) *Adam garth* (v. garðr), *Maken close, Priests close, Seavye close* (v. sef), *Whynnye closes* (v. whin); in 1292 (*Ass*) *Swynesethals* ('pig sætr' and hals); in c. 1210 (StBA) *Birchehevd* ('birch tree headland,' v. bi(e)rce, hēafod), *fontem Susanne*; in 1195 (*FF*) *kirkefen* ('church fen'), *Olebec* (possibly a compound of ON *Óli*, a short form of ON *Óláfr*, and bekkr), *Oustwic* and *Oustwibec* ('east wīc'), *cruce Sundwize* (presumably a weak feminine form corresponding to the strong masculine personal name *Sundvíss*, which is recorded in Lind).

24. Ennerdale and Kinniside

ENNERDALE

Anenderdale c. 1135 (early copy) *Lowther*[1], *Ananderdale* t. Ric 1 (1308) Ch

Enderdale 1303 Pat, *Eghnerdale* 1321 Ipm, *Eynordale* 1322 Cl, *Eghennerdale* 1323 MinAcct, *Eynerdale* 1334, 1352, 1363 Ipm, 1338 Cl

Enerdale 1395 Pat, 1476 FF

Ennardale 1523 LP, *Ennerdalle* t. Hy 8 AOMB, *Ennerdale or Enderdale* 1777 NB

Ynnerdale 1574 CantW iii

ENNERDALE BRIDGE is *Bridge in Enerdall* 1656 PR (Lamplugh). In the parish was *Ennerdale Parke al. the Fence* 1650 ParlSurv.

The earlier name, as suggested in DEPN, was ON *Anundar-dalr*, '*Anund*'s valley.' The later name, as first suggested by Lindkvist (41), is 'valley of the Ehen' (v. *supra* 13). Both names show the ON genitival inflexion -ar, v. Introduction.

GREAT BORNE. The medieval bounds of the woodland of Loweswater (1230 Scotland) suggest that Great Borne is identical with a hill there called *Hardecnut*. The latter name is identical with Hardknott *supra* 344.

CROSSDALE is *Crossedale* 1279 Ass (p), *Crozedal* 1294 Cl (p), *Cros(s)dale* 1593, 1608 CW xxxi, *Crosdell* 1605 Ct, *Crosdaill* 1606 ib., *Crosedaile* 1633 PR (Lamplugh), *Crowsdale* 1744 ib., *Croesdale* 1776 ib. 'Valley marked by a cross,' v. dalr.

HOW HALL is *Carswelhowe in Ennerdale* 1523 LP, *Caswaldhowe* 1576 S, 1672 Blome, *Castlehowe* 1578 Cocker, *Caswellhow* 1623 CantW vi, *Castle-How* 1794 H, 1816 Lysons, *Castle-How, Caswell-How or How*

---

[1] The copy in StB (No. 8) gives the reading *Avenderdale*.

Hall 1842 AllerA. Apparently, in origin, OE **cærse w(i)elle**, 'cress spring,' to which ON **haugr** has been added. Cf. Carswell (Berks).

KINNISIDE (6″)

Kynisheved 1321 Ipm, *Kynesheved* 1334 ib., 1338 Cl, *Kenesheued*, *Kynesheued* 1323 *MinAcct*, *Kynysheved* 1363 Ipm
Kyneshed 1363 Ipm
Kenysyde 1502 *Cocker*, *Kynysyde* 1541 FF

KINNEYHOW CARR (6″) is *Kinhowe karr* 1578 *Cocker*. *v.* haugr, kiarr. KINNISIDE COP (6″). Cf. *two little hilles called Keniside and Wasaborowe* ib. There was also in the neighbourhood a lost *moram de Kynesyde* 1570 *ExchKR*.

The first part of this name may be an old hill-name such as underlies Kinmont *supra* 364. If so, 'head of the hill,' *v.* hēafod.

SILVER COVE is *Silfoucon, Silfhucone* (sic MS) 1338 Cl, *Silver Cowe* (*or Coue*) 1578 *Cocker, Silver Coves* 1650 *ParlSurv*. The forms are too late for any certain interpretation. The first part of the name resembles Silpho (PN NRY 115), but the meaning of the latter is itself doubtful.

SIMON KELL is *Simonkeld(e)* 1279 *Ass* (p), *Simundekelde* 1292 ib. (p), *Semonkell, Semenkell* 1578 *Cocker*. 'The spring (*v.* kelda) of *Sigemund* (OE) or, more probably, of *Sigmundr* (ON).'

BANK HO (6″) is *Banckhowse* 1578 *Cocker*. BANNA FELL is *Bannyfell* 1609 DKR xxxviii, *Banafell, Benefell* 1610 ib. BECKFOOT (6″) is so named in 1765 (*LowtherW*). BIRK MOSS is so named in 1593 (CW xxxi). *v.* bi(e)rce, mos. BLACK POTS (6″) is *le Blakepottes* 1338 Cl, *Blackpotts* 1578 *Cocker*. 'Black pits.' BLAKELEY (6″) is *Blake lee* ib. *v.* Whorl Gill *infra* 388. BLAKELEY RAISE is *Blake lee Raids* ib. *v.* hreysi. BOAT HOW (6″) is *Bawthow, Bawethow* ib., *Balthow* 1650 *ParlSurv. v.* haugr. BOWNESS is *Bownas* 1765 *LowtherW*. A curved headland, cf. *supra* 123. BRACKEN WREAY (6″) is *Brakenwray* 1578 *Cocker*. 'Bracken-covered corner,' *v.* (v)rá. BRANDRETH (6″) is *the threefooted Brandreth* 1805 *Brayton*. This contains the word *brandreth* (from ON *brand-reið*, 'grate'), meaning 'gridiron, tripod.' The hill may have been named from some three-legged grate on it for a beacon fire. Cf. *Brandreth stone* in Westward *supra* 332. BUCK HOLE (6″) is *Buckhoole* 1578 *Cocker*. CATHOW is *Katthay* ib. Apparently 'wild-cat enclosure,' *v.* catt, (ge)hæg, and cf. Cathays Park (Cardiff)

(NCPNW 162). Caw Fell is *Cawffelde* ib. Probably 'calf-field.'
Cockhow is so named ib. *v.* haugr. Crag is so named in 1606 (*Ct*).
Croftbrow is *Crofte browe* 1578 *Cocker.* Dryhurst (6″) is *Dryhurst*
ib., *Drist* 1754 CW xxi. Presumably 'dry hyrst.' Fellend is so
named in 1593 (CW xxxi). Flatfell End is *Flatt fell ende* 1578
Cocker. Friar Moor (6″) is *frier moore* ib. Gill is so named in 1605
(*Ct*). *v.* gil. Gillerthwaite is *Gillerthwait* 1604 CW xxxi. Low
Gillfoot (6″) is *Lowgill-foot* 1796 PR (Lamplugh). Graystone (6″)
is *Graye stone* 1578 *Cocker.* Green Cove (6″) is *Grenecove* 1570
ExchKR. v. cove. Greenthwaite (6″) is *the greenthwate* 1578 *Cocker.*
v. þveit. Hay Stacks. Cf. West (130)—"The more southern is by
the dalesmen, from its form called *Hay-rick.*" Lavrick Hall is
Laverick Hall 1608 CW xxxi. Lizza Brow (6″) is *Leasabrough* 1578
Cocker, Leasiebrow 1726 PR. Longlands (6″) is *Langlands* 1578
Cocker, Longlands 1762 PR. Longmoor (6″) is *Lange Moore* 1578
Cocker, Longmoor 1716 PR. *v.* mōr. Longmoor Head (6″) is *Long-
moreheade* 1578 *Cocker.* Meadley is *Medlay* ib., *Meedley* 1712 PR.
High Merebeck (6″). Cf. *Lowmeerbeck* 1696 PR and Mere Beck
supra 21. Mireside is so named in 1608 (CW xxxi). Moorend is
so named in 1593 ib. Pillar is so named in 1783 (Donald). It may,
as suggested by W. G. Collingwood (CW xx, 244), be (*ad altum*)
Delhertgrene 1322 Cl (sic MS). Poukes Moss (6″). Presumably
'goblin's moss,' *v.* pūca. Raven Crag (6″) is *Raven Cragg* 1805 *Brayton.*
Red Pike is *le Rede Pike* 1322 Cl. Routen is *Routon* 1608 CW xxxi.
Sampson's Bratful. This is a heap of stones about which the legend
is that it was brought here in the devil's apron (brat). Scarth Gap
is *Scarf Gapp* 1821 G. *v.* skarð, gap. Sillathwaite is *Sillithwate or
Sirrithwate* 1578 *Cocker.* If the latter form is correct, this may be
'*Sigriðr's* þveit.' Cf. *supra* 383. Standing Stones is so named in
1691 (PR). Steeple is so named in 1783 (Donald). Stockdale
Moor. Cf. *Stokedalebek* 1540 *LRMB.* Swinside is *Swinsyde, Swain-
side, Swanside* 1578 *Cocker, Swain-side* 1770 CW xvii. Swinside End
is *Swinsidend* 1671 PR, Thwaites (6″) is *Thwaits* 1656 CW xiv. *v.*
þveit. Toddle Bank (6″) is *Toddall banke* 1578 *Cocker.* Tongue
(6″) is *le Brinttenng'* 1322 Cl. Near by is Brin Crag (6″). High and
Low Waterside (6″) are *Watersyde* ib., *Highwaterside* 1675 PR.
Whinns is *Whins* 1794 MapH. *v.* whin. Whitebanks (6″) is *White
bancke* 1578 *Cocker.* White Esk (6″) is the name of a hill immediately
north of the head waters of the Calder. It gave rise to the stream-
name *White Eskebekk* 1578 *Cocker.* Cf. *le Whiteskford* 1338 Cl. The

hill-name presumably arose from a white ash tree, *v.* eski. WHORL GILL (6″) rises in Blakeley (hill) *supra* 386, which is well rounded and may have been named *Whorl* from hwyrfel. WIND GAP (6″) is *le Windȝate* 1322 Cl. Cf. *le Wyndeyaterigg* 1338 ib. 'Pass through which the wind sweeps.' The early forms are from OE windgeat, recorded in BCS 1066 and found also in Winnats (Db). WOODFOOT is *Woodfoote* 1625 *Ct.*

FIELD-NAMES

(b) In 1765 (*LowtherW*) *Moorside* (*Moorsid*' 1604 CW xxxi. *v.* mōr); in 1628 (CW xxxi) *Gardends* (*Gardenes* 1625 *Ct*); in 1606 (*Ct*) *hollyngs* (cf. *holling thorne* 1578 *Cocker*); in 1578 (*Cocker*) *Abiltree, biggarth, bigg knott* (*bygknotte* 1541 *MinAcct*. 'Barley garth' and 'barley hill,' *v.* bygg, garðr, knǫtt), *bitts, Blaford, Bone landes, bonam banckes, Cokey gill* (*v.* gil), *the Coupe, Coupland Closse, Crosse browe, Dainelandes, farrethwate* (*v.* þveit), *gill grawng-head, Hare shawe* (presumably 'hare wood,' *v.* sceaga and cf. Haresceugh *supra* 216), *hempe garth* (*v.* garðr), *Kildrellhowe* (*le Geldramshowe* 1338 Cl. *v.* haugr), *Kirkhowe* ('church hill,' *v.* kirkja, haugr), *meane inge* ('common meadow,' *v.* (ge)mǣne, eng), *Mowtkey banck, the potts, the riddings* (*v.* hryding), *the Strandes* (*v.* strand), *the Walt closse*; in 1540 (*MinAcct*) *greslond*', *Rawfeldholme* (*v.* holmr); in 1338 (Cl) *le licheyate* (sic MS) (also *le Lycheyate*) (OE lic and geat, 'lich-gate,' of which the earliest example in NED is dated 1482–3), *Oxlesgate* (also *le Oxelesgate*) (probably 'track (*v.* gata) to the ox pasture,' the first part of the name being OE oxa and lǣs. Miss M. C. Fair believes this to be the old drove road fording the Calder and crossing the moor to Wasdale and Gosforth), *le Wrengilheved* (in which OE hēafod has been added to ON (v)reina gil, 'stallion ravine,' *v.* (v)reini, gil and cf. Wrynose *infra* 437). Under each of the following dates there is one field-name: *heighburne* 1539 *MinAcct*, *the Mereend* 1608 CW xxxi, *Water Cragge nouke* 1609 ib., *Wyndgill* 1605 *Ct* (*v.* gil).

25. Eskdale and Wasdale[1]

ESKDALE occasionally [eʃdəl]

> *Eskedal(e)* 1285 StBA *et freq* to 1368 IpmR, (*in Coupeland*) 1301 GDR, *Eschdale* 1445 Pap, *Eskdale* 1578 *Cocker*
>
> *Asshdale* 1461 Pat, *Asshedale* 1544 ib., *Ashedale* 1570 *ExchKR*
>
> *Esshedaille* 1504 HMC x, *Esshedale* 1519 *FF*, *Esshdale* 1535 VE, *Eshdell* 1606 DKR xxxviii, *Eshdale otherwise Eskdale* 1642 HMC iv

Originally 'valley of the Esk' (*supra* 14), *v.* dalr. Later there was confusion with *esk*, 'ash-tree,' from ON eski, and anglicising to *esh*

---

[1] Birker (*supra* 342) was added in 1934, but part of Eskdale and Wasdale was transferred to Nether Wasdale (*infra* 440) in 1934.

and *ash*. The lost *Eskedale* in the Isle of Man, 1154 *Eschedala* (PN IOM 294), is apparently from *eskidalr*.

BOOT is *Bout*, *(the) Bought* 1587 *Eskdale*, *Bought* 1627, 1795 *PR*, *Boot* 1791 ib. Cf. *close called boughte de bekk* 1578 *Cocker* (in Nether Wasdale). This is ME *bouȝt*, 'bend, turn,' aptly descriptive (as Professor Tait noted for us) of the acute re-entrant angle which the valley makes at Boot above the confluence of the Whellan Beck with the Esk. Cf. *bought* in NED; the form *byht*, whence *bight*, recorded in OE, had *i*-mutation.

ESK HAUSE is *Eskhals* 1242 Furness, 1322 Cl, *Long Eske hawse* 1540 *LRMB*, *Eskhowse* 1578 *Cocker*, *Esk horse* 1821 G. 'The hals, or pass, at the head of the river Esk' (*supra* 14).

GREAT GABLE is *le Heye del Mykelgavel, le heye del Mikelgaule* 1338 Cl, *Great Gavel* 1783 Donald. The modern name 'Great Gable' is an accurate translation of the 14th-century *Mykelgavel*. The first element here is OE *micel*, or more probably ON *mikill*, 'great'; the second is ON *gafl*, 'gable,' an appropriate description of the sharply cut triangular mountain so called. Another example of this name appears in GREAT GABLE in Above Derwent, for which no early forms have been found. The element *gafl* also enters into the names GREEN GABLE in Ennerdale and GAVEL FELL in Ennerdale, which is so named in 1609 (DKR xxxviii). The *heye* of *Mykelgavel* was probably a forest enclosure beneath the mountain (*v.* (ge)hæg).

MITERDALE

> *Meterdal* 1294 Cl
> *Miterdale* 1334 Ipm *et passim, Myterdell* 1473 AD iv, *Myterdale* 1570 *ExchKR, Mitredale* 1610 Denton, 1769 CW xxi
> *Mitterdale* 1519 FF, *Mytterdale* 1586 CW x

MITERDALE HEAD is *Myterdale head, Mytredale head* 1570 *ExchKR*. 'Valley of the Mite (*supra* 22),' *v.* dalr. The *-er* represents the ON gen. sg. in *-ar, v.* Introduction.

RYSEBRIGGE (lost). *Rysebrigge, Rise-bridgeyeat* 1578 *Cocker* make an addition to the list of names, discussed in PN Sx 258, in which OE hrīs, 'brushwood,' is followed by brycg. The best recorded of the series is the hundred-name Risbridge in Suffolk (EHN i, 95). 'Bridge' in this compound is more likely to mean a causeway of brushwood than a bridge in the usual sense of the word.

Sca Fell [scɔ·] is (*frithes or fences called*) *Skallfeild* 1578 *Cocker*, *Scoffield-Rana* 1750 Pococke, *the mountain Scofell or Scowfell* 1794 H. In spite of the 16th-century form *Skallfeild*, the second element here is clearly fiall. The first may well be the ON *skalli*, 'bald head.' Skalla-Grímr of Njálssaga was so nicknamed because he showed a bald head at an early age.

Strenshal (6″) is in a bend in the Esk. No mention of the name has been found before the 19th century (*Stential* 1837 *Surveyors Accounts*), but the name seems to be identical with Strensall (WRY) and *Streonæshalch*, the original name of Whitby (PN NRY 126). The first element seems to be related to OE *gestrēon*, 'profit, gain,' but the sense in which it was used in these compounds is uncertain.

Wasdale [wɔsəl] occasionally [wɔʃdəl]

> *Wastedal(e)* 1279 *Ass* (p), 1322 Cl, 1323 *MinAcct*, *Wast Dale* 1653 CantW vii
> *Wassedale* 1279 *Ass* (p), 1310, 1397 Pat, 1336 *Ass*
> *Wacedale* 1285 *For* (p), 1369 Ipm, *Wascedale* 1321, 1334, 1363 Ipm, *Wasedale* 1405 Pat, *Wasdell* 1608 DKR xxxviii, *Wastall* 1671 Fleming

Wasdale Hall is on the site of *Daker End* 1783 Donald. Wasdale Head is *Wascedaleheved* 1334 Ipm, *Wassedaleheved* 1410 Pat, *Wasdale Hede* 1448 AD iii, *Wasshedaylehed* 1519 *FF*, *Wastedale heade* 1540 *LRMB*, *Wastellhead* 1628 PR (Crosth).

Ekwall (DEPN) suggests that this is ON *vat(n)s dalr*, 'valley of the lake,' from ON *vatn*, 'water,' which occurs again in Loch Watten in Caithness. See further Wastwater *supra* 36. The Icelandic name *Vatnsdalr*, *Vazdalr*, is of the same origin, and there is a duplicate of Wasdale itself in Wasdale (We), with *Wascedale* and *Wassedale* as medieval forms.

Acre Hows (6″) is *Acrehowes* 1587 *Eskdale*. Cf. *little Acrehows* 1660 ib. Arment Ho is *Armithow* 1578 *Cocker*, *Harmothow(e)s*, *Harmethowes* 1587 *Eskdale*,[1] *Armont Ho* 1821 G. Presumably 'hermit hill,' *v.* haugr. Bakerstead (6″) is *Bakerste(a)d* 1570 *ExchKR*. *v.* stede. Banklands (6″) is *Bankelandes* 1578 *Cocker*. Great and Little Barrow (6″). Cf. *the Barrow* 1587 *Eskdale*. *v.* be(o)rg. Beckfoot is *Bekkfoote* 1578 *Cocker*. Beckhead (6″) is the head of *Beksneuell*, *Beksueuel* (sic MS) 1338 Cl. This is an inversion compound, but the

---

[1] Add: *Harmuthhows* 1788 *PR*, *Armuthhows* 1794 ib., *Hermenthouse* late 18th *ChwAccts*.

second part of the name cannot be determined. BELL CRAG (6") is
belled Cragg 1587 *Eskdale*. BIRDHOW is so named in 1660 ib. BLACK
COMB (6") is *Blackcombe* 1578 *Cocker.* It is referred to in *Le Blackoumb-
heved* 1322 Cl, *le Blakecombek* 1338 ib. *v.* hēafod, camb, bekkr, and
cf. Black Comb *infra* 449. BLACK SAIL (6") is *Le Blacksayl* 1322 Cl.
v. Sail Beck *supra* 26. BLAKE BANK (6") is *Bleakbank* 1587 *Eskdale*.
BLEABECK (6") is so named ib. *v.* Blea Beck *supra* 5. BLEATARN HILL
(6"). Cf. *the How on the northside of Bleatarne, Bleatarne head, Blea-
tarnefoot* ib. *v.* Blea Tarn *supra* 32. BOAT HOW is referred to in *the
Low Bothhow* ib. Apparently 'booth hill,' *v.* bóþ, haugr. BORROW-
DALE PLACE (6") is *Boroughdale place* 1570 *ExchKR, Borradailplace*
1587 *Eskdale*. The name has probably been transferred from Borrowdale *supra* 349. BROAD TONGUE is *the Broadtongue* ib. *v.* tunge.
BROWN BAND (6") is so named ib. BROWNHOW (6") is *Brownhowse*
1570 *ExchKR, Brownhow* 1660 *Eskdale*. Cf. *Brownhowstoppe* 1587 ib.
BULL HOW (6") is so named in 1660 ib. *v.* haugr. CAT COVE (6") is
the Foot of Catscove ib. *v.* cove. CHRISCLIFFE KNOTTS (6") is *Crasshe-
clyfte, Crasheclyfte* 1570 *ExchKR, Christcliffe* 1578 *Cocker, Christ Clift*
1628, 1797 *PR,* 1754 CW xxi, *Christclift* 1789 *PR*. CHURCH HO (6")
is so named in 1676 *PR*. CLOVEN STONE (6") is *the cloven gray
stone* 1587 *Eskdale*. COCKLY PIKE (6"). Cf. *Cockley Mossfoot* ib.
COMMONS CRAG (6"). Cf. *Comons* 1578 *Cocker*. DAWSONGROUND
CRAGS (6") is probably to be associated with *Dawson place* 1570
ExchKR, a house which is now represented by the Woolpack Inn.
DOW CRAG (6") is *Dove cragg* 1587 *Eskdale, Doe-Cragg* 1794 H.
'Pigeon crag.' ELLER HOW (6") is *Eller How, Ellerhowes* 1587 *Eskdale*.
v. elri, haugr. FELL END (6") is *the feildende* 1578 *Cocker*. GATE HO
(6") is *Yatehouse* 1570 *ExchKR, Yatthouse* 1724 *ChwAccts*. GILL
BANK is *Gilbank* 1570 *Exch KR*. GREAT and LITTLE (6") GRAIN GILL.
Cf. *the Green at Graingillfoot* 1587 *Eskdale. v.* grein. GREAT
HOW is *the Greathow* ib. *v.* haugr. GREEN CRAG (6") is *the Green
Cragg* 1587 *Eskdale*. GREEN HOW is *the greene howes* 1578 *Cocker,
the Greenhow* 1587 *Eskdale. v.* haugr. HARD RIGG is (*the*) *Hardrigge*
ib. HODGE HOW (6") is *Hogehowe* 1578 *Cocker*. HOLLING HEAD (6")
is *Hollenhead* 1570 *ExchKR, Hollinghead* 1587 *Eskdale*. 'Holly head,'
v. holegn. HOLLINGHOW (6") is *Hollenhowe* 1570 *ExchKR, Hollinghow*
1587 *Eskdale*. 'Holly hill.' HOLLOWMIRES (6") is *Hollow myre* 1578
Cocker. v. mýrr. HOW may be *le Howe* 1570 *ExchKR. v.* haugr.
HOWS is *le Howes* ib. ILLGILL HEAD is *head del Ilgill* 1338 Cl. Presumably 'evil gil.' KETTLE COVE (6") is *Ketle Cove* 1578 *Cocker*.

v. **cove.** Kirk Fell is *Kerkefell, le egge of Kirkefelle* 1338 Cl. *v.* kirkja, fiall (under fell). Lambford Bridge is *Lambford, the Lambfoard* 1587 *Eskdale*. Lingmell is *Lingmale* 1578 *Cocker*. Longrigg Green (6″) is *Langrogreen, Langregreen* 1587 *Eskdale, Langreygreene* 1656 CW xiv, *Langregreen* 1660 *Eskdale*. Low Holme is *Laweholme* 1570 *ExchKR, the Lawholme in Myterdale* 1586 CW xiv, *Lowholme, the Lowhome* 1587 *Eskdale*. *v.* holmr. Low Longrigg is *Langrigge, the Longrigge* 1587 *Eskdale*. Low Place is *Lowe place* 1570 *ExchKR*. Maiden Castle (6″) is so named in 1587 (*Eskdale*). It is on a track from Eskdale to Wasdale Head, but there is no obvious trace of any ancient earthwork which might have given rise to the name. Oliver Gill (6″) is so named in 1587 (*Eskdale*). Paddock Wray is *Paddockwraye* 1570 *ExchKR*. 'Toad corner,' *v.* (v)rá. Peel Place (6″) is *Pyle place* ib., *Peelplace* 1587 *Eskdale, Peopleplace* 1769 *ChwAccts*. Pens End (6″). Cf. *the Penns* 1587 *Eskdale*. Pickle Coppice (6″). Cf. *Pighill, a little pighill* 1578 *Cocker*. *v.* pightel. Rake Rigg (6″) is *Rake Rigge* ib. *v.* reik, hryggr (under hrycg). Randlehow (6″) is *Randall howe* 1570 *ExchKR, Rondalehow, Rondallhowe* 1578 *Cocker, Randlehow* 1587 *Eskdale*. *v.* haugr. Rough Crag (6″) is *Rughcrag* 1338 Cl, *the Rough Cragg* 1587 *Eskdale*. Rough How (6″) is *the Roughhow* ib. *v.* rūh, haugr. Round How is *the Roundhow upon Longrigg* 1660 ib. *v.* haugr. Row Head (6″) is *Roehead* 1754 CW xxi. The Screes is *Screes* 1783 Donald, *Eskdale Screes* 1794 H. This contains *scree* (*v.* NED), 'precipitous stony slope upon a mountain side,' from ON *skriða,* 'landslip.' The screes in question may have given rise to the name *Scrithesedge* in this parish, recorded in 1587 (*Eskdale*). Slight Side is so named in 1578 (*Cocker*). Spout Ho is *Spouthouse, Spoutehouse* 1570 *ExchKR*. Standing Stones (6″) is *the standing stones* 1587 *Eskdale*. Thorns (6″) is *Thornes* 1570 *ExchKR*. This is now known locally as Fold End. Tongue. Cf. *Tonge bridge* 1540 *LRMB*. The 'tongue' is between two streams. Tongue Moor. Cf. *ye Tounge feelde* 1578 *Cocker*. There is a high tongue-shaped hill here. Wha Ho is *Whawes* 1570 *ExchKR, Whaes* 1587 *Eskdale, Whose* 1700 *ChwAccts*. Cf. *the Whawbottom* 1587 *Eskdale*. Whin Crag (6″) is *Whinny Cragge* ib. 'Gorse crag,' *v.* whin. White Moss (6″) is *the White Moss* 1660 ib.

FIELD-NAMES

(*a*) Allan (*great Allen (al. Iland*) 1578 *Cocker* (*v.* allan), Coal (cf. *Colemoss* 1587 *Eskdale*), Doola Ting, Goodend, Gues Field (cf. possibly *gest feilde* 1578

Cocker), Kagat, Mean Wood (*v.* (ge)mǣne), Moral (cf. *morrell wood* 1578
Cocker), Rake Ring (*v.* reik), Rampshole, Red Becks (cf. possibly *Redbefoard*
1587 *Eskdale*), Ridding (*Riddinge* 1578 *Cocker. v.* hryding).

(*b*) In 1660 (*Eskdale*) Bangarth (*Bangarth* 1570 ExchKR, the *bende garth*
1578 *Cocker. v.* garðr), *Care Moss* (cf. *Carrmire* 1587 *Eskdale. v.* kiarr,
mýrr), *Clattergap, Evilrakehow* (*v.* reik, haugr), *the Gilderbeckescove* (cf.
gilderbeckhow 1587 *Eskdale*, possibly containing ON *gildri*, 'snare'), *guddum
Peatskales* (cf. *guddy close* 1578 *Cocker*), *Horpinhow, Minigatehow, the Pinnes,
Sleape Stone* (probably slǣp, 'slippery place'), *the Thorne Rake* (*v.* reik), *the
Whitehow* (*Withhow* 1587 *Eskdale. v.* haugr); in 1587 (*Eskdale*) *Bandhow,
Boshow, Brenthowes, Broadthorne, Cafell Gate, Caplecragge* (probably ME
capel, 'nag'), *Catterbeckfoot, Cookriggemoss, Coppedhow* ('flat topped hill,'
from haugr and the OE adjective *coppede*, well recorded in Anglo-Saxon
charters with reference to trees which have been polled or topped), *the
Crossgriens* (*v.* grein), *cross Waynegate* ('waggon road'), *Eelearke*[1] (*piscatus
vocatus an Ile ark* 1570 *ExchKR*), *Eskhowfoot* (*v.* haugr), *Garbethowes, Gray
Cragg, Greathow Steele, Hardstone yeat, Hindreth, Lindslack* (*v.* slakki),
Longhow Hights, Readgill, Readmire end (*v.* mýrr), *Saddle of the Whinnes*
(*v.* whin), *Shearegreen, Starbeckgreen* (*v.* star-, bekkr), *Taythes foot, Thorn-
scarth* (*v.* skarð), *Threaptongue* (*v.* þrēap- and tunge), *tree Esh, Whinny
style* ('whin grown path,' *v.* stīgel), *the White Borran* (*v.* burghan), *White
Rake* (*v.* reik), *White Scarrehow* (*v.* skarð, haugr); in 1578 (*Cocker*) *bere pott
holme* (*v.* holmr), *borans* (*v.* burghan), *Cokman hole, deedhowe* (*v.* haugr),
dragg myre (*dragg* may represent the ON *drag* mentioned under Drigg *supra*
377, with reference to a track along which a sledge could be drawn across the
mýrr), *Eller Crooke* (apparently 'elder tree crook of land,' *v.* elri, krókr), *the
gynnie crofte, howe myre* (*v.* haugr, mýrr), *the Lanes, Long Lades, outrake*
('out drove,' *v.* reik), *Petticote, Preest howe* (*v.* haugr), *silke mire* (*v.* mýrr),
Stoodfall-lees (*v.* stōdfald), *Tippie closse, Wokam slake* (*v.* slakki); in 1570
(*ExchKR*) *Akelsted* (*v.* stede), *Cunegarth* (*v.* coninger), *Thedes, Thollous*
(probably 'hole house,' with NCy *t'* for *the*); in 1322 (Cl) *Holgil* (*Hollegill*
1294 ib. 'Deeply cut ravine,' *v.* ON holr, under holh, and gil).

26. Gosforth

GOSFORTH

Goseford c. 1150 StB *et freq* to 1396 FF
Gosford c. 1170 StB *et freq* to 1440 FF
Gosseford c. 1225 StB *et freq* to 1514 BM
Gouseford, Gowseford c. 1225 StB
Gosforth in Coupeland 1388 Pat, *Gosford al. Gesforth in Coupeland*
  1405 ib., *Gossefurth* t. Hy 8 *AOMB, Gosfurthe* 1540 *MinAcct,
Gosfoorth* 1578 *Cocker, Gosforth or Gosford* 1777 NB

---

[1] A contrivance for catching (or perhaps for storing) eels. *v.* NED *eel*[5], *ark*[5].
This carries the word *eel-ark* 300 years behind the earliest references in NED.

GOSFORTH GATE (6″) is so named in 1660 (CantW viii). GOSFORTH HALL is so named in 1778 (CW iii).

OE *gōsa-ford*, 'geese's ford.' The final *-th* in the modern name is due to Scandinavian influence. In view of the strongly Scandinavian character of the district, shown in the decoration of the famous Gosforth cross, the change from *ford* to *forth* had probably occurred in local speech many generations before it is first recorded in documents; it occurs also in Gosforth (PN NbDn 95).

BOLTON HALL

> *Boutonam* c. 1170 StB
> *Bouelton* c. 1230 StB, *Boulton* 1279 *Ass*
> *Bothelton* 1251 FF, 1279 *Ass*, *Botheltona* c. 1300 *Netherhall*
> *Bolton* 1294 Cl *et passim*, (*in Coupland*) 1310 Greenfield iv, 1318 AD iv, *Bolton Hall* 1497 Ipm
> *Boleton* 1364 Ipm

BOLTON HEAD is *Boltonheued* 1282 StB. HALL BOLTON is so named in 1637 (CW (OS) viii). Cf. *infra* Hallsenna.

'tūn marked by a **bōōl** or building,' *v.* **bōōltūn.**

BRIDGE PETTON is *moram de Brigerpetin* c. 1285 Netherhall, *Briggepeting* 1303 Pat, *Briggpetton* 1586 CW (OS) viii, *Brigg Petton* 1596 PR. This seems to be an inversion compound, with ON *bryggja* as the first element. But the medial *-er-* of the first form complicates the derivation, unless the plural *bryggjur*, 'quays', be postulated, and the name must be left unexplained.

GREASON COTTAGE (6″). It is possible that this name may represent the *grossa grisa petra* and the *altera grisa petra* mentioned in a number of 13th-century documents in StB. If so, the name means 'grey stone' or 'stones.' It appears as *Greystan, Graystan* elsewhere in StB. It might, however, represent the local pronunciation of Greysouthen *infra* 397.

HALLSENNA [hɔ·senə]

> *Sevenhoues* c. 1225 StB (p), 1278 *Ass* (p), 1293 FF (p), c. 1310 HMC x, *Sewenhauis* c. 1285 *Netherhall, Seuenhoghes* 1292 *Ass* (p)
> *Sevenhous* c. 1225 StB (p), *Sevenhouse* c. 1230 ib. (p), c. 1300 CW xli, *Seuenhouses* 1302 *Ass* (p)
> *Sennthouues* c. 1260 StB (p), *Senthowes* 1278 *Ass*
> *Seynhouse* 1428 CW xii (p)

Synoshall 1569 FF
Halseonhouse 1662 *PR*, *Hall Senhouse* 1668 CW viii

In the neighbourhood was *Becksenowyate* 1657 CW xiv.
Originally 'seven hills,' *v.* haugr, and cf. Sewborwens *supra* 228.
For the prefixed 'hall,' cf. *infra* 417.

MURTHWAITE MOOR (6″) is connected with *Morthweyt bec* c. 1235 StB,
Morthaitbec c. 1300 ib. 'Moor clearing,' *v.* mōr, þveit.

NEWTON is *Neuton in Goseford* c. 1225 StB, 1278 *Ass*, (*in Coupland*)
c. 1225 StB. 'New tūn.'

STUBSHEAD HILL (6″) is named from *the land of Stubsat* 1318 AD iv.
'Stubby pasture,' *v.* stubb, sætr.

THISTLETON is *Thystilton* 1318 AD iv. 'Thistle tūn.' There are
earlier examples of this compound in Thistleton (R), DB *Tisteltune*,
and Thistleton (La), 1212 Fees *Thistilton*.

THORNBANK is *Thornbanc, Thornbank* c. 1230 StB.

BENGARTH (6″) may possibly be associated with the family of Alice
Ben (1583 PR) and Joseph *Benn* (1720 ib.). It is *Bengarth* 1733 ib.

ADDY HOUSE (6″) is *Adde House* 1671 *PR*. BLEAWATH is *Blaywathe* 1596
PR. *v.* blár, vað. BLENG BRIDGE (6″) is *Blenge Bridge* 1641 CW xv.
BLENGDALE (6″) is so named in 1655 (*PR*). BLENG TONGUE (6″) is
Blenktonge 1540, 1544 *MinAcct, Blentonge* 1542 ib., 1578 *Cocker,
Blentounge* 1578 *Cocker, Blaing Tongue* 1783 Donald. Cf. also *Blanke
tonge Fote* 1540 *LRMB*, the foote of *Blentonge* 1578 *Cocker. v.* tunge
and Bleng R. *supra* 5. BOLTHOW is *Boathow* 1715 PR. *v.* haugr.
BOONWOOD is *Bounwood* 1692 (*PR*). BOW BRIDGE (6″) is *Bow Brigge*
1609 ib., presumably so named from its shape. BROOM is so named in
1731 ib. CHERRY GARTH (6″) is *Chirry garth* 1578 *Cocker*. DENTON
HILL (6″) was named after the Rev. Christopher Denton who in 1696
married the heiress of Gosforth Gate (CW iii, 231). FLEMING
HALL is *Flemynghall* 1419 StB, possibly so named from the family
of le Fleming of Rydal, lords of the manor of Beckermet. HALLSTEADS
(6″) is *Gosfoorth hallstead* 1578 *Cocker. v.* h(e)all, stede. HAWKBARROW
FM (6″) is *Hawkesbarrowe* 1598 (*PR*). HERMONS HILL (6″) is said by
Parker (60) to be *Hagworm's Hill* in 1673 (*PR*). Probably 'viper's hill,'
from ON *hǫgg-ormr*. Cf. *supra* 325. HURLBARROW is *Hurlebarrow*

K

1638 (*PR*). It may have reference to the round-shaped Bleng Fell, *v.* **hwyrfel** and **be(o)rg.** JULIAN HOLME is *Julianholm* 1365 AD iv, *Gillianholme* 1600 CW (OS) viii, *Gillen home* 1606 ib. *v.* **holmr.** KELLBANK (6″) is *Keldebank* 1376 AD iv (p), *Keldbanke* 1653 CW xviii. *v.* **kelda.** KEMPLERIGG is so named in 1731 (PR). LACONBY [leikənbi] is *Lakynbye, Lakenby* 1548 *SP.* The forms are late, but the name may well be an ancient formation in -bȳ. It may be identical with Lackenby (PN NRY 159), in which the first element seems to be OIr *Lochán.* LINGBANK is *Nethergwhynbanke al. lyngbanke in Newtona in Gosford* p. 1500 StB. *Lingbanck* 1598 (*PR*). LOWCRAY (6″) is *Lacrey* 1604, *Locrye* 1635 ib. LOWERCRAY BANK (6″) is *Locraybanck* 1570 FF. MEOLBANK is *Mealbanck* 1605 PR. *v.* **melr.** PARK NOOK is so named in 1575 (CW (OS) viii). PEEL PLACE is (*del*) *Pyel* 1365 AD iv (p), *Peel place* 1639 CW (OS) viii. *v.* **pele.** RAINORS (6″) is *Raynrosse* 1597 *PR*, *Rainors* 1772 ib. ROW is *Rawe in Gosforth* 1600 CW xiv. *v.* **rāw.** SCALE (6″) is *Scale* 1365 AD iv (p). *v.* **skáli.** SCAR BROW (6″) is *Skarbrow* 1657 PR. SCOTT HALL (6″) is *Scott hooll* 1597 *PR.* SERGEANT FORD is *Sergeaunts Foord* 1578 *Cocker.* SILVER HOW is so named in 1727 (PR). *v.* **haugr.** SPOUT HO (6″) is so named in 1597 *PR.* TARNHOW is so named in 1782 (PR). There was formerly a tarn here (Parker 44). *v.* **tiǫrn** and **haugr.** WALK MILL (6″) is *walke millne* 1653 CW xviii, i.e. 'fulling-mill.' WHINNERAY is *Wynwarrowe* 1599 *PR.* WIND HALL (6″) is so named in 1639 (CW (OS) viii).

FIELD-NAMES

(*a*) Carolina, Claremont, Danish Camp, Outgang (*v.* **ūtgang**), Red Stile, Windermeresteel (*Windermirestyle* 1783 PR. *v.* **stigel**).

(*b*) In 1571 (CW (OS) viii) *Totteriggs* (*Toddolrygholms* late 13th *Netherhall, Toddelryg* 1472 AD iv. The first part of the name may be a compound of ME *tod,* 'fox,' and *hol,* 'hole'; the second is hrycg); in 1391 (*Netherhall*) *le Byssopgarth'* (*v.* **garðr**), *Stokdalebek'*; in 1382 (StB) *le Couperacre* (*v.* **æcer**. The first element is apparently *couper* (from ME *coupe(r)*, ON *kaupa*), 'dealer (usually in horses or cattle).' The first example quoted in NED is dated 1581), *Fleteland* (presumably from **flēot**); in late 13th (*Netherhall*) *Gumerholm* (the first element seems to be the personal name *Gumer*, recorded in northern England. Its origin is uncertain, but it may represent OE *Gūðmǣr,* ME *Guthmer*), *laykwylgra*...; in c. 1300 (*Netherhall*) *le Hevit* (*v.* **hēafod**), *le Houe* (*v.* **haugr**), *duos knottos* (sic) (*v.* **knǫtt**); in 1278 (*Ass*) (p) *Hou Groucok* (cf. *Grucokgille* c. 1225 StB, *Groucokgile* c. 1270 ib., *Grucocgile* c. 1275 ib. *Hou Groucok* is an inversion compound of haugr and possibly the ME *Grewcok* (from Fr *grue*), from which is derived the surname *Grewcock, Groocock* (Weekley, *Surnames* 91–2)); in c. 1270 (StB) *Stellerun* ((*le*) *Scel*(*e*)*run*, *Stel*(*e*)*run*, *Sceleirun*, *Scalerun* c. 1225 ib. The second element is ME *ron*, from ON runnr, 'thicket.' The first element can hardly be, as suggested by Ekwall (ScandCelts 94), OE stigel. If the form *Scalerun* be correct, it should be interpreted 'thicket by a shieling,' *v.* skáli); in c. 1260 (StB) *Setikonoc* (*Seteknoc* c. 1240 ib. This is apparently an inversion compound consisting of sætr and OIr *cnocc*, the whole meaning 'shieling on a hillock'); in c. 1250 (StB) *schalingam in Butoft, Strivland, Thornborhe*[1]; in c. 1245 (StB) (*ad*) *Canchem* (*le Chance* c. 1225 ib.)[2]; in c. 1240 (StB) *Blindbec* ('bekkr hidden by vegetation'), *g'tigat, Houthenhou* (also *Houthunhou*. This possibly contains the Anglo-Scandinavian personal name *Ouþen* (from ON *Auðun*), which sometimes appears as *Houden*. *v.* haugr); in c. 1230 (StB) *Borthheuid* (*v.* héafod), *Helewynherge* (the second element is erg. The first element may be the ME personal name *Herlewin*, from OFr *Herluin*, with loss of *r* before *l*, as in Bec *Hellouin*, which is derived from the name of *Herluin*, the founder of the abbey), *Thornheued, Whitrais, Whiterais* ('white cairn,' *v.* hreysi); in c. 1225 (StB) *le Brathaurane, Gillebanc* (also *Gillibanc*), *Gillebec, Hayusbanc* (*v.* hēg, hūs, banke), *Hessepile, Holeslac* (ON holr, slakki), *Kylnebannch* (*v.* cyln, banke), *Lickebuske, Likebulbec, Ran, fons sancte Helene, Stainraisse* (*v.* steinn, hreysi), *Wetteberck* (also *Wetebanc*). Under each of the following dates there is one field-name: *Cunning Holes* 1742 CW x, *Conyholes* 1596 *PR* (presumably 'rabbit holes'), *Dirthole* 1663 *PR, Elvinhowe* 1577 ib. (presumably elves' haugr), *Garboclandes* 1396 AD iv, *Hegardynlande* 1382 *Netherhall, Hunterplace* 1731 PR, *Jacktrees* 1671 *PR, Romend* 1657 CantW viii, *Sandyhill* 1657 PR.

27. Greysouthen

GREYSOUTHEN [greisu·n]

Craykesuthen c. 1187 *HolmC, Creiksuthen* 1230 Scotland, *Craicsuthen* c. 1258 StB (p)

Creisuth, Craysuth, Creysuth 1278, 1279 *Ass*

Cressewen 1278 *Ass*

Kreyksuchen (sic) 1279 *Ass* (p)

Graykesothen, Craykesothen 1292 *Ass*

Craysuthen, Creysuthen 1292, 1301 *Ass, Craysothen, Creysothen* 1293, 1299 FF, 1304, 1306 Ipm, 1307 Cl, *Craysothin* 1308 Ipm

Graysothen(*e*) 1299 FF, 1332 SR, 1395, 1406 *Ass, Graysothyn* 1306 Greenfield iv

Graysone 1505 *Cocker, Grasoone* c. 1510 ECP, *Graysuen* 1519 *FF, Graysome als. Greysothen* 1635 Hudleston, *Greysoon* 1765 PR (Crosth)

Greswithen 1794 H

[1] Add: *Kerlingsik*, 'old woman's stream' (ON *kerling*, sík).
[2] 'a type of ditch', or in Cu, 'depression' (StB 159).

'*Suthán*'s rock or cliff,' from MIr. *craicc*, as suggested by Ekwall (DEPN *s.n.*). *Suthan* is an early Irish personal name of which other instances are recorded in England.

TOWNEND. Cf. Robert *Attetounhend* (1332 SR).

TIFFIN WOOD (6″) may be associated with the family of *Tyffyn, Tyffen* (1570 *ExchKR*), a common name in this part of Cumberland.

COLIN GROVE (6″). Cf. *Collen banke* 1578 *Cocker*. MELGRAMFITZ WOOD (6″). Cf. *Mettgram fitts* ib. *v.* fit. MILLBANKS (6″) is *Millne bancks* ib. *v.* myln.

FIELD-NAMES

(b) In 1578 (*Cocker*) *Cirringham, hingthorne Intake* (*v.* intak), *hurrock more* (dial. *hurrock*, 'a piled up heap of loose stones'), *Muthey* (possibly a compound of (ge)mōt and (ge)hæg), *Ousthaile* ('east haugh,' *v.* austr, h(e)alh), *Tranlei mire* (*v.* mýrr), *Ulphei knotts* (*v.* knǫtt); in c. 1335 (*Hesley*) *Crokelandemire* (*v.* krókr, land, mýrr), *Halleker* (*v.* h(e)all, kiarr), *la Moselonde* (*v.* mos, land).

28. Haile[1]
HAILE [hial]

Hale c. 1180 *Hesley* (p) *et passim* to 1584 FF, (*al. Hele in Copeland*) 1479 Pat, *Hayll* t. Hy 8 *AOMB, Hayle* 1569 FF, *Haille* 1584 ib.

HAILE BANK (6″) is *Halebank* 1359 FlemingMem, *Hailebank* 1657 CW xiv. HAILE HALL is *Hale-Hall* 1794 H.

'Nook, corner,' *v.* h(e)alh. Cf. Hale Grange (We).

STOCKBRIDGE is *Stoke Bridge* 1578 *Cocker*. An earlier reference to the name occurs in *Stokbriggeholm* 1251 FF. *v.* stocc, brycg.

ULDALE FM is *Uldale* 1656 CantW vii. It is connected with *Uluedale-bech* c. 1205 CW (OS) i, facs., *Uluedalbec* 1291 ib. 'Wolves' valley,' *v.* Uldale *supra* 327.

WILTON is *Wiletun* c. 1205 CW (OS) i, facs., 1212 Cur (p), *Wiletona* c. 1205 CW (OS) i, facs. (p), *Wilton'* 1212 Cur (p) *et passim, Wylcton'* 1279 *Ass* (p), *Wylton* ib. (p), 1334 Ipm. In view of the form *Wylcton'*, this is probably 'willow tūn,' *v.* welig.

RIDDING WOOD (6″). Cf. Roger *del Riddyng* (1368 FF). *v.* hryding.

BROAD LEYS is so named in 1828 (PR, Gosforth). *v.* læs. HORSECLOSE WOOD (6″) is named from *Horseclose* 1538 *AOMB*. TOWN END is

[1] Part of Haile (which is spelled *Hale* on the 1″ O.S. map) was transferred to St Bridget Beckermet (*supra* 338) in 1935.

so named in 1679 (CW xv). WINDER is so named in 1578 (*Cocker*). It probably has the same origin as Winder *infra* 406.

FIELD-NAMES

(b) In 1578 (*Cocker*) *Ackhowe, Adamhowe* (*v.* haugr) and *Adam Riddings* (*v.* hryding), *Brakenroot Croft, Clugwth meadow, denstray, hows towne, Sowerbutts* (*v.* saurr), *the Stawe, wanegate* ('waggon road,' *v.* gata), *Wathgate* (*v.* vað), *Waresike* (*v.* sic). Under each of the following dates there is one field-name: *Belhousbanckes* c. 1290 *Hesley* (probably OE *bellhūs*, 'belfrey'), *Gybyorte* 1448 HMC xxv, *Morcote* 1446 ib. (*v.* mōr, cot(e)), *Stanton in Hale* 1294 Cl (*v.* stān, tūn), *Suremire* c. 1260 StB (OE *sūr*, 'sour,' and mýrr).

29. Harrington[1]

Halfringtuna c. 1160 StB

Haueringtona c. 1160 (early copy) *Lowther*,[2] *Hauerington* c. 1175 StB, 1279 *Ass*, *Haueringtun* c. 1180 StB, c. 1200, c. 1205 CW (OS) i, facs. (p), *Haueryngton* 1396 Pap

Hafrincton c. 1200 StB, *Hauringtona* c. 1235 ib.

Hauirringtona c. 1265 *Hesley*

Haiuerington' 1279 *Ass*

Harington 1292 Cl (p), *Haryngton* 1428 FA

Haveryngham al. Haryngton 1549 *Work*

Harmton 1672 Blome

The *l* in the first form never appears again, and can hardly be taken seriously. An *l*, which is equally meaningless, appears in *Halfrebrek*, the earliest form of Haverbrack (We), where the first element is undoubtedly ON *hafri*. All the other forms of Harrington point to derivation from an OE *Hæfringtun*, containing the personal name *Hæfer*, found in Haversham (PN Bk 8). *v.* ingtūn.

BECKSIDE is so named in 1671 (PR). BLACKETHOLME GATE (6″) is *Blackettholme yate* 1703 *LowtherW*. CROFT HEAD (6″), EAST CROFT, FORELAND (6″), GRAYSON GREEN, STOCKSHILL (6″) and WEST END (6″) are so named in 1725 (*Work*). CROSS HO (6″) is so named in 1726 ib. GREYSTONE COTTAGES (6″). Cf. *Gray Stone* 1725 ib. HALLCAT (6″) is *Hallcott* 1657 CantW viii, *Hall-catt* 1708 PR. HOLLINS (6″) is

---

[1] Part of Harrington was transferred to the borough of Workington (*infra* 454, where its name is preserved in one of the municipal wards), and the remainder was re-named Lowca, in 1934.

[2] The copy in StB (No. 107) gives the reading *Haveryngton*.

Hollings 1725 *Work, Hollins* 1733 ib. *v.* **holegn.** KILNGREEN (6″) is *Killgreen* ib. *v.* **cyln.** LOWCA [laukə] is *Loweowe* (sic) t. Ed 3 (t. Eliz) *Cocker, Lowkay* 1655 PR, *Lowcoe* 1658 *Work, Lowker* 1673 ib., *Lowcoe al. Lowker* 1746 ib. LOWCA HEIGHTS (6″) is *the Height of Lowca* 1703 *LowtherW.* The forms are too late for interpretation. MICKLAM is so named in 1660 (*Work*). SCAW is *Skaw* 1652 PR. HIGH and LOW SCAW (both 6″) are HIGH and LOW SCOW 1725 *Work. v.* skógr. SIKE WHINS is *Sike Whinnes* 1723 ib. *v.* sík (under sīc), whin. WESTGILL is *Weskell Well* 1725 ib. WHINS is *Whinns* ib. *v.* whin.

FIELD-NAMES[1]

(a) In 1815, Bear Gate (*Bearyeatt* 1725), the Pykeys or the three Pykeys (*Pyke* 1660 (early 18th), *Pykey* 1725).

(b) In 1728, *Brunton-House-end, Rogeresse* (*Rogeresses* 1725; cf. *Rogers-Head* ib.), *Steggon-Steell* (*Stoggon-Steele* ib. *v.* stigel); in 1727, *Buts al. Spout Croft, Cepplemoor* (*Copplemoor* 1725), *Crooked Barmara, Cross-end, Jennett Close* (*Genatt Close* 1725), *Langery-head* (*Langery-head al. Dobby Close* 1725. Cf. *Langrey Mead* 1703, *Langrey* 1725), *Loose-plott* (*Lowseplett* 1682. *v.* hlōse), *Pantwell al. Midtown, Wakehow* (*v.* haugr); in 1725, *Barkmouth, Bridgestone, Broad Ing* (*v.* eng), *Collinsteel* (*v.* stigel), *Covensty* (*v.* stig. The first element may be ME *coven,* 'company,' 'gathering,' as in 'coven of witches'), *Flask-head* (*v.* flasshe), *Fould, Garth-Nook* (*v.* garðr), *Kendalls, Leekhouse Green* (id. 1703), *Mooryeatt* ('moor gate,' *v.* mōr, geat), *Pow Stones, Smiddy Hill, Stubbing-Brow, Surdum Street, Woodcockhow* (*v.* haugr); in 1703, *the Crooke of Cragg, the Topp of Borran* (*v.* burghan), *Islam, the Pann Brow;* in 1702, *Coatgarth* (*v.* cot(e), garðr), *Preistgate;* in 1682, *Langslake* (*Langslacke* 1658. 'Long valley,' *v.* slakki), *Wetherigg al. Weiriggs* (*Wether-riggs al. Weighriggs* 1658. *v. infra* 456); in 1673, *Rothery Rowe* (*v.* rāw); in 1660 (early 18th) *Stockbridge* (*v.* stocc, brycg), *Thackwood* (*v.* þak), *Yewriggs;* in n.d. (Whellan) *dowff Scarth* (*v.* skarð), *Hornhow Gyll* (*v.* gil).

30. Hensingham[2]

HENSINGHAM [hensigəm]

Hensingham c. 1170 StB *et passim*, with variant spelling *-yng-*
Helsingham c. 1170 StB, *Elsingham* 1301 GDR
Hunsingham c. 1170 StB
Ensingham 1276 FF
Henzingham 1292 *Ass*

---

[1] Where no source is given, the reference is to *Work.*
[2] In 1934 Hensingham was divided between St Bees (*infra* 430), Weddicar (*infra* 443) and the borough of Whitehaven, where it gives its name to a municipal ward (*infra* 450).

This, like Addingham *supra* 193 and Whicham *infra* 443, is an ancient Anglian name ending in -ingahām. But it is difficult, if not impossible, to reach a convincing explanation of the name on the basis of the existing material. If the solitary form showing *u* in the first syllable can be trusted, the name can, formally, be derived, as by Ekwall in DEPN, from a personal name *Hȳnsige*, a hypothetical form of the recorded *Hūnsige*, in which the first element has undergone *i*-mutation as in *Hēmgils* which goes back to *Hāmgils*. But it is not impossible that the origin of the name may lie, beyond discovery, in one of the archaic names of *provinciæ* or *regiones* recorded in early sources relating to northern England, of which many are etymologically obscure. In any case, the name is historically important as an indication of Anglian settlement in the extreme west of Cumberland at a date which cannot reasonably be placed later than the first quarter of the 7th century (*v. Trans. R. Hist. Soc.* NS XXII, 21).

LINETHWAITE is *Lynthwayt* 1338 Cl, 1359 Pat, *Lynthwaite* p. 1500 StB. 'Flax clearing,' *v.* līn, þveit, and cf. *supra* 359.

HIGH and LOW WREAH are (*del*) *Wra* 1350 *Lowther* (p), *Wray(e)* 1540 *MinAcct*, *High Wrey* 1673 CaineCl. They lie in the eastern angle of Hensingham parish, *v.* (v)rá.

CARTGATE (6″), THE CROSS, GOOSE BUTTS (6″), HOLLINS, NETHEREND, OVEREND and WHELPSIDE (6″) are so named in 1728 (*LowtherW*). CHAPEL HO is *Chapplehouse* 1657 CantW viii. FOULYEAT (6″) is so named in 1823 (PR). *v.* fūl. GALEMIRE (6″) is *Gaylemire* 1616 CaineCl. Probably 'bog-myrtle mýrr,' from OE *gagel*. INGWELL is so named in 1842 (AllerA). It is on the site of *Starmier* 1660 Caine. The latter name is 'sedge mýrr,' from ON star-. LOWHOUSE MILL (6″) is so named in 1819 (CaineCl). MILLHILL (6″) is *Millhills* 1728 *LowtherW*. SUMMER GROVE is so named in 1808 (CaineCl). WOODEND is *Wodend* 1387 IpmR.

FIELD-NAMES

(*a*) Dene Hole, Padstow Field, Share Meadow, Toddle's Field.

(*b*) In 1738 (*Work*) *Borrans Close* (*v.* burghan); in 1728 (*Work*) *Kelbriggs* (*v.* kelda), *Neatholm Grainge* (presumably 'cattle holmr,' *v.* nēat), *Rakes* (*v.* reik), *Seggs*, *Scratgate* (*Scradgate* 1673 CaineCl. Probably 'goblin road,' from ON *skratti*, 'goblin, spectre,' and gata).

IRTON

31. Irton with Santon[1]

Yrton c. 1225 StB (p), *Irton* ib. *et passim*
Hyrton, Hirton 1225 StB (p), 1278 *Ass* (p), 1285 *For* (p), 1399
    IpmR, 1496 Pat
Yirreton 1228 Gray
Urton c. 1250 StB, 1512 LP
Iryton 1292 QW
Erton 1747 CW x

IRTON HALL is so named in 1675 (CW x).
'tūn on the Irt' (*supra* 17).

EASTHWAITE

Ustethayt 1292 *Ass* (p), *Usteatt* 1665 CW x, *Usthwaite in Irton*
    1673 ib.
Ouesthwait in the town of Santon 1338 Cl, *Ostethwayte* 1387 IpmR
Ewsted 1570 *ExchKR, Ewsthwate* 1578 *Cocker*
Easthwaite 1731 PR (Gosforth)

'East clearing,' from ON **austr**, replaced by English 'east,' and
þveit.

GATESGARTH or GASKETH [gasket] is *Catescart* 1278 *Ass* (p), [ ]*catescart*[2]
1279 ib. (p). 'Goats' gap,' *v.* **geit, skarð**. The name is identical with
Gatesgarth in Buttermere *supra* 356.

HEADS WOOD (6″) represents 2 *acres of wood called Le Hevedes* 1294
Cl. *v.* **hēafod**.

MOSSTHWAITE (6″) is *Mosethueytbec* c. 1260 StB, *Mosthwat* 1615 CW x
'Moss clearing,' *v.* **mos, þveit, bekkr**.

SANTON

Santon c. 1235 StB *et passim, (in Coupland)* 1381 *Ass, Gt. or Magna*
    Santon 1584 FF
Sampton 1279 *Ass* (p), 1332 SR
Saunton 1540 *LRMB*
Saynton 1569 FF
Sancton 1610 CW (OS) xv

SANTON BRIDGE is so named in 1673 (CW x). HALL SANTON is *Hall*

---

[1] The detached part of Nether Wasdale (*infra* 440) was transferred to Irton in 1934.
[2] The initial letter has been rubbed out in the MS.

Santon 1710 ib., *Hale Santon* 1718 ib. This is a formation similar to Hall Bolton and Hallsenna *supra* 394, and Hallthwaites *infra* 417.

'Sand tūn.' Parker (172) notes that the place is not particularly sandy, but Miss M. C. Fair notes for us that there are several patches of sand in the neighbourhood, and that within half a mile of Santon is the only sand-pit in the district producing silver-sand.

THUEITDOUNEGALEG' (lost) is *Thwitengales* c. 1235 StB, *Thueitdounegaleg', Thitdunegalieges, Chaitduneleg', Chaitdunegalheg, Chaitmegalheg* c. 1260 ib. This is an inversion compound of which the elements are OWSc þveit and the Old Irish personal name *Dungal*, which is found also in Duncansbay (Caithness) and, probably, nearer home in Dunglaston (PN Dumf 46). To 'Dungal's þveit,' ME *haye*, 'enclosure,' was later added. See also ScandCelts 35–6.

CADDY WELL and PORTERTHWAITE (6″) may be associated with the families of Roger *Cady*, parochial chaplain of Irton (1472 AD iv) and George *Porter* (1570 *ExchKR*). Cf. CW xiv, 91–2.

AIKBANK is *Aikbanke* 1718 CW x, *Oakbank* 1775 ib. *v.* eik. BRIDGE END FM (6″). Cf. *bridge ende* 1578 *Cocker*. COOKSON PLACE is *Cookstone Place* 1713 CW x. CRAG is *the Cragg* 1646 ib. CRAGHOUSE is *Santon Craggehowse* 1563 FF. CUBBEN is *Cubboone* 1668 CW x, *Cubbon* 1691 ib., *Cubban* 1723 ib. EELBECK GROUND is *Eilbecke Ground* 1662 CW x, *Elbecke Ground* 1665 ib., *Elebeck Ground* 1692 ib. GALLY'S BEDSTOCK (6″). These, known locally as *Gally's Bedstocks* ('Goliath's bedposts'), are four large recumbent stones (*ex inf.* Miss M. C. Fair). GATERIGGHOW (6″) is *Garterhow* 1681 CW x, *Gaiterhow* 1690 ib., *Gatrighow* 1728 ib., *Gatrickhow* 1728 PR (Gosforth), *Gaithrigghow* 1736 CW x. 'Goat ridge haugr,' *v.* geit, hryggr (under hrycg). GILL HO is so named in 1692 CW x. GREENGATE (6″) is so named in 1718 ib. GUBBERGILL. Cf. *Gubbergillheade* 1657 ib. xiv. HALL FLATT (6″) is *Hallyflatt* 1693 ib. x, *Hall Flatt* 1697 ib. HANGING HOW (6″) is *Hanginghowe* 1741 ib. *v.* haugr. HEWRIGG is *Hewrig* 1647 CW x, *Hurigg* 1686 ib., *Hawrigg* 1701 ib., *Hewrigg in Erton* 1747 ib. HOLLINS is *Hollings* 1741 ib. IRT COTTAGE (6″) is *Irt cote* 1578 *Cocker*. *v.* cot(e) and Irt R. *supra*. KEYHOW is so named in 1679 ib. KIRKLAND is *Kyrkeland* 1472 AD iv. *v.* kirkja. KITCHEN GROUND is *Kitchin Ground* 1688 CW x. It is there given as the property of John *Kitchin*; this family first appears in Irton in 1583, though John and Nicholas *Kechyn* are mentioned as tenants in Gosforth in 1466 (AD iv).

MAINSGATE is *Maynesgate* 1626 CW x. *v.* mains.[1] MILL PLACE is so named in 1673 (CW x). MITESIDE is so named in 1702 ib. *v.* Mite R. *supra* 22. MOOR END is *Moore End* 1662 ib. MOORGATE is *Moor Yeatt* 1675 ib. MOORSIDE (6″) is so named in 1776 ib. NEWLANDS WOOD (6″). Cf. *the house Newlands* 1705 ib. PARKGATE is *Parkyeate* 1659 CantW viii. PARSONAGE FM (6″). Cf. *the Parsonage* 1697 CW x. PLUMGARTH is so named in 1615 ib. 'Plum-tree garth.' An early example of this compound has become a village name in Plungar (Lei), *Plungard* c. 1125 (c. 1220) *Sloane Roll* xxxi, 7. PUGHOUSE WOOD (6″). Miss M. C. Fair suggests that this may be a place where tiles or bricks were made. The heating of clay for pot-making is locally termed 'pugging.' SLAPESTONES (6″) is *Sleapstones* 1694 CW x, *Sleepstones* 1718 ib., *Slaipstones* 1757 ib. 'Slippery stones,' *v.* slæp. SLEATHWAITE is *Slapwhaite* 1690 ib., *Slatwhaite* 1774 ib. 'Sloe clearing,' *v.* slá(h). SORROWSTONES is *Sorrowstone* 1647 ib. For a possible origin of this name *v.* Parker 62. STANGENDS (6″) is *Stangendes* 1563 FF. WARDWARROW is *Wardwarey* 1676 CW x. WOOD END is *le Wodend* 1363 Ipm.

FIELD-NAMES

(b) In 1717 (CW x) *Gaskow* (*Garscogh* 1399 IpmR, *Garscoue* 1614 CW x. Possibly OE *gār*, 'spear,' or *gāra*, and skógr); in c. 1260 (StB) *Wluehou* ('wolves' haugr'), *le Yuinhat*. Under each of the following dates there is one field-name: *Boghous* 1472 AD iv, *Burnbooth* 1700 CW x (*v.* búð, under bōþ), *Condygarthlands* 1722 ib. (probably from coninger), *Copeland* 1514 LP, *Crookhurst* 1679 CW x (*v.* krókr, hyrst), *Dragghurst* 1597 ib. (*v.* hyrst), *Foulesyke* 1722 ib. (*v.* fūl, sīc), *Garstone* 1615 ib. ('enclosed meadow,' *v.* gærstūn), *Gilleremire* 1717 ib., *Katch Ground* 1718 AllerA, *Litilknaphou* 1290 StB ('little cnæpp' and haugr), *Muntons* 1733 CW x, *Retrawtell* 1399 Denton, *Stonhangere* 1279 Ass (probably 'stān hangra.' Cf. Clayhanger (Ch, St)).

LAMPLUGH [lamplə]

32. Lamplugh[2]

Lamplou c. 1150 StB, 1212 Cur, 1278, 1279 *Ass*, *Lamplo* 1182 P (p), 1212 Cur

Lamplogh c. 1160 StBA, 1419 Pat, *Amploh* 1210 Cur, *Lampelogh* 1283 Pat

Lanplo 1181 P (p)

---

[1] Add: MELTHWAITE is so named in 1679 ib. *Melthwaite Side* appears on the maps of Hodskinson (1774) and Greenwood (1823) but not on the earliest OS. *v.* mel(r), þveit, as *supra* 359.

[2] Salter (*infra* 432) was added to Lamplugh in 1934.

Landplo(h) c. 1200 StB (p), 1241 Cl (p), 1266 Pat, *Landplogh*
  c. 1200 CW (OS) i, facs. (p), *Landplou* 1230 Scotland, 1292 QW,
  Lantploch c. 1250 StB, *Landeplogh* 1359 ib., *Lanteplogh* 1401
  Furness
Lamplod 1201–30 DuLa
Lanploch c. 1210 StB (p)
Langplogh, Langplugh 1292 *Ass*, *Langeplogh* 1309 Greenfield iv
Lamplewe 1419 Pat, *Lamplewgh* 1570 FF, *Lamplugh* 1580 ib.,
  Lamplage 1657 CantW viii

LAMPLUGH CROSS is *ye Crosse* 1694 PR, *Lamplugh Cross* 1781 ib.
LAMPLUGH HALL is so named in 1617 ib. It is *Lampley Hall* 1675
Ogilby. LAMPLUGH MILL (6″) is *Lamplugh-mill* 1699 PR, (*Miln*) 1734
CW xxxviii.

This is a British name, the first element being **landā*, 'enclosure',
as in *Vindolanda*, Chesterholm Nb.[1] Ekwall (DEPN *s.n.*) takes the
second element to be a word corresponding to Welsh *plwyf*, 'parish'
(from Latin *plebs*). But the forms ending in a back spirant are too
numerous and well recorded for this etymology. No Welsh word
corresponding to these forms is known, and the meaning of the
second element must be left an open question.

KELTON (6″)

Keltona c. 1150, c. 1200, c. 1210, c. 1280 StB, 1201 *HolmC*, (*ad*)
  Keltonam c. 1205 StB, *Keltone* c. 1250 ib., *Kelton* c. 1270 ib.
  et passim, (*in Coupland*) 1397 FF, *Kelton'* 1279 *Ass*, *Keltun* 1292
  ib.
Chelton 1174–5 HolmC
Kelton or Ketelton 1610 Denton, *Keteltwone al. Kelton* 1665 CW
  xxxviii

KELTON HEAD is so named in 1582 (PR).
It was said by Denton (28) that this name took its origin from the
Cumbrian thegn *Ketel*, son of Eldred, but the early forms do not
support this view. It is unusual for the name *Ketel* to be reduced to
Kel as early as the 12th century. Certainty is impossible, but ON
kelda, 'spring,' is the most probable origin of the name. The form
Keteltwone comes from a badly written note appended to a pedigree,
and has no authority. *v.* tūn.

---

[1] The meaning 'church' (as in Welsh *llan*, Cornish *lan*, Breton *lann*) is a later
development.

LUND. The only form which definitely refers to this place is *the Lund* 1604 PR. The following forms—*Lund* c. 1150 StB (p), *Lunde, Lunda* early 14th StMaryY, *Lound* 1308 StB, *the Lund* 1374 Cl—probably belong here, but may possibly refer to LUND BRIDGE (6″) in Nether Wasdale parish, for which we have a form *Lunds* in 1578 (*Cocker*). *v.* lundr.

MURTON

Morton' 1203 Cur *et freq* to 1585 FF, (*iuxta Langplugh*) 1292 *Ass Moreton(e)* 1294, 1338 Cl, 1334 Ipm, *villa...vocatur Moreton' et non Morton'* 1391 *Ass, Moreton' in Cleater* 1543 *MinAcct Murton juxta Lamplogh* 1335 StB

KNOCK MURTON is *Knockmorton* 1783 Donald. The name consists of OIr *cnocc*, 'hillock,' and Murton. It refers to a pile of stones on the top of Murton Fell.
'Moor tūn,' *v.* mōr.

ROWRAH is *Rowra* 1583 PR. Cf. *Rucwrabek* 1248 StB. 'Rough corner,' *v.* rūh, (v)rá.

WINDER is *Winderye* c. 1200 StB, *Wyndergh* c. 1210 ib., 1285 *For*, (*in Coupland*) 1271 StB, *Wynderve* 1277 CW x, *Wyndeyre* 1285 *For*, *Wynder* 1535 VE. WYNDER GATE (6″) (in Arlecdon) is *Wynder-gat* 1594 PR. WINDER GILL (6″) is so named in 1598 ib. Cf. also *Wynder Scotle* 1410 AllerA. 'Wind(y) shieling,' *v.* erg.

BANKEND is so named in 1591 (PR). BECK (6″) is *the Beck* 1584 ib. *v.* bekkr. BENTHOW is so named in 1581 ib. *v.* beonet, haugr. BIRD DYKE is *Birkdyck* 1586 ib., *Bird Dike* 1809 ib. The first element is clearly birki, 'birch.' BLAKE FELL is so named in 1783 (Donald). COCKAN is *Cockan* 1636 PR, *Cockin* 1650 ib. COCKLEYGILL (6″) is *Cocklay-gill* 1581 ib. *v.* cokelayk. CROFT HO (6″) is *Crofte* 1657 ib. DOCKRAY NOOK. *v. supra* 333. FELLDYKE is *Fell Dike* 1581 ib. Possibly 'turf dīc,' from Scots *fail*. FOUMART GILL (6″) is 'polecat gil,' from ME *fulmard*. GATRA is *Gateway* (sic) 1582 PR, *Gatray* 1605 ib., *Gateray* 1756 ib. Probably 'goat corner,' *v.* geit, (v)rá. GILL is *the Gill* 1582 ib., *Gill in Kelton* 1681 *Ct. v.* gil. GREEN (6″) is *the Green* 1581 PR, *T'greene* 1655 ib. HAVERCROFT is *Havercrofte* 1600 ib. 'Oats croft,' *v.* hafri. HAWES is *Haws in Kelton* 1613 ib., *Hawes* 1617 ib. HIGH HO (6″) is so named in 1753 ib. HIGH PEN (6″) is *the overpene of Midlefell* 1609–10 CW xxxi. It possibly contains the OW *pen*, 'hill,' though this word is distinctly rare in Cumberland place-names. *Midlefell* is MIDDLE FELL in this parish. HIGH TREES (6″) is *Hygh-trees* 1583 PR. HODYOAD[1] is so named in 1730 ib. HOLEDALE is *Holdaile* 1598 ib., *Hooledaile* 1632 ib. HOLLINS is *the Holing* 1591 ib., *Hollins* 1594 ib., *the Hollinges* 1597 ib. 'The hollytrees,' *v.* holegn. HIGH HOWS, HOWS WOOD (both 6″). Cf. *Howes* 1588 ib. *v.* haugr. HUNTER HOW is so named in 1591 ib. *v.* haugr. KIRKLAND is so named in 1586 ib. *v.* kirkja. LANEFOOT is *Lonenfoot* 1734 ib., *Lanefoot* 1737 ib. *v.* lonning. HIGH, MIDDLE (6″) and LOW LEYS are *the lyes* 1583 ib., *Lease* 1586 ib., *the Leyes* 1608 CW xxxi, *High Leyes* 1638 PR, *Middle Leys* 1756 ib., *Law Lees* 1615 ib. *v.* læs. LINGCROFT is *Lyngcroft* 1584 ib. *v.* lyng. PRIEST HOW (6″) is so named in 1751 (*LowtherW*). 'Priest haugr.' REDHOW is *Readhow* 1589 PR, *the Readhowe* 1598 ib. *v.* haugr. SADDLER'S KNOTT is *Sadlemoore Knotte* 1609–10 CW xxxi. It is so named from the shape. *v.* cnotta (under knǫtt). SCALESMOOR is *Skelsmyre* 1586 PR, *Skeelsmoor* c. 1732 AllerA, 1816 Lysons. The first element is skáli. SCALLOW is *Skallay* 1582 PR, *Skallow* 1588 ib., *the Scallowe* 1606 ib. Probably 'bare hill,' from ON *skalli*, 'bald head,' and haugr. SMAITHWAITE [smiaθwæ·t] is *Smathat* 1586 ib., *Smaithait* 1596 ib. 'Small clearing,' *v.* ON smá(r) and þveit. STOCKHOW HALL is *Stackay* 1581 PR, *Stockey* 1599 ib., *Stockhow* 1602 ib., *Stockahall* 1780 ib. STONYWATH is so named in 1588 ib. 'Stony ford,' *v.* vað. HIGH STOWBANK is *Stawbank* 1583 ib., *Stallbank* 1693 LowtherW, *High Stowbank* 1761 PR. Cf. *Low Stawbank* 1772 ib., *Lowerstawbank* 1780 ib. STREETGATE (6″) is *Streetgat* 1581 ib., *Strat-gat* 1584 ib. THACKMOOR WOOD (6″). Cf. *Thackmoor-gate* 1737 ib. *v.* þak. TODHOLE [tiadəl] is *Todhol* 1582 ib., *Teadholes* 1602 ib., *the Toadhole* 1606 ib. Probably 'toad hole,' in spite of the earliest form. TOM BUTT (6″) is so named in 1751 ib. WHINNAH is *Whyney* 1583 ib., *Winnah* 1675 *Ogilby*. WOODEND is *the Woodend* 1582 PR.

FIELD-NAMES

(a) In 1809 (*EnclA*) Cop Thorn (*v.* coppede), Gale, Honey Pott, Lattaray, Outrigg, Red Ing (*v.* eng), Watley Bank, Wineatte; in 1806 (PR) Teas (*Teathes* 1628 ib., *Toathes* 1733 ib., *Toes* 1792 ib.).

(b) In 1781 (PR) *Lagaran wod* (*Ladkerton Wood* 1629 ib., *Lackerton Wood* 1655 ib.); in 1777 (PR) *Millgillhead* (*Mylgill-head* 1583 ib.); in 1690 (PR) *Youdhole* (*Yawdhole* 1608 ib. dial. yad, 'nag'); in 1592 (PR) *the Hock, Kyrkholm* (*v.* kirkja, holmr); in c. 1250 (StB) *Sputekelde* (ME spoute (of

---

[1] Probably of the same origin as *Hadyad*, 'hold-nag.'

which the earliest reference in NED is dated 1392) and kelda), *tostelterun*.
Under each of the following dates there is one field-name: *Collier-yeat* 1688
PR, *le Crounk* c. 1290 StB, *Dubhalle* 1635 PR (*v.* dub), *Gledemerthueit* c. 1210
StB ('clearing by the kite mere,' from OE *glida, gleoda*, 'kite,' mere and
þveit), *Houngrelle* 1624 PR ('hunger hill'), *The Meadow Shawe* 1681 CW xv
(*v.* sceaga), *Rollohead* 1604 PR, *Royndergill* 1593 ib., *Teydall* 1642 PR,
Undergarth 1292 *Ass* (*v.* garðr).

33. Lorton

HIGH and LOW LORTON

> *Loretona* c. 1150 (early copy) *Lowther, Loretuna* 1171–5 (1333)
>   CW iii, *Loreton* 1230 Scotland
> *Lortun*(*a*) c. 1160 StB, *Lorton*(*e*) 1197, 1198 P *et passim*, (*parua*)
>   1279 *Ass* (p), (*in Braythweit*) 1316 Ipm, *Overlorton* 1365 Pat,
>   *Lorton Inferior* 1399 IpmR, *Lortonhighside* 1596 FF, *Nether Lorton*
>   1597 CW (OS) xii, *Oud Lorton* 1669 PR
> *Lorenton*' 1195 FF
> *Loorton* 1540 *MinAcct, Lurton, Lowe Lurton*' 1570 *ExchKR*

LORTON LOW MILL (6″) (in Whinfell parish) is *Lorton Mylne otherwyse called Whynfell Mylne* 1586 *Cocker*. In the parish were *del Crag
de Lorton* 1292 *Ass* (p) and *Hede de Lorton* 1473 *Cocker*.

v. tūn. For the first element Ekwall (DEPN) suggests ON *Hlóra*,
'roaring,' found as a Norwegian stream-name *Lora* (Elvenavne 148)
and as a mythical feminine personal name.

ARMASIDE is *Harmondesheved* 1368 Ipm, *Hermudesheved* 1369 ib.,
Hermethside 1578 *Cocker, Armesyde* 1600 CW (OS) xii, *Armaside* 1608
ib., *Harmeside* 1647 ib. The two medieval forms vary too widely for
any certain explanation, but the name may contain the ON personal
name *Hermundr*. The second element is OE hēafod, 'head.' The later
forms have clearly been influenced by ME *ermite*, 'hermit,' found in
the various Armathwaites in the county.

BLAZE BECK and BRIDGE (both 6″). The 'Blaze' in question may be
recorded in the name of Edward *del Blees* (1325 *Ass*). If so, it may
well be identical with the Norwegian *bles* which occurs in Blaze Fell
supra 220. The bridge is *Whinlatter Bridge* 1753 CW (OS) xv.

HOBCARTON is *Hopecartan* 1260 *Rental, Hobbecartan* 1290 *MinAcct*.
This is a difficult name. There is little doubt that it is an inversion
compound of which the second element is the OIr personal name
Cartán. The alternation of *Hope-* and *Hobbe-* in the early forms makes

the meaning of the first element uncertain. The name as a whole probably refers to the hill which culminates in Hobcarton End, and it is at least possible that the first element should be associated with the word *hobb* or *hobbe* which Ekwall (Studies[2] 177–8) suggests for the first element of Hautbois (Nf). A cognate of the word is recorded in Frisian with the sense of a 'piece of rising ground surrounded by marsh.' Its history is obscure and its meaning cannot be defined closely, but its general sense seems to have been 'hill.'

LORD'S SEAT is *Lauerdesate* 1247 *FF*, *the Lordseatt* 16th CW xiv, *Lord's Seat* 1821 G. The first form shows that this name, which clearly means 'lord's pasturage' (*v.* sætr), is at least of early medieval origin. The first element is OE *hlāford*, 'lord.'

SWINSIDE is *Swynesheued* 1260 *Rental*, 1292 *Ass*, *Swyneside high close* 1578 *Cocker*. 'Swine's headland,' *v.* hēafod.

WHINLATTER is *Whynlater* 1505 *Cocker*, *Whinlatter* 16th CW xiv, *passes of Whinlate* 1794 H. 'Furze-covered slope,' *v.* **whin** and Latrigg *supra* 321.

BOONBECK (6″). Cf. *Boonhouse* 1681 *DandC*. CASS HOW (6″). Cf. *Casse place* 1578 *Cocker*. Cf. *supra* 303. CLINTS WOOD (6″) is named from *Clynte* ib. *v.* klint. CRAGGED HEAD (6″) is *Cragge of the head* ib. HOW WOOD (6″) is *the How* (a wood) ib. *v.* **haugr**. WONSUL HOW (6″) is *woornstale howe* ib. *v.* **haugr**.

FIELD-NAMES

(b) In 1681 (*DandC*) *Cattrood-lands*, *Langdraughts* ('Long draught,' i.e. "a place where a net (for fish) is wont to be drawn," *v.* NED, *s.v. draught* sb. III, 7 b, where the first example of the word used in this sense is dated 1895); in 1674 (*DandC*) *Beneathbeck*, *Beneathgate*; in 1578 (*Cocker*) *Avenhe*, *the Butts*, *the Coollopp holmes*, *Croke of the Howe* (*v.* haugr), *Doungerley*, *grayles*, *harrowe close*, *the healds* (*v.* h(i)elde), *Hornell groves* (*Thornell grove*, *hornehill grove* 1570 *ExchKR*), *Intack* (*v.* intak), *the Langaldside*, *Lingthwate* (*v.* lyng, þveit), *Ranckdale*, *the Raynes* (*v.* rein), *Rebell ryke* (sic), *Sawghill* (also *Saughkell*) (perhaps identical with *Salkeld supra* 236), *Scarborowe*, *Swathes garth* (*v.* garðr), *Thickthornes*, *Towneman dale*, *Ulwray* (*v.* (v)rá), *Walkmill Leate* ('fulling mill stream'), *Whames Inge* (*v.* hvammr, under hwamm, eng), *the Wringe*; in 1570 (*ExchKR*) *Flates*, *Stockdale*. Under each of the following dates there is one field-name: *Gainebankes* 1682 *DandC*, *Slatwharrall* 1584 CW (OS) xv ('slate-quarry', *v.* NED *quarrel*, sb.[2]), *Stangends* 1651 ib. xiv.

34. Loweswater

LOWESWATER [lauzwɔtə]

> *Lousewater* c. 1160 StB, 1303 *GDR*, 1323 Ch, 1383 Pat, 1385 FF
> *Laswater* (sic) c. 1160 (early copy) *Lowther*.[1]
> *Losewater* 1247, 1556 FF
> *Lowswater* 1186 StB, *Lowswatter* 1656 CantW vii
> *Laweswater, Laweswatre* 1188, 1189 P, 1397 Pat, *Laueswat'* 1190–5 P
> *Loueneswater* t. Ric 1 (1308) Ch
> *Loweswatre* 1230 Scotland, 1279 *Ass*, 1366 Pat, *Loweswater* 1367 Ipm
> *Louswater* 1281 Wickwane
> *Lauswatre* 1357 FF, 1389 ib. (p), *Lawswatyr* 1388 StB (p), *Lawswater* 1764 CW xli

> *v.* Loweswater *supra* 34.

KIRKHEAD is *Kirkeheued* 1279 *Ass* (p), *Kirkeheved* 1286 StB. 'Church headland.' Loweswater church is about a quarter of a mile to the north-east.

LATTERHEAD is *Laterheued* 1260 *Rental*. The second element is OE **hēafod**. For the first see Latrigg *supra* 321.

MARSHALFLATE and SERGANTESHOU (both lost). It is a curious coincidence, though it may well be no more, that two field-names in Loweswater—*Marshalflate* 1539 MinAcct (*v.* flat) and *Serganteshou* 1230 Scotland (*v.* haugr)—have first elements which reflect the organisation of feudal society. *Marshal* stands for OFr *marechal*, originally meaning 'a servant who looked after the stables,' from which a later sense 'farrier' developed. The medieval *sergeant* was normally a man rendering some form of direct personal service to a lord.[2] As, however, there is no feudal centre in the neighbourhood of Loweswater, no stress can be laid on these names, and *Marshalflate*, for which there is no medieval form, may be derived from a family-name.

MOCKERKIN

> *Moldcorkyn, Moldcorkin* 1208 FF, *Molcorkilne, Molkorkilne* c. 1225 StB, *Molcerkyn* 1369 Ipm, *Molkorkyn* 1370 ib., *Molkirkyn* 1390 Cocker

---

[1] The copy in StB (No. 107) gives the reading *Loswater*.

[2] Sergeant Knowe across the Border was called after a member of the Beattie family who was King's Sergeant and Officer of Eskdale in 1552 (PN Dumf 39).

Morcorkin 1230 Scotland
Molcornekynne 1285 *Ass, Moltcornkyn* 1292 ib.
Mokerkyn 1505 *Cocker, Mockerkin* 1578 ib.

As suggested by Ekwall (ScandCelts 29), this is an inversion compound. The first element is identified by Ekwall with OWSc **moldi*, well recorded as a hill-name in Norway. Like the OE *molda*, of which it is a cognate, the word seems to have meant literally 'top of the head' (see Ekwall, Studies[2] 195), and it could have been appropriately applied to the neighbouring MOCKERKIN How. The second element is probably a diminutive in *-án* of the OIr personal name *Corc* which occurs in Corby *supra* 161.

SCRAITHEGIL (lost) is *Sorachegil*[1] 1254 StB, *Scraithegil* 1256 ib. The meaning is 'ravine in which there has been a landslide.' The second element is gil, the first is ON *skreið*, standing in ablaut relation to *skriða*, 'landslip,' which is recorded as an Icelandic place-name (Kålund ii, 225). The word *skreið* seems to occur in Scrafield (L), for which there are numerous medieval forms showing *-ei-* in the first element. See also under Burnhope Seat (*supra* 176).

SOSGILL is *Solrescales* c. 1203 (n.d.) StBA, *Saurestaħs* 1209 FF, *Saurescoles* 1230 Scotland, *Sourescal* 1278 *Ass, Sourscales* 1301 Pat, *Sorescale* 1507 *Cocker, Soskell* 1609 CW xxxi, *Sosgill* 1782 PR (Lamplugh). 'Muddy shieling,' or 'shielings,' *v.* saurr, skáli. The first *l* in the first form is presumably an inverted spelling for *u*. The second element was obscured through lack of stress and confused with gil.

STARLING DODD, DODD and LITTLE DODD. *v.* dod. In 1230 (Scotland i, 203) the boundary of the woodland belonging to Loweswater ran in part from Blea Tarn to the path of *Styalein*, by this path to the slope of the hill called *Hardecnut* (cf. *supra* 344) and *le Dod de Gillefinchor*, and from the same Dod as far as *the other high Dod of Gillefinchor*. As is usual, these boundary marks cannot be identified with absolute precision, but their succession suggests very strongly that the modern *Starling* of Starling Dodd represents the *Styalein* of 1230. The latter name is an inversion compound, meaning '*Alein*'s path,' from the Breton personal name *Alein* (cf. Allonby and Ellonby *supra* 261, 240) and OE stīg. The medieval *stīg* seems to be preserved in a modern footpath along this hill.

---

[1] The 1254 form is either a corruption or a scribal error.

L

The Dod and *the other high Dod of Gillefinchor* cannot be fixed so nearly, but they may well be identical with the hills called Little Dodd and Dodd, between Starling Dodd and Buttermere. Ekwall (Scand-Celts 25) takes the *Gille* of *Gillefinchor* to represent the ON *gil*, 'ravine', as in *Gillecamban* (196), *Gillegarran* (375). The second element is the ON personal name *Finnþórr*.[1] The *c* in *-finchor* is undoubtedly due to the common medieval misreading of *t* as *c*. As Professor Ekwall points out, the name is apparently still in use in the corrupt form Gillflinter (Beck).

THACKTHWAITE is *Tacthwayte, Thacthwait* 1220 StB, *Thakkethweyt* 1279 *Ass, Thakthwaite* 1279 FF, *Thackwhat* 1519 *FF*. 'Clearing where reeds for thatching grow,' *v.* þak, þveit.

WATEREND is *dil Waterende* 1292 *Ass* (p), *atte Waterende* 1302 Pat (p), *Water end* 1578 *Cocker*. It is at the north end of Loweswater (lake).

BARGATE, CRABTREE BECK (6″) (place), HIGH NOOK, THRUSHBANK (6″) and WATERGATE are so named in 1794 (MapH). BLACK CRAG, BLEA CRAG (6″) (*v.* blá(r)), CARLING KNOTT (*v. infra* 440). HIGHCROSS, LOW FELL (6″) and MELLBREAK are so named in 1784 (West). FANGS is *ffanges* 1602 CW (OS) xii. FOULSYKE (6″) is *Foul sike* 1794 MapH. *v.* fūl, sīc. GODFERHEAD is *Godfred* ib. HIGH PARK is *the high parke* 1578 *Cocker*. LING CRAGS are *Ling Crag* 1821 G. *v.* lyng. MILL HILL is so named in 1758 (DKR xlii). It is probably *Milnehow* 1550 NB. PEEL is *the Peele* 1631 CW xxxvi. SCALE FORCE is *Scaleforce or Highforce* 1794 H. *v.* skáli, fors. SPOUT HO (6″) is so named in 1578 (*Cocker*). *v.* spoute.

FIELD-NAMES

(b) In 1794 (H) *Kirkstall, Michihowe* (*v.* haugr); in 1390 (*Cocker*) *Dumbek, layroksyke* (*Layrocsyk* c. 1203 (n.d.) StBA. Probably 'lark sīc'). Under each of the following dates there is one field-name: *Craples hall* 1675 Sandford, *Dubwra* a. 1256 StBA (*v.* dub, (v)rá), *Dupwath* 1286 StB (*v.* vað), *Fernnbigg'* 1333 *Cocker* (may be 'fern bigging'), *le fryth* 1507 ib. (*v.* fyrhþ(e)), *la More* 1292 *Ass* (*v.* mōr).

[1] Recorded in Cu (StB 317).

35. Lowside Quarter[1]

LOWSIDE QUARTER (6″). This was originally part of St Bees parish.

BRAYSTONES

> *Bradestanes* 1247 StB (p), 1279 *Ass* (p), *Braydestanes* 1278, 1279 ib., 1294 Ipm
>
> *Braystanes* 1279 *Ass et freq* to 1391 HMC xxv, with variant spellings *Brai-, Brey-, Braystones* 1279 *Ass, Braistones* 1540 *MinAcct*
>
> *Braythestanes* 1294 Cl, *Breithstanes* 1300 ib., *Braihcstanes* 1363 Ipm

'Broad stones,' *v.* breiðr, steinn, with the second element replaced by OE stān.

BRIG STONES (6″) is *Brighestaynes, Bruggestaynes* c. 1260 StB. Brig Stones is by the sea, and *Brig* here represents ON *bryggja*, 'jetty, quay.' The second element is steinn.

COULDERTON

> *Culdretun* c. 1180 *Hesley, Culdertun* c. 1200 CW (OS) i, facs., *Culderton(e)* 1294 Cl *et freq* to 1395 Pat, *Culdreton* 1363, 1370 Ipm
>
> *Culterston* 1207 P, *Culderston* 1369 Ipm
>
> *Culdirton* c. 1260 StB
>
> *Couderton* 1474 Pat, *Nether Cowderton* 1585 FlemingMem
>
> *Coulderton, midle and ouer Colderton* 1578 *Cocker*
>
> *Coutherton* 1758 *LowtherW*

In the neighbourhood were *Cultercoubeck* and *Culterton'-ose* (sic print) 1294 Cl.

The first element here, as in Holm Cultram *supra* 288 is, as noted in DEPN, the British word corresponding to Welsh *culdir*, 'narrow strip of land,' with reference to the long tongue of land between Ellergill Beck and the sea. Hence 'tūn on a site known as *Culdir.*'

CROFTHEAD (6″). Cf. *Croft foote, the Crofte* 1578 *Cocker.* MIDDLE and LOW EHENSIDE are *Ehenside* ib., *Endside* 1754 *LowtherW. v.* Ehen R. *supra* 13. GILL HO (6″). Cf. *the gill closse* 1578 *Cocker. v.* gil. HANGING BANK (6″) is *hanginge banck* ib. NETHERTOWN is *Nethertowne* 1720 PR (Millom). Cf. *Overtownefeilde* 1578 *Cocker.* ROTHERSYKE is *Roderscicke* 1658 CantW viii, *Rodersyke* 1717 CaineCl. *v.* sīc.

---

[1] Part of Lowside Quarter was transferred to St John Beckermet (*supra* 340) in 1935.

FIELD-NAMES

(a) Near and Far Adams, Castlabank, Duke Butts, Feulow, Maiden Castle (v. supra 255), Standing Stone, Tarn Whins (v. tiǫrn, whin).

(b) In 1578 (Cocker) Aslabanck, belbutt (cf. supra 382), bromock, burnt hewes, Cranebutt, headlaslake, healyslake, Heke flatt, Hewland browes, Kerster (also Kirster) flatt (conceivably 'kirkju staðir'), Rauensey (may be 'raven's ēg'), Mid and Low Sowra, Sleabanck, Wandowbanck holme (v. holmr), Warskales (v. skáli), Waterley, Whynie howe (v. haugr), Wythingkeld (v. kelda); in 1474 (Pat) (township of) Bondage (possibly a parallel to Bongate in Appleby (We) (13th Bondegate), which is described in a charter of King John as Vetus Appulbi ubi villani manent); in 1338 (Cl) Eyngarth (v. Ehen R. supra 13), Mitegarth (v. Mite R. supra 22 and cf. Fishgarth supra 79), Thurnpot (probably 'thorn pot').

36. Millom and Millom Rural

MILLOM

> Millum c. 1180 Furness et freq to 1550 FF, with variant spellings
>   Mil-, Myll-
> Muluum (sic) 1189–94 LaCh, Mullum 1205 ib. (both p)
> Miluun 1183–1216 DuLa
> Milnum c. 1205, 1287 Hesley, 1300 Pat, 1334 Ipm, 1338 Cl,
>   Mylnom 1279 Ass, Milnom ib., 1282 DuLa
> Millun 1251 Pipe, Milloun 1278 Ass, Millon, Milon 1279 ib., Milun
>   1338 Cl
> Melon, Mellon, Melom 1279 Ass, Mellom 1405 Pat
> Millom 1303 FF et passim
> Mill Holme 1533–8 ECP
> Mylneham or Mylham 1565 FF

MILLOM CASTLE is the castle of Millom 1513 LP.

The early forms make it clear that this is 'at the mills,' from mylnum, dative plural of myln, a useful parallel being Kilham (PN ERY 97), from cylnum. The numerous forms showing -ln- and the occasional appearance of u in the first syllable are conclusive. Millom and Millom Rural are distinguished as Above Millom, Beneath Millom 1625 PR.

The present name is not recorded till c. 1180, and it is likely that, as W. Farrer argued in Trans. of the Lancashire and Cheshire Antiquarian Society xviii, 94 and 97, it was earlier called Hougenai, the dative plural of haugr with the addition of ēg. Hougun, a manor held by Earl Tosti in 1065 and comprising five vills (with nineteen teamlands, four in Hougun, four in Bootle, four in Whicham, six in Hougenai and one in Kirksanton), was later represented by the manor of Millom. The site of *Hougenai* was perhaps at Millom Castle.

ARNABY is *Arnolvebi* c. 1230 Furness, *Arnolby* 1292 ib., *Arnoldeby* 1292 *Ass*, *Arnolfby* 1301 Furness, *Arnaldby* 1411 Pat, *Arnabye* 1605 PR, *Annoby* 1633 ib. ARNABY MILL is so named in 1664 ib. '*Arnolf*'s bȳ.' This personal name was extremely common in ON in the forms *Ǫrnolfr*, and in the present context may certainly be regarded as of Norse origin. The corresponding form *Arnulf* in which the name appears in ODan and OSw, is comparatively rare, and most of the examples are late.

DUDDON is *villa de Dodene* 1279 *Ass*. DUDDON BANK (6") is *Duddenbanke* 1601 PR. DUDDON BRIDGE is *pontem de Duden*, *Doden* 1292 *Ass*, *Dodenbrig* 1332 SR (p), *Duddonbridge* 1610 PR. DUDDON HALL is so named in 1703 ib. *v.* Duddon R. *supra* 11.

DUNNINGWELL (6") is *Duningekeld* c. 1210 Furness, *Dunnyngwell* 1599 PR. The first part of this name is probably the Old and Middle English personal name *Dunning*. The second element in the oldest form is clearly ON kelda, 'spring.' By the end of the 16th century it had been replaced by the English 'well.'

HAVERIGG is *Haverich* c. 1170 StB, *Haverig(g)* c. 1180 Furness *et passim*, *Heuerig* c. 1195 Cockersand, *Hevrigge* 1600 PR, *Haveridge* 1612 ib. 'Oat ridge,' *v.* hafri, hryggr (under hrycg).

HESTHAM is *Hestholm* 1250–93 DuLa (p), *Estholm*, *Hestholm* 1278, 1279 *Ass* (both p), *Heston* 1628 PR, *Hestholme*, *Hesthamme* 1655 ib. 'Stallion meadow,' *v.* hestr, holmr, and cf. *supra* 120, 302.

KIRKSANTON [kʌrsantən]

> *Santacherche* 1086 DB
> *Kirkesant'* a. 1152 Furness, *Kirkesantan* ib. *et passim* to 1333 *Ass*, *Kirksanton* 1175–90 DuLa, *Kyrksanton* 1278 *Ass*, *Kirksanton* 1333 ib., *Kirksancton* 1629 PR
> *Kyrkesande* 1292 *Ass*

In the parish was *holmum de Kirkesantan* 1175–94 Furness. *v.* holmr. The Rev. W. S. Sykes tells us that the holm in Kirksanton is known locally as *Monksholm*, from the monks of Furness.

'Church of St Sanctan,' *v.* kirkja. The name *Sanctán* was borne by more than one early Irish saint. There is an exact parallel to this name in the parish-name Kirk Santon in the Isle of Man (PN IOM 133),

13th *ecclesia Sancti Santani*. It has been suggested (Sedgefield 71) that a corruption of the name *Santan* into *Saint Anne* may explain the dedication of the chapel of Thwaites in this parish to the latter saint at its consecration in 1724. There is a recorded example of such a corruption in the name Kill St Ann in county Dublin, which represents an earlier *Cill Easpuig Sanctáin* (PN IOM *loc. cit.*).

LACRA is *Lawcray, Lowcray, Loucray* 1403 *Deed, Lacra* 1611 PR, *Lacrae* 1623 ib., *Lacrey* 1629 ib., *Lackra* 1641 ib., *Lawcrey* 1655 ib., *Lakerey* 1774 ib. Probably, as Professor Ekwall suggests, ON *lauk-*(v)rá, 'garlic (v)ra'.

LANGTHWAITE (6″) is *Langetwait* 1170 Furness, *Langethwaith* 1250 ib. There is in the parish also LONGTHWAITE (6″), and the forms *Long-thwayte* 1462 *Netherhall, Longthwatt* 1614 PR may refer to either place. The meaning of both is 'long þveit.'

LAYRIGGS is *duas Leiriggas, duas Layriggas* 1175–94 Furness, *duas Lairiggas* 1190–1204 ib., *Layrigges* 1623 PR. Apparently 'muddy ridges,' from ON leirr and hryggr.

LOW SCALES [lɑskəlz]

    Loftcales 1332 SR (p)
    Loscalez 1570 *LowtherW, Loskels* 1591 PR, *Loskills* 1598 *Star Chamber, Loskelles* 1607 PR, *Neather Loscalls* 1694 ib., *Low-Loscalls* 1702 ib., *Netherloscailes* 1702 *Netherhall, Low Lascals* 1774 Donald

HIGH LOWSCALES is *Upper Loskeles* 1630 PR, *High-Loscalls* 1734 ib., *High Lascals* 1774 Donald.

If the first form can be trusted, this is 'shielings with a loft,' *v.* lopt, skáli.

MELES (fields) is *Melis, Meles* 1175–94 Furness, *Molas* a. 1290 ib., (*le*) *Meles* ib., 1292 ib., 1410 HMC x, c. 1840 *TA, le Melis* 1397 DuLa, *Meales* 1537 Furness. 'Sandhills,' *v.* melr and cf. Eskmeals *supra* 345. The name is now given to fields lying by High and Low Layriggs in Kirksanton (*supra*) (*ex inf.* Rev. W. S. Sykes).

POSTLETHWAITE (*TA*) is the name of a field in Mirehouse, and clearly corresponds to what is called the *manerium de Postelthayt, Posteltwaith* 1278 *Ass, Postelthweyt* 1279 ib. In the latter case, the plaintiff said it was a manor, but the defendant said it was part of the vill of Kirksanton. There is no other recorded example of this place-name, but it is presumably the origin of the widespread Cumbrian family-name

Postlethwaite. Unfortunately, the derivation of the name is obscure. Formally, it may contain the ON *postoli*, 'apostle,' but there are no known religious associations of the site. The name should possibly be associated with Postle Meadow, a mile and a half to the south. *v.* þveit.

SALTHOUSE is *Salthus in Caupland* 1247 Furness. 'Salt-house'; that is, apparently, a building in which salt was stored.

STANDING STONES is *lapides stantes* 1260–80 Furness, *the Standing Stones* 1587 PR (Whicham).

STAYNLENOK (lost) is *Staynlenok* 1260–80 Furness. This is apparently an inversion compound of ON steinn and **Lennóc*, a diminutive of OIr *Lend*, the whole name meaning '*Lennóc*'s stone.' See further ScandCelts 34–5.

SUNKENKIRK (6″) is *Chappell Suke* 1624 PR, *Chapel Sucken* 1642 HMC iv, *Sunken Kirks* 1794 H, *Sunken-Kirk* 1816 Lysons. This is the site of a stone circle (*v.* CW ii, 57–76), to which the name may possibly refer. Unfortunately, the name does not seem to be found before the 17th century, and the original form and meaning cannot be determined.

SWINSIDE is *Swynesat* 1242 FF, *Swinside* 1608 PR. 'Swine pasture,' *v.* sætr.

THWAITES FELL derives from *Thueites* c. 1170 StB, *Thuaites* 1183–1216 Furness, *Tweites in Copland'* 1210 Cur, *Twaytis* 1449 AD iv (p), *Thwaytes* 1466 Netherhall, *Thwaits up in the head of Millome* 1675 Sandford. 'Clearings,' *v.* þveit. THWAITES MILL (6″) is *Thwayte Myll* 1632 PR. THWAITE YEAT is *Thwet-yeat* 1610 ib. *v.* geat. HALLTHWAITES is *the Hall of Thaytis* 1449 AD iv, *Halthwett, Halthwettes* 1608 PR *Halthetes* 1611 ib., *Hall-thwayte* 1629 ib., *Hawthwaites* 1657 CW xiv. This is a case, as in Hall Bolton and Hallsenna *supra* 394, in which the word 'hall' has become prefixed to an existing place-name. The form of 1449 shows the first stage in this combination.

WRINGE (lost) is *Wrengis de Haverig* c. 1250 StB, *Wringes* 1604 PR, *Wringe* 1633 ib. No suggestion can be offered, if it is not OE *wringe*, '(cheese)press.'

COOKSON'S PLANTATION (6″), DRINKALDS[1], GORNAL GROUND[2] (6″), STEEL GREEN[3] and TOWSEY HOLE (6″) are probably to be associated

---

[1] *Drinkall* 1630 Sykes, *Drinkals* 1678 PR.   [2] *Gurnalground* 1631 ib.
[3] *Stealgreene* 1627 ib.

with the families of Richard *Cookson* (1594 PR), John *Drincall* (1592 ib.) and Milo *Drinkall de Wayside* (1646 ib.), Jenet *Gurnell* (1593 ib.), Anthonye *Steele* (1597 ib.) and Frances *Towsay* (1668 ib.).

APPLEHEAD (6″) is *Aplehead* 1629 PR. ASH HO is *Ashouse* 1642 ib. BANKSIDE is *Banksid* 1679 ib. (Whicham). BECK is *Becke* 1603 PR. BECK BANK (6″) is *Beckbanke* 1608 ib. BECKFOOT is *Beckfout* 1669 ib. HIGH BECKSTONES MILL (6″) is *Upper-beck-stones mill* 1816 Lysons. BLEA MOSS (6″) is *Blemos* t. Hy 8 *DuLa. v.* mos. BOADHOLE is *Boad holle* 1626 PR, *Board-whole* 1680 ib. Cf. the same name *supra* 372. BOGHOUSE is so named in 1609 ib. BORWICK RAILS is *Barret-Rayls* 1728 ib., *Burick Rails* 1757 ib., *Burwick-rails* 1763 ib., *Borwick-rails* 1793 ib. BRIDGE END is *Bridgend* 1607 PR. BROADGATE is *Brodyett* 1609 ib., *Brod-yaitt* 1610 ib., *Brodgaite* 1619 ib., *Broadegate* 1622 ib. *v.* brād, geat. BUCKMAN HALL (6″) is so named in 1608 ib. It is *Buckmanhowe* 1609 ib., *Buckmanhale* 1632 ib. BURNFIELD is so named in 1772 ib. CRAG HALL is *Crag(g) Hall* 1599, 1610 ib., *Crag hale* 1607 ib., *(in Thwaits)* 1657 CW xiv. CRAG HO (6″) is *Craghous* 1646 PR. THE CROFT (6″). Cf. *Croftes juxta mossam* 1190–1200 Cockersand. CROSS (6″) is *Crosse* 1604 PR, *Crosse below Myllom* 1629 ib., *the Cross in Millom* 1652 ib. (Whicham). CROSS HO is *Crosho* 1609 PR, *Cros-house* 1614 ib., 1646 *LowtherW*. DASHATGATE is *Dasshettyeat* 1570 *LowtherW*, *Dyshet yeat* 1607, 1617 PR, *Dashet yeat* 1630 ib., *Dashat-yate* 1646 *LowtherW*, *Dashatgate* 1647 PR, *Dyesat-gate* 1784 ib., *Dyeset* 1784 *Sykes*. ELF HALL[1] is *Elfe-hole* 1631 PR, *Elphole* c. 1840 *TA*. Cf. *Elfe Cragge* 1631 PR, *Elfgate* 1633 ib. Apparently 'elf hole.' FENWICK (local) is *Fenacke* 1630 ib., *Fenwicke* 1654 ib. GRAYSTONE HO (6″) is *Grayston Ho* 1629 ib. THE GREEN is *Green* 1781 ib. (Whicham). HALL BANK is *Hallebanck* n.d. AD iv. HALL GREEN (6″) is *Hall greene* 1664 *LowtherW*. HARRATH (6″) is *Harroth* 1579 *Star Chamber*, *Harrats* 1794 H. HAWS is *Hawes* 1599 PR. HIGH BROW is *Hebbero* 1608 ib., *Heberah* 1667 ib., *Hebberaw* 1671 ib., *Hebrah* 1695 ib. The forms suggest that the original name may have been OE hē(a)h be(o)rg, 'high barrow,' but they are too late for certainty. THE HILL is *(the) Hill* 1597, 1657 ib. HODBARROW is *Hodbarrow* 1620 ib., *Het-brow* 1634 *Sykes*, *Hotbarrow* 1799, 1808 PR, *Hob(b)erow* 1646 *LowtherW*. HOLE HO is *Holhouse* 1602 PR, *Wholehouse* 1710 ib. The first element seems to be OE holh, 'hollow.' INTAKE WOOD(6″). Cf. *Intack* 1645 *LowtherW. v.* intak. KNOTTEND is *Knotend* 1608 PR. LADY HALL is

---

[1] Cf. *Elfa-hills* (*supra* 209) and Elva Hill (*infra* 435). The Rev. W. S. Sykes tells us that this is the probable site of the Furness Abbey salt works.

Ladye hall 1604 ib. LIMESTONE HALL[1] (6″) is so named in 1798 (CW xxiv). Low Ho is so named in 1770 (PR). MAINS BROW (6″). Cf. *Maynes* 1595 ib. *v.* mains. MARSHSIDE is *Marshseede* 1604 ib., *Marshside* 1612 ib. MIDLOW HILL (6″) is *Medlowe* 1664 *LowtherW*. MIRE HO. Cf. *Mirehouse Grange* 1537 *AOMB*. THE MOOR is *More* 1604 PR. Probably the *vastum de Mylnom* of 1279 *Ass*. MOOREND (6″) is so named in 1781 (PR). MOSS SIDE (6″) is *Mosseside* 1678 ib. NEW FIELD (6″) is so named in 1734 ib. NEW HALL is so named in 1733 ib. THE OAKS is *Ake* 1570 *LowtherW*, (*the*) *Oakes* 1609, 1616 PR. OXENBOWS is *Oxenbow* 1634 ib., *Oxenbowe* 1647 ib. GREAT PADDY CRAG (6″) is *Great Paddy Cragg* 1821 G. PANNATT HILL (6″) is *Pannethill* 1645 *LowtherW*, *Panethill al. Bare-arse* 1720 PR. PARKHEAD (6″) is *Parke-heade* 1694 ib. PIKEWELL (6″) may be *Pighelle* 1537 *AOMB*. *v.* pightel. PO HO is *the Powlehouse* 1586 PR (Whicham), *Powhouse* 1596 PR, *Poowhous* 1640 ib., *Pohous* 1641 ib. The poll is Whicham Beck. POHOUSE BANK (6″). Cf. *Powbanke* 1593 ib., *Poolebancke* 1617 ib. RAYLANDS (6″) is *Ray-lands* 1703 ib. ROANLANDS (6″) is *Rowlandes* 1588 ib. (Whicham), *Rollande* 1619 PR, *Rawnlands* 1646 *LowtherW*, *Ronalandes* 1653 PR, *Rowenlandes* 1657 ib., *Rownlands* 1733 ib. SCALE HOOK (6″) is *Scalhouke* 1604 ib., *Skelhook* 1611 ib., *Skoolhooke* 1623 ib. *v.* skáli. HIGH (6″), MIDDLE (6″) and LOW SHAW are *Shawe* 1602 ib., *High Shaw* 1686 ib., *Middle Shaw* 1803 ib., *Law Shaw* 1801 ib. *v.* sc(e)aga. SLAPESTONE (6″) is *Slepstones* 1605 ib., *Slepestone* 1611 ib., *Slaipestones in Thwayts* 1701 ib. 'Slippery stones,' *v.* slǣp. SMALLTHWAITE [smaˑəʍæˑt] is *Smalthwett* 1611 ib. *v.* þveit. SPUNHAM is *Spooname* 1624 ib., *Sponenham* 1649 ib., *Spunham* 1767 ib. STILE HILL (6″). Cf. *Style* 1629 ib., *Stial* 1650 ib. *v.* stigel. STILE SIDE (6″) is so named in 1657 ib. STONESIDE HILL (6″) is *Stones Head Fell* 1783 Donald. STRANDS (6″) is so named in 1700 PR. *v.* strand. TARNHEAD (6″) is *Tarnehead* 1664 ib., *Tarnheud in Havrigg* 1699 ib. *v.* tiǫrn. UNDER HILL (6″) is *Underhill* 1624 ib., *Wonderhill* 1633, 1640 ib., *Woonderhill* 1646 *LowtherW*. WATERBLEAN (6″) is *Waterblane* 1591 ib., *Waterblene* 1618 ib., *Waterblayne* 1626 ib., *Watterbleane* 1646 *LowtherW*. WHINS (6″) is *Whines* 1605 PR, *Whinnes* 1643 ib. *v.* whin. WHITRIGGS CLOSE is *Whitrygges* 1466 *Netherhall*, *Whitrigg close* 1630 PR, *Whitriges Close* 1657 ib. 'White ridge,' *v.* hryggr (under hrycg). WINDY SLACK is *Windislacke* 1607 ib. *v.* slakki. WOOD HO is so named in 1623 ib. WOODS is so named in 1735 ib.

[1] The Rev. W. S. Sykes tells us that there is a small outcrop of limestone here.

FIELD-NAMES

(a) Adam Knott, Allans (v. allan), Bannet Hill (cf. *Banotehead* 1633 PR), Beevers, Boon Goats, Boon Tarn, Breeches Peice (sic), Brida, Budge Parrock, Burnbarrow (there is a charcoal heap here), Calleras, Cranberry Marsh, Crellin Field (id. c. 1840 *TA*), Cringling, Deerham (*Dearnanne* 1636 PR, *Deareham* 1645 *LowtherW*, *Dearnam* 1683 PR), Doups, Fardy Meadow, Gallows Bank (*Gallowbank* 1774 PR), Garbutts (v. gāra), Gilder's Bank, Gillermire (v. mýrr), Gladam Holm (v. holmr), Gleadon Field, Hagger Slack (v. slakki), Heathwaite (v. þveit), Heator, Honey Pot, Kirkthwaite (*Kirthat* 1646 *LowtherW*. v. kirkja, þveit), Lag Brow, Lowthwaite (*Lowthwaytrigge* 1675 *LowtherW*. v. þveit), Lunnun Hills, Lyreas Field, Mace lands, Mains (*Maines houses* 1678 *LowtherW*. v. mains), Mean Ing (v. (ge)mæne, eng), Monk lands, Mount Pleasant, Nickle, Ormandy Field[1], Out Rake (v. reik), Peg's Whey, Poo Banks, Rag Slack (v. slakki), Redding (v. hryding), Robin Well (id. 1779 *Sykes*), Scalethwaite (v. skáli, þveit), Gallows Sewell and Long Sewal (*Sewal* c. 1330 *Hesley*. This is apparently sǣ-w(e)all, which in OE means not 'sea wall,' but 'cliff by the sea'), Silver Field, Sour Field (v. Des), Spice Brow, Stords (v. storð), Summer Ridding (*Somyrridding* c. 1200 Furness. v. hryding), Tenter Holme (id. 1779 *Sykes*. v. tenter, holmr), Trotten and Troughton Marsh, Wafford Meadow, Wallet, Washing Mire (v. mýrr); in 1842 (AllerA) Holborn Hill (*Holborn-hill* 1735 PR, *Holboran-hill* 1738 ib., *Holburen hill* 1750 ib.); in c. 1840 (*TA*) Boak Piece, Cunning Garth (v. coninger), Goath Meadow (id. 1798 CW xxiv), Huron (may be *Horrum* a. 1152 Furness, possibly the dative plural of horh (or *horu*), 'filth'), Micklethwaite (id. 1798 CW xxiv. 'Big þveit,' v. micel), Strait Field; in 1812 (PR) Blawith; in 1810 (PR) Greedy-gaite.

(b) In 1798 (CW xxiv) Big Rigg ('barley ridge,' v. bygg, hryggr, under hrycg), Bower Gardens, Halfpenny Butts and Greaves, Steward Ing (id. 1681 PR. v. eng and cf. supra 410); in 1794 (H) Netherbeck (*Neather becke* 1645 *LowtherW*), Overbeck (*Upperbeck* ib. v. bekkr), Scots-Croft (there is a local tradition of a battle here (H i, 530)); in 1785 (PR) Whaiteyeat (*Whaytyeat* 1612 ib.); in 1748 (PR) Wyer-head (*Wirehead* 1683 ib.); in 1730 (PR) Whoas (*Whowes* 1597 ib.); in 1728 (PR) Braconhill (*Brakenhill* 1610 ib. v. braken); in 1717 (PR) Bouthwaite Nooke (sic) (cf. *Banthwaite* 1630 ib. v. þveit); in 1675 (*LowtherW*) Hallford, Kellflatt (v. kelda), Seatefield, Whineways; in 1664 (PR) Curleygarth (v. garðr), the Marlelands, Marshford (*Marsh-foord* 1630 PR), Narr Crofte, the Wisters; in 1646 (*LowtherW*) Armating ('hermit meadow,' v. eng), Croftbladen (apparently an inversion compound), Crosabanck (*Crosshowbanke* 1570 ib. v. haugr), Flask (v. flasshe), Girsham, Graymaynes (*Graymayns* 1570 ib. v. mains and cf. the same name infra 426), the greapes (possibly ON greip, v. infra 446), Murthatgrene (v. þveit), Newcowme, Penhousbowe, Tuttoground (*Totoground* 1639 PR, in the possession of Cristofer Toto in 1607 (PR) and Widow Tutto in 1646 (*LowtherW*)), the Whay; in 1645 (*LowtherW*) Layrey, Preistman ground; in 1643 (PR) Toothouse (*Tootoes* 1638 ib., *Touttes* 1641 ib. Apparently from tote, 'look-out'); in 1633 (PR) Pastermouth (*Pasturemouth* 1605 ib.); in 1630 (PR) Sanworth, Shoonam; in 1623 (PR) Knotte (v. knott), Oakma; in 1570 (*LowtherW*)

[1] The Rev. John Ormandy became incumbent of Thwaites in 1822 (AllerA 176).

Crokerylbek' (cf. *Crokenbek* 1292 *Ass*), *Reddy halle*, *Sowth seyle*; in 1392 (HMC x) *Ravenesfors* (*Ravenfors* 1285 Cl. Either '*Hrafn*'s waterfall,' or 'waterfall frequented by ravens,' *v.* fors); in 1300 (Pat) *Barkerhals*[1] (id. c. 1235 StB. *v.* hals); in 1287 (StBA) *le Rutandpull* (*v. supra* 25, poll), *Sandflos* (*v.* flasshe); in 1279 (*Ass*) *le Cokelayk'* (*v.* cokelayk), *Sandscarth* (*Sandscarth* c. 1180 StBA, *Sandscarth, Sandscard* 1175–94 Furness. 'Sand scarð'), *Qywytemos* (presumably 'white mos'); in 1260–80 (Furness) *le Blakedik* ('black dīc'), *Couepul* (*Cimepul* c. 1260 ib.), *Forkebriggesik* (*Forcebriggesyk* c. 1260 ib. *v.* fors, brycg, sīc), *Layrwatpul* (also *Layrwath*) (*Lairpul* 1183–1216 DuLa, *Lairwath, Lairwathpulle* c. 1220 Furness, *Layrpul, Lairwaith* c. 1260 ib. 'Muddy pool' and 'ford,' *v.* leirr, pōl, vað); in 1210 (Furness) *Lahethwaitsig* (*v.* lágr, þveit, sík, under sīc), *Ulfeldac* (also *Ulfeclake*) (the forms seem to be corrupt, but the meaning may be *úlfaleikr*, 'place where wolves play'); in 1190–1204 (Furness) *Sleuenmira* (*Sleuenmire* c. 1180 StBA, *Slevenmire* 1175–94 Furness. *v.* mýrr); in 1175–94 (Furness) *Crochenges* ('Meadows in a bend,' *v.* krókr, eng), *Fitesik* (and *Fithesik*) (*v.* fit, sīc). Under each of the following dates there is one field-name: *Aunays* 1337 Ipm, *Becksonen* 1702 PR (apparently an inversion compound, but recorded too late for safe interpretation), *Blaholme* c. 1230 Furness (*v.* blár, holmr), *Brockbergh* 1777 NB (*v.* be(o)rg), *Buckhowe* 1610 PR (*v.* haugr), *Calhocke* 1642 ib., *Dent* 1632 ib. (possibly another example of the OIr *dinn, dind*, found in Dent in Cleator *supra* 358), *fons sancte Trinitatis*[2] 1183–1216 Furness, *Hase* 1663 PR, *Houberghe* 1338–9 Furness (apparently OE be(o)rg added to ON haugr), *Linriddinge in Staynton in Millum* 1250–93 DuLa (*v.* lin, hryding), *Loueside* 1679 PR, *Thorneburgh* 1347 HMC x (*v.* þorn, ðurh), *Totelhow* 1650 PR (*v.* haugr), *Wodridding* c. 1260 Furness (*v.* wudɹ, hryding).

MORESBY [mɔrizbi]

37. Moresby[3]

Moresceby c. 1160 StB (p), 1400 Cl, *Morisceby* c. 1225 *HolmC*, 1291 CW (OS) i, facs. (p), *Morisseby* 1291 Tax

Moricebi 1195 P (p), 1252 Cl *et freq* to 1428 FA, with variant spellings *Moryce-*, *Morise-*, and *-by*

Moricheby 1265 LaAss (p), 1295 StB

Moresby 1498 Ipm

MORESBY HALL is so named in 1777 (NB). In the parish is CROFT-MORRIS which is referred to in *croftum Mauricii anglice Croft morez* p. 1500 StB.

'bȳ of *Maurice*,' a French personal name from Latin *Mauricius*, a saint popular on the continent. The Romano-British name was probably GABROSENTVM (*v.* Appendix).

---

[1] The first element is perhaps the genitive *Barkar*, hence the hals of *Bǫrkr*, an ON personal name.

[2] The earliest church of Millom is dedicated to the Holy Trinity.

[3] Part of Moresby was transferred to Whitehaven (*infra* 450) in 1934.

ADAMGILL HEAD (6″). A grant to Holm Cultram, made c. 1225 by Adam de Harrais, refers to the stream *qui descendit de magno fonte meo*, and in a grant by his daughter Agnes, the land is said to be 'south of Adam's spring.' On the 6-inch map a spring is marked just about 250 yards south of Adamgill Head, to the north of Harras Moor. *Adam* of the gill and spring is probably to be identified with the Adam de Harrais (Harrays) mentioned in the grants.

FARMLANDS (6″) is *Fermelaundes* 1292 *Ass* (p), *Farmlands* 1698 Terrier. The first element is apparently the OFr *ferme*, 'rent.' The second seems to be 'land' represented in the first form by launde. The exact meaning of the compound is uncertain.

BONNY (6″) is *Boney* 1774 Donald. HIGH and LOW COMMONGATE (both 6″) are *High* and *Low Commin Yate* 1743 *LowtherW*. GILL-BROW, GOOSEGREEN and HOWGATE (all 6″) are so named in 1698 (Caine). GILLHEAD, THE HIGH, and MIDDLEGILL are so named in 1743 (*LowtherW*). *v.* gil. MOORGATE (6″) is *Mooryate* 1713 ib., *Moorgate* 1727 ib. ROSE HILL is so named in 1802 (Caine). ROTH-MIRE (6″) is *Routh Moor* 1698 ib. *v.* rauðr. TOWLOW (6″) is *Tool How* ib. ULGILL is so named ib. Probably 'wolf gil,' *v.* úlfr.

FIELD-NAMES

(a) Bendale, Blind Lonnen (a 'dead-end' lane. *v.* lonning), Browel's Field, Cubby Meadow, Kennel or Candle Fields, Latter Field, Monastines, Yowart's Park.

(b) In 1743 (*LowtherW*) Bleerbank, *Fawlaw*, *Grindalls* (*Grindall* 1698 Terrier), *Lucas How*, *Rase Leys* (*v.* hreysi, læs), *Stockbridgehall* (cf. *Stocke-briggil* c. 1225 *HolmC*. *v.* stocc, brycg), *Troughton Close* (id. 1698 Terrier); in 1698 (Terrier) *Birkett* (*v. supra* 4), *Cross* (cf. *high crosse hill* 1578 *Cocker*), *Rake Bank* (*v.* reik), *Scaled Hill Close* (*v. supra* 318); in p. 1500 (StB) *Withemyre* (*Witemire* 1254 ib., *Whitemire* 1256 ib., *Wythemir* c. 1280 ib.). Under each of the following dates there is one field-name: *Ackbanke* 1659 *CantW* viii (*v.* āc), *Picts holes* 1777 NB (possibly prehistoric pit dwellings. NB (ii, 47) describes them as caverns).

MOSSER

38. Mosser[1]

Moserg(e) 1203 Cur, 1220 StB, *Mosergh(e)* 1279 *Ass et freq* to 1541 *MinAcct*
Moserwe 1212 Cur (p), 1279 *Ass*

[1] Added to Blindbothel (*supra* 345) in 1934.

Musergh 1294 Cl (p), *Mesergh* 1296 FF
Mosehare 1397 FF, *Mosser* 1575 ib.

'Shieling on the moss,' *v.* mos, **erg**. Identical with Moser in Whit-well (We).

FELL SIDE is so named in 1653 (CantW vii). GRAYTHWAITE is *Magna, Parva Grathwayte* 1563 FF, *Gratwhat* 1631 PR (Lamplugh). *v.* þveit.

FIELD-NAMES

(*b*) In c. 1203 (n.d.) (StB) *Capeltrebek* (possibly from *capel*, 'nag,' trēo(w) and bekkr), *Dubbes* (*v.* dub), *Raysethwaytbec* (*v.* hreysi, þveit, bekkr), *Ulnescarthbec* (probably for *Ulu-*, '*Úlfr*'s scarð,' *v.* bekkr).

MUNCASTER
39. Muncaster

Mulcastre t. Hy 1 (1412) Furness *et freq* to 1509 LP, with variant spelling *-caster*, *Mulcastel* 1292 Ass (p), *Mulkaster* 1363 Ipm
Molecastre 1185–1201 DuLa, *Molecastr'* c. 1200 LaCh, *Molecastre* 1265 Cl (p), 1278 Ass
Mulecastr' 1210 Cur, 1252 Cl (p), 1279 Ass, 1301 Ch, *Mulecastre* 1246 LaAss (p)
Mullecaster 1278 Ass (p)
Mulncastre 1278 Ass (p)
Melecastre 1279 Ass
Mulcastr' et non Moncastel, Monescastre, Monecastr' 1292 Ass (p), *Mulcastre vel Moncastre* 1389 IpmR, *Munkaster* 1397 DuLa, *Moncastre* 1436 Fine, *Moncastre al. Mouncastere al. Mouncastell* 1505 Pat, *Montcastre* 1508 ib., *Monkcaster* 1525 CW xiv, *Momaster* 1576 S
Monkastle 1675 Sandford

MUNCASTER FELL is *Moulcastre fell* 1578 *Cocker*. MUNCASTER MILL (6″) is *Mulcaster-milne* 1658 PR (Lamplugh).

The second element in this name is OAnglian **cæster**. As in *Palmcaster supra* 330, the first element seems to be a personal name. Formally, it may be OE *Mūla*, recorded in *Mulantun* (Moulton, Nf). But OE personal names are very rare in the place-names of this county, and it is much more probable that the first element of Muncaster is the ON by-name *Múli*, recorded in the north from the 10th century. The suggestion in DEPN that the first element may be the ON *múli*, 'crag,' is made unlikely by the absence of any trace of this word in the numerous hill-names of Cumberland. The change from *Mul-* to *Mun-* is probably due to the common French interchange of *l-r* to *n-r*, or to change of *l-l* to *n-l*, arising in forms in which OFr -*castel* has replaced the earlier -*caster*. A change of this kind would be natural in the name of an important feudal site. The forms *Monescastre* and *Monecastr'* from the 13th century show that the change was not due to the influence of the word 'monk.'

BARNSCAR is *Remains of the City of Barnsea* 1774 Donald, *Barnscar, or Bardskow in the maps, Barnsea* 1794 H. This is the site of an ancient settlement, but the forms so far found for the name are too late and too varied to admit of interpretation.

BIRKBY (6")

>   *Bretteby* c. 1215 StB *et freq* to 1323 Cl, (*in Coupland*) 1316 FF, *Breteby* 1278 Ass, *Bretotby* 1279 ib., *Britby* c. 1290 Furness, 1425 Cl, 1431 Ass, *Bretby* 1337 Ipm, 1411 Pat
>
>   *Bertby* 1332 SR, *Brytbye or Byrtbye* 1565 FF, *Birbie* 1659 CW xiv

'bȳ of the the the Britons.' After metathesis of *r* had taken place, the first element was in modern times wrongly associated with *birk*, 'birch.' The name is identical with Birkby in Crosscanonby *supra* 282.

ELLERBECK is *Ellerbank* c. 1215 StB, *Ellerbecke in Birkby* 1678 LowtherW. Apparently 'elder-tree bank' (*v.* elri), for which *beck* has been substituted.

LINBECK is *Lindebecke* c. 1280 StBA, *Lindebeck* 1350–60 ib., *Linbeck* 1660 LowtherW. 'Lime-tree beck,' *v.* lind.

MONKGARTH POOL (local) is *Mitegarth* 1338 Cl, *Mytgarth* 1363 Ipm, *Monkgarthe* 1368 IpmR, *le Monkgarth* 1369 Ipm, *Monkegarth* 1538 AOMB, *Monkyngarth* 1544 ECP, *Monk garth* 1570 ExchKR, *Mankegarth* (sic) 1578 *Cocker*. This fishery, on the estuary of the Mite (*supra* 22), belonged to Calder Abbey. The garth has disappeared, but Miss M. C. Fair informs us that the pool is still drawn at times with a seine net.

NEWTOWN is *Newton, Neweton* 1509–10 LP. 'New tūn.' NEWTON KNOTT (6"). It has been suggested by the Rev. W. S. Sykes (CW xxvi, 85) that this is identical with the *Editheknot* in Ravenglas on which Conishead Priory received land from a local grantor (Dugdale vi, 558). The latter name means '*Edith*'s hill,' from the OE feminine personal name *Ēadgȳþ*, and cnotta (under knott).

RAVENGLASS

Rengles c. 1180 CW xxix (three times)

Renglas 1208 ChR, 1208, 1210 Pipe, 1292 QW, 1292 *Ass*, *Renglass* 1209 FF

Reynglas c. 1240 StB

Ranglass c. 1240 StB (p), c. 1250 ib., *Ranglas* ib., 1278, 1279 *Ass*, c. 1290 StB, 1294 Cl, c. 1310 BM, 1323 *MinAcct*, *Ranglasse* 1292 *Ass*, 1294 Ipm

Rayneglas c. 1270 StB

Ringlas 1278 *Ass*, *Rynglas* 1279 ib.

Raynglas 1279 StB

Ravenglas 1297 Cl, 1321, 1334, 1370 Ipm, 1540 *MinAcct*, *Raven-glasse* 1298, 1321, 1334 Ipm, 1338 Cl, 1540 *MinAcct*, *Ravengles* 1334 Ipm, *Ravenglasce* 1369 ib.

Ravynglas 1364 Ipm, 1440 Cl, *Ravinglas* 1364 Ipm, *Ravyn Glasse* t. Hy 8 *AOMB*

Rawnglasse 1654 CantW vii

RAVENGLASS CROSS (1800 CW xxi) is *the Market Cross* 1774 ib. Cf. *crucem in Renglass* c. 1225 StB.

This is probably a compound of OIr *rann* and the Irish personal name *Glas*. Such a name, meaning '*Glas*'s part, lot or share,' has an exact parallel in the lost south Scottish *Reinpatrik*, in which the element *rann* is followed by the personal name *Patrick*. The name is discussed at length by Ekwall (ScandCelts 92–3. See also DEPN) who shows that its earliest forms can all be explained by this derivation. Owing to extensive changes in the coast-line, it is impossible to recover the ancient topography of the site, and in any case, no topographical explanation that has so far been suggested will adequately account for the forms which are on record. The forms beginning with *Raven-* are clearly attempts to make intelligible a name which has lost its meaning.

For the Romano-British name of Ravenglass *v*. Appendix.

ROUGHOLME is *Rouholm* 1278 *Ass*, *Rucholme* 1279 ib., *Rugholm* ib. (p), *Rougholme* 1641 CW xviii. 'Rough holme,' *v*. rūh, holmr.

BARROW LODGE (6″) is *Barrow* 1641 CW xviii. *v*. be(o)rg. BRANKEN WALL is *Brankin Wall* 1679 PR (Whicham). BROAD OAK (6″) is so named in 1660 (*LowtherW*). CRAG is *Cragg* 1769 *Sykes*. CROPPLE HOW is so named in 1766 (AllerA). *v*. haugr. DYKE, HOWBANK and

KNOTT END are so named in 1769 (*Sykes*). FOREST MOSS (6″) is *Mosse called Forrest mosse* 1578 *Cocker*. GRAYMAINS is *Graymaines* 1698 CW ii. *v.* mains. HINNING HO is so named in 1769 (*Sykes*). Cf. *Hennin myre, the hennins* 1578 *Cocker. v.* haining. THE KNOTT. Cf. *Knotland* 1570 *ExchKR. v.* kno̦tt. MILLBRIDGE PLANTATION (6″). Cf. *Milne bridge* ib. MURTHWAITE is *Murthat* 1748 CW x. Cf. *Morewhat Greene* 1604 PR (Whicham), *Murthatgreene* 1649 ib., *Moorthwait greene* 1656 ib. 'Moor clearing,' *v.* þveit. STAINTON is *magna Staneton* 1569 FF, *Stainton* 1769 *Sykes*. 'Stone tūn,' *v.* stān (or steinn). WALLS is *Waw* (sic) *castell* 1578 *Cocker*. Cf. *Wawes closse* ib.

FIELD-NAMES

(*a*) Eskgarth (*Eskgarth* 1338 Cl. This is described in 1338 as a fishery (cf. Fishgarth *supra* 79) and it is still in commission as such).

(*b*) In 1578 (*Cocker*) *Ardasike* (*v.* sīc), *the butts, Chesall flatt* (possibly OE ceosol, 'gravel, shingle'), *Collcrofts, Elseycroft* (*Aylficroft* Dugdale vi. '*Ailsi*'s croft.' *Ailsi* is the OE personal name *Æðelsige*), *gilder flatt, Gretowe, hie riddinge* (*Heyriding* c. 1150 StB. *v.* hē(a)h, hryding), *Reedfoorth Closse, Stainewray* (*v.* steinn, (v)rá), *Stubbake riddinge* ('stub-oak hryding'), *Urtriggs* (presumably hrycg near the estuary of the Irt (*supra* 17)), *Whitewrayes* (*v.* hreysi); in 1545 (*MinAcct*) *Kerkgill* (*Korkgill* 1542 ib., *Corgill* 1543 ib., *Kergill* 1544 ib. Apparently '*Corc*'s gil,' from the OIr personal name *Corc*, cf. *supra* 161); in 1338 (Cl) *Casteland* (*Castelland* t. Ed 3 (t. Eliz) *Cocker*. 'Castle land'), *Knoclandes* (*v.* cnocc); in c. 1250 (StB) *Likokeryding* (*Likekeriding* ib. *v.* hryding), *Watsadding*; in c. 1215 (StB) *Manrigthwayt* (*v.* þveit), *Setforn*' (apparently an inversion compound, identical in meaning with Fornside *supra* 312, '*Forni*'s sætr'); in Dugd vi, *Grastamflet* ('gray stone stream,' *v.* fljót), *Hulotbec* (probably 'owlet bekkr'), *Kirksti* (*v.* kirkja, stīg), *Watelandes* (apparently 'wheat lands,' *v.* hwǣte).

40. Parton

PARTON is so named in 1794 (H).

41. Ponsonby

Puncunesbi c. 1160 StBA, c. 1205 *Hesley* (p), *Puncuneby* c. 1185 StB, *Pouncounbi* 1285 StBA

Punchunebi c. 1180 *Hesley, Punchunby* c. 1202 StB *et freq* to 1565 FF, *Pynchonby* 1321 Ipm

Punzunby c. 1170 StB, (*in Coupland*) 1271 ib., *Punzanby* 1243 FF
Ponzonbi 1228–43 DuLa (p)
Punsoneby 1243 Cl, *Punsunby*, *Ponsunby* 1279 *Ass*, 1300 Cl
Possenby 1279 *Ass*, *Ponsonby* 1338 SR (p)
Punceby early 14th StMaryY

PONSONBY HALL is so named in 1794 (H).

This is a late bȳ-formation, *v.* Introduction. *Puncun* is a French personal name, used in England in the 12th century and later. Johannes filius *Puncun* or *Punzun* is mentioned in the Pipe Rolls for Cumberland from 1178 to 1185.

CALDER and CALDER ABBEY[1] [kɔ·də]

Forms for the place are

Calder 1178 P (p) *et passim*, *Kaldir* c. 1190 StB, *Cauder towne* 1554
  CW xvi
Caldra 1228–43 DuLa

Forms for the Abbey are

Caldram 1152 Furness, c. 1205 CW (OS) i, facs., *Kaldra* 1216–32
  Dugd v, *Kaldre* 1231 Ch, *Caldir* c. 1240 Furness, *Caldre* 1242
  FF *et freq* to 1338 Cl, *Kaldir* 1300 Pat, *Kalldri* 1393 Pap
Chaldra c. 1180 *Hesley*
Caudre 1300 Ipm, *Cawdre*, *Kauder* 1536 LP, *Cawder Abbey* 1684
  CW i
Caler 1412 Fine

CALDER BRIDGE[1] is *pons aque de Calder* t. Hy 8 *AOMB*, *Calder Bridge* 1644 CW xv. CALDER HALL is so named in 1578 (*Cocker*). *Calderdale* appears in 1247 (FF), *Calderbank* in c. 1215 (StB), *Calderforde banke* in t. Ed 3 (t. Eliz) *Cocker*, *Calder Lopp* in 1723 CW (OS) v. *v.* Calder R. *supra* 7.

SCARGREEN is *Skargreene* 1656 CantW vii, *Scairgreen* 1754 *LowtherW*. The skarð, or cleft, in question is mentioned in the Middle Ages as *Scart* 1212 StB, *Scarth in the vills of Ponsonby and Gosforth* 14th HMC x (iv) (abstract). The road through, or to, the cleft appears as *Scharthgate* 1444 StB.

TOWN END (6″) is recorded in the name of Robert *dil Tunhende de Punconby* (1292 *Ass*). *v.* tūn.

[1] Calder Abbey and Calder Bridge are in the parish of St Bridget Beckermet.

M

IN FELL (6") is so named in 1842 (AllerA). LAVEROCK HOW is *Laverick Howe* 1828 PR (Gosforth). Although the development of the name cannot be traced, it is not unlikely that this represents the *Lauerdeshou* mentioned in c. 1215 StB. If so, the meaning is 'lord's hill,' *v.* hlāford, haugr.

FIELD-NAMES

(b) In 1664 (*Work*) *Swainsonplace* (John *Swainson* 1583 ib.); in c. 1270 (StB) *Harthkyn* (*Ardekin* c. 1212 ib. The form of 1212 suggests the possibility that this name may have arisen from Gaelic *àrd choin*, 'height of the dog.' Cf. Ardkinglas (Argyllshire)); in c. 1215 (StB) *Whitekelde* (*Widekeldeflat* c. 1202 ib., *Qwhitekeldflat* c. 1212 ib. 'Level ground by the white spring,' *v.* kelda, flat); in c. 1215 (StB) *Aldegail* (apparently 'old geil'), *Apiltrewaht* (*v.* æppel, trēo(w), and vað or þveit), *Crocland* (*v.* krókr, land), *Kirkebergh* (*v.* kirkja, be(o)rg), *Likrestinge*, *Moshouflat* (*Mosouflath* Dugd vi, *v.* mos, haugr, flat), *Northschoh* ('north wood,' *v.* skógr); in c. 1212 (StB) *Hayuirig* (*v.* hrycg), *Ulvescroft* (*Ulvescrophe* c. 1202 ib. '*Ulfr*'s croft.' Identical with Ulverscroft (Lei)); in Dugd vi, *Crucem de Haukesker* (possibly 'hawk crag,' *v.* sker), *Saithegile* (the first element here seems to be ON seiðr, 'spell' or 'incantation'; the second is gil), *Stanbrigg* (*v.* stān, brycg). Under each of the following dates there is one field-name: *Fishers yate* 1606 Ct, *grangia Haymeri* c. 1202 StB (probably '*Aymer*'s barn'), *Hirstedes* 1228–43 DuLa, *Langakyrs* 1444 StB ('long æcer'), *Wellsplace* 1641 *Work.*

PRESTON (6")
42. Preston Quarter [1]

Prestun c. 1135 (early copy) *Lowther* [2], *et passim*
Prestona t. Ric. 1 (1308) Ch, *Preston* c. 1210 StB *et passim*, *Preston Quarter* 1705 CW (OS) ix

PRESTONHOWS is *Preston Howse* 1535 VE, *Preston Howes* 1695 Caine. 'Priest or priests' tūn.' This was originally part of St Bees parish.

HUTBANK (6") is *Hudbank* 1770 *LowtherW.*

ROTTINGTON
43. Rottington [3]

Rotingtona c. 1125 StB, *Rotingtun* c. 1135 (early copy) *Lowther* [4], *Rotington* c. 1135 StB *et passim* to 1610 Denton, *Rotingtuna* t. Ric. 1 (1308) Ch, *Rotynton'* 1279 *Ass*, *Rotyngton* c. 1280 StB, 1334 Ipm, 1338 Cl, 1496 StB, 1535 VE, *Rotincton* 1207 StB (p)

[1] Divided between Rottington and Whitehaven (*infra* 450) in 1934.
[2] The copy in StB (No. 8) gives the reading *Preston*.
[3] Parts of Preston Quarter and Sandwith (*infra* 433) were added to Rottington in 1934.
[4] The copy in StB (No. 8) reads *Rodingtun*.

Rodintona c. 1125, c. 1130 StB, *Rodinetun* c. 1135 ib., *Rodington*'
1279 *Ass*, 1289 ib. (p), *Rodyngton* 1422 FF, 1474, 1496 StB,
Roddington 1640 CW xix
Redintona c. 1130 StB, *Rettingdon* 1606 DKR xxxviii
Rothinton' 1279 *Ass*, *Rothyngton* 1397 Fine (p)
Rottington 1295 FF

ROTTINGTON HALL is *aula de Rotington* 1258 StB.

This is clearly an OE compound in -ingtūn, like Harrington in this
neighbourhood. Its first element seems to be the OE personal name
Rōta which is not found independently, but lies behind Rooting (K)
and Rottingdean (Sx). It seems to be an early by-name, meaning the
pleasant or merry one.

FLESWICK BAY [flezik] (6"). Although no early forms have been
found, there seems no doubt that this name is identical with Flesh-
wick, Isle of Man. The latter name is discussed by Marstrander
(112–14) and derived by him from ON *flesiu-vík*. The second
element is ON **vík**, 'bay,' a word of which there seems to be no other
example on the Cumbrian coast. The first element is a Norwegian
word *flesja*, of which the commonest meaning seems to be 'slab' or
'flat stone.' This sense would be appropriate to the situation of
Fleswick, which is a bay among the sharply stratified rocks of St Bees
Head.

PATTERING HOLES (6") may be connected with *Poteruns* 1258 StB and
Potronkirke 1261 ib. *v.* runnr. There does not seem to be any
tradition which would account for the *kirke* in the form of 1261.

SOUTH HEAD. No early forms have been noted, and it has been
suggested by the Rev. James Wilson (StB, 419) that the original name
of this headland was *Houtbergh, Houtheberh, Houburgh* c. 1250 StB,
Howthberwe, Howtbirwe 1258 ib. The latter name consists of OE
be(o)rg or ON **berg**, preceded by an element which may well be the
ON **hofuð** contained in Whitehaven *infra* 450. This word has developed
in a similar way in Howth, Co. Dublin, Ireland.

TOMLIN is so named in 1821 (G).

FIELD-NAMES

(b) In 1754 (*LowtherW*) Langrigg ('long hrycg'), *Paulfleck*; in 1474 (StB)
le Knapehowe (*Michelknaphowe* 1258 ib., *Knaphou* 1261 ib. Probably **cnæpp**
with haugr added later. *v.* micel), *le Rayse* (*Raise* 1261 ib. *v.* hreysi); in

1261 (StB) *Astinhole*[1] ('*Asten*'s holh or hóll,' from ON *Hásteinn*, ODan *Hasten*, or possibly ON *Ásketill*), *Brundeshole* (also *Brunildhole*) (the first element is the well-known ON personal name *Brynhildr* which is known to have been current in England in the 12th century. The name occurs again in the inversion compound *Rigbrunild* c. 1207 in Stainton (We). As the site of *Brundeshole* is unknown, it is, as in the case of *Astinhole*, impossible to be certain whether the second element is OE holh, 'hole, hollow,' or ON hóll, 'hill' (*v. supra* 249). The topography of the parish perhaps makes the latter more probable); in c. 1250 (StB) *Bernardhou* (*v.* haugr. The first element is either OE *Beornheard* or, more probably, OFr *Bernard*), *Brezhou* (apparently '*Bret*'s haugr'), *Friday landes* (probably barren fields. Cf. *Friday* in compounds in NED, and *v.* also PN Sr 278–9, 410–11), *Garebrad* (*v.* garbrede), *Kenelflat* (possibly the first element is *kennel*, 'drain' (*v.* NED *s.v. kennel* sb.[2]) or *kennel*, 'shelter for dogs' (NED *kennel* sb.[1])), *terram sancte Bege que vocatur Kirkeland*, *Meysihwra* (*v.* (v)rá), *Seberth*, *Wynnefoth*.

ST BEES

44. St Bees[2]

Cherchebi c. 1125 StB, *Kirkeby* ib. *et freq* to 1404 ib., *Kirchebi* c. 1170 ib. (p), *Kerkebi* 1195 P (p), *Kyrkeby* c. 1260 StB, 1395 Pat, *Kirkeby infra Coupelaund* 1292 QW, *eccl. Sce Bege de Kirkeby* 1292 Ass, *Kirkeby al. St Bees* 1578 Cocker

eccl. Sce bege que est in Caupuland c. 1135 (early copy) Lowther, *eccl. Sce' Bege* 1154–81 ib., 1279 Ass, *Sancta Bega* 1259 Cl, 1279 Ass, *Sce Beghe* ib., (*apud*) *Sanctam Begam* 1281 Wickwane, *Seynt Beys* 1434 Pat, *St. Bege al. St. Be* 1536 LP, *Saynt Bees* 1556 FF, *St Beghes* 1568 CW xv

Kirkebibeccoch t. Ric 1 (1308) Ch, *Kirckebybechoc* 1288 Ass, *Kirkebybeghog* 1331 StB, *Kyrkebybeghok* 1334 ib., *Kirkebybecok* 1335 ib. *et freq* to 1393 IpmR, *Kirkebybeghok* 1359 Pat, *Kirkeboghok'* 1377 GDR, 1388 StB, *Kirkeby Beycok* t. Hy 8 AOMB, *Kirckeby Beacocke al. St. Beghes* 1585 Jackson, *Kirbye Beacock al. St. Beeghes* 1593 ib.

Bechockirke c. 1210 StB (p), *Beyhogkirke* 1278 Ass, *Behokirk* 1291 Tax, 1403 Pat, *Beghokirk(e)* 1319 Carliol, 1336 Ass, *Beghokkirk' in Allerdal* 1330 Carliol, *Bughokirke* 1540 AOMB, *Bughookyrke* 1541 MinAcct

ST BEES HEAD (in Sandwith parish) is *Berh* 1261 StB, *lez berghe* 1496 ib., *saincte bees hede* 1523 StBA, *the Barugh or St Bees head* 1777

---

[1] Cf. Alstonby (*supra* 102).
[2] Part of Hensingham (*supra* 400) was added to St Bees in 1934.

NB. These forms show that the original form of St Bees Head was simply ON berg, 'hill.' The old name survives in CLOVEN BARTH (6″) on the headland south of St Bees Lighthouse. ST BEES STONE (6″) is described as *signum sancte Bege insculptum in lapide positum in via tendentem* (sic) *versus Cleter* (StB 368). In the neighbourhood were *Kyrkbyhaven* c. 1258 StBA, *Kirkehaven* 1261 ib. (cf. Whitehaven *infra* 450), *Kirkebypol* 1279 *Ass*, and *Kyrkebyskales* p. 1500 StB.

The earliest recorded name of this place appears to have been *Kirkiubýr*, 'bȳ with, or near, a church' (of St Begu, mentioned by Bede, *Historia Ecclesiastica* iv, 21). To this was added *Beghóc*, the Irish diminutive of the name of the saint, which gave an inversion compound (cf. *Killebeccocestun* in Eddleston, Peebleshire (Watson, Celtic PN Scot 151)). The diminutive was also prefixed to *kirke*, which gave a Germanic compound of the normal type.

For the Romano-British name of St Bees Head *v.* Appendix.

NOTE. FINKLE ST. *v. supra* 47 and *infra* 455.

CONEYSIDE HO may be *Cuningishow* c. 1135 StB, *Cuningeshou* c. 1140 ib., *Coningshou* c. 1260 ib. The three medieval forms represent ON *konungs haugr*, 'king's mound' (*v.* haugr). The identification with Coneyside is probable, but no early modern forms have so far appeared to confirm it.

FLATT HO (6″) takes its name from *terra que vocatur Flatth* c. 1210 StB, *the flatt* 1578 *Cocker*. The first quotation is an early example of the word flat used independently.

LOUGHRIGG is *Loukerig'* 1288 *Ass* (p), *Lokerigge* 1540 *MinAcct*, *Lockrigg* 1657 CW (OS) xiv, *Lowkrigg* 1680 PR. The solitary medieval form suggests that the first element may be ON *laukr*, the cognate of OE *lēac*, 'leek.' The second element is hryggr.

PETEGROVES (lost) is *le pete grovis* 1474 StB, *Petgroffes* 1498 ib., *Petegroves* t. Hy 8 *AOMB*. 'Peat pits,' *v.* gróf.

HIGH and LOW WALTON are *Walton* c. 1160 StB, *Walton in Kirkbybeghok* 1378 ib., *Low Walton* 1723 CW (OS) v. LOW WALTON WOOD is so named ib. The absence of any forms showing an *e* between the *l* and the *t* makes it unlikely that this is OE *w(e)ala tūn*, 'tūn of the Britons.' It probably means 'walled settlement.' The origin of the name is unknown.

HIGH HO is so named in 1621 (PR). SEACOTE (6″) is *le Seecote* 1474 StB. 'Cottage(s) by the sea,' *v.* sǣ, cot(e).

FIELD-NAMES

(b) In 1722 (PR, Gosforth) *Brackenthwait* (*Brakenthwaitt* p. 1500 StB, *Brakenthwate* 1578 *Cocker*. v. braken, þveit); in 1660 (early 18th) (*Work*) *Holmes* (*Holme* t. Hy 8 *AOMB*. v. holmr); in 1650 (Jackson) *Deepslackes* (v. slakki), *a Tangle Scare called Moore Scare* (cf. *Skarrs or rokes* 1578 *Cocker*, in this neighbourhood. v. skarð), *Tare Broad*; in 1578 (*Cocker*) *Jordan close* (cf. *Jordani crosse* p. 1500 StB. 'Jordan's cross'), *the meere ditche* ('boundary ditch,' v. (ge)mǽre); in t. Hy 8 (*AOMB*) *Benehowe* ('bean haugr'), *Grenehowflat* (cf. *Grenecaphou* c. 1250 StB, *Grenehougap* 1261 ib., *Grenehowgapp* 1474 ib. v. grēne, haugr, and ON gap, 'a break or opening in a range of mountains' (v. NED s.v. gap sb.¹, 5). The earliest example of gap in NED in any sense is c. 1380, in this sense 1555), *Middellwallflatt* (cf. Walton *supra* 114), *Sikerre*, *Stanylathe* (v. hlaða); in p. 1500 (StB) *Brasewykegyll* (v. wīc, gil), *Coltman crosse*, *Coltman kylne* (v. cyln), *Craikhowe* (v. haugr), *crux franchisie* (presumably a boundary cross marking the limit of the liberty or franchise of St Bees), *Ellerbec crosse* (v. elri, bekkr), *magnum lez* (v. lǽs), *Skalegyll* (v. skáli, gil), *le bec stanez*, *Whynnys* (v. whin), *Wynewell*, *Wythmore* (v. wīðig, mor); in 1480–90 (StBA) *Dowghscotte* ('pigeon cote'), *ye Spetyll thorne* (preserving the memory of a lost *spitel* or hospital). Under each of the following dates there is one field-name: *the Hindhouse* late t. Eliz *Lowther*, ...*kluepenhou* 1289 ib., *Rattenby Castle* 1794 H, *Sowdam* 1795 PR (Lamplugh), *Starrara* 1720 ib. (Milburn), *Wray* 1732 ib. (Harrington) (v. (v)rá).

45. Salter[1]

SALTER (6″) [sɔ·tə]

Salterge c. 1150, c. 1180 StB, *Saltergie* c. 1150 ib., *Salterghe* c. 1160 ib., *Saltargha*, *Salterga* c. 1190 ib., *Saltherge* t. Ric 1 (1308) Ch, *Salterg*' 1278, 1279, 1292 *Ass*, *Saltergh* 1279 ib. (p)

Salterre c. 1200 StB, *Salterra* c. 1205 ib., *Salter* c. 1210 ib., t. Hy 8 *AOMB et passim*, *Saltere* c. 1210 StB

Salterw 1279 *Ass*

Sater 1591 PR (Lamplugh)

SALTER HALL is so named in 1766 (PR, Lamplugh). In the neighbourhood were also *Salter-yet* 1602 ib., *Salter yatte* 1627 ib. and *Sawtor Pyke* 1410 AllerA. v. pīc.

'Salt shieling,' v. erg.

ESKETT is *Eskat* 1760 PR (Lamplugh). The solitary form is too late for any interpretation to be profitable.

MILLGILL BRIDGE (6″). Cf. *ye foot of Millgille* 1410 AllerA, *Mylgillhead* 1583 PR (Lamplugh), *Milngillhead* 1631 ib. 'Mill ravine,' v. myln, gil.

---

[1] Added to Lamplugh (*supra* 404) in 1934.

46. Sandwith[1]

SANDWITH [sanəθ]

Sandwath 1260 *Rental* (p) *et freq* to 1607 DKR xxxviii, *Sandewath* 1294 Cl (p), *Sandwith* t. Hy 8 *AOMB*, *Sandwaith(e)* 1548 *SP*, 1723 CW v

'Sandy ford,' *v.* vaδ.

BYERSTEAD (6") is *Byrstede, Byrestede* 1279 *Ass* (p), *Byerstede* 1548 *SP*, *Byresteede* 1607 DKR xxxviii. The forms suggest an original *byre-sted*, with reference to a piece of land on which a byre or shed had been built. *v.* bȳre, stede.

MIDTOWN FM (6") is *Mid-towne* 1685 CW xvii.

47. Seascale

SEASCALE

Sescales c. 1165 Weth (p), 1497 Ipm, *Leseschalis* c. 1210 StB *Sescale* 1278 *Ass* (p), *Seaskaill* 1576 CW (OS) viii

SEASCALE HALL is *Seascall Hall* 1576 S, *Seaskall Hall* 1610 Denton. SEASCALE HOW is *Seaskalehow* 1731 PR (Gosforth). *v.* haugr.

This is correctly explained by Denton (21) who speaks, of "Seaskall Hall...which is so called of this word Skale, drawn from the latin *Scalinga ad mare* a Scale or Skeele, for cattle and sheepcot at ye sea." *v.* sǽ, skáli.

LAKING HOW (6"). Until recent times games were played on this hill, and the name probably contains NCy *laking*, 'playing' (*v.* EDD), and haugr. WHOLE HO is *Whole* 1658 CW xiv. It lies in a hollow, *v.* holh.

FIELD-NAMES

(*a*) Acerles, Birka Moor, Grey Croft, Todals (probably 'fox holes').

48. Setmurthy[2]

SETMURTHY

Satmerdac 1195 *FF*, *Satmerdoc* c. 1240 Fountains (p), *Satmerthoc* c. 1265 HolmC, *Satmerthag, Satmerdak, Satmerthach* 1273 *MinAcct*, *Satmerhagh* 1369 Ipm, 1399 IpmR

[1] Sandwith was divided between Rottington (*supra* 428) and Whitehaven (*infra* 450) in 1934.
[2] Part of Cockermouth (*supra* 361) was added to Setmurthy in 1935.

Satmyrthac c. 1220 Fountains (p), *Satmyrthath* (sic) 1246 FF,
Satmirthoc c. 1265 *HolmC*, *Satmirthac* 1281 *MinAcct*, *Satmirtack*
1290 ib., *Sadmyrdagh*, *Satmyrthagh* 1292 *Ass*, *Sathmirthaugh*
1293 *MinAcct*, *Satmyrthake* 1305 Parl, *Satmyrthawe* 1310 Ipm,
Satmirtha 1391 *GDR*
Satmurda c. 1255 Hosp (p), *Satmurthac* 1260 *Rental*, *Satmurdak*
1279 *MinAcct*, *Sadmurdagh* 1292 *Ass*, *Satmurchak* 1302 Pat
Sadmardak 1270 *MinAcct*
Sakmorthow 1447 *Netherhall*, *Sackmorther* t. Eliz ChancP
Satmorthowe 1519 *FF*
Setmurther 1567 PR (Crosth), *Setmurthy* 1589 FF
Seckmurthy 1654 CantW vii

In the parish was *boscus de Satmyrthagh* 1292 *Ass*
This well-recorded inversion compound means 'Murdoch's pasture,'
v. sætr. The name *Murdoch* represents OIr *Muiredach*, current in
the north in the 11th and 12th centuries. This interpretation, first
suggested by W. G. Collingwood, was accepted by Sedgefield
(99–100). It is abundantly confirmed by the numerous early forms
now available. Cf. *Karcmurdath* in Hayton *supra* 91.

HEWTHWAITE HALL

Hotweyt 1260 *Rental*, *Hothweyt* 1290 *MinAcct*, *Hothuuayt* 1312
Lowther (p), *Hothwait* 1366 Ipm, *Hothwayt* 1369 ib.
Huthweyt 1266 *MinAcct* (p), *Huthwayt* 1268 ib. (p), 1383 *Ass*,
1399 IpmR, *Hewthayt* 1369 Ipm, *Hutwhayte* 1542 *MinAcct*,
Hewthat 1622 Brayton, *Hughthwait* 1777 NB

'Hill clearing,' *v.* hōh, þveit, as in the lost *Hothwait* in Whitehaven
(453), Huthwaite (PN NRY 177) and (Hucknall under) Huthwaite
(PN Nt 119–20).

OUSE BRIDGE

Hewsbridge 1560 *Cocker*
Oosbridge 1578 *Cocker*, *Ouse Bridge* 1671 Fleming
Usebrige 1579 PR (Crosth), *Eusebridge* 1587 *Cocker*, *Ewsebridge*
1695 ib., 1753 CW xv, *Ewes bridge* 1772 NB, *Euse-bridge*, *Ewes
Bridge* 1816 Lysons
Woose Bridge 1675 Ogilby
Eversbridge 1750 Pococke

In the neighbourhood was *Usegarthe* 1610 *Brayton*, *Euse* 1687
CW xv.

The second element of this late-recorded name is **brycg**, which suggests that the first, with which we may compare Ousemire in Barton (We), is a river-name, perhaps of similar origin to the Nb Ouse Burn (RN 318).

ROTHERY PLANTATION (6″) is perhaps to be associated with the family of Alan *Rotherey* of Cockermouth (1570 *ExchKR*).

BARKHOUSE and HIGH BARKHOUSE (6″) are *the lowe Barkehouse, high Barkhouse* 1578 *Cocker, Lawbercus, Lawbarcus* 1675 Ogilby. Presumably a house in which bark for tanning was stored. BULLY HO (6″) is *Buly house* 1654 CantW vii. DUBWATH (6″) may be *Dobwra* 1292 *Ass. v.* dub, (v)rá. DUNTHWAITE is *Dunthwayte* 1570 *ExchKR, Dunthat, Dunthewater* 1660 CantW viii. *v.* þveit. ELVA HILL. For this name Sedgefield (47) quotes a form *Elfhow* (1488 Ipm), but this refers to a place in the neighbourhood of Hutton in the Forest (*supra* 209). It may of course be that the present is another example of the same name, meaning 'elf hill.' Cf. also Elf Hall *supra* 418. HOW DIKE (6″) is (*the*) *Howedyke* 1578 *Cocker*. KIRKHOUSE is *Kirkehous* 1543 *MinAcct.* 'Church house,' *v.* kirkja. LOWFIELD is *Lowefielde* 1578 *Cocker*. THE RUDDINGS (6″) is *Le Reddinges in Satmerhagh* 1399 IpmR. *v.* hryding.

FIELD-NAMES

(*b*) In 1794 (MapH) *Brathahill* (*Bratheyhill* 1654 CantW vii. This may be *Brathowe* 1399 IpmR. 'Broad hill,' *v.* breiðr, haugr), *Peat Wick* ('peat wic'); in 1578 (*Cocker*) *Alby Closes, Bleacocke house, Eddy Close, Forne gill, Gudha, Howes* (*v.* haugr), *Iredale, Longefett* (*v.* fit), *Nowtifoote, Owner, Oxe castle, Ruffold*; in c. 1265 (*HolmC*) *Arkylcroft* ('*Arkil*'s croft,' cf. Arkleby *supra* 310), *Hallestede* (*v.* h(e)all, stede), *Langeland', Ormescroft* ('*Orm*'s croft'). Under each of the following dates there is one field-name: *highorake* 1507 *Cocker, Suynsate* 1325 *Ass* (apparently 'pig sætr').

49. Stainburn[1]

Steinburn c. 1135 (early copy) *Lowther*, c. 1180 StB, *Steainburna* t. Ric 1 (1308) Ch, *Steynburn'* 1279 *Ass*
Staynburn c. 1220 StB, *Stainburn* 1227 ib. *et passim, Staynborn* c. 1265 *Hesley, Stayneburne iuxta Wirkington'* early 14th StMaryY
Stanburn' 1279 *Ass, Stanburne* 1535 VE
Staneburn 1279 FF

[1] Divided between Winscales (*infra* 454) and the borough of Workington (*infra* 454) in 1934.

The original form of this name was probably OE stān-burna, 'stony stream.' The first element has generally been scandinavianised to steinn, as in the modern form.

CRANBERRY MOSS (lost) is apparently *Traneberimos* 1227 StB, *Tranbermosse* c. 1227 ib., *Cranberry Moss* n.d. Whellan. 'Cranberry mos,' cf. Sw *tranbär*, Da *tranebær*. *Tranberamyr* is recorded in Middle Norwegian.

KIRKEBY CROSSAN (lost). A place of this name is mentioned in a mid-13th-century grant to St Bees in which Patrick son of Thomas of Workington grants 5 shillings from his rent of *Kirkeby crossan* (StB 68). Other 13th-century charters in the St Bees Register refer to lands in *Kirkecrossan* and *Kyrcros*. The full form *Kirkecrossan* is clearly an inversion compound. It probably meant 'Crossan's church,' *Cros(s)án* being an Old Irish personal name. It seems clear that a church or chapel existed on the site before the 13th century, but nothing seems to be known of its history (v. ScandCelts 28, StB 339).

MOOR HO is *Morhuses* 1279 *Ass.* 'Moor houses,' v. mōr, hūs.

PRIOR HOW is *Priorhouue* c. 1270 StB. This is clearly 'prior hill' (v. haugr), presumably with reference to the Prior of St Bees, but the significance of the name is not evident.

WEST LEYS is *West Leeys* 1550 (1687) Whellan. v. lǣs. THE YEARL (6″) is *Hearl Dubb under Stainburn* n.d. Whellan, *Hearl* 1705 ib. v. dub.

FIELD-NAMES

(a) High, Middle and Low Fitz (*Fitts* 1762 *LowtherW*. Cf. also *Millfitt* 1705 Whellan. v. fit), Far and Near Laws (v. hlāw), Mains Field (v. mains).

(b) In 1770 (*LowtherW*) *Aron How* (v. haugr), *Hole in the Mire* (v. mýrr), *Upper Kirkgates* (v. kirkja), *Stubbings*, *Teas*; in 1550 (1687) (Whellan) *Byorlathe* (v. hlaða), *Esthus* (apparently 'east hūs'), *Haithkeld* (*fontem qui vocatur Hothekeld* c. 1258 StB. This is probably OE hōd, 'shelter,' which has been Scandinavianised, and kelda. For the first element cf. PN ERY 225–6), *Hest Gill* (v. gil), *ditch of Hungill*, *Neyldringe*, *the Storthe Rayne* (v. storð, rein), *Trindells of Rothmer*, *Wangappe* (v. gap); in c. 1270 (StB) *Avena'croftes* ('crofts formed out of land taken in from the waste,' v. afnám), *Bigbere* (v. bygg), *Gilmoreboug* (the first element, as suggested by Ekwall (ScandCelts 69), seems to be the OIr personal name *Gillamaire* or *Gillamuire*, 'servant of Mary.' The second element is probably miswritten, and cannot be corrected with certainty), *Owthirthgate*. Under each of the following dates there is one field-name: *Holgate* c. 1258 StB (*v.* holr, under holh, gata), *Hungerig* 1227 ib. (probably from hungor and hrycg (or hryggr)).

50. Ulpha

ULPHA [uˑlfə, uˑfə]

Wolfhou 1279 *Ass* (p), *Ulfhou* 1337 Ipm
Ulpho 1449 AD iv, *Ulpha* 1625 CW (OS) iii, *Ulphay* 1638 PR (Millom), *Ulfay* 1646 *LowtherW*, *Ulpha or Ouffa* 1777 NB
Uffay 1695 M

ULPHA PARK is *Uffay Park* 1576 S, *Uffay or Woolfhay Park* 1610 Denton.
'Wolf hill,' *v.* haugr. Cf. *woolfehowe* 1578 *Cocker*, a meadow in Netherwasdale.

BOWSCALE is *Buskall* t. Eliz ECP, *Bouskell* 1646 *LowtherW*, *Bouskall* 1724 PR (Millom). *v.* boga, skáli, and cf. the same name *supra* 181. Cf. also *Bowesscard* (*v.* skarð) and *Bowesfell* (*v.* fjall, under fell), both 1242 Furness, on the Birker-Ulpha boundary.

HARTER FELL is *Herter fel* c. 1210 Furness. 'Hart's fell,' from ON *hjartar fiall*, with preservation of the gen. sg. in -*ar*.

MOASDALE (6″) is *Mosedale* c. 1210, 1242 Furness. *v.* mosi, dalr, and cf. Mosedale *supra* 304.

RAINSBARROW WOOD (6″) is *Ravenisberg* 1273 AD iv, *four high hills there called Rainsbarrow Breary* 1683 *Hudleston*. The first element is ON *hrafn*, 'raven,' possibly used as a personal name. The second element is ON berg, 'hill.'

THREE SHIRE STONE is *Shirestones upon Wrenose* 1576 S, *the Shire Stones upon the mountain Wrynose at the head of Dudden where it first meeteth with the county of Westmorland* 1610 Denton. This marks the place where Cumberland, Westmorland and Lancashire meet.

WRYNOSE is *Wrenose* 1576 S, 1610 Speed, *the mountain Wrynose* 1610 Denton, *Wrey Nose a great fell* 1671 Fleming, *wrye knott* 1675 Sandford, *Wry-Nose* 1789 Clarke. The meaning of the name is shown by the early forms *Wreineshals* 1157–63 LaCh, *Wrainshals* 1170–84 ib., recorded for Wrynose Hawse (We). According to Ekwall (DEPN), the elements are ON (*v*)*reini*, 'stallion,' and hals. But ON (*v*)*reini* is a weak noun, and the -*s*- will be difficult unless we can assume that the 1157–63 form represents ON (v)*rein-nes*, the second word, ON nes, being used in the sense of 'spur of land.' hals is frequently used in Cumberland place-names in the sense of 'pass.' The modern name Wrynose results from an attempt to change the unintelligible (v)*rein-nes* into a word which conveys some kind of meaning.

BASKILL (6″) is *Baskell in Ulfay* 1664 *LowtherW*, *Baskall* 1774 Donald. BIGERT MIRE is *Biggatmire* 1646 *LowtherW*, *Brigetmire* 1664 ib., *Bigertmyre* 1722 PR (Millom), *Beggar Mire* 1774 Donald. BLACK HALL is so named in 1610 (Denton). BRACKENTHWAITE (6″) is *Brackenthwate in Ulfay* 1664 *LowtherW*. v. braken, þveit. BRANDY CRAG (6″). Miss M. C. Fair notes that this name preserves the memory of a cache for smuggled goods brought from Ravenglass along the ancient packhorse road south of the Esk to Penny Hill. BRIGHOUSE is *Brigghouse* 1657 CW xiv. THE CROOK is *Crooke in Ulpha* 1655 PR (Millom)[1]. FOLDS is *Foulds* 1717 ib. v. fal(o)d. FROTH POT (6″). Cf. *Froth Hall* 1774 Donald. GRASSGUARDS (6″) is *Grasgarth* 1646 *LowtherW*. 'Grass garðr.' GRIMECRAG is *Gryme Crag* ib. HAZEL HEAD is *Hazel Head* 1738 PR (Millom), *Hasell Head* 1774 Donald. v. hæsel. HOLE HO is *Whole House* 1689 *Sykes*. HURST and LOW HURST (6″) are *Hirst in Ulfay* 1660 *LowtherW*, *Law-Hirst* 1786 PR (Millom), *Lowhirst* 1792 ib. v. hyrst. LONG GARTH is *Langarth* 1646 *LowtherW*, *Longegarth* 1661 PR (Millom). v. garðr. OLD HALL is so named in 1738 ib. PANNEL HOLME (6″) is *Panelholme* 1646 *LowtherW*. v. holmr. THE PIKE is *Pike* 1737 PR (Millom). v. pīc. WALLOWBARROW is *Wallobarrow* 1646 *LowtherW*, *the Walley barrey* 1660 ib. v. be(o)rg. WHINFIELD GROUND (6″) is *Whinfeild* 1664 ib., *Whinfell Ground* 1710 PR (Millom). v. whin. WOOD-END (6″) is so named in 1606 ib. This may be *the Woodhend* c. 1441 StBA (p).

FIELD-NAMES

(a) Allen Meadow (v. allan), Baythorpe Meadows, Borrans (v. burghan), Branderas, Buck Buske (v. buskr), Castle How or Hall, Crowberry How (v. haugr), Dope, Eam Parrock (cf. Yanfold *supra* 55), the Frith (v. fyrhþ(e)), Gale or Gaily Close, Gallows Field, Gold Rill, Know Hill (v. cnoll), Lag Ley, Meadow Platt, Ontridge, Penn, Pinfold (v. pundf(e)ald), Rake (v. reik), Old Rerrocle, Seven Oaks, Sineath, Sour Earth (v. *infra* Des), Tenter Lands (v. tenter), Thin Ling, Tup Close, Waterloo, Witch.

(b) In 1664 (*LowtherW*) Denislacke (*Dennislacke* 1646 ib. v. slakki), Gilderholme (v. holmr), *ye lawe* (v. hlāw).

[1] Add: CROSBYTHWAITE (6″) is so named in 1748 PR (Millom).

51. Waberthwaite[1]

WABERTHWAITE [wɔ·bərθwət]

Waybyrthwayt' c. 1210 *Netherhall* (p), *Wayburthwayt* c. 1215 StB, 1279 *Ass* (p), *Wayburthueit, Waybyrthueyt, Waybirthueit* c. 1260 StB (p), *Weyburgthwayt* 1266 Cl (p), *Waiburgthwayt* 1267 ib. (p), *Weyburghthwait, Wayburgthwait* c. 1270 ib. (p), *Weyburtheyt* 1278, 1279 *Ass*, *Wayburgthweyt* 1278 ib. (p), *Weyburtheweyt* 1279 ib. (p), *Weyburthweyt* 1280 FF (p), 1295 Cl (p), *Wayburthuayt* 1281 Wickwane, *Wayburgthwayt* 1290 Cl, *Weyburthwyt* 1292 *Ass* (p), *Wayburthwayt* 13th HMC x (p), *Wayberthwait* 1383 ib., *Wayburthwait* 1392 ib.

Warthebuthewait c. 1230 StB (p)
Werbuthethwait c. 1230 StB (p)
Weibuththwait c. 1230 StB (p)
Waybuthethwait c. 1250 StB (p)
Waybouthueit c. 1250 StB (p), *Waybuthwayt* 1347 CW xli, *Waybuthat* 1382 ib., *Waybuthait* 1383 ib.

Waithbuthwait, Waithbutwait c. 1255 StB (p), *Waythbutwait* c. 1258 ib. (p)

Waburtheyt 1259 Pipe (p), *Wabertweyt* 1292 *Ass* (p), *Waberthwait* 1341 Ipm, *Wabyrtwayt* 1391 *Netherhall*, *Wabirthwayth* 1406 HMC x, *Wabarthwait* 1552 CW (OS) viii, *Waberthwayte* 1565 FF

Waythebuthwayt, Waythebutwat c. 1260 StB (p), *Waythebutwayth* c. 1260 *Hesley* (p), *Waythebuthwait* c. 1290 Furness (p)

Wumburthweyt 1279 *Ass* (p)
Weburthweyt 1279 *Ass*
Wabrethwayt 1348 HMC x
Wawburthwaite 1576 S
Wyberthwaite 1794 H

HALL WABERTHWAITE is so named in 1779 (PR). Cf. *supra* 417.
The numerous forms of this name vary too widely to establish its precise origin. As observed by Lindkvist (127), the first part of the name is ON *veiði-búð*, a compound of búð with a word *veiðr*, meaning 'hunting' or 'fishing.' The chief difficulty presented by the forms is the frequent appearance of an *r* in the second syllable. It is probably a remnant of *-ar*, the gen. sing. of *búð*, which occurs in Bowderdale *infra* 440, but its persistence is remarkable, and it has given rise to

---

[1] Corney (*supra* 364) was added to Waberthwaite in 1934.

forms in *burg* and *berg* which are at variance with the other materials for the history of the name. But the series of forms as a whole confirms Lindkvist's derivation, and the name may be translated 'þveit by the hunting or fishing booth.'

CROSS is *Crosse in Waberthwaite* 1680 *LowtherW*. NEWBIGGIN is *Newbigginge* 1678 CW (OS) iii. 'New building,' *v.* bigging.

FIELD-NAMES

(a) Barrs (*v. supra* 70), Becka Stile, Caddy Leys (*v.* lǣs), Carbett Close, Flook Head, Hagg (*v.* hǫgg), Harry Fields, Haver Folds (*v.* hafri), Humour Close, Ing Meadow (*v.* eng), Noddles, Pinders Sike, Near and Far Row Burden, Sim, Skelding Meadow, Spout Meadow (*v.* spoute), Wigh.

52. Nether Wasdale[1]

NETHER WASDALE is *Netherwacedal, Netherwasdale* 1338 Cl, *Netherwashedale* 1540 *MinAcct*, 1570 *ExchKR, Netherwasdaill* 1552 CW viii. *v.* Wasdale *supra* 390.

BOWDERDALE is *Beutherdalbek, Boutherdalbeck* 1322 Cl, *Bouthdale* 1338 Cl, *Bouderdaleclose, Bowderdale Close* 1540, 1541 *MinAcct, Bowlderdale* 1578 *Cocker*. For further forms, *v.* Over Beck *supra* 23. As stated by Lindkvist (7), this name represents an ON *búðar dalr*, 'valley of the booth.' The form *búðar*, which is represented in both the earliest and the modern forms, is the genitive singular of ON búð. The name occurs again in Bowderdale in Ravenstonedale (We), *Bowdardall* 1595 PR, *Boutherdaile* 1636 ib.

CARLING STONE (6"). This name may contain ON *kerling*, 'old woman.' There is a clear south Cumberland example of this word in the lost *Kerlingsik* c. 1250 StB, 'old woman's stream,' *v.* sík (under sīc), in Bolton in Gosforth *supra* 397. Carling Knott *supra* 412 may have the same origin.

DROPPING CRAG (6") is *Le Droppingcrag* 1322 Cl. The 1322 form, as printed, appears as *Droppingerag*, and the manuscript is not clear, but *Droppingcrag* appears to be the correct reading. The word 'dropping' may be used here in the sense of 'dripping.' Three other

---

[1] The detached part of Nether Wasdale was transferred to Irton (*supra* 402), and part of Eskdale and Wasdale (*supra* 388) was transferred to Nether Wasdale, in 1934.

examples of the name are found in south-west Cumberland, but no early forms have been found for them.

GOWDER CRAG is *Gouthcrag* 1338 Cl, *Cowter Cragg* 1578 *Cocker*. The solitary medieval form suggests that the first part of the name may be ON *gauð*, 'barking,' presumably in the sense of 'echoing,' but no certainty is possible. GOWDER CRAG in Borrowdale and GOWDER BARROW (6″) [gɔdər] in Muncaster may have the same origin, but no early forms have been found for these names. It is, however, noteworthy that in a *Guide to the Lakes* (1830), reference is made to the notable echo from Gowder Crag and Shepherds Crag in Borrowdale.

LUND BRIDGE (6″). See Lund *supra* 406.

SCOAT FELL is *le Scote in Bouthdale* 1338 Cl, *Leescote of Bowlderdale* 1578 *Cocker*. Professor Ekwall derives from ON *skot*, 'projecting piece of land, especially high land,' 'rising hill,' sometimes 'place where timber is shot down a hill,' well evidenced in Norway (NG v, 288, xiii, 135).

YEWBARROW is *le Mikeldor de Yowberg* 1322 Cl, *le Durre de Youbergh* 1338 ib., *Yeweberrowe, Yewberie hill* 1540 *LRMB*. The medieval boundary of the free chace of Kinniside and Nether Wasdale proceeded from Over Beck (*supra* 23) "usque le Nose de Cambe de Youbergh et sic sequendo sursum per le Cambe de Youbergh usque le Durre de Youbergh." The 'nose' of Yewbarrow is the southern projection of the mountain, and the passage supplies a good example of OE *nosu*, 'nose,' used in a topographical sense. The 'cambe' is the long ridge of the mountain itself (*v.* camb). The 'door' (from OE *duru*, cf. Lodore *supra* 350) is the depression between the northern end of Yewbarrow and the fells which lie between Bull Crags and Black Comb (*supra* 391). It appears now as DORE HEAD. The name Yewbarrow itself seems to be a compound of OE *eōwu*, 'ewe,' and be(o)rg.

BROAD GAP (6″) is *Bradgapp* 1570 *ExchKR*, *Brodegapp* 1578 *Cocker*. Cf. *supra* 432. BROWFOOT (6″) is named from *the browe* ib. BROWN HOW (6″) is *the Browne howse* ib. BUCKBARROW is *Buckeborowe* ib. *v.* be(o)rg. FOSTER BEDS (6″) is *Foresterbedd, le Forstbeddes* 1338 Cl, *Forster bed* 1578 *Cocker*. FOULSYKE (6″) is connected with *Foulesikehead* 1570 *ExchKR*. *v.* fūl, sīc. GALESYKE is so named ib. *v.* sīc. The first element may be geil, but more probably it is *gagel*, 'bogmyrtle.' GAP is *del gap* 1539 *MinAcct*, *Gape in Neither Wasdaill* 1659 CantW viii. *v. supra* 432. GILL is *le gyll* 1570 *ExchKR*. *v.* gil.

GRAY CRAG (6″) is *Gray Cragg* 1587 *Eskdale*. GREENDALE is probably *Grindale* 1332 SR (p), *Gryndell* 1570 *ExchKR*. *v.* dalr. HANGING STONE (6″) is *Hingingstone* 1587 *Eskdale*. HARROW HEAD (6″) is *harrowehead* 1570 *ExchKR*. Cf. Harras in Ainstable *supra* 169. HAYCOCK is *Hay Cocks* 1783 Donald. This is probably a descriptive name, derived from the shape of the hill. How END (6″) is so named in 1578 (*Cocker*). *v.* haugr. INTAKE WOOD (6″). Cf. (*the*) *intake* ib. *v.* intak. KIDBECK is *Kydbek in Wassedale* 1397 Pat. *v.* Kid Beck *supra* 18. KIDBECK How (6″) is *Kidbekhowe* 1578 *Cocker*. *v.* haugr. MILL How (6″) is *ye milne howes* ib. MILL PLACE (6″) is *Mylne place*, *myll place* 1570 *ExchKR*. MORT is *Moorte, highe morte* 1578 *Cocker*. SCALE is *le Scale* 1570 *ExchKR*. *v.* skáli. SEATALLAN is *Settallian* 1783 Donald. Presumably a late record of an inversion compound meaning '*Alein*'s sætr.' Cf. Starling Dodd *supra* 411. STARHOLME (6″) is *Sterholme* 1570 *ExchKR*, *Stare holme* 1578 *Cocker*. 'Sedge holmr,' *v.* star-. STOCKDALE HEAD (6″) is *Stokedalehead* ib. Cf. *Stokedalebek* 1540 *LRMB*. STRANDS (6″) is *Strand of Irt* 1578 *Cocker*. *v.* strand. It is named from its position in relation to the river Irt (*supra* 17). STRANMOSS WOOD (6″) is named from *Tranmorse* 1570 *ExchKR*, *Tranemosse* 1578 *Cocker*. 'Crane mos,' from ON trani, 'crane.' WINDSOR is *Wyndsore* 1570 *ExchKR*, *Windsor, Winsore* 1578 *Cocker*, *Windsor* 1783 Donald. The history of this name is unknown. WOODHOW is *Woodhawe* 1570 *ExchKR*, *Woodhowe* 1578 *Cocker*. YEWTREE is *Ewtree* ib.

FIELD-NAMES

(*b*) In 1578 (*Cocker*) the *Aldegarth* ('old garðr'), *balesbanke, barstilltre, Birkettlees, Blakebell feilde, Bone sike* (*v.* sic), *Bornes* (*v.* burghan), *Boughtde bekk* (*v.* bekkr), *Capmer butts, the Carr* (*v.* kiarr), *Clewes, the Cringle* (*the Cryngill* 1570 *ExchKR*. *v.* kringla), *the Crookin, Dead tarne* (*v.* tiǫrn), *Darnell Ings* ('darnel meadows,' *v.* eng. Darnel is first recorded in northern texts), *Ehenshawehowe* (*v.* sceaga, haugr), *Eshton Shawe* (*v.* sceaga), *flaught howe* (*v.* haugr. The first element is ME *flaught*, 'turf'; conceivably this was a hill where turf was cut for burning), *the gardes* (*v.* garðr), *gardspare, hanger-flatt, Lath croft* (*v.* hlaða), *Longmanhowes, Lyneholme* (*v.* lín, holmr), *Mershe-howe* (*v.* haugr), *Outrake* ('outer droveway,' *v.* reik), *Pirscoate, Scordhow mosse, Scotts Croft, Seghill, Sindrell Closse* ('cinder-hill,' probably the site of a bloomery), *Spoonehead, Stabsty closse, Stewthowe, Tenter garth* (*v.* tenter, garðr), *Thrusshhowe* (in view of several clear cases in which *thrush* represents OE þyrs or ON þurs, 'giant,' it is not unlikely that this name means 'giant's hill,' *v.* haugr), *Trote well, le Wanes, Water ruddinge* (*v.* hryding), *Woolfehowe* (*v. supra* 437); in 1570 (*ExchKR*) *bough barre, brinneale, Broadgarre, Chaper-steald, Foulegapp* (*v.* fúl, gap), *gylbrough, howemunck* (possibly an inversion compound of haugr and *monk*), *Lurry rygge* (*v.* hrycg. It is difficult to see in what sense dial. *lurry* is used topographically), *Prytcote, Rotongill* (also *Rowtongill*) (*v. supra* 25), *Sommerford* (possibly a ford usable only in summer), *Sternehowe* (*v.* haugr), *Thornehowe* (*v.* haugr), *Toystall, Wynstre*; in 1540 (*MinAcct*) *Borrowdalelond* (held by Henry *borowdale*), *Brokelbank', grisland'* (presumably gríss); in 1540 (*LRMB*) *Brotherdale* (possibly connected with Thomas de *Brotherdal* 1278 *Ass*); in 1322 (Cl) *le Bradstarth* (probably 'broad skarð'), *le Castok* (conceivably ká-stokkr, 'jackdaw stump'), *le Punfald* (*v.* pundf(e)ald).

53. Weddicar[1]

WEDDICAR (6″)

Wedaker c. 1160 (early copy) *Lowther et freq* to 1363 Ipm, with variant spellings *-acer, -acre, -akre, Widacre* 1458 IpmR

Weddaker 1292 StB, *Weddacre* 1493 HMC x (iv)

Wod(e)acre 1334 Ipm, 1338 Cl, 1476 FF, *Woodacre* 1570 *ExchKR*, *Wadacre* 1578 *Cocker*

Weddikre 1406 FlemingMem, *Weddikar* 1583 FF, *Widdiker* 1623 PR (StB)

WEDDICAR HALL is *Weddiker Hall* 1613 CaineCl.

This represents OE *wēodæcer*, 'weedy field' (*v.* æcer), as in DEPN.

CROFTEND is *Croftende* 1279 *Ass* (p), *the Croft end* 1726 *LowtherW*.

ACRE WALLS is *Akerwalls* 1712 *LowtherW*. BOGHOLES (6″) is *Bogholes* 1726 ib., *Bogels* 1774 Donald. KEEKLE BANK is *Kyklebank* 1635 CW (OS) v, *Keekleybanck* 1657 CW xiv, *Keeklebank* 1726 *LowtherW*. *v.* Keekle R. *supra* 18. LOSCA is *Loskow* ib., *Loska* 1783 PR (Lamplugh). Probably, like Loscoe (Db), ON *lopt í skógi*, 'loft in the wood.'

FIELD-NAMES

(b) In 1755 (*LowtherW*) *High Simond Field* (cf. *Low Symond Feild* 1727 ib.).

54. Whicham[2]

WHICHAM

Witingham 1086 DB *et freq* to 1291 Tax, with variant spellings *Wyt-* and *-yng-*

Wintinghaham c. 1130 StB

Hwithingham c. 1175 StB, *Whittingham* 1279 *Ass*, *Whytingham* 1292 ib., *Whityngham-in-Coupland* 1332 Cl, *Quytyngham* 1396 Pap

---

[1] Part of Hensingham (*supra* 400) was added to Weddicar in 1934.
[2] Whitbeck (*infra* 447) was added to Whicham in 1934.

Whetynham 1462 *Netherhall*
Wytineham, Wyteneham 1279 *Ass*
Wycheham 1550 FF, *Whyttyngham al. Whycham* 1573 ib., *Whitcham*
    1552 CW (OS) viii
Whytyam 1570 *LowtherW*
Whitesham 1657 CW (OS) vi

WHICHAM HALL is *Whittingham Hall* 1504–15 ECP, *Whicham Hall*
1634 PR. WHICHAM MILL (6″) is *Whicham Milln* 1723 ib.

OE *Hwītinga hām*, 'the hām of *Hwīta's* people.' The modern form
shows that the *g* was palatalised, as in Whittingham (Nb, PN NbDu
214), which has the same origin, and in several other Old Northumbrian names of this type. On the historical importance of the name,
v. Introduction.

CROFTBATHOC (lost). Although this place is described as *villa de
Croftbathoc* (c. 1205 StBA), no other reference to it has been found,
and its site is unknown. The name is clearly an inversion compound.
The distinguishing element is probably a personal name, presumably
of Irish origin, though no name which corresponds precisely to -*bathoc*
has so far been found. The name is discussed in ScandCelts 22.

HELLPOOL BRIDGE (6″) [helpɑ] is *Helpoolbrigge* 1666 PR, *Helpowbridge*
1679 *LowtherW, Hill-pool Bridge* 1777 PR (Millom). *v.* Kirksanton
Pool *supra* 19.

KIRKBANK (6″) is *Kirkebaunk* 1278 *Ass* (p), *Kirkbank(s)* 1653, 1654
PR. *v.* kirkja.

SATHERTON (lost) is *Sathertun* c. 1260 *Hesley, Satherton'* 1278, 1286,
1289 *Ass, Satherton* 1278, 1292 ib., c. 1296 *Furness*, 1338 Ipm,
Sacherton 1292 QW, *villa de Saterton* n.d. *Furness, Saterton* 1538
Hudleston, Kirkby Santon al. Satterston 1649 ib., *Satterton al. Sotherton al. Satherton* 1741 ib. *v.* tūn. The forms do not suggest any definite
etymology for the first element, unless ON *sǫð*, feminine of *saðr*,
'sated,' can be used as a nickname, in which case '*Sǫð's* tūn' is formally
possible.

SILECROFT

Selecrotf (sic) c. 1205 StBA, *Selecroft* 1211 Pipe (p) *et freq* to 1358
    GDR, *Sellecroft* 1279 *Ass, Sealcrofte* 1578 *Cocker*
Selcroft 1278 *Ass* (p) *et freq* to 1579 FF

Salcroft 1292 *Ass*
Sillcroft 1770 BeethamRep

This is probably a compound of OE **sele**, 'hall, building,' and **croft**.

WHOLE PIPPIN is *Whirleppin* 1646 *LowtherW*, *Whirnepepin* 1646 PR, *Whinnepepin* 1651 ib., *Whirlepippen* 1659 ib., *Whorlepepin* 1719 ib. The second element is English *pipkin*, of doubtful origin, found in dialect as *pippen, pippin*, 'a round and deep earthenware pan.' Like *Whirlepott* (*supra* 281), the name evidently means a pot-hole in a stream. Cf. a pool in the (East Lothian) Tyne called "Saint Baldred's Whirl" (Ritchie, *St Baldred* 124). *v.* EDD *s.v. whirl* sb[8].

CAMPSTONES[1], HODGSON'S GREEN[2] and KELLET HO (all 6″) may be associated with the families of Elizabeth *Cumpstone* (1584 PR), Andrew *Hogshon* (1570 ib.) and Thomas *Kelleth* (1576 ib.).

BALDMIRE is *Baldmyre* 1651 PR, *Bouldmyre* 1668 ib. *v.* **mýrr**. BANK HO (6″) is *the bankhouse* 1656 ib. BAYSTONE BANK FM (6″) is *Bakestone banke* 1570 *LowtherW*, *Basting banke* 1597 PR, *Bastonbanckes* 1603 ib., *Beaston bancke* 1646 *LowtherW*, *Bastonbank* 1651 PR, *Backstonbank* 1655 ib., *Baistonbank* 1720 ib. 'Baking stone bank,' from ME **bak-stān**. BECKSIDE is so named in 1649 ib. CHAPPELS FM is *the Chappell* 1661 ib., *Chappells* 1718 ib. (Millom). CROSS BANK (6″) is *Crossabanck* 1585 PR *et freq*, *Croswaybank* 1704 ib. FELL BROW (6″) is *the felbrowe* 1585 ib. FORE SLACK is *Foreslack* 1646 *LowtherW*, *Forslack* 1651 PR, *Forceslacke* 1686 ib. *v.* **slakki**. GATE SIDE is so named in 1651 ib. GRICE CROFT is *Groscrofte* 1571 ib., *Grisecroft* 1585 ib., *Gricecroft* 1684 ib. The first element here seems to be ON **gríss**, 'young pig.' HALL-BECK is *Holebecke* 1655 ib., *Hoalbeck* 1671 ib., *Wholebeck* 1798 ib. (Appx). 'Hollow beck,' *v. supra* 17. HILL END is *the Hillend* 1654 PR. KELDBANK (6″) is *Kelbanke* 1585 ib. Probably 'spring bank,' *v.* **kelda**. MILLHAW WOOD (6″) is named from *the Milhall* 1595 ib., *the Myll-haw* 1629 ib. (Millom). MIRE MOUTH (6″) is *the Myremouth* 1592 PR. *v.* **mýrr**. PARSONAGE BREAST (6″) is *Parsonag Breast* 1778 Terrier. Upon this the Rector had pasturage for 200 sheep (ib.). For *breast, v.* EDD *s.v. breast* sb.[2] RALLISS is *Rallies* 1769 PR. Cf. *Rally-green* 1716 PR (Millom), *Ralley-ground, Rallystreet* 1729 PR. SLED-

---

[1] *Compston grounds* 1673 PR, *Cumpstons* 1721 ib., *Cumpstones* 1774 Donald. Cf. Cumpstone Ho in Stainmore (We), which is connected in 1573 with Rychard *Compston*.

[2] *Hogshons* 1784 PR.

BANK (6″) is *Sledbanke* 1654 ib. *et freq*, *Slatebank* 1805 ib. SOUTH-FIELD is *Southfeyle* 1570 *LowtherW*, *the Sowth-feild* 1590 PR. TOWNEND KNOTTS (6″) is named from *the Townend* 1656 ib. WHITE HALL KNOTT (6″) is named from *Whitehall* 1569 ib., *Whithaw* 1696 ib.

FIELD-NAMES

(a) Boon Town (may be *Above Town* c. 1840 *TA*), Hartrees, Havera, Ink Pot Meadow, Mains (*the Meanes* 1586 PR. Cf. *Mayneshouses* 1653 ib. *v.* mains); in c. 1840 (*TA*) Askham, Brankin Wall Moss, Bumless Field, Cockle Moss, Cotley, Croon Dales, Cross Ends and Hill (cf. *the Crosse* 1666 PR), Doup (*v.* doup), Dowan, Foul Ford Meadow, Goody Way, Groops (*Growpas* 1588 PR, *Gropes* 1671 ib. ON *greip*, 'three- or four-pronged fork' may, like grein, be used in a topographical sense. *Gropes* may possibly be derived from the cognate English *grāp*), Groove Meadow, Harry Guards, (*v.* garðr), Hickle Meadow, Hill Sack Field, Hirts, Hoase Croft, Hole Slack (*v.* slakki), Hurday (*Hordays* 1778 Terrier), Kirthwaite (probably another example of the compound kirkja and þveit), Lando Blado, Leece Parrock, Plack Acre, Radon, Red Butts, Skiddaw Hill, Sour Earth, Spout Meadow, Swang (*v.* swang), Toddles, Turf Pot, Turton Hill, Whay Meadow (*the Whae* 1588 PR, *Thwa* 1606 ib.), Worgam, Wormbrak Field.

(b) In 1702 (PR) *Fellend* (*Felend* 1670 ib.); in 1678 (PR) *Whaend* (id. 1652 ib.); in 1676 PR *Gill* (*the Gyll* 1602 ib. *v.* gil); in c. 1205 (StBA) *Cregehoued* (possibly containing Gaelic *creag*, 'crag' and hǫfuð), *Gillecroft* (probably '*Gille*'s croft'), *Gillemihelecroft* ('*Gillemihal*'s croft.' The OIr personal name, meaning 'servant of (St) Michael,' was in use in Cumberland in the 12th century. The compound occurs again in *Gilmyghelcroft* (1332) in Pennington (La). See ScandCelts 22, 69, 71); in Dugd vi, *Capsiholm*, *Colterflat* (presumably *coulter*, 'part of a plough' and flat), *Bigridding* ('barley clearing,' *v.* bygg, hryding), *Forsse* ('waterfall,' *v.* fors), *Labote*, *Raveness Fosse* (probably '*Hrafn*'s, or raven's fors'). Under each of the following dates there is one field-name: *Alyre* 1698 PR, *Heps* 1748 ib.

WHINFELL (6″) ## 55. Whinfell[1]

Wynfell c. 1170 HolmC, *Winefel* a. 1179 ib., *Wynnefelle* 1185 ib., *Winnefeld*' 1244 Cl

Whinnefelde 1230 Scotland, *Quinefel(l)* 1260 *Rental*, 1292 *Ass*, *Quinfel* 1268 *MinAcct*, 1308 Ipm, *Quinefeld* 1285 *For*, *Whynfel(l)* 1292 *Ass*, 1307 Pat, *Qwynfelles* 1318 *MinAcct*, *Whinfel* 1324 Cl, *Whynfeld* 1570 *ExchKR*

WHIN FELL is *the Fell* 1658 Cocker. WHINFELL HALL is *Whinfell*

---

[1] Added to Blindbothel (*supra* 345) in 1934.

Halle 1602 CW (OS) xii. Wood Fm. Cf. *boscus de Whynefel, boscus in Quinfel'* 1292 *Ass.*

'Gorse fiall', *v.* whin. Whinfield (PN La 211) and Whinfell (We), 12th *Qwynfell*, are identical in meaning.

Bank is *le Bank'* 1293 *MinAcct. v.* bank.

Toddell (6″) is *Toddeholes* 1293 *MinAcct, Toddall place* 1658 *Cocker.* 'Fox-holes.'

High (6″) and Low Rogerscale are *Rogerscales* 1260 *Rental* (p), 1292 *Ass* (p), *Rogerscale* 1293 *MinAcct, Rogerskell* 1597 CW (OS) xii. '*Roger*'s shieling,' *v.* skáli. This must be a post-Conquest compound, and shows that local names could be formed from *skáli* in the 12th century or later.

Birk Bank is *Birkbancke* 1652 *Cocker.* 'Birch-tree bank,' *v.* birki. Brow (6″) is *Browe* 1636 CW (OS) xii, *Brough* 1686 *Cocker.* Crag End (6″) is *Cragg End* 1724 ib. Cringley Hill (6″) is named from *Cringley* 1660 ib. *v.* kringla. Sandy Beck (6″) is *Sandiebecke* (a meadow) 1693 ib.

FIELD-NAMES

(*b*) In 1723 (*Cocker*) *Cold Coat* (*Caldcoat* 1681 ib., apparently 'cold cottage,' *v.* cot(e)); in 1692 (*Cocker*) *Ellers* (*v.* elri), *Redding* (*v.* hryding); in 1681 (*Cocker*) *Meare Gill* (*v.* (ge)mǣre, gil), *Rispah*; in 1660 (*Cocker*) *Barhead, Cornebarr Yeate, Littlebar Yeate, Kidam* (conceivably 'kid holmr'), *Leazeinge, Leesay, Watter Southerne*; in 1652 (*Cocker*) *Cradlebush, Okedale.* Under each of the following dates there is one field-name: *Benhow* 1693 *Cocker, piscar voc. Blyng* 1539 *MinAcct, Ceealey Banke* 1719 *Cocker, Ingparrocke* 1654 ib. (*v.* eng).

56. Whitbeck[1]

Witebec c. 1160 (early copy) *Lowther*[2] *et freq* to 1292 *Ass*, with variant spellings *Wyte-* and -*be(c)k, Wytebech* 1236 *DuLa*
Wetebec c. 1200 Furness
Whitebec c. 1200 LaCh, *Quitebec* c. 1250 Furness, *Whytebek* 1261 FF, 1279 *Ass*
Witbec 1228–43 *DuLa*
Quitbek 1382 Pat, *Whitbek'* 1383 *Ass, Whitbeck* 1568 FF

---

[1] Added to Whicham (*supra* 443) in 1934.
[2] The copy in StB (No. 107) gives the reading *Wytebek*.

WHITBECK MILL (6″) is *Whitbeke mylle* 1538 *DuLa*
'White beck,' from *hvít(r)* (ON equivalent of OE hwīt) and **bekkr**.

ANNASIDE

Ainresate c. 1145 StB, *Aynerset* c. 1150 ib., 1242 FF, 1340 *GDR*,
    (p), *Ainresete, Aynnerset* 1228–43 *DuLa* (both p), *Ainersathe*
    1261–72 ib. (p), *Eynersate* 1278 *Ass* (p), *Aynirset* 1382 Pat
Enresate c. 1150 StB
Andersetta c. 1170 StB
Annerside 1503 *Norfolk, Anerset* 1526 *DuLa, Annasyde* 1658 CW
    xiv, *Anneseed* 1679 *LowtherW, Anns's Side* 1774 Donald, *Anderset,*
    now called Agnes Seat 1777 NB

'*Einarr*'s sætr,' from the common ON personal name *Einarr.*

BARFIELD is so named in 1794 (H). It is apparently to be identified
with *Scalgarthbare* 1462 *Netherhall, Skalgarth Barn* c. 1500 CW (OS)
xii, *Skalgarsbarre* 1515–29 *CP, Scougarbar* 1654 ib., *Scrogar-bar* 1744
Hudleston, Barfield or Scrogar Bar 1776 ib., though Hutchinson
(i, 561), in referring to *Scoggarbar*, does not make this identification.
v. skáli, garðr, be(o)rg.

GUTTERBY

Godrikeby 1209 FF, *Godrykeby* 1228–43 *DuLa, Goderygby in the*
    liberty of Coupeland 1298 Ipm, *Godrikeby, Goderikeby* 1305 ib.,
    Godrykeby 1305 Parl, *Godrygby* 1324 Ipm, *Godrigby* 1383 *Ass*
Cudrikby 1396 Pap
Guderbye, Gudderbie 1526 *DuLa, Godderby* 1536 *MinAcct, Goderby*
    1538 *DuLa*
Gutterbie 1593 FF

v. bȳ. The earliest forms suggest that the first element here is the
OE personal name *Gōdrīc.* Cf. the same name *supra* 380.

HALL FOSS is *Hall-foss* 1721 PR (Bootle), 1794 H, *Hall Force* 1732
Hudleston. It is possible that this place may appear as *Fors* c. 1245
StB, *Forsce* 1472 AD iv, *Lez fforce* c. 1500 CW (OS) xii. In any case
the name is clearly ON fors,' waterfall.' There is a reference in two
13th-century charters (AD iv and v) to the land of *Midilfors in Coupe-*
land, which must have been in this neighbourhood, but cannot now
be identified.

MONK FOSS is *Fossa* 1135–54 *DuLa, Fossa(m)* 1135–52 Furness,
Munkfossam c. 1200 ib., *Munkeforse* c. 1220 ib., *Fors in Coupland*

1242 ib., *Mounkfors* c. 1280 ib., *Mountfosse* 1460 Pat, *Monk Force* 1610 Denton, *Monkffoss* 1738 CW (OS) xvi. The origin of this name is shown by a series of charters in the Furness Coucher (ii, 522–3), in the earliest of which Godard de Boivilla grants *quandam carrucatam terre in Cauplandia, Fossam nomine* to the monks of Furness. This carucate, or ploughland, appears again in an original charter of 1157–8 recording its surrender, as *una carucata in Copelanda que dicitur Fossa*, by the monks of Furness to Michael le Fleming (LaCh 307–8). The monks subsequently recovered this ploughland, and by the end of the 12th century, it had come to be known from their ownership, as *Munk fossa*. The original name was simply the Latin *fossa*, 'ditch.' The later name *Monkeforse*, *Mounkfors* is probably due to the influence of the name Hall Foss (*supra*), a short distance to the north, deriving from fors.

STANGRAH is *Stangerhovet* 1180–1210 Furness, *Stangarhawe, Stangarhay* 1526 *DuLa, Stangerhowe* 1536 *MinAcct*, 1687 *Hudleston, Stangar* 1537 *DuLa, Stangrey* 1673 PR (Whicham). The earliest form shows that this is a compound of *stangar*, genitive of ON *stǫng*, 'pole,' and *hǫfuð,* 'headland.' Cf. Stanghow (PN NRY 146) and *Stangerhau* in Ravensmeols (PN La 250).

BLACK COMB is *Blackcoum* 1671 Fleming, *Blackcomb* 1777 NB, *Blackcoume* 1778 Terrier. Jefferson (AllerA 127) says that this takes its name from the blackness of the heath growing on it. *Comb* is OE camb, 'crest.' Cf. Black Comb *supra* 441. HOLEGILL is *Holgill* 1571 FF. KIRKSTONES (6″) is a monument composed of thirty stones (AllerA 122). MIDTOWN (6″) is *Midtown Whitbeck* 1702 *LowtherW.* MOOR GREEN (6″) is *the Moorgreene* 1661 PR (Whicham). POOLFOOT is *Powfoot* 1702 *LowtherW. v.* poll. STANDING STONES (6″)[1] is *Standyng(e)ston(e)s* 1528 *DuLa.* TOWN END (6″) is so named in 1661 (PR). WAYSIDE is *Wayside* 1645 *LowtherW, the Whaside* 1669 PR (Whicham), *Whaeside* 1697 ib. It probably takes its name from *the Whae* 1599 PR (Whicham), *Thwa* 1606 ib., *the Whay* 1646 *LowtherW, Whaend* 1652 PR (Whicham).

FIELD-NAMES

(a) Bream (may contain ME *breme*, 'rugged,' as in Sir Gawayne and the Green Knight, v. 2145), Carrier, Firth (*v.* fyrhþ(e)), Rhaebuck, Rope Field, Roundabout[2]; in c. 1840 (*TA*) Alpella, Boonwood, Burnt Moor, Drown

---

[1] 'The remains of a Druidical monument' (AllerA 121).

[2] Common in other counties for a field surrounded by a wood or containing a clump of trees.

Sheep, Eglands, Featherstone, Goodystook, Grains Field (*v.* grein), Mickleton, Nuckisons, Ray, Reddings (*v.* hryding), Roe Bank, Stye Dale, Tangle Field, Tongue (*v.* tunge); in 1842 (AllerA) Blacklegs (rock) (id. 1794 H).

(*b*) In 1228–43 (*DuLa*) *Hesilgyle* (*v.* hesli, under hæsel, gil), *sichet called Muclesalc* (sic), *Mikelslac* (*v.* mikill, under micel, slakki), *Stainlandes* (*v.* steinn), *le Stainraise* (*v.* steinn, hreysi); in c. 1220 (Furness) *Crokerbec* (*v.* krókr, erg, bekkr), *Druthergile* (*v.* gil), *Stanebrede* (*v.* stān, brǣd); in 1180–1210 (Furness) *Dunemsbech, Edrikescroft* ('*Ēadrīc*'s croft'), *Gisse*. Under each of the following dates there is one field-name: *Ackescroft* 1220–1300 *DuLa* (*v.* āc), *Alditcroft* 1261–72 ib. ('*Aldgyþ*'s croft,' from OE *Aldgȳþ*, fem. personal name), *Karkebucholm* WestF (inversion compound of OWelsh *carrecc*, 'rock' and bukkr, holmr), *Waitewra* 1190–1200 Cockersand (*v.* hveiti, (v)rá).

57. Whitehaven[1]

WHITEHAVEN, *olim* [ʍitən, ʍitheivən]

Qwithofhavene c. 1135 StB, *Hwithothavene* 1203 FF, *Whithofthaven* c. 1240 StB, *Whitouthavene* c. 1260 ib., *Quitonthavene* (sic print) 1304 Cl, *Whitofhaven* 1323 Pat, *Whittofthaven in villa de Kirkeby* 1329 StB

Withofhavene c. 1140 StB

Witehovedhafne c. 1140 StB, *Wythod-, Wythothauene* 1279 *Ass*, *Wytetavene* 1323 Cl

Withoue c. 1180 StBA

Witenhauen 1278 *Ass*

Wythauene, Whytehauene 1279 *Ass*, *Wytehauen* c. 1280 StB, *Whitehhavene* 1334 Cl, *Wittehauen* early 14th StMaryY, *Whithaven* 1535 VE, *Whithauin* 1576 S

The origin of this name is correctly stated by Denton (25): "Whithaven or Whit-toft-haven is a creek in the sea at the north end of a great bergh or rising hill there which is washed with the flood on the west side where is a great rock or quarry of white hard stone which gives name to the village and haven." This rock was known as 'white headland' (ON hvít hǫfuð). Before 1150 a harbour had come into being under the headland and had given rise to the triple compound *hvíthǫfuðhafn*, of which the second element was early lost. The word 'haven' is of Scandinavian origin (Björkman, *Scandinavian Loan-words in Middle English*, 242). It is not recorded in England

---

[1] The borough of Whitehaven now includes parts of Hensingham (*supra* 400), Moresby (*supra* 421), Preston Quarter (*supra* 428) and Sandwith (*supra* 433). Hensingham and Sandwith, as also Bransty *infra* 452, have given their names to municipal wards.

before the 11th century, and Whitehaven is a remarkably early example of its appearance in an English place-name. Cf. also *Kyrkbyhaven supra* 431.

In contrast to this 'white headland,' a second promontory on this stretch of coast, which cannot now be identified with certainty (it has been suggested by the Rev. J. Wilson (StB 31) that it may be Swartha Brow between Whitehaven and Hensingham), was known in the 12th century as the 'black headland,' from ON svart and hǫfuð. The name appears in the 12th century as *Swartahof* c. 1125 StB, *Suuarta-hoft* c. 1135 (early copy) *Lowther*, *Swartof* c. 1170 StB, *Suarthoved* t. Ric 1 (1308) Ch, and survived at least until the reign of Henry VIII in the form *Swarthow* (*AOMB*).

WHITEHAVEN STREET-NAMES[1]

ADDISON ST is *Addisons Allen* (sic) 1758. Henry and Mary Addison, relatives of Joseph Addison, lived at Mount Pleasant (*infra*) c. 1700 (cf. CW iii, 361). CARTER LANE is so named in 1758. CATHERINE ST is so named in 1758, probably from a member of the Lowther family of that name. CHAPEL ST, so named in 1758, is on the site of a chapel, shown in a print of 1642. CHARLES ST, DUKE ST, KING ST and QUEEN ST, all so named in 1758, commemorate Charles II, his queen, Catherine of Braganza, and his brother James, Duke of York, afterwards James II. CHURCH ST, so named in 1758, derives its name from the church of St Nicholas (built in 1693). COLLEGE ST is *Colledge St* 1758. A college, which later became a carpet factory, was built here by John, first Earl of Lonsdale (CW iii, 353). COATES LANE is so named in 1770 from Thomas Coates, an original trustee of the Town and Harbour Trustee Board, formed in 1705. CROSS ST, EAST STRAND and FOX LANE are so named in 1758. FLATT WALKS. The walks by *Flatt* c. 1690 CW iii. GEORGE ST is *Georg Street* 1758. This includes *Hartley Street* 1758, named from the owner of a rope-walk here. GINNS, BACK GINNS. Cf. *Gin Close* 1758. These owe their name to the old horse ginns by which coal was drawn from the pit before the introduction of steam engines (Caine 103–4). GRANBY ROW, HAMILTON LANE and KELSICK LANE are so named in 1770; the last two from local families. HIGH ST and HOWGILL ST (*v. infra*) are so named in 1758. IRISH ST and SCOTCH ST are so named in 1758. In a letter written (c. 1700) to Sir John Lowther by his steward, at the time when the former was town-planning, it was suggested that these streets should be thus named as an inducement to traders of those nationalities to settle there. LOWTHER ST (from the family name of the Earls of Lonsdale, the principal landowners), MARK LANE, MARLBOROUGH ST, NEW ST, NEW TOWN, PETER ST, PIPEHOUSE LANE (the site of a former tobacco pipe factory), PLUMBLANDS LANE (near Plumblands Beck), SCHOOLHOUSE LANE and SENHOUSE ST (*v.* Tangier St

---

[1] Where no source is given, the reference is to *LowtherW*. For information with regard to many of these street-names, we are indebted to Mr W. Watson. All the references in this paragraph to CW iii are to the Old Series.

infra) are so named in 1758. MARKET PLACE includes *James Street* 1758 (named from James II) and *Poe Street* 1758 (named from Pow Beck *supra* 24). MICHAEL ST is *St Michaels Lane* 1758. MOUNT PLEASANT, so named in 1790 (MapH), from its beautiful grounds (Caine 46). ROPER ST is *Roper Lane* and *Alley* 1758, from the rope spinners who worked here. Cf. *Rope-Walks* 1770. TANGIER ST. In 1685 Captain Richard Senhouse (*v.* Senhouse St *supra*) returned from Tangier and in 1688 built *Tangier Ho* (CW iii, 365 ff.); the family derived their name from Hallsenna (394), *Sevenhoues* in c. 1225.

Lost street-names are *Love Lane* 1790 MapH, *Milbank Lane* 1758, *Norman Lane* ib., *Rosemary Lane* 1790 MapH, *Tickell Lane* 1758, called after the family of the poet, Thomas Tickell (1685–1740), *Williamsons Lane* 1770.

ARROWTHWAITE (6″)

Hayringthwait c. 1170 StB, *Ayringthwait* c. 1230, c. 1260 ib., *Haringthwait* 1323 ib., *Aringthwait*, *Harinthwait*, *Eyringthwait* 1324 ib., *Ayrinthwait* 1331 ib.

Harathwaite c. 1690 CW (OS) iii, *Harrathwaite* 1774 *LowtherW*

The forms suggest an original *eyringa þveit*, 'clearing of the people on the eyrr,' or gravelly shore. *v.* þveit.

BRANSTY ROAD, ROW and STATION preserve traces of the name of the district of Bransty (*Bransti* c. 1215 StB (p), 1338 Cl, *Branstibec* c. 1225 *HolmC*, c. 1260 StB, *Branci*, *Brancy* (sic) 1279 *Ass*, *Brandestie* 1294 Cl, *Brantsty* 1321 Ipm, *Bransty* 1334 ib., *Branesty* 1364 ib., *Bransty Beck* 1790 MapH). *Bransty* is from OE *brant-stīg*, 'steep path,' and was originally the name of the old road to Cockermouth which made its way direct along the present Bransty Road to Bransty toll-bar, before the new road was made. It ascends steeply.

CORKICKLE (6″)

Corkekyll c. 1210 StB, *Corkykyll* 1321 Ipm, *Corkikel* ib., 1334 ib., 1338 Cl, *Corkekel* 1334 Ipm, 1338 Cl, *Corkekyll in villa de Egremont* c. 1382 StB, *Corkeckle* 1566 FF

Corketel, *Corketol* 1279 *Ass*

Corkeele 1578 *Cocker*

Ekwall (ScandCelts 88) suggests that this name was originally given to the spur of hill between Corkickle and the river Keekle, and that the first element is the Middle Irish *corr*, 'point, peak.' For the second element *v.* Keekle R. *supra* 18.

HARRAS

Harras c. 1220 StB (p), 1338 Cl, *Harres* 1447 StB, *Arras parke* p. 1500 ib., *parcus de Harres prope Branstye*, *Harris* 1540 *MinAcct*

Harrais c. 1220 StB *et freq* to early 14th StMaryY, with variant spellings *Harrays, Harreys* c. 1220 HolmC (p), 1285 *Ass* (p), *Hareys* 1288 Orig (p)

Herres 1544 *MinAcct*

In the neighbourhood was *Harashowe* p. 1500 StB. This is probably, as Professor Ekwall suggests, ON *hær, 'stone,' as in Harome (PN NRY 70), hreysi.

HOTHWAIT (lost) is *Hothwait* c. 1140 StB *et passim*, with variant spellings *-twait, -thewat, -thweit, -tha(i)te*. 'Hill clearing,' *v.* hōh, þveit, and cf. *supra* 434. It is identical in situation with BRACKENTHWAITE (*Bra(c)kenthwaite* 1690 CW iii, 1758 *LowtherW*), the site of which is now occupied by the streets opposite Bransty railway station (StB 41 n.). For this latter name *v.* braken, þveit.

HOWGILL (6″) is *Holgile, Holegyll* c. 1170 StB. 'Deeply cut ravine'. Cf. Hole Gil *supra* 336.

PRIESTGILL is *Prestegile* c. 1180 StB, *Prestgill* p. 1500 ib., *Pries Gill* 1698 Terrier, *Priestgill* 1743 *LowtherW*. 'gil of the priests.'

YEW BANK is probably recorded in the name of Waldef de *Yuebanc* (c. 1258 StB).

AIKBANK is *Akebank* 1743 *LowtherW*. 'Oak bank.' BEARMOUTH (6″) is referred to in "*three holes, called Bear Mouths*, through which the men and horses go down to the coal works" 1794 H (ii, 69). SALTOM PIT (6″) is *Saltom* 1737 CW (OS) iii. SANDS CLOSES (6″) is *Sands Close* 1713 ib. SCILLY BANK is *Scilly Bank* 1743 *LowtherW, Silly Bank* 1774 Donald. TOM HURD ROCK is so named in 1794 (H). WHITE PARK (6″) is so named in 1815 (LysonsM).

FIELD-NAMES

(*a*) The Big Waite.

(*b*) In 1772 (*LowtherW*) *Harmless-Hill, Pickering-Bank*; in 1743 (*LowtherW*) *Scab'dhill, Wenthead* (*v.* went); in 1578 (*Cocker*) *butts dale, Clough riggs* (*v.* clōh), *dowan rigge, the knotts* (*v.* knǫtt), *rod rigge, wysinge dale*; in 1329 (StB) *le Bradeheng* (*le Bradehyng* 1315 ib. 'Broad meadow,' *v.* brād, eng), *foulknot* (*v.* fūl, cnotta), *le terne* (*v.* tiǫrn); in c. 1260 (StB) *Helkocmire* (*Helcocmire* c. 1215 ib. *v.* mýrr), *le Waterfal*; in c. 1170 (StB) *Haigescoc* (also *Eikescoc*) (probably 'oak wood,' *v.* eiki, skógr), *Pol* (*v.* poll). Under each of the following dates there is one field-name: *Baccusfield* 1758 *LowtherW* (apparently 'bake-house field'), *Edgers* 1770 ib., *le Foulesike* (*v.* fūl, sīc), *Jack-a-Dandy Hill* 1794 H, *Langaran* 1694 Gilpin.

WINSCALES

58. Winscales[1]

Wyndscales 1227 StB *et freq* to 1334 Ipm, with variant spelling *Wind-*, *parva Wyndscal* c. 1258 StB, *Windescales* 1278 *Ass*, *Vyndchales* 1321 Ipm

Wynskales 1254 Cl *et passim*, with variant spelling *Win-*, *parva Wynscales* c. 1258 StB, *Wynskels* c. 1495 ECP

In the parish was *Winscales Tarn* 1550 (1687) Whellan. *v.* tiǫrn. 'Windy shielings,' *v.* skáli.

THE CUT STONE (6″), on the parish boundary, is apparently *Custes Stone* n.d. Whellan. GALE HO is *Gaile, Gaile-head* 1725 *Work. v.* geil. HUNDAY COTTAGE is *Hunday* 1660 (1723) CW (OS) v. LOW HO, SOUTHFIELD (both 6″) and EAST TOWNEND are so named in 1725 (*Work*). MIDTOWN is *Mid-Town, Middle-Town* ib. MOREDIMPLE (6″) is stone called *Moredimple* 1550 (1687) Whellan. *Dimple* may represent the OE **dympel*, 'pool,' 'hollow,' of obscure origin, found in Dimlington (PN ERY 17–18). WYTHEMOOR is *Withmoor* 1578 *Cocker*, *the marras of Withmire* n.d. Whellan. WYTHEMOOR HEAD (6″) is *Wythmoorhead* 1725 *Work. v.* wīðig, mōr (or possibly mýrr).

FIELD-NAMES

(b) In 1750 (*Work*) *Raythfoot* (*Rauthfoot* 1725 ib.); in 1736 (*Work*) *Farehill* (*Farrhill* 1676 ib.); in 1725 (*Work*) *Harrgill* (*v.* gil), *South-Ings* (*South Inges* 1651 ib. *v.* eng), *Whinngill* (*v.* whin, gil); in 1638 (*Work*) *the Loneinge* (*v.* lonning).

59. Workington and Workington Rural[2]

WORKINGTON [wʌrkitən]

Wirkynton c. 1125 StB *et freq* to c. 1540 Leland, with variant spellings *Wirkin-*, *Wirken-*, *Wyrkin-*, *Wyrken-*, *Wrykinton* 1275 FF (p), *Wrykynton* 1512 LP

Wirkyngton c. 1130 StB (p) *et freq* to 1564 FF, with variant spellings *Wirking-*, *Wyrking-*, *Wyrkingthon* 1277 *Netherhall* (p), *Wrykington* 1279 *Ass*

---

[1] Part of Stainburn (*supra* 435) was added to Winscales in 1934.
[2] Parts of Harrington (*supra* 399) and Stainburn (*supra* 435) were added to Workington in 1934. Harrington has given its name to a municipal ward. So has Seaton—the ecclesiastical parish of West Seaton on the north bank of the Derwent (*supra* 319), which was earlier absorbed in 1899. See also Cloffocks *supra* 361.

Wirchintuna c. 1130 StB, t. Ric 1 (1308) Ch, *Wirchinghetona* c. 1150
StB, *Wirchintona* c. 1160 (early copy) *Lowther*[1]
Wirketon' 1211 Cur
Workington 1564 FF, *Woorkyngton* 1569 *SP*

WORKINGTON HALL is so named in 1777 (NB). CASTLE LODGE (6″).
Cf. *the castle of Wyrkyngton* 1402 Pat. In 1380 ib. licence was given
to crenellate the manor house of *Wirkyngton*.

This contains a personal name *Weorc* or *Wyrc* which enters into
many place-names in the Anglian parts of England. The one individual
who is known to have borne a name formed from this element—an
abbess called *Verca*, mentioned in Bede's Life of St Cuthbert—lived
near the river Tyne. If stress is laid on the form *Wirchinghetona*, the
present name can be translated 'tūn of *Weorc*'s people,' but the other
forms suggest that the *-ing-* was uninflected, and it is doubtful whether
it can have had more than the force of a simple genitive. It may be
added that for historical reasons the form *Wurcingtun* in BCS 815
cannot be identified with Workington, as in DEPN. It probably
refers to Warkton (Nth).

NOTE.[2] BELLE ISLE ST is named from Belle Isle in Windermere which is
owned by the Curwens, lords of the manor of Workington. BRIDGE ST,
CHRISTIAN ST and RAMSAY BROW are so named in 1793 (MapH). Christian
St is so named from the family of *Christian* of the Isle of Man, a member
of which married a Curwen. CROSSHILL is *Crossehill* 1725. CURWEN ST is
named from the family of *Curwen*. FINKLE ST. *v. supra* 47. FROSTOMS
RD. Cf. *High* and *Low Frostam* 1725, *Frosthams* 1821 G. MARKET PLACE is
Markett Place 1725. MILLRIGG ST. Cf. *Mealrigg* 1660 (1723) Jackson.
Probably 'sandy ridge,' *v.* melr. NOOK ST. Cf. *Nooke, Carmalt al. Nooke*
1725, *Kirmalt oth. Nook* 1749. *v.* Caermote *supra* 326. PINFOLD ST. Cf.
Pynfould-Side 1725. *v.* pundf(e)ald. POW ST is so named in 1793 (MapH).
v. poll. Lost street-names are *Moot-Hall-Lane* 1730, *Priest Gate* 1793 MapH
(*Priestgate* 1660 (early 18th), *Preistgate* 1673 (early 18th), 1725), *Uppergate*
1775 (id. 1725). *v.* gata.

GILDERSKUGH (lost) is *Gilderschoh* 1258 StB, *Gilderscow* 1550 (1687)
Whellan, *Gilderskew* 1660 *Work*, *Gilderscow Beck* n.d. Whellan,
Gilderskugh 1705 ib. In the neighbourhood was *Gylderstainflatt*,
Gilderstanflat 1227 StB. In both these names the first element is
ON *gildri*, 'snare.' In *Gilderskugh* the second element is skógr, in
Gilderstainflatt the other elements are steinn and flat.

---

[1] The copy in StB (No. 107) gives the reading *Wyrchynton*.
[2] Where no reference is given, the reference is to *Work*.

BANKLANDS (6″) is so named in 1603 (*Work*). BURROW WALLS (6″) is *Burrough Walls* 1794 H. CALVA HILL (6″). Cf. *Calvey Yate* 1717 *Work*, *Calva Closes* 1749 *LowtherW*. Probably 'calf hill,' *v*. haugr. CHAPEL BANK is *the Chapple Bank* 1731 *Work*. CLAY FLATTS (6″) is *Clay Flatt* ib. LILLY HALL (6″) is so named in 1821 (G). MOORCLOSE is so named in 1723 (CW (OS) v). NEWLANDS (6″) is so named in 1725 (*Work*). PARKEND (6″). Cf. *Workington park* 1777 NB. ST MICHAEL'S MOUNT overlooks the sea and was apparently the site of a medieval station for guarding the coast. The chapel which is recorded on this site as *Watch Chapell* 1569 *SP*, *St Michael's Chappel* 1731 *Work*, was dedicated to St Michael, patron of high places. St Michael's Mount may have received its present name in imitation of the well-known St Michael's Mount in Cornwall, but the connection of the site with St Michael is probably of high antiquity. Whellan records a *How Michael* on or near this site. SCHOOSE is *Scowes* 1660 (1723) CW (OS) v, *water of Skewes* n.d. Whellan, *the Scows* 1705 ib. *v*. skógr. STONYHAUGH (6″) is *Stonyhugh* 1725 *Work*. *v*. h(e)alh. SUNNY BROW (6″). Cf. *Sunnybank* 1550 (1687) Whellan. WESTFIELD (6″) is *Westfields* 1723 CW (OS) v. WETHER RIGS is *Weatheriggs* 1723 Jackson. Cf. the same name *supra* 400.

FIELD-NAMES[2]

(b) In 1789, *the Hame of Mowa* (*Moway* 1731, *the Mowa* 1739); in 1779, *Buckermire* (*Buckermer*, *Bucker Moor* 1749); in 1749, *Naddale* (*Naddall* 1725. Cf. Naddle *supra* 313); in 1743, *Barrott Howes Rigg*, *Bridgetts Well*; in 1742, *Larepotts* (*v*. leirr), *Swinedales*; in 1740, *Grayson-Barf* (*Grayson-Baurgh* 1725. Probably 'grey stone hill,' *v*. berg), *Hag-Hill*; in 1737, *Coat-Garth* (*v*. garðr), *Wenthouse* (cf. *the Lane or Went* 1734. *v*. went); in 1727, *the Bitts*, *Flat* (*v*. flat); in 1725, *Barrow Croft* (*v*. be(o)rg), *Butts*, *Copt-stone*, *Ennon*, *Fredales*, *Lowseyrigg*, *Tarngunerigg* (apparently an inversion compound of tiorn and '*Gunnar*'s hryggr'); in 1660 (early 18th) *Hening* (*Henyngs* 1543 Rich-Wills, *Henning Gate* 1550 (1687) Whellan, *Hayuynge rayse* n.d. ib. *v*. haining and hreysi), *Labouras* and *Labramoor*, *Ridding* (*v*. hryding), *Sowter*, *Stairfit* (*v*. fit); in n.d. (Whellan) *the Alyne Fytt* (*v*. fit), *ymp garthes* ('young plant garðr,' *v*. NED *s.v. imp* sb.[8]), *Kyblan Stone* (the foot of Derwent), *a dub called the Patturde*, *ege of Pimdar Banks*; in 1550 (1687) (Whellan) *Monkwath* (*Monekewath*, *Monekthwayth*, *Monkwayt* 1279 *Ass*. 'Monk ford,' *v*. vað). Under each of the following dates there is one field-name: *Dikes Towne* 1675 Sandford, *France Close* 1739, *Millfitt* 1705 Whellan (*v*. fit), *Readlands* 1744, *Simy Close* 1754, *Waytcroft* 1777 NB ('wheat croft'), *Well-Dote* 1734.

WYTHOP [widʌp] (6″)

60. Wythop

Wizope 1195 FF (*ter*)
Wythorpe 1260 Scotland, *Withorp* 1381 Pat, *Wythorp* 1383 *GDR*,
 Withorppe 1777 NB
Wythope 1279 *MinAcct et passim*, with variant spellings -*hop*(*p*),
 (*in Braithwayt*) 1370 Cl
Wythehop 1307 Pat, *Wythehope in Derwentefelles* 1318 ib.
Whethope 1383 Pat, *Wethop* 1505 *Cocker*
Wedoppe 1537 CW (OS) xiv, *Wedupp*(*e*) 1566 *Lowther*, *Widdopp*
 1575 PR (Crosth), *Widdup al. Withop* 1601 DKR xxxviii
Widehope 1576 S

WYTHOP HALL is *Wythopall* 1619 CantW v. WYTHOP MILL (in
Embleton parish) is *Wythoppe mill* 1578 *Cocker.* WYTHOP MOSS is
probably the *mussa* of 1195 FF. WYTHOP WOODS is *boscus de Wydehop'*
1292 *Ass.*

'Withy valley,' cf. wīðig, hop. The name is correctly explained by
Denton (37) as "salicum convallis." The later forms suggest that the
first element was taken to be *wide*. The -ʒ- in the 1195 form indicates
the Anglo-Norman pronunciation of OE -ð-.

LOTHWAITE (6″) is *Loftweic, Loftwic* 1195 FF. The first element here
is clearly ON lopt, 'loft.' The second may possibly be þveit, but the
document of 1195 is an original Final Concord, in a hand which
distinguishes between *c* and *t*.

CASTLE HOW (6″) is so named in 1784 (West). v. haugr. CHAPEL is
the chapel of Wythop 1777 NB. DARLING HOW is *Derlingow'* 1541
MinAcct. v. haugr. ESKIN is *Eskyn* 1578 *Cocker.*

FIELD-NAMES

(*a*) Burgh How (*v.* burh, haugr), Hanger Bannock.

(*b*) In 1578 (*Cocker*) *the Strandes* (*v.* strand), *Vnnthwate* and *Brownthwate*
(*v.* þveit); in 1573 (*Lowther*) *Cauldhowse* (*Caldehuse* 1276 ib. *v.* cald, hūs);
in 1276 (*Lowther*) *Bekewra* (*v.* bekkr, (v)rá), *Harescogbek* (*v.* hara, skógr,
bekkr, and cf. Haresceugh *supra* 216), *Helerheuide* (*v.* elri, hēafod, perhaps
replacing hǫfuð), *kylneflatmyre* (*v.* cyln, flat, mýrr), *mikilbek* (*v.* mikill, under
micel, bekkr), *minerdalebek, Staynscaghe* (*v.* steinn, skógr), *vlueshouse* ('*Úlfr*'s
hūs'). Under each of the following dates there is one field-name: *Adscall*
1619 CantW v, *Sawyers Cragg* 1789 Clarke.

Rows 279, 283

→ Forms 313, 119

Late Caer love Cocanusta 326, 455   cf 264

heath (Ham) 398 (cf 476)

Hamer Hall (hām) (309)

pig sacta (Brigham 35)

Roecomi (hmm) 334